This is a study of the life of Margaret Beaufort, mother of Henry VII and the foundress of two Cambridge colleges. It is at once the first biography of Lady Margaret to explore the full range of archival sources, and one of the best-documented studies of any late-medieval woman.

Lady Margaret's early experiences of the medieval 'marriage market' anticipated the turbulent political world in which she reached maturity. Deeply involved in the Wars of the Roses, a conspirator against Richard III, she was to become the foundress of one of England's greatest ruling dynasties. Her considerable wealth, much of it derived from her son's triumph, was used to finance education at Oxford and Cambridge, and her lasting memorials are the Cambridge colleges of Christ's and St John's. Behind her activities as both politician and benefactress can be discerned a vigorous, sometimes ruthless, but always enterprising personality, which left a deep impression on her contemporaries.

This is a biography of unusual character which brings to life an extraordinary personality under a great variety of aspects, illuminating in depth the political, social, ecclesiastical and academic history through the life of one of the most remarkable women of the age.

THE KING'S MOTHER

The head of Lady Margaret Beaufort,
from her tomb effigy in Westminster Abbey

THE KING'S MOTHER
LADY MARGARET BEAUFORT,
COUNTESS OF RICHMOND AND DERBY

MICHAEL K. JONES
Assistant Master, Winchester College
MALCOLM G. UNDERWOOD
Archivist, St John's College, Cambridge

CAMBRIDGE
UNIVERSITY PRESS

Published by the Press Syndicate of the University of Cambridge
The Pitt Building, Trumpington Street, Cambridge CB2 IRP
40 West 20th Street, New York, NY 10011-4211, USA
10 Stamford Road, Oakleigh, Victoria 3166, Australia

First published 1992
Reprinted 1992

Printed in Great Britain at the University Press, Cambridge

A catalogue record for this book is available from the British Library

Library of Congress cataloguing in publication data
Jones, Michael K.
The king's mother: Lady Margaret Beaufort, countess of Richmond and Derby/Michael K.
Jones and Malcolm G. Underwood.
p.   cm.
Includes bibliographical references and index.
ISBN 0 521 34512 X
1. Beaufort, Margaret, countess of Richmond and Derby, 1443–1509.
2. Henry VII, King of England, 1457–1509 – Family.   3. Great Britain – History – Wars
of the Roses, 1455–1485 – Biography.   4. Great Britain – History – Henry VII.
1485–1509 – Biography.   5. Great Britain – Nobility – Biography.   6. Tudor, House of.
I. Underwood, Malcolm G.   II. Title.
DA330.8.R5J66 1992
942.04′092 – dc20   90-25937   CIP

ISBN 0 521 34512 X hardback

UP

CONTENTS

ILLUSTRATIONS

Frontispiece
The head of Lady Margaret Beaufort, from her tomb effigy in Westminster Abbey, by permission of the Warburg Institute, University of London

Between pages 134 and 135

1 Calendar of the the Beaufort Hours, showing the date of Lady Margaret's birth, 31 May 1443, BL Royal MS 2A XVIII, fol. 30, by permission of the British Library.

2 Portrait of Lady Margaret in the master's lodge at Christ's College, by permission of the Master and Fellows, photograph by Christopher Hurst.

3 Portrait of Lady Margaret by Roland Lockey, in the hall at St John's College, Cambridge, by permission of the Master, Fellows and Scholars.

4 Miniature of Lady Margaret by Lucas Hornbolte, by courtesy of the Collection V de S.

5 Rose emblem at head of PRO, SC6/Hen. VII/1771, with the permission of the Controller of Her Majesty's Stationery Office.

6 Aerial photograph of the site of gardens at Collyweston palace, by permission of the Cambridge University Collection of Air Photographs.

7 Presentation inscription in the book of hours given by Lady Margaret to Lady Shirley, St John's College Library MS N.24, fol. 12v, by permission of the Master, Fellows and Scholars.

8 The badge of Thomas Stanley and arms of Lady Margaret in their book of prayers, Westminster Abbey MS 39, fol. 1, by courtesy of the Dean and Chapter.

PREFACE

This book is the product of the long-standing interest of the authors in the life and work of one of the most famous English medieval women. Their shared interest has grown from different perspectives. In the case of Michael Jones the springboard was his knowledge of the part played by the Beaufort family in the Hundred Years War, and in the politics of the reigns of Henry VI and Edward IV. The interest of Malcolm Underwood was first aroused by the light which the varied riches of the archives of St John's College, Cambridge, throw on the career and household of Lady Margaret Beaufort, its foundress.

We have adopted a thematic approach to our subject, in an effort to explore the range of Lady Margaret's concerns: her attitude towards both lines of her family; her involvement with the shifting loyalties and unstable dynasties of late medieval England; the administration of her properties, and her fortunes in a succession of marriages; the life of her own household in widowhood; her interests in forms of devotion, in chivalry and ceremonial, and in the universities. We have sought to place her in the context of her times, as politician, landowner, patron and benefactress.

We owe a great debt to specialists in many different fields, in university departments, archives and libraries. We cannot hope to do justice here to them all, but would like to acknowledge particularly the help and advice of the following: Dr Stuart Airlie, Dr Rowena Archer, Mark Ballard, Professor C. N. L. Brooke, Professor A. L. Brown, Pat Coulstock, Anne Crawford, Professor R. B. Dobson, Maria Dowling, Dr Eamon Duffy, Philippa Glanville, Professor Ralph Griffiths, Kate Harris, Mr F. Hepburn, Dr Rosemary Horrox, George Keiser, Kay Lacey, Veronica Lawrence, D. J. Lloyd-Guth, Mr J. Mitchell, Dr Nigel Morgan,

Dr D. M. Owen, Dr Carole Rawcliffe, Dr Richard Rex, Dr Colin Richmond, Nicholas Rogers, Dr J. A. F. Thomson, Livia Visser-Fuchs. We are grateful to D. J. Lloyd-Guth for transcripts of muniments at Sizergh Castle, and to Dr Carole Rawcliffe for transcripts of material relating to the Stafford family.

Especial mention is necessary of two scholars who have substantially enriched this work: Miss M. M. Condon and Mr T. B. Pugh. They have read and commented on a number of the chapters, generously contributed many references and shared with us their insights.

Acknowledgement is due to the following for allowing us access to their archives and libraries, the patience and diligence of whose staffs have been indispensable to the project: the Masters and Fellows of Christ's College, Clare College, Peterhouse, Queens' College and St John's College, Cambridge; the Marquis of Exeter for permission to use the records at Burghley House; the Spalding Gentlemen's Society; Mrs Strickland for permission to use the records at Sizergh Castle; the Dean and Chapter of Westminster Abbey.

The following bodies have afforded financial assistance and facilities to pursue our research: the British Academy, the Carnegie Trust, the Glasgow University Research Funding Committee, St John's College Cambridge.

Last, but by no means least, we are grateful to our families and friends for giving us their support and encouragement.

M.K.J.
M.G.U.

ABBREVIATIONS

ADN	Archives Départementales du Nord
AN	Archives Nationales
BIHR	*Bulletin of the Institute of Historical Research*
BL	British Library
BN	Bibliothèque Nationale
BRUC	A. B. Emden, *A Biographical Register of the University of Cambridge to 1500* (Cambridge, 1963)
Brunet	J. C. Brunet, *Manuel du Librairie*, 2nd edn, 4 vols. (Paris, 1814)
BRUO	A. B. Emden, *A Biographical Register of the University of Oxford to 1500*, 3 vols. (Oxford, 1957–9)
Cal. Papal Registers	*Calendar of Papal Registers*
CCR	*Calendar of Close Rolls*
Cooper	C. H. Cooper, *The Lady Margaret: A Memoir of Margaret, Countess of Richmond and Derby*, ed. J. E. B. Mayor (Cambridge, 1874)
CP	*The Complete Peerage*
CPR	*Calendar of Patent Rolls*
CUL	Cambridge University Library
DNB	*The Dictionary of National Biography*
DRO	Dorset Record Office
EETS	Early English Text Society
EHR	*English Historical Review*
HMC	*Historical Manuscripts Commission*

KRO	Kent Record Office
L and P	*Letters and Papers Illustrative of the Reigns of Richard III and Henry VII*
L and P Henry VIII	*Letters and Papers of the Reign of Henry VIII*
Mornynge Remembraunce	'Mornynge Remembraunce had at the moneth mynde of the Noble Prynces Margarete Countesse of Rychemonde and Darbye emprynted by Wynkyn de Worde', in *The English Works of John Fisher, part I*, ed. J. E. B. Mayor, EETS, e.s., 27 (1876), 289–310
Notes	*Notes from the College Records, Continued from The Eagle [St John's College Magazine], vol. xxxvi*, ed. R. F. Scott (St John's College, 1915)
Oration	Oration made at Cambridge by John Fisher, in J. Lewis, *Life of Dr. John Fisher*, 2 vols. (London, 1855), II, 263–72
PCC	Prerogative Court of Canterbury
PPC	*Proceedings of the Privy Council*
PRO	Public Record Office
RCHM	*Reports of the Royal Commission on Historical Monuments*
RP	*Rotuli Parliamentorum*
SANHS	*Proceedings of the Somerset Archaeological and Natural History Society*
SJC	St John's College Cambridge, archives
STC	*Short Title Catalogue of English Books, 1475–1640*, 2nd edn, ed. W. A. Jackson, F. S. Ferguson and K. F. Pantzer, 2 vols. (London, 1963–76)
TBGAS	*Transactions of the Bristol and Gloucestershire Archaeological Society*
TCWAS	*Transactions of the Cumberland and Westmorland Archaeological Society*
THSLC	*Transactions of the Historic Society of Lancashire and Cheshire*
VCH	*Victoria County History*
WAM	Westminster Abbey Muniments

Will   Will of Lady Margaret Beaufort, printed in the St John's College Quatercentenary volume *Collegium Divi Johannis Evangelistae, 1511–1911* (Cambridge, 1911), 103–26

GENEALOGICAL TABLES

I   The Beauforts

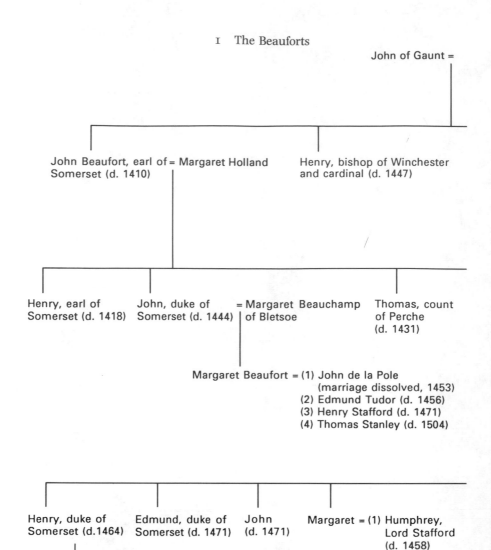

(3) Katherine Swynford

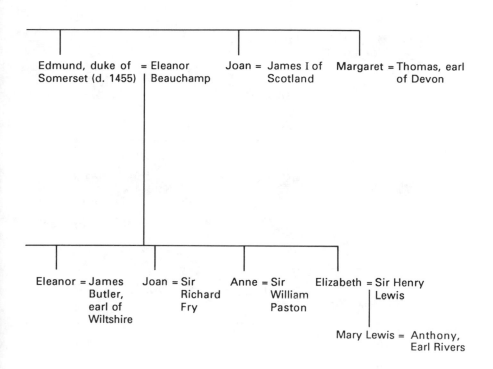

Thomas, duke of = Margaret Neville   Joan = (1) Robert Ferrers
Exeter (d. 1426) of Hornby   (2) Ralph Neville,
                   earl of Westmorland

Edmund, duke of = Eleanor Joan = James I of Margaret = Thomas, earl
Somerset (d. 1455) | Beauchamp   Scotland   of Devon

Eleanor = James Joan = Sir Anne = Sir Elizabeth = Sir Henry
    Butler,   Richard   William | Lewis
    earl of   Fry   Paston
    Wiltshire

                    Mary Lewis = Anthony,
                          Earl Rivers

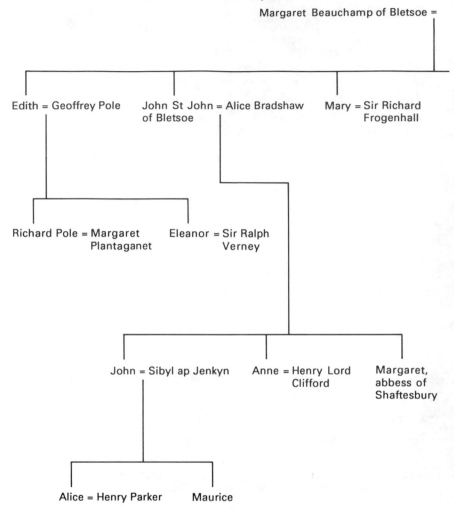

(1) Oliver St John

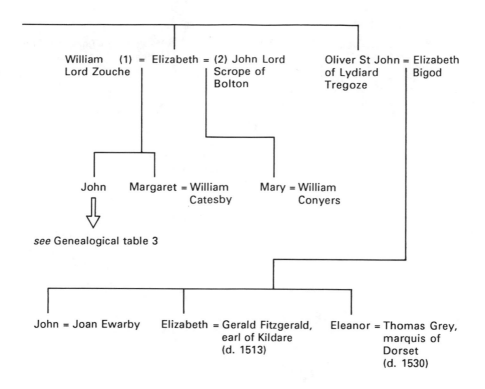

William   (1) = Elizabeth = (2) John Lord   Oliver St John = Elizabeth
Lord Zouche | | Scrope of   of Lydiard | Bigod
            | | Bolton   Tregoze

John   Margaret = William   Mary = William
  ⇓   Catesby   Conyers

see Genealogical table 3

John = Joan Ewarby   Elizabeth = Gerald Fitzgerald,   Eleanor = Thomas Grey,
                                    earl of Kildare   marquis of
                                    (d. 1513)   Dorset
                                                                      (d. 1530)

3   The Zouches

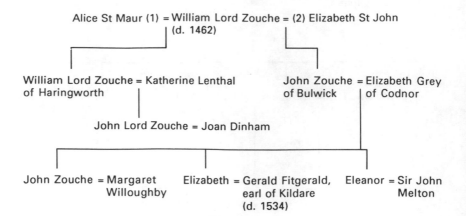

Alice St Maur (1) = William Lord Zouche = (2) Elizabeth St John
                      (d. 1462)

William Lord Zouche = Katherine Lenthal   John Zouche = Elizabeth Grey
of Haringworth   of Bulwick   of Codnor

John Lord Zouche = Joan Dinham

John Zouche = Margaret   Elizabeth = Gerald Fitgerald,   Eleanor = Sir John
              Willoughby   earl of Kildare   Melton
                                             (d. 1534)

4 The Welles

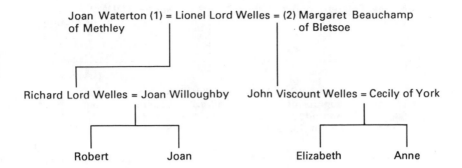

Joan Waterton (1) = Lionel Lord Welles = (2) Margaret Beauchamp
of Methley   of Bletsoe

Richard Lord Welles = Joan Willoughby   John Viscount Welles = Cecily of York

Robert   Joan   Elizabeth   Anne

5 The Staffords

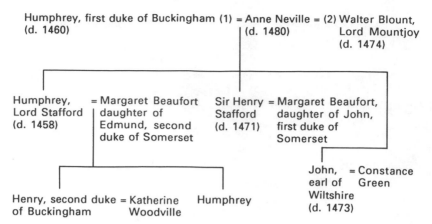

Humphrey, first duke of Buckingham (1) = Anne Neville = (2) Walter Blount,
(d. 1460)   (d. 1480)   Lord Mountjoy
                                                                     (d. 1474)

Humphrey,   = Margaret Beaufort   Sir Henry = Margaret Beaufort,
Lord Stafford   daughter of   Stafford   daughter of John,
(d. 1458)   Edmund, second   (d. 1471)   first duke of
                   duke of Somerset   Somerset

                                                      John,   = Constance
                                                      earl of   Green
Henry, second duke = Katherine   Humphrey   Wiltshire
of Buckingham   Woodville   (d. 1473)

6   The Stanleys

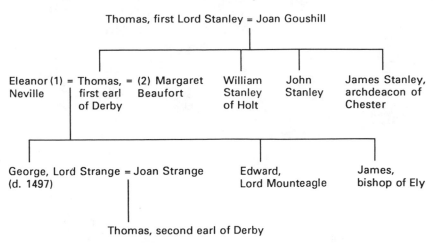

Thomas, first Lord Stanley = Joan Goushill

Eleanor (1) = Thomas, = (2) Margaret   William   John   James Stanley,
Neville   first earl   Beaufort   Stanley   Stanley   archdeacon of
          of Derby   of Holt   Chester

George, Lord Strange = Joan Strange   Edward,   James,
(d. 1497)   Lord Mounteagle   bishop of Ely

Thomas, second earl of Derby

INTRODUCTION

The figure of Margaret Beaufort has always fascinated chroniclers and historians. They have been attracted partly by the varied circumstances of her life, which led her through four marriages, made of her a conspirator and her husband's prisoner, and eventually the mother of a king and revered benefactress of universities. Great-granddaughter of John of Gaunt through his liaison with Katherine Swynford, and heiress of a disgraced military commander, she was to see her son and grandson kings of England. She seemed a living exemplar of the changeability of fortune so beloved of medieval moralists. Her own awareness of this, shown by the tears of foreboding she often shed in times of triumph, was noted by John Fisher, her chief confidant and confessor, in his sermon preached a month after her death.[1] Historians have also been struck by her fortitude, that blend of classical stoicism and Christian patience which was regarded as the appropriate response to the turning of fortune's wheel and the acts of providence.

Bernard André, first historian of the Tudor dynasty, combined these elements in his dramatic story of how Lady Margaret preserved the life and inheritance of her young son, the future Henry VII. André depicts a woman of courage and foresight, 'steadfast and more stable than the weakness in women suggests'.[2] It is she who, fearing for Henry's safety, sends him away into exile in the wake of the final overthrow of

---

[1] *Mornynge Remembraunce*, 305–6.

[2] 'Supra quam muliebris fragilitas posceret firmius et constans.' Bernard André, 'Vita Henrici Septimi', in *Memorials of King Henry VII*, ed. J. Gairdner, Rolls Series (London, 1858), 14–16.

the Lancastrians by Edward IV in 1471. She is given a farewell speech, standing on the quay at Tenby, in south Wales. She commits Henry to the care of his uncle, Jasper earl of Pembroke, saying that she wishes him in safer hands than her own, for women are known for imprudence, weakness and instability. André wrote with the prejudices and the literary conventions of his age, explaining Margaret's achievement by making her qualities seem exceptional. As chronicler and poet, celebrating the rise and reign of Henry VII, he tended to overdraw her vulnerable yet heroic isolation, her deep-seated hatred of the Yorkist court and her personal distrust of Edward IV.

Allowing for André's polemic, however, he grasped a dynamic quality about Margaret which others have felt and expressed. Another early Tudor historian, Polydore Vergil, a drier observer, gave Margaret no speeches but allowed her an even more active role as instigator of the conspiracy of the duke of Buckingham against Richard III. 'She', he wrote, 'being a wise woman, after the slaughter of King Edward's children was known, began to hope well of her son's fortune...She uttered to Lewis (her physician) that the time was now come when King Edward's eldest daughter might be given in marriage to her son Henry.' King Richard might now easily be deprived of the throne, and therefore Margaret asked Lewis 'to deal secretly with the queen of such affair'. After the collapse of the revolt and the attainder of Richard's enemies, 'it went very hard that Thomas Stanley was not accounted amongst the number of the king's enemies, by reason of the practices of Margaret his wife...who was commonly caulyd the head of that conspiracy'.[3]

Shakespeare, deriving his history from the work of Vergil and Thomas More through Edward Hall, was to leave a vignette of Margaret, the active political partisan, in *Richard III*. There Edward IV's queen voices the traditional picture of her antipathy to the Yorkist house:

> STAN. God make your Majesty joyful as you have been.
> ELIZ. The Countess Richmond, good my lord of Derby,
>   To your good prayer will scarcely say Amen;
>   Yet, Derby, notwithstanding she's your wife,
>   And loves not me, be you, good lord, assur'd
>   I hate not you for her proud arrogance.

---

[3] Polydore Vergil, *Three Books of English History*, ed. Sir H. Ellis, Camden Society, o.s., 39 (1844), 195–204.

Later, Richard himself warns the earl of Derby of his wife's activity against him and on behalf of her son:

K. RICH....Dorset is fled to Richmond...
BUCK. I hear the news, my lord.
K. RICH. Stanley, he is your wife's son. Well, look unto it...
    Stanley, look to your wife; if she convey
    Letters to Richmond, you shall answer it.[4]

Sir George Buck, the early seventeenth-century antiquary who came from a family friendly to the Yorkist cause and set about redressing Richard's evil reputation, took a sinister view of her political activity. His Lady Margaret was a 'politic and subtle lady' by whose malign influence Henry duke of Buckingham, her nephew, was persuaded to head the rebellion against Richard. It is likely that Buckingham really needed little persuasion to assume a leading role, and himself had aspirations to the throne, but Margaret's skill in using him as political cover for her son's ambition cannot be denied. Buck's was a more realistic appraisal of her role than that of Tudor commentators who presented Buckingham simply as a willing supporter of Henry Tudor.[5]

Buck also launched a more scathing accusation than that of political duplicity. He claimed that Margaret had been involved in a plot with her chaplain, later cardinal, John Morton, and others to cause the deaths by sorcery and poison, of the princes in the Tower. The plot was portrayed as part of Buckingham's conspiracy revealing the lengths to which Margaret's pitiless ambition for her son would take her. One of those accused was Thomas Nandyke or Nandick of Cambridge, conjurer. He had graduated bachelor of medicine in 1476–7 and so could be imagined to have had access to drugs and potions necessary to the plot. Nandyke was described in the act of attainder against the conspirators of 1483 as 'a necromancer late of Cambridge, in the following of the Duke of Buckingham'. He was reprieved by the reversal of the attainder in 1485.[6]

Unfortunately Buck's case was founded partly upon 'an old manuscript book' which was never produced, but he was not alone in his estimate of her dangerous character. Sir William Cornwallis

---

[4] *King Richard III*, ed. A. Hammond, *The Arden Shakespeare* (London, 1981), Act I, Sc. III, 152; Act IV, Sc. II, 269.
[5] Sir George Buck, *The History of King Richard III*, ed. A. N. Kincaid (Gloucester, 1979), 64; cf. below, pp. 63–4.   [6] Buck, *Richard III*, 54, 85, 163; BRUC, 418–19.

criticized Richard III's action in allowing her to be kept in close custody
by her husband rather than executed. He saw it as an indication not
of her innocence but of Richard's foolish clemency, a 'weakness' in his
rule which led to his fall.[7]

The transition from celebrating Margaret's qualities as superior to
those commonly expected in women to crediting her with demonic
resources is perhaps not as sharp as it may seem. In the political world
of the early sixteenth as of the seventeenth century women were rarely
leaders. Those who were, usually gained their place as a result of the
failure of the male line, or of early widowhood and their consequent
key place in the dynastic marriage market. Because their influence was
normally indirect, their overt political activity was regarded with
suspicion, astuteness being all too easily associated with 'woman's
wiles'. Like Margaret Beaufort, Margaret of York, duchess of Burgundy,
was credited with 'magic arts' which she used to trouble King Henry
VII by raising up the ghost of Richard duke of York to haunt him, in
the shape of Perkin Warbeck. 'Magic arts' is a term used ambiguously
by Sir Francis Bacon to describe Margaret's schemes and wiles to
educate and further Warbeck. He recalls that the king's friends called
her Juno to his Aeneas, since she stirred 'both heaven and hell to do
him mischief'.[8] The tradition of the duchess's constant political
interference to the hurt of the first Tudor went back to Polydore Vergil
who depicted her as having 'the spirit of a man and the malice of a
woman'. It was also founded on remarks made by the king himself,
obsessed with her 'great malice', and possibly haunted by the fear of
Burgundy both as a refuge of Yorkist conspirators and a source for
independent claims to the English throne.[9]

In the course of his history of Henry VII's reign Vergil noted
Margaret Beaufort's continued importance: she was a person to whom
Henry 'allotted a share in most of his public and private resources'.[10] The ambassadors of Spain and Venice at Henry's court
included her among the persons of greatest influence with whom they

[7] Buck, *Richard III*, 243.
[8] Sir Francis Bacon, *History of the Reign of King Henry the Seventh*, ed. R. Lockyer (London, 1971), 130.
[9] C. Weightman, *Margaret of York, Duchess of Burgundy, 1446–1503* (Gloucester, 1989), 153–6.
[10] Polydore Vergil, *Anglica Historia*, ed. D. Hay, Camden Society, n.s., 74 (1950), 7, 24.

had to deal.[11] For two other contemporaries who were closer to her, John Fisher and her former cupbearer, Henry Parker Lord Morley, her public position was backed by a responsible use of power: Fisher in his month-mind sermon and Parker writing Margaret's encomium in his old age both stressed her active care for her household and other dependants, and her wisdom where tactful handling of people was required.[12]

The dynamic, politically active, side of Lady Margaret has always retained some hold on historians, but it has usually been submerged by attention to her stoical and pious qualities. To succeeding generations the image of the conspirator turned matriarch of the dynasty proved less potent than that of the pious benefactress. Her reputation as a saintly widow and patron of learning took central place in the memoir of her by Thomas Baker, the historian of St John's College, Cambridge.

Baker published the memoir as preface to an edition of John Fisher's sermon at Lady Margaret's month mind.[13] It was written as an act of piety towards the foundress of his college, and was mostly devoted to an account of the early history of St John's. Baker was a natural antiquary, sympathetic to the foundress and other benefactors of the college: 'I have more regard to our founders and benefactors that are dead and gone than I have to the present college now living.'[14] He was amazed that 'amongst so many hundreds, I may say thousands, as have eat her bread, no grateful hand has yet been found to do her right'.[15] His own stand as a non-juror against the Whig establishment of his day no doubt intensified this feeling, and also made him more prepared to tolerate and even praise Lady Margaret's piety, a strand in her life not amenable to the anti-papal climate in which he lived.[16] Nevertheless he was constrained throughout his narrative to apologize for her 'Romishness'. The vow of chastity which she took, a fairly

---

[11] *Calendar of State Papers, Spanish, I, Henry VII, 1485–1509*, ed. G. A. Bergenroth (London, 1862), 163, 178; *Calendar of State Papers, Venice, I, 1202–1509*, ed. R. Brown (London, 1864), 264.

[12] *Mornynge Remembraunce*, 296–7; BL Add. MS 12060, fols. 21–3.

[13] *A Mornynge Remembraunce had at the Monethe Minde of Margarete Countesse of Richmonde*, ed. T. Baker (London, 1708); reprinted, incorporating Baker's notes on the manuscript copy of *Mornynge Remembraunce* in a register at St John's (SJC, D91.23, 97–109), in *The Funeral Sermon of Lady Margaret Beaufort*, ed. J. Hymers (Cambridge, 1840).

[14] *Funeral Sermon*, ed. Hymers, 52.   [15] *Ibid.*, 1.

[16] In the process he noticed the wider context of her piety: her membership of a number of religious confraternities. Such facts are now known to be commonplace, but were not in Baker's day.

common practice among widows in her day and a recognition of their standing in the Church, was not to be judged other than 'as an efflux of the purity of her mind'.[17] Baker felt the need to explain that in printing Fisher's sermon he was not himself commending Roman Catholic doctrines: they were merely 'some few Romish mixtures interwoven with the Lady's character'. References to her death-bed affirmation of belief in the real presence were, he says, included simply as report, not as evidence of his own position.[18]

Baker, drawn to the foundress of his college by her munificence and its lasting effects, agreed with Fisher in seeing her bounty as the fruits of personal sanctity. He went further, stressing the humility that made her uninterested in 'titles', despite her relationship to 'thirty kings and queens in the fourth degree'. Her private virtues and public charities were 'the only crowns she affected to wear'.[19] It is by no means certain that Fisher, the late medieval prelate for whom it was as important to mention Margaret's nobility of lineage as to dwell on her nobility of character, would have understood this sentiment. For him she was the womb of kings, and like Martha who held 'the castell of Bethany', her public and private personae lent each other dignity. The combination of the royal and Beaufort arms and badges, proudly reared above the gateways of her colleges and in the backgrounds of her portraits, would not seem to indicate a lack of interest in titles. If she did not wear the crown but reserved it for her son, she certainly wore a coronet. Baker, however, was creating an intimate portrait after his own fashion. It was that of the princess of learning who cared not for state and glory, and who was tenderly regarded by the king her son, as their surviving correspondence showed.[20]

If Baker was living in something of an ivory tower in his belief that Margaret shunned regality, his portrait of hallowed learning had a lasting effect. William Wordsworth, in a sonnet commending to St John's the gift of a portrait of himself, bade it

> Go faithful portrait, and where long hath knelt
> Margaret, the saintly foundress, take thy place.[21]

Long before Wordsworth, however, her learning had been ably appraised and set in the context of its time by George Ballard who, in

---

[17] *Funeral Sermon*, ed. Hymers, 16; below, pp. 153, 187–8.
[18] *Funeral Sermon*, ed. Hymers, 58–9.   [19] *Ibid.*, 3.   [20] Below, p. 74.
[21] 'To The Author's Portrait', Misc. Sonnets, XXIV, *The Poetical Works of William Wordsworth*, ed. E. de Selincourt and H. Darbishire (Oxford, 1946), II, 50.

1752, produced his *Memoirs of Learned Ladies*, with a second edition in 1775. Ballard reviewed her patronage of scholarship and provided a list of her translations and the literary works with which her name was associated. His knowledge of the achievements of other learned ladies enabled him to present a balanced view. He considered that the education of Lady Margaret was 'according to the custom of that age, not very extraordinary'. He drew attention to the literary interests of the duchess of Buckingham, revealed in her legacy of books to Margaret, her daughter-in-law.[22]

Ballard's sound work could not be neglected, and Horace Walpole, treating of Lady Margaret in *Royal and Noble Authors*, referred his readers to it, leaving him free to attack his subject in a lighter vein. Walpole was an iconoclast in the Gibbonian mould, a champion of the innocence of Richard III against the contemporary assumption of his guilt. He treated Lady Margaret patronisingly as 'the mother of Henry VII to whom she seems to have willingly ceded her *no* right to the crown, while she employed herself in founding colleges and in acts of more real devotion and goodness than generally attend so much superstition'.[23] He went on to ridicule the account of her vision of St Nicholas by whom, according to Fisher's witness, she said she had been guided in her choice of Edmund Tudor as husband:

> On so nice a point, the good young lady advised with an elderly gentlewoman, who, thinking it too great a decision to take upon herself, recommended her to St. Nicholas, who, whipping on some episcopal robes, appeared to her and declared in favour of Edmund. The old gentlewoman I suppose was dead, and St. Nicholas out of the way; for we hear nothing of the Lady Margaret consulting either of them on the choice of two other husbands after the death of Edmund, by whom she had King Henry.

Very different was the mood of Edmund Lodge, who included a notice about Lady Margaret in his brief memoirs to accompany portraits of famous personages between 1821 and 1834.[24] Lodge's view was that history had treated her 'with complacency rather than justice'. It was not only that he rejected the 'wanton and misplaced ridicule' used by Walpole. He also suggested that she in a remarkable

[22] G. Ballard, *Memoirs of Learned Ladies* (London, 1775), 6–17.
[23] H. Walpole, *A Catalogue of the Royal and Noble Authors of England, with Lists of their Works* (Edinburgh, 1796), 289–92.
[24] E. Lodge, *Portraits of Illustrious Personages of Great Britain*, 4 vols. (London, 1821–34), II, 1–2.

way allowed her strict piety and moral virtue to discipline her power, which she had used before Henry VII's accession to considerable effect. He owed his throne to her and ruled 'in the opinion of no small party' by her tacit appointment. Moreover her piety was not gloomy or morose, as such 'superstition' had been regarded by Walpole and his contemporaries. She did not abandon the court but was present at its ceremonies, domesticating grandeur in her good relations with her son. Her behaviour was marked by caution, however. 'She stepped widely, it is true, out of the usual sphere of her sex to encourage literature by her example and bounty, but she cautiously confined herself within it, to avoid any concern in the government of the state after Henry had mounted the throne.'

Lodge's plea to take Margaret seriously not only as a learned but as a political figure, was amplified in 1839 by the work of Caroline Halsted.[25] Halsted's essay won a prize awarded by the directors of the Gresham Commemoration of Victoria's accession, and there is no doubt that the presence of a young queen, 'to whom the females of Britain look with duty and affection, with pride as women, with devotion as subjects', helped to inspire the study. Halsted, like Baker and Lodge, was struck primarily by Lady Margaret's moral qualities: 'It is her Christian character, her moral virtues, her high integrity during that dark period when temptations to disloyalty and ambition assailed the collateral branches of royalty...that has secured for this illustrious princess so exalted a position among the most dignified females of England.'[26]

Halsted, however, began with a wider interest than her predecessors in the general history of England. She was also the authoress of a biography of Richard III, in which she repudiated the story of his deformity as a slur of adverse propaganda. Historically alert, she was not content with pointing up Margaret's virtues and achievements as a patron of learning, but wished to investigate her impact on that 'dark period', so the study inevitably had a major political dimension. Halsted took a critical view of her sources, attributing the scant attention previously paid to her subject to 'the defective and confused state' of the records of the period.

With the printed sources and manuscripts of the British Museum at her disposal she formed some acute judgements, which can be

---

[25] C. Halsted, *Life of Margaret Beaufort, Countess of Richmond and Derby* (London, 1839).
[26] *Ibid.*, Preface, x.

confirmed from other sources, about Margaret's political capacity. Halsted depicted her efforts to provide for her son and strike an alliance with Edward IV after Stafford's death in 1471, as a result of 'strong judgement and acute perception, which influenced her conduct in all matters of emergency'.[27] In stressing her achievement she painted the enmity between Margaret and the Yorkist court in colours too lurid: it is now clear that Margaret's attitude to Edward IV, both when she was married to Stafford and later, was one of cautious support, rather than thinly veiled hostility. Nevertheless, the prudence of Margaret's attitude, in contrast to that of another branch of the Beauforts, is beyond question.[28] Halsted also understood that the real bitterness between Margaret and the ruling house centred not upon Edward who, despite his displacement of Henry VI, had a claim to legitimacy, but upon his brother, Richard, because of his act, or rumoured act, of infanticide.

Halsted at times exaggerated Margaret's initiative: her own prudence as an isolated female is said to have led her to marry Stafford after Edmund Tudor's death, whereas we are fairly certain that the alliance, a politically important one, was also discussed between her brother-in-law Jasper Tudor and Humphrey duke of Buckingham when Jasper and Margaret visited him at Newport in March 1457.[29] It is far-fetched to associate Margaret's literary efforts, the evidence for all of which post-dates Henry VII's accession and in which the scope of her personal literary contribution was limited, with her work of 'superintending Henry's education' in Wales in the 1460s.[30]

In another important respect Halsted's portrait of Margaret the politician has to be modified. Concurring with Lodge, she wrote that 'the establishment of King Henry on the throne appears to have been the signal to his admirable parent for retiring from all matters connected with public affairs.'[31] She became, like a devoted Victorian lady, the example of obedience and submission, only appearing at court as an affectionate parent to grace her son's state. While there is evidently much truth in this picture of Margaret's devotion to her son, the relationship was far more of an active partnership. Her

---

[27] *Ibid.*, 92, 108.   [28] Below, pp. 45–6.
[29] Halsted, *Life of Margaret Beaufort*, 65; cf. below, pp. 40–1.
[30] Halsted, *Life of Margaret Beaufort*, 95; cf. below, p. 162.
[31] Halsted, *Life of Margaret Beaufort*, 162.

establishment at Collyweston was not a condition of seclusion; she
continued to take an interest in political affairs, and, through her
judicial power, to consolidate her son's regime. She was, for example,
fully aware of ways in which her own family financial interests in
France could be used to benefit the king, and was active in pursuing
them for this reason.[32]

Halsted's work was published at the same time as, and probably
forestalled, a study of Margaret by the antiquary and topographer John
Britton.[33] It survives as an incomplete manuscript memoir and notes in
Cambridge University Library.[34] Its chief interest lies in being the only
informed study of Margaret to present her in an unfavourable light.
Britton looked back to Horace Walpole's scepticism, with which he
agreed, but his approach was more systematic. Britton's scepticism was
part of a larger thesis rooted in his view of the age in which Margaret
lived, a view in some ways refreshingly different from the neo-Gothic
adulation of his own. Her age, he deemed, was one in which men were
solely preoccupied with war and religion and in which the people were
'held in vassalage to a tyrannical priesthood'. All accounts of her had
ignored the distorting lens of a false piety; the eulogistic tradition began
with Fisher, a Catholic priest intent on creating an image of sanctity to
accord with that piety, and therefore not be trusted.

Britton was protesting at the acceptance in 'modern' nineteenth-
century Protestant England of a medieval Catholic picture of Lady
Margaret. His attempted demolition of her reputation for virtue was
based on his conviction that, at worst, she was dominated by pure
superstition and the observance of 'formal and in fact pantomimic'
ceremonies. At best, her charitable deeds were motivated by 'a
mistaken idea of benefiting the repose of her own soul and an
ostentatious love of the influence derived from extensive patronage'.[35]
While one may reject as too narrow the terms of Britton's dismissal of
the age of Caxton, Margaret of York, and the Master of Mary of
Burgundy, his perspective affords a detailed critique of Margaret's
saintly image which needs consideration. It is a subtle charge, though
difficult to confirm or deny, that she felt an excessive personal pride in
the scope of her influence. It should certainly become clear in this book,

---

[32] Below, p. 82.
[33] In 1836 he had published, with Edward Brayley, *The Ancient Palace and Houses of
Parliament at Westminster*, and was issuing a successor to Lyson's *Magna Brittania*, *The
Beauties of England and Wales*.   [34] CUL, MS Oo.6.89.   [35] *Ibid.*, 10.

however, that she had wider opportunities for cultivating it than has generally been thought; that she was no recluse but very familiar with the panoply of court and high office.

Britton saw no humility in Margaret's apparent willingness, mentioned by Horace Walpole and stressed by Edmund Lodge, to cede her own title to the throne to her son and abdicate any part in state affairs. He suggested that for a queen to reign at that time was a practical impossibility, and that had she tried to do so she would immediately have been pre-empted by Yorkist claimants. Instead she chose a sure method of advancing her own status and ambition by arranging the marriage of Henry and Elizabeth of York.

The correspondence of the king and his mother afforded for Britton no compelling evidence of closeness between them. He found Henry's letters formal and distant and Margaret's imbued with a wish to conciliate which banished real affection. Her willingness that he should reap the benefits of the debts due to her family in France, and Henry's grateful reply in which he tells her that the debts may one day be useful in dealing with the French king, are seen only as the manifestations of Henry's avarice, and of a mutual cunning. Britton did not consider the episode as a demonstration of their political co-operation.

He also detected Margaret's shrewdness, verging on trickery, in a letter in which she asked the king to write commanding her to retain men for the benefit of Prince Henry (the duke of York), the command itself to be an excuse for 'my lord and hosbond'. In the same way that she thus deceived the earl of Derby, Britton conjectured, she might have deceived Fisher when she told him that a vision of St Nicholas guided her choice of husband. A woman of such good sense, Britton argued, would not have believed in such a vision; if she did, her superstition was contemptible.[36]

Such an opinion of Margaret's shrewdness was akin to that of Buck, but it recognized ability as well as guile. It was unlike the picture of a stable and honest character painted by Halsted who, though she granted Margaret's political qualities, grounded them in courage and endurance rather than duplicity. Britton's notes were vitiated by his general antipathy to medieval religion, but at times they brought a refreshing iconoclasm into the subject. He was dealing with an image of majesty coupled with saintliness which had not been seriously

[36] *Ibid.*, 15–16.

questioned since Buck's time: for the chroniclers of the sixteenth
century Margaret had been the nurturer of the ruling dynasty, for the
romantics of the nineteenth she was the simple but indomitable
protectress of her child. Britton was the first to add a purely pragmatic
dimension. His notes show that during 1838 he was actively pursuing
enquiries with a number of eminent antiquaries, but the result was an
abbreviated memoir which remained unpublished. The applause was
taken instead by Caroline Halsted, writing on behalf of her early
champion of womanhood and motherhood.

In contrast to Britton, the Cambridge antiquary Charles Cooper
preferred in his study of Lady Margaret to avoid overt expressions of
opinion in favour of the chronicle approach. Town clerk of Cambridge
and writer of its annals, he amplified Halsted's portrait by reference to
a far wider range of sources. As an historical work it lacks the vigour
and direction of Halsted's; Cooper's main interest was in gathering as
much knowledge as possible about a figure of legendary importance to
his town and university. At Cooper's death his manuscript was offered
to St John's College for publication. Before being published in 1874 it
was annotated by John E. Mayor with references to the State Papers,
and provided with a calendar of records in the college relevant to the
subject.[37] Mayor's editorial additions continued the work of John
Hymers, who had published Thomas Baker's *Funeral Sermon*, with
Baker's additional notes and his own work on the early history of the
college, illustrated with various documents, in 1840.

Renewed university interest in Lady Margaret the Foundress and her
connection with Fisher and the nascent St John's, should not, however,
obscure Cooper's own achievement. This was to show that Margaret's
influence spread through many localities besides Cambridge: that her
power and jurisdiction reached Kent, the marshes of Lincolnshire, the
city of Coventry. Cooper's diligence led him to enlarge on well-known
episodes: a footnote to the entertainment of Spanish nobles at
Coldharbour in 1501 investigates the mansion using a variety of
sources from printed royal wardrobe accounts to a notice in *The
Gentleman's Magazine*.[38] Some of his references may not have been very
discriminating, indeed were exploratory jottings, but as a guide to the
many dimensions of Margaret's activity his study was the most
comprehensive yet undertaken. Mayor's notes and calendars also

[37] Cooper.   [38] *Ibid.*, 71–2 n. 4.

pointed firmly in the direction of a wider treatment of her life and importance than had hitherto been attempted.

Some of the clues given by Cooper were picked up by E. M. G. Routh in her *Memoir of Lady Margaret*, published in 1924.[39] The book was written as a pious commemoration to help the appeal then in progress for Lady Margaret Hall, Oxford, and the countess presented by Routh is a personable lady to whom one could certainly feel loyalty, and whose domestic life could to some extent be reconstructed. Routh herself considered that an important contribution of her book was its account of the part played by Margaret in gaining the crown for Henry VII. Detailed as it is, however, it makes essentially the same points as Halsted, repeating the suggestion, dismissed by Britton, that Margaret actively sacrificed her own claim to the throne in order to advance her son.[40]

Routh also found Margaret's social concerns arresting: 'had she lived in later times, one could easily imagine her as successfully managing a Red Cross hospital, or a canteen'.[41] The ghost of Margaret's 'Romishness', which had troubled every previous treatment of her piety and good works, was banished by concentrating on her homely charitable concerns. The spirit of co-operative goodwill appropriate to aiding one of the newer colleges at Oxford was seen to have existed in the earlier efforts of its patroness. The 'homeliness' of Lady Margaret was also illustrated by a sketch of her married life with Henry Stafford. For this Routh broke new ground by obtaining, with the aid of Canon Westlake, details of their household itinerary during 1466–71 from the records at Westminster Abbey. Her account of life at Collyweston drew on household expenses printed by Cooper and on help from the Master and Librarian of St John's College, although she did not see personally 'the stores of material in Cambridge' which might throw more light on Margaret's daily life.[42] Gripped by her theme, Routh overdid her picture of a contented middle-class nanny: 'All the arrangements in the royal nurseries were the special care of the Lady Margaret, who settled down very happily to the role of grandmother.'[43] Her deeper investigation of life at court and at Collyweston, however, helped to revise the

---

[39] *A Memoir of Lady Margaret Beaufort, Countess of Richmond and Derby, Mother of Henry VII* (Oxford, 1924). [40] *Ibid.*, Preface, 6; 11. [41] *Ibid.*, 25.
[42] *Ibid.*, 77; Preface, 5.
[43] She may have been responsible for certain ordinances for the use of the royal household, but of special care for nurseries we have found no evidence. See below, pp. 149, 187.

dominant image of Margaret's seclusion from worldly affairs after 1485.

A recent biography by Linda Simon adds little new material to the older studies, but brings to bear a contemporary perception of Lady Margaret as a beleaguered woman in a society where widowhood alone gave her any legal power.[44] Halsted, however, had noted the strength of Margaret's position as *femme sole* by act of parliament in 1485, which did in fact give her the right to hold property and sue, although still married to the earl of Derby.[45] Simon relates the political circumstances of Margaret's early life in exciting detail, and explores her personal life at a modern psychological level untouched by Routh. She describes the travail of late medieval childbirth and the impact of Margaret's youthful marriages and motherhood.[46]

The present book aims to explore further the political involvement of Lady Margaret in the national and local scene, and to examine in the context of her time her other activities, in the realms of literature, education and the conduct of her household. Lady Margaret's biographers have been unanimous in praising her political skill as survivor in a dangerous age, and her interest in scholarship and literature, but she has been seen as an isolated beacon of endurance possessing rare talents and vision in a world of barbarism. So in the political sphere her important connections with the court of Edward IV have been overlooked, while her life after 1485 has been pictured as one of quiet seclusion. In fact her household at Collyweston, which Routh was unable to examine fully, was a hub of activity: in the administration of justice, projects for building and endowment, fen drainage and estate management. Even her own cultural pursuits cannot be divorced from wider circumstances: her position as patron of literature and learning has to be seen in the context of fifteenth-century book production. It was a period of highly competitive activity between printers for an aristocratic market.

The cultural interests of Lady Margaret were not unique among her sex. This emerges most clearly when she is considered alongside some of the other women of power, piety and learning who flourished as her contemporaries. Their accomplishments were noted in the late

---

[44] L. Simon, *Of Virtue Rare: Margaret Beaufort, Matriarch of the House of Tudor* (Boston, Mass., 1982).   [45] Halsted, *Life of Margaret Beaufort*, 166.
[46] The birth-date of 1441, given by Halsted, inclined to by Cooper and followed by Simon is incorrect: below, p. 34.

eighteenth century by Ballard. He cited, for example, the literary output of Juliana Berners, prioress of Sopwell, a cell of St Albans Abbey. This lady wrote treatises on hawking, hunting, fishing and heraldry which were printed in 1481, with a second edition in 1486, and were still in demand enough to be printed once more in 1595.[47] Acquaintance with such ladies had taught Ballard that, contrary to Britton's view, the late middle ages was not wholly a time of barbarous ignorance.[48]

Ballard's limited insight has been extended in our own time by greater familiarity with the fifteenth-century phenomenon of a learned and devout upper-class English laity. Lady Margaret and her contemporaries, such as Lady Hungerford or the literate church-going merchants' wives described in *The Italian Relation*, had no deep knowledge of the Latin sources of their Christian heritage.[49] Their achievement lay in using what they found in the liturgy and devotion of the Church to increase awareness of their own part in worship. Sometimes, as in the case of Lady Margaret, their resources and position allowed them to expand this awareness so as to have a considerable effect on their age: it was almost a generation before Margaret's and William Atkinson's translation of the *Imitation of Christ* was superseded.

In both the realms of learning and politics Lady Margaret can be compared with English and French ladies of her own and the succeeding generation. She was as active at maintaining her own interest and that of her son as was Elizabeth Woodville in advancing her relations, and Cecily, duchess of York, in supporting her husband. On the other hand, she never presided directly over the political scene like Margaret of Anjou or Margaret of York, duchess of Burgundy. The duchess of Burgundy had an equal reputation for piety and learning and a personal collection of twenty-five books, far larger than the number associated with Margaret Beaufort. Margaret of York, however, was able to profit from the cultural riches of her adopted home in Burgundy.[50]

Louise of Savoy, the mother of Francis I of France, was both more politically active, actually reigning as regent during his captivity, and,

[47] Ballard, *Memoirs of Learned Ladies*, 3.   [48] *Ibid.*, 6.
[49] *A Relation of the Island of England about the Year 1500*, transl. and ed. C. A. Sneyd, Camden Society, o.s., 37 (1947), 23.
[50] Weightman, *Margaret of York, Duchess of Burgundy*, 204–5.

from surviving records, more explicit in devotion to her son's cause. She recorded his political progress in her journal and spoke of 'mon roy, mon fils, mon seigneur et mon Cesar'. As Margaret Beaufort's tears of apprehension greeted climactic moments in her son's life so Louise followed with agitation Francis's every political move. Louise also was a figure around whom artists and scholars clustered as she dwelt on her domains, while retaining contact with the world's affairs.[51] Like Lady Margaret, she had a childhood pierced by difficulty and sorrow: she lost her mother at the age of seven, was married at twelve, and widowed at eighteen.[52] Her daughter, Margaret of Navarre, patron of Clement Marot and for a short time of Calvin, composed both a confession of faith, the 'Mirroir de l'Ame Pechéresse', and 'The Heptameron' a cycle of stories which were not merely translations but original efforts in the manner of Boccaccio.

Margaret of Navarre belonged to a generation more thoroughly imbued with classical models than either her mother or Lady Margaret Beaufort. Her piety, too, had begun to pass from a pattern of meditation within the framework of the Church's sacraments evident in Lady Margaret's 'Mirror for the Sinful Soul', to a self-contained, individualistic faith which brought accusations of heresy in its train. The poems written by both Louise of Savoy and her daughter voicing devotion to Francis I, find no parallel from the pen of Margaret Beaufort. The mutual regard of Henry VII and Lady Margaret was briefly, though intensely, expressed in the course of business letters. Yet like Louise and Francis, Margaret and Henry came from outside the direct royal line; in both cases their bonds were formed by the necessity to challenge and assert their right. In the case of Margaret Beaufort her background taught her both to assert her right and to be circumspect in doing so. She was the heiress of a family whose existence had on occasions posed a threat to the other descendants of Edward III. It was not a Yorkist, but a Lancastrian king, Henry IV, who had first tried to exclude the Beauforts from succession to the English throne.

[51] A. Deneuil-Cornier, *The Renaissance in France* (London, 1969), 68–71.
[52] *Ibid.*, 117.

THE FAMILY BACKGROUND

The Beaufort family was the offspring of an adulterous liaison between John of Gaunt, duke of Lancaster, and his mistress Katherine Swynford, who later became his last duchess. The affair began in 1371, and continued throughout much of the duke's second marriage to Constance of Castile. Their relationship had become public knowledge by 1378, when John's open acknowledgement of his mistress provoked indignation and outrage. For several days in November 1379 Gaunt's ducal warrants were dated at Katherine's house at Kettlethorpe (Lincs.) and the mayor of Leicester, in a clear recognition of her influence with the duke, made payments to her for expediting the borough's business.[1] When, in a dramatic meeting with Constance in 1381, Gaunt agreed to give up Katherine it was not through any repentance for his sinful lifestyle, but a renewed concern to advance his claim to the Castilian throne.[2]

The bastard children, three boys and a girl, were born between 1372 and 1381 and given the name Beaufort after Gaunt's castle and lordship in the Champagne. The choice was an unusual one. Beaufort and Nogent had become part of the Lancastrian estate on the marriage of Blanche of Artois and Edmund earl of Lancaster in 1276 and had become sole property of Henry, the third earl, in 1336. Gaunt had acquired the lordship on his marriage to Henry's younger daughter (and eventual sole heiress) Blanche in 1359. Yet it had never been more than a peripheral part of his properties. There is no evidence that

---

[1] S. Armitage-Smith, *John of Gaunt* (London, 1964), 358, 390–3.
[2] P. E. Russell, *The English Intervention in Spain and Portugal in the Time of Edward III and Richard II* (Oxford, 1955), 283–301.

he ever visited it and stayed in the castle where romantic legend places the birth of the children. In his great march through France in 1373 he crossed the Aube further down-river, at Plancy. By then the lands had been lost to the French. John Wyn, who had taken a lease on the lordship in 1365, paying Gaunt an annual rent of £100, went over to the enemy on the re-opening of hostilities in 1369.[3] It has been suggested that in choosing the title of a French *seigneurie* Gaunt was envisaging the creation of a French appanage to endow his bastard line. The more pragmatic and likely explanation must be that the association with a lordship long-lost to the French would not prejudice the rights of his legitimate heir.

John of Gaunt's first marriage to Blanche of Lancaster had produced three sons and two daughters. Two of the boys, John and Edward, had died in infancy leaving Henry of Bolingbroke (born 1366) as the sole surviving male heir. Gaunt's second marriage to Constance of Castile in 1371 gave him another son (John, born 1374) but he too died at a very early age. Yet despite the insecurities of the male succession Gaunt never at any stage contemplated creating a land-base for the Beauforts from his own estates. Instead he concentrated his interests on Bolingbroke. By 1381 he had secured for Henry the marriage of Mary Bohun, coheiress of the de Bohun earldoms of Hereford and Essex: the Bohun badge of the Swan was to become one of Bolingbroke's chief emblems. In contrast, he envisaged for his Beaufort children marriages with well-to-do gentry families. By 1392 Joan Beaufort's marriage had been arranged with Sir Robert Ferrers of Oversley; four years later Thomas, the youngest son, was united with Margaret Neville of Hornby. There was nothing unusual in this; indeed it was regarded as the proper way to make provision for the bastard progeny of the upper nobility. William Montagu, earl of Salisbury had made a bequest of 500 marks for the upbringing and marrying of his bastard son, again enabling a match with a member of a prosperous gentry family.

Gaunt's relations with his Beaufort children were considerate. They were recognized as members of his family and never ostracized, even if in the early 1380s it was deemed prudent to transfer them for a while

---

[3] Armitage-Smith, *John of Gaunt*, 198–9. The suggestion made by A. Tuck, *Richard II and the English Nobility* (London, 1973), 206, that Gaunt may have hoped to bestow a newly created appanage of Aquitaine on John Beaufort, was only a possibility for a brief period between 1394 and 1395.

to Mary de Bohun's household. Here the four bastard children received fine liveries of scarlet and white silk furred with miniver.[4] In the early 1390s John Beaufort, the eldest of the three brothers, participated with distinction in a number of crusading enterprises. In May 1390 he led the English contingent in the Barbary crusade, an honour that marked his social acceptance in an exclusive aristocratic preserve. By this period John of Gaunt had begun to live openly with Katherine again. Gaunt's household lists for 1391 show Katherine Swynford and the Beauforts John, Henry, Thomas and Joan in attendance along with Henry Bolingbroke.[5] The unfortunate Constance, who had separated from Gaunt in 1389, died on 24 March 1394.

Constance's death opened the way for marriage with Katherine Swynford, and plans to make appropriate landed provision for the Beaufort offspring without damaging the estate of the true heirs. John Beaufort accompanied Gaunt on his visit to the duchy of Aquitaine, which commenced in November 1394. Gaunt may have envisaged a possibility of settling this appanage on the Beauforts. But by the summer of 1395 such notions were fast becoming unrealistic. John's estate was to rest on a purchase Gaunt made from William Montagu, earl of Salisbury (by 1395) of the Somerset manors of Curry Rivel, Langport and Martock in reversion.[6] It was hardly a substantial endowment and Gaunt could certainly have bought more from Salisbury.

On Gaunt's return to England, after consultation with Richard II, he married Katherine at Lincoln early in 1396. An aura of scandal hung over this event, caught well by one chronicler: 'the wheche weddyng caused mony a mannus wonderyng, for, as hit was seyde, he haad holde heere longe before'.[7] The couple immediately petitioned the pope to secure its confirmation, in view of the adulterous relationship they had enjoyed during Gaunt's second marriage. In September 1396 the pope ratified the contracted marriage and declared its offspring, past as well as future, legitimate. These developments were to transform the Beauforts' position. Yet bastardy was a complex issue and one in which

[4] C. Given-Wilson and A. Curteis, *The Royal Bastards of Medieval England* (London, 1984), 149.

[5] Printed in J. T. Rosenthal, *Nobles and the Noble Life, 1295–1500* (London, 1976), 153.

[6] G. L. Harriss, *Cardinal Beaufort* (Oxford, 1988), 3–6.

[7] *An English Chronicle of the Reigns of Richard II, Henry IV, Henry V and Henry VI*, ed. J. S. Davies, Camden Society, o.s., 64 (1856), 114.

fourteenth-century developments in common law had begun to undermine the jurisdiction of the Church. The power of the papal bull represented a spiritual purging of the infamy of bastardy. It did not enable the succession of lands or office. To protect more fully the Beauforts' property rights and enable their promotion to the ranks of the nobility Gaunt had their legitimacy confirmed by act of parliament. In February 1397 the pope's legitimation of Sir John Beaufort, his brothers and sister was declared, followed by the king's own wish to pronounce them *muliers* (the subsequent offspring of a man who has married the mother of his bastards). To counter their asserted lack of birthright they were to be raised and admitted to dignities and offices as if they were born in lawful matrimony.[8]

The act represented an important disposal of royal favour. The king addressed the Beauforts as 'consanguineos suos', recognizing his cousinage or blood-link with the family. John Beaufort, the eldest of the offspring, was now showered with honours. The day after the act he was created earl of Somerset. He quickly became a Knight of the Garter and received a stream of royal offices. On 20 November 1397 he became constable of Wallingford castle, on 5 February 1398 constable of Dover castle and warden of the Cinque Ports and on 29 August 1398 he was appointed king's lieutenant in Aquitaine. A prestigious marriage had been secured by September 1397 to Richard II's young niece, Margaret Holland (who became in 1408 coheiress of Edmund earl of Kent), linking him to some of the greatest aristocratic houses. On 29 September he was further elevated to the rank of marquis. The transformation was mirrored in the change of John Beaufort's coat-of-arms. His arms before 1397 were a bend of England (gules charged with three lions *passant guardant or*) with a label of France, against a plain background. In fourteenth-century usage the paternal arms on a bend, against a plain background, were the common designation of illegitimacy. After February 1397 John quartered his father's royal arms on the shield itself, within a *bordure compony*: a denotion of legitimate cadency.[9]

Despite the elevation of the Beauforts, and their rapid acceptance amidst the ranks of the aristocracy, their bastardy was never completely forgotten. The mocking nickname 'Fairborn' was still in use at the end of the fifteenth century. It is with John that the problems of the

---

[8] *Cal. Papal Registers, 1364–1404* IV, 545; *RP*, III, 343.
[9] *CP*, XII, i, 41–2; Given-Wilson, and Curteis, *Royal Bastards*, plates 6a and 6b.

Beauforts' origins are particularly found. His date of birth in 1372 is confirmed by the grant of an annuity to him as king's knight twenty years later. This meant he was probably born of double adultery. Gaunt had married Constance in September 1371; Katherine's husband Sir Hugh Swynford did not die until 11 November. This chronology fits with the chronicler Froissart's statement that the liaison began during Gaunt's second marriage, and also while Katherine's own husband was still alive.[10] Adultery on the part of the woman as well as the man carried a far greater stigma and accounts for the slander of Katherine's reputation by some of the chroniclers. Its consequences could be seen in the case of Thomas Swynford. Thomas (born *c.* 1368) was son and heir from Katherine's first marriage. After the death of his mother in 1403 his attempts to gain possession of lands in Hainault devolving upon him were thwarted because of doubts expressed about his own legitimacy. He had to appeal to Henry IV, who provided letters patent authenticating that Thomas was 'begotten in lawful matrimony'.[11] Conversely, there would always be an element of doubt as to whether John was a Beaufort or a Swynford.

John's position was compounded by the length of time that had elapsed between his birth and the marriage of his parents. After he had been born the liaison between Gaunt and Katherine Swynford seems to have been interrupted. Constance of Castile gave birth first to a daughter, and then in 1374 to a son. Sadly he died in infancy and evidence points to the affair with Katherine being resumed in 1375. Thus John was several years older than the other Beaufort children and had already come of age before the marriage of Gaunt and Katherine early in 1396. These aspects were to leave a taint that the process of legitimation could not completely remove, when Henry IV inserted the 'excepta dignitate regali' clause into the patent of legitimation in 1407.

This event illustrated the complexity of the relationship between John Beaufort and Henry IV. An element of tension existed at the very start of the reign. Beaufort had not openly opposed Bolingbroke's exile in 1398 and the confiscation of his estates. In July 1399 he had been one of the few peers prepared to support the duke of York's attempts to raise an army to counter Henry's landing at Ravenspur. John had

---

[10] *CPR,* 1391–6, 63; Armitage-Smith, *John of Gaunt,* 462–3.
[11] *Excerpta Historica,* ed. S. Bentley (London, 1831), 158–9.

taken £200 from the treasury to enlist 300 men to resist the invasion.[12]
In 1399 John Beaufort was one of the poorest English earls; his estate,
largely limited to the Somerset manors Gaunt had purchased from
William Montagu, earl of Salisbury, four years earlier, was insufficient
to support his title. Beaufort's hopes for a major landed endowment
kept him loyal to Richard II and he was willing to exploit the political
problems facing his half-brother to his own advantage. In John of
Gaunt's will, of 3 February 1398, a clear distinction had been
maintained between Henry and John Beaufort. The conveyances to the
Beauforts were of acquired property, and Gaunt's reluctance to grant
any of his own lands had stemmed from a scrupulous concern not to
diminish Bolingbroke's expectations. John Beaufort may have hoped to
profit materially from Henry Bolingbroke's exile. Yet the situation was
complex. According to the *Traison et Mort* chronicle, in the summer of
1399 the Percies had wished to see John Beaufort executed. But in a
dramatic gesture Henry had produced a letter written to him during his
exile, in which Beaufort had shown his secret goodwill. Given the
double-dealing that characterized the last years of Richard II's reign
this story seems plausible. He was on probation at first. In November
1399 he was appointed king's chamberlain during pleasure. In the
parliament in the same month he and his heirs were degraded from the
rank of marquis, a creation too closely associated with the policies and
favourites of the previous king, but he retained the title of earl of
Somerset. But in February 1400, after he had shown his loyalty in the
first major plot of the new reign, he was re-appointed chamberlain for
life.[13] From then on he was to prosper remarkably.

John Beaufort's record of service in the new reign was exceptional.
He was often at court, attended the council, was a member of
diplomatic and family missions and held active commands in Calais
and Wales until his death in 1410. His close association with the
Lancastrian royal family was demonstrated by the ceremonial duties
he undertook. He escorted the king's elder daughter Blanche to
Cologne for her marriage with the Count Palatine in July 1402 and
accompanied Joan of Navarre, Henry's second wife, from Brittany to
England in January 1403. He shared with the king a strong chivalric
outlook: both a fellow-crusader and a member of the tourney, he
represented the Garter Knights in a joust with Jean de Werchin of

[12] A. L. Brown, 'The reign of Henry IV', in *Fifteenth-Century England, 1399–1509*, ed. S. B.
Chrimes, C. D. Ross and R. A. Griffiths (Manchester, 1972), 6.   [13] *Ibid.*, 6–7.

Hainault at Smithfield in July 1409. The king in return accorded him especial favour. In November 1401 he stood as godfather for Beaufort's son and heir, named Henry after the king. Strikingly, he granted him and his heirs male an annuity of 1,000 marks, to be replaced by an annuity of £1,000 three years later, which helped buttress the Beauforts' rather shaky landed position.[14]

However important financially, the annuity still left John Beaufort heavily dependent on the crown. His landed position was transformed in 1408 when his wife, Margaret Holland, became one of the coheiresses of the earldom of Kent, a possibility that could hardly have been envisaged in 1397. The earldom, one of the greatest of the fourteenth century, had become extinct after the death of earls Thomas (d. 1400) and Edmund (d. 1408). The properties that descended to Margaret Holland were of vital importance to the Beaufort family and came to form the heart of its landed identity. Successive partitions of the Holland estate continued to augment the Beaufort inheritance throughout the first half of the fifteenth century. It was her right to these Holland properties that made Margaret Beaufort a great heiress.

It seems likely that by 1401 Somerset had become the magnate closest to the king and was to remain so for the remainder of his life. John Beaufort's strong sense of identity with the Lancastrian house was revealed in the book of hours he commissioned in the early 1400s. He shared Henry IV's devotion to St Thomas of Canterbury, shown in the elaborate nature of the prayers to the saint, occupying no less than six pages. Indeed John wished to be buried in Canterbury cathedral, as close as possible to Henry's resting place. The book also included memoria to St John of Bridlington, a saint venerated by the house of Lancaster, and the altars dedicated to St John at St Nicholas' church, Dover, and St Peter's, Sandwich, were established when John Beaufort was constable of Dover castle and warden of the Cinque Ports.[15]

With the public acknowledgement of the closeness of the Beauforts to the royal family the possibility arose that they might be eligible for

---

[14] Harriss, *Cardinal Beaufort*, 17–18.

[15] N. J. Rogers, 'Books of hours produced in the low countries for the English market in the fifteenth century' (Cambridge MLitt, 1982), 87. The notion that the Beaufort motto 'Souvent me souvient' was based on that of Henry IV rests, however, on a misreading of the king's motto 'Soverain': E. Danbury, 'The decoration and illumination of royal charters in England, 1250–1509', in *England and Her Neighbours 1066–1453*, ed. M. Jones and M. Vale (London, 1989), 173–4.

succession to the throne. Their legitimation in 1397 had been unconditional. Yet the enabling act referred to property, office and noble rank. Although it accorded the right to dignities it conferred no royal interest or right and title to the throne. Here the language of the act was significant. It used no words of empire, majesty or sovereignty, such as 'regnum', 'summa potestas', 'corona' or 'maiestas' that would enable a man to be an heir of a kingdom. That possibility may have been remote in 1397. It assumed a far greater relevance after the succession of Henry IV. As early as 1400 there had been a plot to kill the king and his sons. At the end of 1406 a detailed discussion of the issue of succession had seen the designation by statute of the crown on the king's sons and the heirs of their body. No mention was made of any remainder to the Beauforts, and continued emphasis was laid on a sense of legitimate succession, 'suis de ipsius corpore legitime procreandis'. There would have been no shortage of candidates if the order was extended beyond the king and his children, including the Mortimers and the house of York, and there were good political reasons for not delineating the issue further.[16] Nevertheless, a desire for a clarification of his position led to John Beaufort petitioning the king in February 1407, requesting an exemplification 'of the tenour of the enrolment' of the letter patent dated 9 February 1397 providing for his legitimation. The royal response was the confirmation of the original letters, with the insertion of the clause, after the enablement of honours and dignities 'excepta dignitate regali'.[17]

This crucial clause was never intended to be a resumption of rights accorded to the Beauforts by the original act of legitimation. The insertion was made on the patent roll, and the wording of the act on the roll of parliament was left in its original form. It was a refinement of the act of 1397, made on the king's initiative, though it did not carry a binding power on his successors. At the time of John Beaufort's petition in February 1407 he already had four sons, Henry, John, Thomas and Edmund. Despite the high regard the king had for his half-brother and the substantial royal favour accorded to him, he did not regard him or his male line as candidates for the succession.

This sense of doubt as to the Beaufort legitimacy lay at the heart of the family's identity. They were loyal servants of the house of

---

[16] The issue is ably discussed in P. McNiven, *Heresy and Politics in the Reign of Henry IV, The Burning of John Badbury* (Bury St Edmunds, 1987), 132–5.

[17] *CPR, 1405–8*, 284; *Excerpta Historica*, 152–3.

Lancaster, active in their military and civil responsibilities and recognized as important members of the broader royal family. When Margaret's father, John Beaufort II, was elevated to the dukedom of Somerset in March 1443, it was ostensibly for his nearness to the royal blood and his willingness to do the king service.[18] Their close sense of identity with Henry IV can be seen in their subsequent association with the chapel of St Michael in Canterbury cathedral, near the burial place of the first Lancastrian king, which became a family shrine. In October 1431 the young Thomas Beaufort was buried there. In January 1440 Margaret Holland was laid to rest with her first and second husbands, John Beaufort and Thomas duke of Clarence. In October 1453 Isabel, a daughter of Edmund Beaufort, second duke of Somerset, was buried in this chapel and it is likely from the scale of Edmund's patronage of Canterbury that he too was intending a fine tomb and memorial there: plans frustrated by his violent death at St Albans.[19] Yet it was the same king, Henry IV, who had made explicit the view that the Beauforts were not able to succeed to the throne.

Speculation inevitably continued over the issue. Early in 1450, at a time of dynastic uncertainty, popular awareness of the Beauforts' closeness to the royal lineage was given public expression. The stalwart service rendered to the Lancastrian dynasty, first by Thomas Beaufort, duke of Exeter, and then by Cardinal Beaufort, had enhanced the prestige of the family, and Henry VI was known to be favourably inclined towards them. The Commons had charged that the duke of Suffolk's hasty marriage of his son to the young heiress Margaret Beaufort was proof of his ambition to gain the throne.[20] If Henry VI had died childless early in the 1450s, Suffolk's son and heir, John de la Pole, would have had a claim through Margaret's position as Beaufort heiress. Early in 1453, when Henry VI had the match between John and Lady Margaret dissolved so that the newly created earl of Richmond could marry her, he may have envisaged Edmund Tudor as his heir, in the right of Margaret Beaufort. Yet the situation was

---

[18] *PPC*, V, 252–3.
[19] All four sons of John Beaufort earl of Somerset and Margaret Holland were once commemorated in the stained glass of the chapel. The paragraph is based on: *The Chronicle of John Stone Monk of Christ Church, 1415–71*, ed. W. G. Searle (Cambridge, 1902), 20–2, 26, 58; F. Woodman, *The Architectural History of Canterbury Cathedral* (London, 1981), 176–9; and information kindly provided by Dr Christopher Wilson.
[20] *RP*, V, 177.

unclear. Many regarded the Hollands, rather than the Beauforts, as closest to the Lancastrian line: only this fact can explain the huge dowry of 4,500 marks (one of the largest marriage portions in late medieval England) Richard duke of York was willing to pay to arrange the marriage of the duke of Exeter's heir, Henry Holland, with his eldest daughter, Anne, in August 1445.[21] The Staffords, descended from John of Gaunt's youngest brother Thomas of Woodstock, were also possible candidates and in 1444 Henry VI had created Humphrey Stafford duke of Buckingham.

There was never any real prospect of a Beaufort claim to the English crown before 1483, when Lady Margaret's only son, Henry Tudor, emerged as Richard III's rival and challenged his right to the kingdom. The Welsh chronicle tradition that Margaret had insisted that her son be named not Owen (in memory of his paternal grandfather) but Henry (in honour of Henry VI his uncle) confirms the close sense of identity with the house of Lancaster.[22] In 1485 Richard III wrote to his chancellor, Bishop John Russell, on the drafting of a proclamation against Henry Tudor. Particular reference was made to his Beaufort lineage, for Richard recognized that it gave far greater credibility than his royal Valois or Tudor descent. The comments were specific: Henry had no interest, right or title to the throne because he was descended of bastard blood, for 'his moder was doughter unto John Duc of Somerset, son unto John Erle of Somerset, son unto dame Kateryne Swynford, and of her in double advoutrow goten; whereby it evidently appereth that noo title can or may be in hym'.[23] The reference to the double adultery indicated that it was the circumstances of John Beaufort's birth that reinforced the stigma of bastardy and impeded any hope of inheriting the crown through his line. When Henry Tudor came to the throne, he confirmed the original 1397 act of legitimation as a recognition of his royal lineage, but did not base his claim to the kingdom on it. The sense of doubt that hung over the family's dynastic position had a strong effect on Lady Margaret, seen in her obsession with pedigree in her son's reign.

[21] J. M. W. Bean, 'The financial position of Richard, duke of York', in *War and Government in the Middle Ages*, ed. J. Gillingham and J. C. Holt (Cambridge, 1984), 195, citing PRO, DL41, 2/8.

[22] R. A. Griffiths and R. S. Thomas, *The Making of the Tudor Dynasty* (Gloucester, 1985), 47–8.

[23] *Original Letters Illustrative of English History*, ed. H. Ellis, 11 vols. (London, 1824–46), 2nd series, I, 164.

Margaret's grandfather John, earl of Somerset, had died in 1410 less than forty years old. The career of her father John Beaufort, first duke of Somerset, was a series of lost opportunities. The early death of his elder brother Henry in 1418 left him as the senior member of the family's second generation. In November 1419 he crossed over to France with his younger brothers Thomas and Edmund. He was not yet sixteen, and it was to be his first experience of active warfare. He was equipped with fine armour and received a special present of two war horses from his uncle Henry Beaufort, bishop of Winchester.[24] It could have been the start of a long and notable military career. Instead it became a disaster. Captured at the battle of Baugé in March 1421, he spent his next seventeen years in captivity in France, the longest period endured by an English aristocrat during the entire Hundred Years War. Somerset was the most valuable English prisoner captured by the French during the war, and the nearest they ever got to taking a royal prince. A number of attempts to arrange his release were made. An exchange mooted with members of the Orléans family (in the period 1421–2) never came to anything. His main hope of freedom lay with the captive John duke of Bourbon. In May 1423 Beaufort had been transferred to the keeping of Marie de Berry, Bourbon's wife. The chance of negotiating his release had been discussed in a meeting of the English council on 10 March 1427. It was decided that Bourbon should secure Beaufort's liberation or give surety for his ransom. Such sums would then be repaid to Henry VI if he so wished. A moving petition from the imprisoned John Beaufort (*c.* October 1427) pressed that parliament should approve the arrangement, adding that no other way of securing his freedom existed and that he had suffered much hardship through his long detention in France.[25]

The agreement was formally ratified with Bourbon in London on 8 February 1429. Fresh disappointments were in store. Bourbon was unable to raise the money. Shortly before his death, on 30 January 1434, he added an important clause to his will. He referred to Beaufort 'long held a prisoner' now to be used to secure the release of Bourbon's stepson the count of Eu.[26] For John Beaufort who had seen his younger brother Thomas, another victim of Baugé, released four years earlier,

[24] WAM, 12163, fols. 12, 12v.
[25] PRO, SC8/141/7018. For the earlier release efforts see A. Joubert, *Négociations relatives à l'échange de Charles, duc d'Orléans et de Jean, comte d'Angoulême, entre les seigneurs anglais* (Angers, 1890); AN, K168/92; PPC, III, 255–6.   [26] AN, P1370, no. 1882.

it was a new setback. All the other English captured in the battle had secured their freedom: Lord FitzWalter in 1426, John Holland, earl of Huntingdon, a year later. The earl of Suffolk and Lord Talbot, captured at the reverses at Jargeau and Patay in June 1429, had been released in 1431 and 1433 respectively. Now Somerset was burdened with fresh difficulties. The count of Eu had refused to accept the treaty of Troyes, and his release during Henry VI's minority had been expressly forbidden in Henry V's last will. In a council meeting of 20 February 1436 the young king 'at the instance and very requeste' of Cardinal Beaufort and his nephew Edmund, initiated practical arrangements to secure the exchange.[27] After complex negotiations Beaufort secured his freedom in the late summer of 1438.

The long saga of these release efforts serves as an important reminder of the series of frustrations that came to jaundice John Beaufort's outlook. Little is known about the conditions of Beaufort's captivity: his confinement was comfortable enough for him to produce a bastard daughter, Tacyn, whilst in France. But the practical problems of paying off his large ransom (at £24,000 the capital value of all his inheritance, including his mother's Holland lands, at twenty years' purchase) were to encumber him for the remainder of his life. Negotiations with the French over the repayment of debts and the recovery of hostages left by him as pledges dominated his last years. His health may well have been affected by his long captivity and in the winter of 1442 he was already suffering illness. A sense of grievance at the high ransom 'whereby he was impoverished' was to dominate his outlook.[28] It led to a tragic debacle.

John Beaufort's long captivity had blighted his prospects of securing an advantageous marriage. He finally secured a relatively modest match, marrying Margaret Beauchamp of Bletsoe around 1442. The Beauchamps of Bletsoe (Beds.) and Lydiard Tregoze (Wilts.) had come to prominence in the reign of Edward III. Roger Beauchamp was a successful soldier and courtier, summoned to parliament by writ from 1363 onwards. But his grandson and heir was never summoned, nor were his descendants. By the mid-fifteenth century, when Beaufort married Margaret Beauchamp, heiress to the family's estates, they had settled into the ranks of the well-to-do gentry.[29] It was a galling contrast with his highly successful younger brother Edmund, who had

[27] A decision referred to retrospectively in PRO, E404/56/329.
[28] *CPR, 1436–41*, 515.   [29] *CP*, II, 44–5.

married the well-jointured Eleanor, daughter of the great Richard Beauchamp earl of Warwick, and widow of Thomas Lord Roos of Hamelak.

Although by now suffering ill-health, in 1443 John Beaufort was offered a chance to improve dramatically his position by leading a major expedition to France. Tough negotiation with the crown saw his elevation to the rank of duke and acquisition of lands worth 600 marks a year, including part of the lordship of Kendal, to bolster his estate. Beaufort's attitude was one of vigilant self-interest. Both in discussions with the king and in his efforts to re-settle through conveyance much of the family property he was prepared to damage the interests of his younger brother Edmund, who may well have withdrawn his support for the campaign. The powers of his commission were also a slight to the authority of the king's lieutenant in France, Richard duke of York. Much was hoped for from Beaufort's expedition. Yet the only motive that seems to explain his conduct was a desire to recoup as much of his ransom as was possible. Resembling one of the meandering *chevauchées* of the fourteenth century, it commenced by levying an illegal transport tax in the Cotentin that created an uproar in Normandy. Worse was to follow. The frontier town of La Guerche in neutral Brittany was captured and held to ransom: an incident that came close to provoking full-scale war with the duchy. The army then occupied the region north of the Loire, not as a base to attack the forces of Charles VII, but to enable Beaufort to levy *appatis* (war taxes) on the entire area. Finally the soldiers were disbanded prematurely.[30] The expedition had cost the English exchequer over £26,000: the result was a misuse of funds comparable with the military fiascos of the later years of the fourteenth century.

Beaufort's reception on his return to England could not have been more hostile. The king was deeply angered and banished him from court. His financial malpractices became the subject of a major government enquiry, and property and goods in both France and England were confiscated. Beaufort retired to the west country in disgrace, where he died shortly afterwards. It was rumoured that he

---

[30] The background comments are drawn from M. K. Jones, 'John Beaufort, duke of Somerset and the French expedition of 1443', in *Patronage, the Crown and the Provinces in later Medieval England*, ed. R. A. Griffiths (Gloucester, 1981), 79–102, and 'L'imposition illégale de taxes en "Normandie Anglaise"': une enquête gouvernementale en 1446', in *La 'France Anglaise' Au Moyen Age. Actes du IIIe Congrès National des Sociétés Savantes* (Paris, 1988), 461–8.

may have hastened his end by suicide.[31] It was a traumatic legacy for his family. Beaufort was buried quietly and without any ostentation in Wimborne Minster. A priest was paid 10d for two days of prayers for his soul and a small commemorative window was erected.[32] A disgraced war commander and perhaps also a suicide was not an easy memory to bear. Margaret came to inherit the martial tapestries owned by her father (including one of the story of the captain Matthew Gough, who had fought with Beaufort in France). They served as a stark reminder of the rapidity of a fall from grace, the mutability of worldly achievement: 'When he was weddyed, and in estate most high... fortune...to grounde hym cast cruellye.'[33]

Margaret had no recollection of her father. But the tragedy of his crippling ransom and exile from court was vividly preserved by the chronicler of Crowland, whose abbot had had to seek an interview with Beaufort over a boundary dispute in Goggisland marsh before his last campaign. It was a source that Margaret (who had been admitted to the confraternity of the abbey in 1465) certainly had access to. His disgrace and subsequent death so soon after his elevation to great honours seemed to exercise a particular fascination for contemporaries. Alongside this unsettling memory Margaret would inherit more general Beaufort traits seen most characteristically in the career of her uncle Edmund Beaufort. Edmund exemplified the combination of loyalty to the Lancastrian house and an acquisitive and rather defensive self-interest that was to be so typical of the family. A handsome and urbane courtier, his affair with Henry V's 'young and lusty' widow, Katherine of Valois, in 1426–7 had created a political scandal. By the mid-1440s he had already achieved great renown in the wars in France. He had been elected to the Order of the Garter after his successful defence of Calais in 1436, and was to be further rewarded by a promotion to the earldom of Dorset. In 1439–40 he presided over the last major English achievements: the relief of Avranches and recapture of Harfleur. Yet there were also disquietening signs of a ruthless concern to safeguard his own position. In 1433 there was a major enquiry into his conduct in Normandy after allegations that he had transported the artillery from Gisors to his own private

[31] *Ingulph's Chronicle of the History of Croyland*, ed. H. T. Riley (London, 1854), 399.
[32] DRO, P204/CW23.
[33] *English Historical Literature in the Fifteenth Century*, ed. C. L. Kingsford (Oxford, 1913), 395–7.

castle of Chanteloup in the Norman Cotentin. His expedition to Maine in 1438 brought forth widespread complaint that it was serving Beaufort interest rather than that of the war effort, and Edmund's conduct was to be bitterly attacked by one of the army's leading captains, that professional soldier of fortune, the landless Roger Lord Camoys.[34] After the death of John Beaufort, Edmund, as heir male, took on the leadership of the Beaufort family. He had close relations with his uncle, the cardinal, and a marriage alliance was forged by the union of his own daughter Margaret and the eldest son of the duke of Buckingham, which seems to have taken place by 1447. His three sons, Henry, Edmund and John, would carry on the male line of the family for another generation.

After John Beaufort's death his wife resided in Bletsoe castle (Beds.) and at Maxey castle (N'hants.). There was some interchange between her household and Edmund Beaufort's. In 1447 Margaret Beauchamp married her third husband, Lionel, Lord Welles. Welles became a loyal supporter of Edmund, serving under him in the Calais garrison in the early 1450s. After Edmund Beaufort's violent death in 1455 his widow Eleanor found shelter at Maxey. She was to remarry with one of Margaret Beauchamp's servants, Walter Rokesley (who was later to be buried at Crowland). But Margaret Beaufort's own sense of family intimacy in her early years was derived from the St John family, the offspring of Margaret Beauchamp's first marriage, to Oliver St John (d. 1437). The numerous children of this match provided Margaret with companionship and familial identity in the early stages of her life. At Bletsoe was an embroidery Margaret had worked, delineating the descent of the St Johns: she had presented it on the occasion of John St John's marriage in 1498, a fitting symbol of her strong personal identification with the maternal side of her family.[35]

The depth of Lady Margaret's interest in her maternal lineage and her Bletsoe ancestry is revealed from two sources closely linked with

[34] AN, Collection Dom Lenoir, 22, fol. 307; PRO, C81/1371/46 (kindly drawn to our attention by Mr John Watt). For Edmund's affair with Katherine see *Incerti Scriptoris Chronicon Angliae*, ed. J. A. Giles (London, 1848), 17; R. A. Griffiths, 'Queen Katherine of Valois and a missing statute of the realm', *Law Quarterly Review*, 93 (1977), 248–62. If Edmund had resumed his liaison with Katherine in 1428, in defiance of the statute of the previous parliament, and fathered her first child (Harriss, *Cardinal Beaufort*, 178–9), he would have run a colossal political risk. It is possible that he acted as godfather to the first of Katherine and Owen Tudor's offspring, who was thus named after him.

[35] SJC, D91.17, p. 19; Cooper, 5.

her. The first was the book of hours she inherited from her mother. The work had an unusual history. The original manuscript was commissioned by Margaret's grandfather, John earl of Somerset. On his death the book was divided: the larger part of the psalter passing into the Holland family, the remainder to Margaret's mother, who incorporated it in a book of hours she had commissioned from the London painter William Abell in the early 1440s. This work then passed into Margaret's hands and became one of her most treasured possessions. She added a particularly large number of entries, rather as if it were a common-place or day book, and bequeathed it to her chapel at Westminster Abbey. These included the obits of the Grandison family, which were copied en masse from a fourteenth-century exemplar. The obits related to the sisters, parents or uncles of Mabel de Grandison, who had married Sir John Patshull of Blestoe (d. 1349). Their daughter Sibyl had married Roger Beauchamp, first Lord Beauchamp of Bletsoe, Margaret's maternal great-great-great-grand-father.[36] The second source was a collection of pedigrees Margaret had commissioned from Thomas Wriothesly, Garter King of Arms, in Henry VII's reign, which were particularly informative on those related to Lady Margaret through the female line. Next to the marriage between Sir John Beauchamp (Margaret's maternal grandfather) and Edith Shottesbroke the Beauchamp lineage was rehearsed, traced back to the same Roger first Lord Beauchamp, 'chamberleyn a le tres noble Roy Edward le tierce'.[37]

Bletsoe provided an occasional residence for Margaret Beauchamp and the St Johns, and her cofferer Ralph Lannoy was to be buried in the parish church in 1458. It was from Bletsoe that a marriage was arranged for Tacyn, the bastard daughter of Lady Margaret's father John, duke of Somerset, who had been secured letters of denizenship in 1443. The match was a good one, with Reginald Lord Grey of Wilton, and Tacyn was to reside in the nearby seat of Bletchley until her death in 1494.[38] A more frequent family dwelling-place was the Fenland

[36] Plate 1, BL, Royal MS 2A XVIII, discussed in Rogers, 'Books of hours', 84–7, which revises the account in M. Rickert, 'The so-called Beaufort Hours and York Psalter', *Burlington Magazine*, 104 (1962), 238–46. Entries from the MS are printed by F. Maddon in *Collectanea Topographica et Genealogica*, 1 (1834), 277–80. For information on the Grandison exemplar we are indebted to Nicholas Rogers.

[37] The collection of pedigrees is found in BL, Harley MS 1074, of which extracts are printed in 'Pedigrees of noble families related to the blood royal', *Coll. Top. et Gen.*, 1 (1834), 295–318.   [38] *PPC*, V, 288; *CP*, VI, 180.

castle of Maxey and here Margaret spent much of her early childhood. Notes in the book of hours of the Fairfax family of nearby Deeping Gate provide a settled picture of family life. The baptism of their child at Stamford in 1445 was attended by two of the daughters of Margaret Beauchamp's first marriage, Edith and Elizabeth St John. Another christening of a Fairfax daughter in St Peter's church, Maxey, was witnessed by Edith St John and Thomas Yerman, the steward of the household at Maxey. Other occasions were attended by Margaret Beauchamp herself, her servant Walter Rokesley (who had married Eleanor, dowager-duchess of Somerset, widow of Edmund Beaufort) and members of the Browne family, wealthy merchants of Stamford.[39] This was Margaret's early milieu, and it forged connections and loyalties she was to maintain all her life.

Margaret Beauchamp's first marriage to Sir Oliver St John had left five children: two sons and three daughters. These siblings of the half-blood became Lady Margaret's adopted family. She championed their interests and gave them prominent positions within her own household. In her patronage of the St Johns she was even on occasion prepared to defy the wishes of her own son, Henry VII. Details of some of the offspring of the elder son John St John were entered into the Beaufort book of hours, including information concerning one of his daughters, Margaret, who became abbess of Shaftesbury.[40] John's eldest son, John II, became Margaret Beaufort's chamberlain after 1504 and was an executor of her will. The younger son of Margaret Beauchamp's marriage to Oliver St John, also named Oliver, inherited the family property at Lydiard Tregoze. He died in 1497 and his tomb, later erected in the chancel of the church of Kirke Rochford (Lincs.) proudly referred to his service as 'sometime squire' to the 'grandame of Henry VIII'.[41] Margaret Beaufort's identification with and support for the broader St John family was noticeable and consistent. Another of the St John daughters, Mary, had married Sir Richard Frogenhall, a close servant to Edmund Beaufort. Frogenhall offspring were supported by Margaret from the 1470s onwards. Elizabeth St John had wedded William Lord Zouche and subsequently John Lord Scrope of Bolton.

[39] Oxford, Bodleian Library, MS Lat. Liturg. e. 10, fols. 1–9, 23–35.
[40] *Coll. Top. et Gen.*, I (1834), 278. In March 1492 Margaret St John received licence to found a chantry at Shaftesbury with prayers for the souls of Henry VII, Lady Margaret, Sir Oliver St John and Margaret, duchess of Somerset: *CPR, 1485–94*, 369.
[41] *Lincs Rec. Soc.*, I (Lincoln, 1911), 204.

Their respective lineages were to encompass some of Richard III's staunchest supporters, including the Catesby and Conyers families. After Bosworth Margaret went out of her way to protect the fortunes of those of her kinsmen under a political cloud. Oliver St John had married Elizabeth Bigod. After 1485 Margaret took another Bigod, Sir Ralph, into her own household, despite his record as a servant of Richard III. Members of the Conyers family were also assisted.[42] No stronger proof could be required for the depth of Margaret's concern for this branch of her family.

The earliest event recorded in the calendar of the Beaufort book of hours was the birth of Margaret herself. The date given was 31 May 1443. The day and month are generally agreed, being those on which she appointed that Westminster Abbey should celebrate her anniversary during her lifetime, but about the year there has been more uncertainty. The antiquary William Dugdale had suggested an alternative year, 1441, based on the rather vague evidence of inquisitions taken at the death of Margaret's father, and this has been followed by most of her biographers.[43] However, there can be little doubt that 1443 is correct. Not only does the calendar provide an intimate contemporary family record, but the date fits the circumstances of the last tragic year of her father's life. In May 1443 he had negotiated with the crown over the wardship of an expected child (i.e. Margaret) should he die on campaign.[44] Margaret was younger than has been realized when undergoing the turbulent events of her childhood. She would have had no memory of her father. At best her mother, who had many children by her previous marriage, and was shortly to marry again, would pass on her own brief recollections. The short time span between Margaret's birth and her father's ill-health and mysterious death imparted a feeling of fragility but also a tremendous sense of destiny.

[42] For Margaret's gift to William, Lord Conyers, grandson and heir of Sir John Conyers of Hornby, on the christening of his child: SJC, D91.20, p. 167. The details of the St Johns and their kindred are to be found in Genealogical table 2, xx–xxi.

[43] *Coll. Top. et Gen.*, I (1834), 278; W. Dugdale, *The Baronage of England*, 2 vols. (London, 1675–6), II, 123. Examination of PRO, C139/114, shows that of sixteen returns, only one gives Margaret's date of birth as 1441, and eleven place it in 1443.

[44] *PPC*, V, 252.

2

THE WARS OF THE ROSES

The birth of Lady Margaret Beaufort, on 31 May 1443, had occurred as her father was preparing to lead a major military expedition to France, an enterprise that soon proved to be the last attempt by the English to reverse their declining fortunes in the final phase of the Hundred Years War. John Beaufort, newly elevated to the dukedom of Somerset, had negotiated long and hard with the king. He had hoped to ensure that in the event of his death the rights to his only daughter's wardship and marriage were to belong to his wife, Margaret Beauchamp of Bletsoe. But his return from the campaign in political disgrace early in 1444 jeopardized these arrangements. Henry VI was deeply angered by Somerset's behaviour in France and banished him from court whilst treason charges were prepared against him. The Crowland chronicle, a particularly well-informed source, reported a current rumour that the duke's death shortly afterwards (on 27 May 1444 at Wimborne in Dorset) was a suicide. Whether there was any truth in this story is hard to tell. But the explanation is no less likely than the one offered by Thomas Basin, writing long after these events, that Somerset succumbed to illness, although he was still only forty years old.[1] There was no doubting the punitive measures taken by Henry against the late duke's estate in both England and France, amidst accusations of corruption and mismanagement made against the discredited commander. In this uncertain period it was Henry VI's own initiative that steered the fortunes of the Beaufort heiress on to a new course.

On 31 May 1444, exactly a year after Margaret's birth, it was the

[1] *Ingulph's Chronicle of the History of Croyland*, 399; T. Basin, *Histoire des règnes de Charles VII et de Louis XI*, ed. J. Quicherat, 4 vols. (Paris, 1933–44), I, 284.

king who revoked his previous agreement, made with Margaret's late father. At his manor of Berkhamstead he decided that the wardship and marriage of the baby child were now to be held by William de la Pole, earl of Suffolk, for his 'notable services' rendered to the country.[2] Henry knew that his envoy was close to success in the negotiations with the French, which culminated in the signing of the Truce of Tours on 28 May. It was an important agreement that offered, in the king's eyes at least, the possibility of an end to the war. Suffolk's reward was a lucrative wardship, that provided him an income from a substantial portion of the Beaufort estates. Since Margaret's mother, the duchess of Somerset, was again pregnant at the time that Suffolk received the wardship, he petitioned the king that whatever the issue, his income from the lands was to remain unaffected.[3] In fact no second child survived and Margaret remained sole heiress. Suffolk was an influential and ambitious figure at the Lancastrian court, able to use his position as steward of the king's household to secure a number of profitable wardships. But there is no evidence at this stage that he intended, as was later claimed (early in 1450) by his enemies in a hostile parliament, to marry Margaret to his own son, John de la Pole, to further his own dynastic ambitions. Rather, Suffolk was the beneficiary of Henry VI's own deliberate policy of patronage. It was the king who was the guiding force in young Margaret's future destiny.

Suffolk's plans for the marriage of his son lay in a different direction. He did not have adequate heritable estates to enable his heir, John, to support the ducal title vested in him in June 1448. Suffolk needed to marry his son to the greatest English heiress of that generation. By 1446 he had secured the wardship of the child Anne Beauchamp, daughter and sole heir of Henry Beauchamp, duke of Warwick. The Lady Anne of Warwick was a wealthier heiress than Margaret, and there seems no reason to doubt Suffolk's own statement to the Commons in 1450 that he had originally intended a marriage between her and his son John.

These hopes were to undergo a sudden and dramatic change. Early in 1450 the Commons in an angry parliament had brought a stream of charges against Suffolk, ranging from corruption to high treason. Their object was the impeachment of the king's chief minister, and despite his answers to the allegations he was arrested and placed in the Tower on 28 January 1450. New charges were drafted and it must

---

[2] *Excerpta Historica*, 4.　　　　　　　　[3] CPR, 1441–6, 283.

have been clear to Suffolk that his position was now desperate. Provision for his son and heir was an obvious priority. The intended match, Anne Beauchamp, had died in 1449 at the age of five. Instead, John de la Pole, a boy of seven, was married to Margaret Beaufort. According to the Commons' own statement this had taken place between 28 January and 7 February 1450, and this is corroborated by a papal dispensation of 18 August of the same year.[4]

Suffolk's decision to marry his only son to Margaret was a product of the difficulties that faced him in the parliament of 1449–50. The marriage between Margaret and John de la Pole was a hasty measure that was destined not to last. In little more than three years the couple's marriage was dissolved and Margaret's wardship and marriage had been transferred to the king's own half-brothers, Jasper and Edmund Tudor. Ironically, the de la Pole line was to develop a dynastic significance, not through the brief Beaufort marriage of 1450–3, but through John's second marriage to a daughter of Richard, duke of York: an alliance that led ultimately to John's own eldest son and heir being recognized as successor to the throne by Richard III in May 1485.

Margaret never understood or recognized the significance of the ceremony that had taken place when she was only six years old. The validity of a child marriage had a suspended quality, with the child having the choice of ratifying or reclaiming (i.e. revoking) the contract at a future date. Dissent was to be made publicly, before witnesses, including a bishop. Margaret was later to recount to Fisher her own version of these proceedings, which gave an insight into the way a young girl might try to make sense of the events around her. According to Margaret's recollections she had been faced with a choice between two suitors, John de la Pole and Edmund Tudor. The king, Henry VI, 'dyd make meanes for Edmund his broder then the erle of Rychemonde'. Unable to decide, she had been advised to pray to St Nicholas, 'the patron and helper of al true maydens, and to besech him to put in

---

[4] *RP*, V, 177; *Cal. Papal Registers*, X, 472–3; T. B. Pugh, 'The Marcher Lords of Glamorgan and Morgannwg, 1317–1485', *Glamorgan County History*, III, ed. T. B. Pugh (Cardiff, 1971), 556–7. Despite the existence of this contract of marriage, referred to in the papal dispensation of 1450, Margaret seems subsequently not to have recognized it. In her will of 1472 Edmund Tudor is referred to as her 'fyrst husband' (SJC, D56.195). Under canon law Margaret was not bound by such a contract if it had been entered into before she had reached the age of twelve, and this gave the king liberty to arrange a fresh contract with Edmund in 1453. C. N. L. Brooke, *The Medieval Idea of Marriage* (Oxford, 1989), 36; below, p. 38 and n. 6.

her mynde what she were best to do…especially that nyght when she sholde the morowe after make answer of her mynde determynatly'. The saint had intimated to her that Edmund would be the appropriate choice. The scenario had a dream-like quality, with a vague memory of a solemn ceremony and a man dressed in white, 'arrayed like a bishop'.[5] This remarkable account provides a nine-year-old's own view of the reclamation of marriage, conducted early in 1453, when its dissolution was arranged shortly before the time of the Reading parliament, and Margaret's wardship and marriage regranted to Jasper and Edmund Tudor. Since a childhood contract need not be permanently binding, Margaret may have genuinely recalled that she was now being presented with a real choice. In reality the crucial factor was not the intercession of a particular saint but Henry VI's own personal initiative, a rare instance of the last Lancastrian king taking a decision by himself and enforcing his will.

It had been the king who had ordered Margaret's mother, the dowager-duchess of Somerset, to come to London at Shrovetide (14 February 1453) and wait there at his command.[6] The duchess almost certainly brought young Margaret with her, for there is no evidence that she had ever left her mother, either during the period of Suffolk's wardship or after the marriage of 1450. It was Henry again who, once the dissolution had taken place, granted her wardship and marriage to his own half-brothers. It is likely that the king already intended Margaret to marry Edmund Tudor. There were sound dynastic reasons for this. Until late in March 1453 there would have been no indication that Margaret of Anjou was pregnant. Henry's initial intention in dissolving Lady Margaret's marriage with John de la Pole may have been to nominate Edmund Tudor as his heir, in the right of Margaret Beaufort. There was also the need to endow Edmund adequately. On 12 May 1453 Henry authorized a payment of 100 marks to his 'right dere and right welbeloved cousin Margaret' for her arrayment.[7] Her lands were speedily parcelled out between Jasper and Edmund.

[5] *Mornynge Remembraunce*, 292–3.
[6] PRO, C81/768/9893. According to one well-informed source, in late February 1453 'the king allowed a divorce between John, son of the duke of Suffolk, and the daughter and heiress of the duke of Somerset', noting in the margin that the divorce was pleaded: J. Benet, 'Chronicle for the years 1400–1462', ed. G. L. and M. A. Harriss in *Camden Miscellany*, XXIV, Camden Society, 4th series, 9 (1972), 209. Margaret's wardship and marriage was granted to Edmund and Jasper Tudor on 24 March 1453.
[7] PRO, E404/69/145.

Margaret's appearance at court in 1453 left a lasting impression. Despite the dark clouds gathering over the Lancastrian dynasty, her memory was of an impressive display of ceremony. The English recovery in Gascony had led to a new mood of confidence, reflected in a strongly Lancastrian parliament and a vigorous celebration of the feast of St George on 23 April. Two things struck the young Margaret during her introduction to the world of politics and power. The first was the significant position accorded to women. The tone of the court was being set by Margaret of Anjou, whose gift-giving, fine jewellery and rich clothes had helped inflate her household's expenditure, in 1452–3, to over £7,500. In the garter ceremony of 1453 she wore a fine new robe of blood-red colour.[8] The queen's example was followed by other Lancastrian ladies, including the duchesses of Somerset and Suffolk and the countess of Shrewsbury. The second abiding memory was of the attention and kindness shown by the king, which may have sparked her later devotion to the cause of Henry VI's sanctity.

Margaret's marriage to Edmund Tudor was to be brief. The couple had travelled to south Wales in the autumn of 1455, taking up residence at Lamphey in Pembrokeshire. Edmund quickly made his twelve-year-old wife pregnant, his wish to secure a life interest in her estates taking priority over any concern for her safety and well-being. He was not to enjoy them for very long. Whilst acting as Henry VI's lieutenant in the region, he was captured by Richard duke of York's retainers Sir William Herbert and Sir Walter Devereux in August 1456, and imprisoned in Carmarthen castle. Although Edmund was later released, his health suffered: he succumbed to an outbreak of plague and died in Carmarthen on 1 November 1456.[9] The widowed Margaret, some six months pregnant, was left isolated and vulnerable in this lawless region of Wales. Her fears were for the safety of the child she was carrying. Many years later John Fisher, in his Cambridge oration to Henry VII, looked back on this time of terrible danger: 'while your mother carried you in the womb you narrowly avoided the plague of

---

[8] Longleat House, North Muniment Room, Misc. MS. I; A. R. Myers, 'The household of Queen Margaret of Anjou, 1452–3', in *Crown, Household and Parliament in Fifteenth Century England*, ed. C. H. Clough (London, 1985), 135–209.

[9] The general course of events is taken from Griffiths and Thomas, *Tudor Dynasty*, 44–8. Edmund's motives in making Margaret pregnant at such an early age are discussed in more detail below, p. 95. The couple were residing at Lamphey from September 1455: PRO, DL29/651/10533.

which your illustrious father died, which could so easily have killed an unborn child'.[10] Margaret was in no fit state to travel and join her mother in England. She took refuge with her brother-in-law, Jasper, at Pembroke castle where she gave birth to her son, Henry, on 28 January 1457.

In his Cambridge oration Fisher indicated that the birth had been a difficult one, mentioning Margaret's young age ('not yet fourteen') and her small size ('not a woman of great stature...she was so much smaller at that stage'). Both Margaret and Henry may have been in danger of losing their lives, and for Margaret, who had conceived before she was thirteen, the event led to lasting physical damage. She was never to give birth again. Her apparently close and happy subsequent marriage to Sir Henry Stafford lasted for fourteen years but produced no children. Similarly the careful and thorough marriage settlement with Thomas Lord Stanley in 1472 made no provision for issue. Physical incapacity is a more plausible suggestion for this than the legend that Edward IV only allowed the union of Margaret and Stanley on the condition that no children were produced. An echo of the physical and mental trauma left by the early conception and birth is found in a report of the Spanish ambassador in the reign of Henry VII, telling how Margaret had opposed the marriage of one of the king's daughters to James IV of Scotland because she feared that James would not wait till the young princess was of suitable age before trying to consummate it.[11] This reaction probably embodied her own experience. The lack of further offspring was to strengthen the bond between Margaret and her only child.

After Edmund Tudor's death another marriage had been arranged with remarkable speed. In March 1457 Jasper Tudor and Margaret Beaufort had travelled from Pembroke to the duke of Buckingham's manor of Greenfield, near Newport in Gwent.[12] The discussions had concerned the possibility of a marriage with Buckingham's second son, Henry Stafford. Not yet fourteen, Lady Margaret was now taking an active part in planning her future. Her chief concern was to protect her own interests and those of her infant son. Humphrey, duke of Buckingham, was the only English magnate as powerful as Richard, duke of York. Margaret's chief aim was to gain Buckingham's protection and avoid another husband being forced upon her. Bishop

[10] *Oration*, 265.   [11] *Cal. State Papers, Spanish*, I, 176.
[12] PRO, SC6/924/25, m. 11; R. A. Griffiths, *The Reign of Henry VI* (London, 1981), 802–3.

Reginald Boulers of Coventry and Lichfield granted dispensation for the match on 6 April, necessary because Margaret Beaufort and Henry Stafford were second cousins (Buckingham's wife Anne Neville was a daughter of Joan Beaufort).[13] The ceremony may have taken place at Buckingham's favourite residence of Maxstoke (Wark.), within the Coventry and Lichfield diocese, on 3 January 1458. Margaret's early life had fitted only too well the pattern of a young and wealthy heiress being treated as a marketable commodity. But from her marriage with Henry Stafford the stability of a long and harmonious relationship was finally to emerge.

In his will of 10 July 1460 the duke of Buckingham had settled 400 marks worth of land on the couple. But their main source of landed wealth was derived from Margaret's own estates and this enabled the pair to enjoy an aristocratic rather than a gentry lifestyle. After Buckingham's death at the battle of Northampton, Sir Henry Stafford had maintained his family's support for the Lancastrians, and fought on their side at Towton in March 1461. But after Edward IV's victory he was quick to make peace with the new regime, securing a general pardon, first for himself and then later his wife.[14] Stafford's reconciliation with Edward IV protected Margaret's estates, which were saved from the acts of resumption of two successive parliaments. But the price to be paid for the Yorkist victory was the long-term separation of mother and son. William Lord Herbert's capture of Pembroke castle on 30 September 1461 was soon rewarded with a royal grant of the wardship and marriage of Henry Tudor.[15]

Herbert was one of Edward IV's staunchest supporters. His victories against the Lancastrians in south Wales and reduction of their strongholds in the region rendered an invaluable service to the Yorkist dynasty. It was not for nothing that the Welsh bard Lewis Glyn Gothi described him as Edward's 'master-lock'. Intensely ambitious, he used his influence at court to secure a number of wardships, including that of the young Henry Percy, heir to the late earl of Northumberland, to advance his own interests and profit. The close favour accorded to him by the king allowed him to arrange lucrative marriages for his own family; the concentration of offices in south Wales led to an almost

---

[13] Lichfield RO, B/A/1/11, fols. 87, 87v. We owe this reference to Professor Ralph Griffiths and the general line of interpretation to Mr T. B. Pugh.

[14] C. L. Scofield, *The Life and Reign of Edward IV*, 2 vols. (London, 1923), I, 203.

[15] *CPR, 1461–7*, 117 (12 February 1462).

vice-regal pre-eminence in the area, symbolized by a magnificent building programme at Raglan castle.[16] It was at Raglan, with its 'hundred rooms filled with festive fare, its towers, parlours and doors, its heaped-up fires of long-dried fuel' that Henry Tudor was to spend much of his childhood, under the careful supervision of Herbert's wife Anne Devereux. Although the estates of the honour of Richmond had been granted elsewhere, the fact that Herbert had paid no less than £1,000 for the wardship of Tudor and clearly intended to marry him to his eldest daughter Maud, is significant. As Herbert planned to ally young Henry's interests to those of his own family it must have been known that the young Tudor heir had a long-term political future. Indeed, the king may well have intimated that an eventual restoration of estates and confirmation of title was likely.[17] For Herbert continued to refer to Henry as 'Lord Richmond', as did his mother, Lady Margaret, and her husband, Sir Henry Stafford. In the meantime, Margaret maintained contact with her son through messages delivered by her servants and the occasional visit.

Edward IV was well aware that at the crucial victory at Towton, the majority of the English peerage had remained loyal to Henry VI. As a result he pursued a pragmatic strategy of conciliation towards many of the chief supporters of the now exiled Lancastrian dynasty. For some, like Lord Rivers and indeed Henry Stafford, Towton had been enough to convince them that the Lancastrian cause was now lost. Edward was keen to secure the support of the surviving members of the Stafford family. The duke of Buckingham's eldest son, Humphrey, had married another Margaret Beaufort, one of the five daughters of Margaret's uncle Edmund duke of Somerset (who had been slain at the first battle of St Albans in 1455). They had produced two sons, Henry and Humphrey. The death of Humphrey earl of Stafford in 1458, and of Buckingham himself in 1460, left his elder son Henry heir to the enormous Stafford estates. The king took a particular interest in the young boy. He was often in the royal entourage, and on one occasion he and Edward were entertained at the fine Stafford residence at Penshurst. The king was to bring him closer into the royal orbit with an early arranged marriage to Queen Elizabeth Woodville's younger

---

[16] The appraisal of Herbert's role is drawn largely from C. D. Ross, *Edward IV* (London, 1975), 75–7.

[17] D. H. Thomas, 'The Herberts of Raglan as supporters of the House of York in the second half of the fifteenth century' (Cardiff MA, 1968), 55–8, 71–2, 289.

sister Katherine. But Edward was also anxious to secure the goodwill of the young duke of Buckingham's uncles, John and Henry Stafford. Since Henry Stafford drew a large part of his landed income from his wife's estates, the king's safeguarding of these (both Margaret's share of her paternal inheritance and the dower portion of the earldom of Richmond) was of obvious political importance.

Edward IV had successfully cemented an alliance with a family who had been stalwart supports of Henry VI in the last, troubled years of his reign. He had a more ambitious plan: to secure a rapprochement with the male line of the Beaufort family, who remained the principal opponents of the newly founded Yorkist dynasty. After the death of Edmund Beaufort duke of Somerset, in 1455, his eldest son Henry had pursued a bitter personal vendetta against the Yorkist party. His secret march north in the winter of 1460 had out-manoeuvred the forces of Richard, duke of York, who had blundered to defeat and death at the battle of Wakefield. In the uncertain weeks that followed, nervous Londoners daubed the Beaufort portcullis badge onto the walls and doors of their houses.[18] But the entry into the capital of the disorderly Lancastrian army never materialized, and, after the defeat at Towton, Somerset fled with the remnants of the Lancastrian party to Scotland. Henry Beaufort, duke of Somerset, had now moved into the uneasy position of a political exile. He had been sent to France in an embassy from Margaret of Anjou. But the death of the pro-Lancastrian Charles VII on 22 July 1461 effectively ended the mission. The duke had moved to Flanders, under the protection of Philip the Good, and set up residence in Bruges. Here he was isolated from other Lancastrians, and amidst occasional clashes between members of his household and English merchants, rumours were soon circulating that he was willing to come to terms with Edward IV. In September 1462 Somerset made overtures to both Edward and Warwick.[19] Although involved in Lancastrian military efforts in the north of England at the end of the year, he showed no stomach for a fight and quickly came to an agreement with the Yorkists.

---

[18] M. K. Jones, 'Edward IV and the Beaufort family: conciliation in early Yorkist politics', *The Ricardian*, 6 (1983), 259.

[19] *The Paston Letters, 1422–1509*, ed. J. Gairdner, 6 vols. (London, 1904), IV, 52: 'my lord Warwyk had sent to the Kyng, and informed hyse Hyghnesse that the Lord Summyrset had wretyn to hym to come to grace'; *HMC, 5th Report* (records of Lydd, 1462), 523: 'Paid for expenses of ledyng up the manne to the Kyng, that wasse take with letters from the Duke of Somerset.'

Edward IV's willingness to agree terms with the leading male member of the Beaufort family was an astute if risky move. Historians have been critical of a policy of reconciliation towards such a bitter opponent of the Yorkist regime.[20] Yet their assessments have failed to consider the international dimension to Edward's strategy. At the beginning of 1463 the king was struggling to secure the long-term future of his dynasty. The exiled Lancastrians retained considerable support, and a number of foreign observers still felt it likely that they would be restored to power. The duke of Somerset was the mainstay of the Lancastrian cause. His defection would have a profound effect on the morale of the remaining Lancastrians and also on international opinion. Somerset and Warwick fighting together at the siege of Alnwick late in December 1462 was as unexpected as it was demoralizing for the Lancastrian garrison, and contributed to the speedy collapse of resistance in the north. Edward now put on a considerable show to emphasize his trust in Somerset. He went hunting with him and Somerset jousted in royal tournaments. Many were surprised at the degree of favour accorded to a former opponent. Gregory's chronicle described how 'the king made full much of him; in so much that he lodged with the king in his own bed many nights'. Somerset's lands and annuities were restored, though the king prudently reserved his former military office of lieutenant of the Isle of Wight for the trusted Yorkist, Geoffrey Gate.[21]

Edward IV's dramatic reconciliation with the duke of Somerset was followed with particular interest in France, where the Lancastrians had set up their court in exile at Koeur. In July 1463 a report to Louis XI noted that Somerset had accompanied Edward to London, and was with him at the time of the parliament when his lands were formally restored. In the tripartite negotiations at Hesdin in October a special clause in the French ambassador's instructions concerned the position of the duke in Edward's regime.[22] These factors made the gamble of restoring Somerset to favour worth taking. They also marked a formal reconciliation with the whole Beaufort family. Henry Beaufort's

---

[20] 'One of those political blunders which mars Edward's record as a statesman': Ross, *Edward IV*, 51–2.

[21] *Historical Collections of a Citizen of London*, ed. J. Gairdner, Camden Society, n.s., 17 (1876), 219–21. The reversal of the act of attainder, with the reversion clause concerning Gate, is printed in full in M. A. Hicks, 'Edward IV, the duke of Somerset and Lancastrian loyalism in the north', *Northern History*, 20 (1984), 36–7.

[22] BN, MS Fr. 6970 (report to Louis XI, 1 July 1463); Scofield, *Edward IV*, I, 296.

younger brother Edmund, a captive for more than two years, was released from the Tower in the summer of 1463. Eleanor, the widowed duchess of Somerset, was pardoned on 18 May 1463 and her annuity returned to her. Trusted Beaufort servants were also welcomed back into the fold. John Martyn of Dartford, who had been the receiver-general for the late Edmund Beaufort, duke of Somerset, and afterwards acted as agent for his widow and also for Margaret's mother, received a pardon, as did Henry Court, who had also served the Beaufort family for two generations.[23] Had Somerset remained loyal to the king, Margaret could have hoped to benefit from her family's newly found re-emergence in Yorkist politics. Yet events were to take an altogether different turn.

At the end of November 1463 Henry Beaufort suddenly defected from Edward IV and fled north to the Lancastrians now in Scotland. It is difficult to gauge the reasons for his decision, for his reconciliation with the Yorkists at the end of the previous year had appeared genuine enough. One chronicler suggested that Edward had not honoured his promise of a full restoration of lands and annuities, but the evidence does not bear this out.[24] More likely is the fact that Somerset had been deeply shaken by an incident at Northampton in July 1463, where the townspeople had rioted and tried to kill him. He had parted from the king and retired to Chirk castle in north Wales, at the heart of his landed estates. Soon he was plotting against the Yorkists, and on his flight to Scotland left rebellion in his wake.[25]

Somerset's defection, after the substantial favours heaped upon him, was a major blow to Edward. He also took it as a deep personal insult. Somerset had broken his oath 'against all nature of gentilesse', and had abused royal trust. As a consequence the king developed an abiding hatred of his adversary, that comes across strongly in the wording of the act of attainder passed against him. When the duke was captured after the battle of Hexham in May 1464 he was summarily

---

[23] PRO, C67/46, mm. 19, 21; Jones, 'Edward IV and the Beaufort family', 260; C. L. Scofield, 'Henry, Duke of Somerset and Edward IV', *EHR*, 21 (1906), 300–2.

[24] The comment is found in J. Warkworth, *A Chronicle of the First Thirteen Years of the Reign of King Edward the Fourth*, ed. J. O. Halliwell, Camden Society, i.s., 10 (1839), 3, and discussed in Jones, 'Edward IV and the Beaufort family', 261.

[25] BL, Add. MS 46399A, fol. 1 (letter of Henry duke of Somerset, Chirk 20 September 1463). The receiver's account for the lordship, 1464–5 (PRO, DL29/634/10) shows that Somerset had reduced rents, no doubt in an effort to win support (drawn to our attention by Mr Pugh).

executed by Warwick's brother John Lord Montagu. Montagu was almost certainly acting on royal orders, and one chronicler attributed his elevation to the earldom of Northumberland specifically to this one execution.[26] It was a sign of Edward's permanent breach with the Beaufort family. Somerset's younger brothers Edmund and John had also fled to Scotland, though they were to survive the rout at Hexham. But all property belonging to the three was confiscated, and their mother, the elderly duchess of Somerset, was imprisoned and suffered some duress.[27] The division was final, and now resumed the nature of a personal feud.

These political vicissitudes led to a sharp dividing of the ways between Margaret Beaufort and others of her family. Her husband's Stafford kin were to be more and more closely associated with the Yorkist cause. Henry, the young duke of Buckingham, had married Katherine Woodville. Stafford's relative, John, Lord Berners, had become Elizabeth Woodville's chamberlain and his son one of her carvers. In contrast Edmund and John Beaufort became the focus for an alternative Lancastrian kinship group, in exile in Flanders. Edmund, now styled duke of Somerset, was to fight for the Burgundians at Montlhéry in 1465 and became attached to the household of the count of Charolais, who by the beginning of 1467 succeeded to the dukedom of Burgundy. Somerset participated in one of the duke's campaigns in the autumn of this year, alongside John Butler, earl of Ormonde, another Lancastrian exile who had escaped originally to Portugal. His elder brother James Butler earl of Wiltshire and Ormonde had been allied to the Beaufort family through his marriage to Eleanor Beaufort, one of Somerset's sisters. Servants of the late earl of Wiltshire were also attracted into service.[28] Although this group, dependent on pensions and gifts from Charles the Bold, duke of Burgundy, operated separately from the court-in-exile of Margaret of Anjou in Alsace, they represented a strongly Lancastrian faction. The duke of Exeter, who held a small Burgundian pension, and also fought on the 1467 campaign, was regarded by many as next in line in the Lancastrian succession after Henry VI and his son Edward. Their partisanship was symbolized by

[26] According to this source he was created earl of Northumberland 'pro honore capitonis dicti ducis Somersetiae': 'Annales Rerum Anglicarum', in *Letters and Papers Illustrative of the Wars of the English in France*, ed. J. Stevenson, 2 vols. in 3, Rolls Series (London, 1864), II, ii, 782.   [27] Scofield, 'Henry, Duke of Somerset', 301–2.
[28] ADN, B2064, fols. 305, 347.

the earl of Ormonde's continued use of the regnal year of Henry VI in his correspondence.

In contrast, Margaret Beaufort benefited from the contacts being forged between Staffords and Woodvilles. In 1466 Henry Stafford and Margaret had obtained by royal grant the former Beaufort manor of Woking, in crown hands from the attainder of Henry Beaufort, duke of Somerset. Its substantial manor house enjoyed easy access by land to wharfsides on the Thames, allowing Henry Stafford, who consolidated his position with further purchases of lands in Old and New Windsor, a more active political role. In May 1467 he rode to a council meeting at Mortlake. Edward IV's foreign policy was becoming strongly pro-Burgundian, with a visit of the Bastard of Burgundy to the capital arranged for June, and the king was clearly wishing to consolidate support in the face of opposition from the powerful Neville family. On another occasion Stafford was summoned to attend the king at Windsor.[29] His alignment behind royal policy can be seen in May 1468, when he and his wife Margaret came up to stay in London at the time of the important meeting of parliament, when Edward's plans for an invasion of France were formally announced. The force was to be led by Walter, Lord Mountjoy, who had recently re-married Stafford's widowed mother, Anne Neville, duchess of Buckingham. Stafford and Margaret arrived in London by boat, and lodged at the Mitre in Cheapside.[30] Yet Edward IV was cautious in his patronage of Stafford, and did not appoint him to the Surrey commissions of the peace. A lingering doubt remained in the king's mind, possibly because he was unsure of the absolute loyalty of Stafford's wife. Faced with a threat against their properties in Kendal, Stafford and Margaret sought a stronger demonstration of Edward IV's favour. In December 1468 the king was entertained at their hunting lodge of Brookwood, Stafford waiting on Edward at Guildford and escorting him to the feast. The occasion allowed Margaret, wearing fine velvet, holland and brabant cloth, her first personal meeting with the Yorkist king.[31]

The role of Margaret in all this political activity was very much a supporting one. But there was no doubting her continued concern for her son's welfare. In 1465 her initiative led to Henry Tudor's admission to the confraternity of the Order of the Holy Trinity (near Knares-

---

[29] WAM, 12185, fol. 104.   [30] WAM, 5472, fol. 5.
[31] WAM, 12186, fol. 42; 5472, fol. 22.

borough in Yorkshire), a body concerned with the redemption of captive Christians imprisoned by the Turks.[32] She kept in regular contact with Henry at Raglan. In September 1467 the couple, on a tour of their west-country estates, decided to pay him a visit. They were ferried across the Severn from Bristol to Chepstow for a sum of 10s before travelling on to Raglan, where they were entertained for a week as guests of Lord Herbert.[33] The following summer, Margaret's fears for her son's safety at the time of Jasper Tudor's raid across north Wales was revealed in a stream of messages. Jasper had landed in the Dyfi estuary near Harlech (which was still in Lancastrian hands) on 24 June 1468 and had struck out towards Denbighshire. Edward IV had reacted quickly, ordering Lord Herbert to raise a massive army to deal with this threat. It seems likely that the young Henry Tudor accompanied Herbert's expedition, witnessing the destruction of the Lancastrian forces at Twt Hill near Caernarfon, and the surrender of Harlech on 14 August.[34]

The qualities of Stafford and Margaret were to be tested to their limit in the period of political crisis between the summer of 1469 and the spring of 1471, a time of instability 'without parallel in English history since 1066'. In July 1469 Warwick rebelled against the king. Lord Herbert, elevated to the earldom of Pembroke as a reward for his capture of the Lancastrian stronghold of Harlech, was summoned to Edward's assistance and marched out of Raglan with a formidable array of Welshmen. The twelve-year-old Henry Tudor was again in his company. But his forces suffered bloody defeat at Edgecote on 24 July and Herbert was captured and executed by Warwick. When news of the battle reached Stafford and his wife a host of anxious messages were sent out from Woking, to ascertain the fate of Herbert, Henry Tudor and also the king, believed now to be in Neville custody at Warwick castle.[35] It was a period of intense anxiety for the couple, since attempts were also being made by the Parrs of Westmorland, with Neville support, to claim the portion of the barony of Kendal held by Margaret. Fortunately news soon arrived of Henry Tudor's safety. He

---

[32] WAM, 6658.   [33] WAM, 12185, fols. 39–45.

[34] WAM, 5472, fol. 7v; Griffiths and Thomas, *Tudor Dynasty*, 65–7.

[35] Henry Tudor's presence at Edgecote and the details of his escape from the battlefield are recorded in a later petition of Sir Richard Corbet, printed in H. Owen and J. B. Blakeway, *A History of Shrewsbury*, 2 vols. (London, 1825), I, 248; for the response of Stafford and Margaret, WAM 5472, fol. 41v. The general course of events and the quotation are drawn from Ross, *Edward IV*, 126–32.

had been led from the battlefield by Sir Richard Corbet, and escorted to the residence of Herbert's brother-in-law Lord Ferrers at Weobley in Herefordshire. Margaret's fears for her son during this period of unrest ran deep enough to be recalled by Fisher nearly forty years later, when he described how Henry's custody had been granted to those caught up in fierce warfare.[36]

The news of Lord Herbert's death and Edward IV's confinement at Warwick threw Henry Tudor's future open. Lady Margaret took a renewed interest in her son's welfare. A party of eight servants, given the troubled state of the kingdom, had travelled first to Raglan and then Weobley, where they found Herbert's widow Anne Devereux and Henry sheltering under the protection of Lord Ferrers. Davy, a man who had waited on Henry Tudor at Weobley, was presented with 20s, and Wakyn Thomas, one of Anne Devereux's servants, received a smaller gift. Another payment was made to Henry, for his 'disportes', to 'bie him bowe and shaftes'.[37] While Henry was practising his archery, the terms of his wardship were under fresh discussion. A thorough study was undertaken of the condition of the original grant. The records of chancery and exchequer were also searched, and one servant was even despatched to south Wales for further 'evidences'. On 21 October 1469, at the Bell in Fleet Street, bread, mutton, ale and cheese were consumed as the legal councils of Stafford and 'Lady Pembroke' met to try and reach an 'accommodation' over Henry Tudor's wardship.[38]

It was during this period of uncertainty that Margaret re-entered the political stage. She was determined to bargain over a title and landed interest for her son. On 24 August 1469, with the king still a virtual prisoner of Warwick and Clarence, she and Stafford rode into London. After consulting her husband she travelled alone to George duke of Clarence's London residence, from where messages could most easily be sent to the duke, now at Middleham in Yorkshire.[39] Clarence held the honour of Richmond and Margaret was no doubt hoping to discuss her son's landed future. Margaret ran a dangerous risk by opening communication with one of the king's captors and her bold decision proved a serious miscalculation. Edward IV was soon able to re-assert

---

[36] *Oration*, 265.   [37] WAM, 5472, fols. 43, 44, 44v.

[38] WAM, 5472, fols. 46–7v; M. K. Jones, 'Richard III and Lady Margaret Beaufort: a reassessment', in *Richard III: Loyalty, Lordship and Law*, ed. P. W. Hammond (London, 1986), 27.   [39] WAM, 5472, fol. 43v.

his freedom of movement. At the end of September 1469 he had arranged that members of his council, including the earl of Essex and Lord Mountjoy, should meet him at York. There followed a progress south that allowed the king to regain the political initiative, approaching London in state. Edward's arrival in the capital offered a worried Henry Stafford a chance to demonstrate his loyalty to the crown. A new hat and spurs were bought for him and sixteen shafts of arrows for his retinue, as he rode to meet the king.[40] Yet the plotting of his wife was not easily forgotten.

During the winter Edward had made some attempts to reconcile the Nevilles and his courtier and household followers. But those who had remained loyal during the rebellion were to benefit from the king's patronage. On 5 January 1470 Henry Stafford's younger brother, John, was created earl of Wiltshire.[41] Henry remained a mere knight. It was a galling moment and a warning of the king's suspicions. His political allegiance was now under royal scrutiny, as was forcefully shown when trouble flared up again. The spark was provided by a series of popular risings in Lincolnshire in the spring of 1470. The disturbances emanated from a private feud between Sir Thomas Burgh of Gainsborough, Edward's master of horse, and Richard, Lord Welles. They were soon to have broader implications. Edward had a personal interest in quelling the unrest, and marched out of London on 5 March 1471. The occasion proved a new political test for Stafford, for the risings involved Lord Welles and his heir, Sir Robert, who were members of Lady Margaret's family on her mother's side. Stafford had hoped to avoid being drawn into the conflict. A royal summons persuaded him otherwise. Stafford hurriedly rode north with a retinue of thirty men and had joined the king's army at Stamford on 12 March.[42]

Henry Stafford had arrived at Stamford in time to witness a particularly brutal and vengeful act. Richard Lord Welles had been summoned to appear before Edward IV on the promise of a royal pardon. It became clear that the king had no intention of honouring his word. As Sir Robert Welles hastened south in a desperate bid to save his father, Richard was summarily executed. The forces of Sir Robert were then routed at Lose-Cote field. Stafford was left with the unhappy task of riding to Maxey to break the news of Lord Welles's death to Lady

[40] *Ibid.*, fol. 45v.   [41] *CP*, XII, ii, 735.   [42] WAM, 12184, fols. 41–7.

Margaret's mother, the dowager-duchess of Somerset.[43] He then rejoined the expanding royal army at a fresh muster-point, at Doncaster, to deal with an insurrection stirred up in Yorkshire by the Nevilles. He was at York with the king's troops between 22 and 27 March, and accompanied Edward on his rapid dash south to Exeter (reached 14 April) to try and intercept the fleeing insurgents.[44] This hectic period in the saddle allowed Stafford to prove his mettle. But it revealed the ruthlessness and cruelty of Edward IV, whose breach of his solemn promise to Lord Welles had shocked contemporaries.

Fresh surprises were in store. Warwick and his party had found shelter in France, where they were supported by Louis XI, who engineered a remarkable alliance between Warwick and Clarence and Margaret of Anjou. As a result of this compact an invasion was now threatened. On 16 July Stafford dined with John Lord Berners, the queen's chamberlain, at Guildford at a time when the commissioners for array had passed through the town.[45] While Stafford was at Woking the king had again moved north, to deal with new disturbances in Yorkshire. It proved to be a disastrous mistake. Edward was unable to oppose Warwick's landing in the west country early in September, or prevent his rapid accumulation of fresh support. The king, out-manoeuvred by the rebels, was forced to flee to Holland. A period of topsy-turvy politics now saw the nominal restoration of Henry VI, who was released from imprisonment in the Tower.

The period of the Lancastrian Restoration presented Stafford and Margaret with new challenges and new opportunities. It was a time of uncertainty and danger. Edward IV was now in exile and they were determined to look to their own interests: first and foremost the safety of Margaret's son, Henry Tudor. During the renewed negotiations over the terms of his wardship Henry had remained at Weobley, and it was from there in October 1470 that Sir Richard Corbet delivered him to the newly arrived Lancastrian Jasper Tudor at Hereford.[46] Jasper and Henry had ridden to London in advance of the opening session of the new parliament (which met on 26 November) and here mother and son were to be briefly re-united.

---

[43] *Ibid.*, fol. 48. Lord Welles had been issued with a royal pardon on 3 March 1470. For his execution see Warkworth, *Chronicle*, 8.   [44] WAM, 12184, fols. 50–72v.
[45] WAM, 12183, fol. 6.
[46] Owen and Blakeway, *A History of Shrewsbury*, I, 248.

On 27 October Henry Tudor was rowed from London to Westminster in Stafford's barge for an audience with Henry VI. Afterwards Henry Tudor, Margaret, Stafford and Jasper dined with Henry VI's chamberlain, Sir Richard Tunstall.[47] The meeting was later invested with much significance. Polydore Vergil related how Henry VI made a miraculous prophecy concerning the young boy's future role in healing the divisions of war. Since Henry had arranged the marriage between Margaret and Edmund Tudor on his own initiative, it is hardly surprising that he remarked on their sole surviving offspring but the dynastic importance of his comments may have been exaggerated in retrospect. In the oration of John Fisher to Henry VII and his mother, Henry VI was again attributed with having miraculously foretold Tudor's accession.[48] At the end of October Stafford, Margaret and Henry returned to Woking. On 5 November the three paid a brief visit to Guildford; a few days later they travelled to Maidenhead and Henley. Young Henry was presented with fine horsecloth for his travels, and on 11 November he bade farewell to his mother and rejoined his uncle Jasper Tudor.[49] Both were to leave for south Wales at the end of the month.

After Henry Tudor's departure Stafford and Margaret recommenced negotiations with George, duke of Clarence, who held the honour of Richmond, to secure a landed settlement for Margaret's son. On 27 November a meeting was held with the duke at Baynard's castle.[50] But their attempts to recover Henry Tudor's inheritance immediately were a failure. The result of these discussions was a compromise. By February 1471 it had been agreed that Henry would succeed to the honour on Clarence's death.[51] Political events were to upturn these provisions. On 14 March 1471 Edward IV landed in Yorkshire with a small army, and cautiously moved south. Warwick held fast in Coventry hoping that some of the Lancastrian lords would defend London, and trap Edward's force between two armies. The leading Lancastrian commander, Margaret's kinsman Edmund Beaufort, duke of Somerset, was to pursue a different strategy.

During his long period of exile Somerset had gained considerable military experience in the service of the duke of Burgundy. He had fought in campaigns in 1465 and 1467; in the following year he and

---

[47] WAM, 12183, fols. 19, 19v.   [48] *Oration*, 269.

[49] WAM, 12183, fols. 20v–3.   [50] *Ibid.*, fol. 25.

[51] M. A. Hicks, *False, Fleeting, Perjur'd Clarence* (Gloucester, 1980), 97–9.

his brother John attended Charles the Bold's court at Brussels. Charles had granted Edmund a substantial monthly pension, and made frequent additional gifts to cover his arrayment and military equipment. The favour shown to Somerset was marked and intimate and set the duke apart from other Lancastrian exiles in Flanders, who lived a somewhat precarious hand-to-mouth existence. According to some chroniclers the special favour accorded to Somerset was a result of Charles's personal friendship with his elder brother.[52] The prominence of Somerset in Burgundian affairs was a source of some concern in Yorkist circles and it was hoped that the marriage alliance between Charles and Margaret of York would dispel his influence. A Paston correspondent described how Somerset had left Bruges in July 1468, the day before Margaret's arrival, to return to Margaret of Anjou's court-in-exile, 'and shal no more come here ayen nor be holpyn by the Duk'.[53] This proved not to be the case. Charles had sent Somerset and Exeter away at the time of his wedding, but they were soon back again. In September 1468 they both served in Charles's army alongside Sir John Courtenay. In January 1469 Somerset was present at the ratification of privileges of the town of Ghent, in the company of many leading Burgundian nobles. In August he was in attendance at Charles's court at The Hague.[54] It was a bizarre situation for Margaret of York, now in close proximity to one of her brother's most determined enemies. The town accounts of Veere give an illustration of Somerset's activity. In January 1470 one of the duke's men arrived with letters concerning the Danzig seaman, Paul Beneke. In March Somerset himself briefly visited the town.[55]

At the beginning of November 1470 Charles the Bold had found himself playing out a difficult balancing act. Early in the previous month Edward IV had arrived in Holland, with his brother Richard

---

[52] ADN, B2064, fols. 52v, 82v, 96v, 247v (and for a payment to Edmund's brother, John Beaufort, attending Charles at Brussels in June 1468, ADN, B2068, fols. 35v–6); G. Chastellain, *Oeuvres*, ed. K. de Lettenhove, 7 vols. (Brussels, 1863–5), IV, 66–8.

[53] *Paston Letters*, IV, 299.

[54] ADN, B2068, fols. 225–6. In June 1468 Charles had paid Somerset and Exeter to leave the court briefly (*ibid.*, fols. 129v–30v). *Collection de documents inédits concernant l'Histoire de la Belgique*, ed. L. P. Gachard, 3 vols. (Brussels, 1833–5), I, 205; *Divisiekroniek: Die Cronycke van Hollandt, Zeelandt ende Vrieslant* (Antwerp, 1530), fol. 322. We owe the last two references to the kindness of Mark Ballard and Livia Visser-Fuchs.

[55] References supplied by Livia Visser-Fuchs from *Bronnen tot de geschiedenis van de handel net Engeland, Schotland en Ireland, 1435–85* (The Hague, 1928).

duke of Gloucester, the Lords Hastings, Rivers, Say, and some 400 of his household men, and were now staying at The Hague thanks to the hospitality of Louis of Gruthuyse. Despite his marriage alliance with the Yorkist house, Charles was at first unwilling to support the exiles openly. His natural inclination had always been towards the Lancastrians, the most prominent of whom, the dukes of Somerset and Exeter, were still at his court. Moreover, he had no wish to antagonize the earl of Warwick and provoke a war. Warwick had formed an alliance with Louis XI, who had declared war on Charles on 17 December. But Charles the Bold still hoped to avoid a conflict with England. On 7 January 1471 the dukes of Somerset and Exeter visited Charles at St Pol and tried to persuade him to support Henry VI.[56] Edward IV was also there to put his own case. Charles's initial reaction was in the Lancastrians' favour, allowing Somerset and Exeter to return to England. But Warwick's declaration of war by 12 February forced his hand. Charles now decided to formally recognize Edward and back his plans to return to England with an invasion force.

For Margaret and Stafford the presence of Somerset in the capital provoked a difficult period of politic diplomacy. Somerset, as a kinsman of Margaret, had paid a courtesy call on her at Woking on 3 March 1471. A request was sent to a London fishmonger for 'dainties' for the duke: fresh salmon, eel and tench.[57] Towards the end of the month discussion became both serious and frantic. With Edward IV waiting at Coventry, Somerset had to decide whether to attempt to hold London (where Edward had strong support) with the few troops at his disposal or raise more substantial forces in the south and await the arrival of Margaret of Anjou in the west country. His distrust of Warwick dictated the latter course and attempts were made to enlist Stafford into the Lancastrian cause. On 23 March Stafford's servant, John Davy, was sent from Staines to London with messages for Somerset. The next day the duke himself arrived at Woking with his retinue of forty men, and stayed for four days.[58] It must have been a tense occasion. Somerset's strategy was to head for Salisbury, which he would use as a recruiting point for an army. Stafford would not commit himself to joining it. The

---

[56] We owe the accuracy of this chronology to Mark Ballard, who has kindly supplied details of Charles's parting gift to Somerset (Archives Générales du Royaume, Brussels, Chambre des comptes 1925, fol. 404v). Somerset and Exeter had returned to England by the end of January, when Exeter was trying to borrow sums of money from the bewildered receivers of his wife's estates: Lancs RO, DDK/1746/14.

[57] WAM, 12189, fol. 58.   [58] WAM, 12190, fols. 77–8.

duke was forced to leave Woking on 28 March without any firm assurance of support. Discussions continued as Somerset moved west. At the beginning of April a body of Stafford's household men travelled from Reading to Newbury for further talks with the duke. Stafford was temporizing. On 2 April he left Woking for London, hoping to avoid the conflict.[59] But Edward IV's decision to march past Coventry and gain entry to the capital forced his hand. On 12 April he suddenly decided to join the Yorkist army. Once again the political careers of Lady Margaret and her male Beaufort kinsmen had taken a sharply divergent course.

The events of the following few weeks were of high drama. Edward, after gathering reinforcements in London, had ridden out of the city in great haste to do battle with Warwick's army. Stafford had been with them. He had left the capital in such speed that he had been unable to gather military equipment or supplies. On 13 April, on the eve of the battle, servants had reached him 'at the field near Barnet' with gussets of mail.[60] As Stafford prepared himself for what would be a dangerous and bloody encounter, he sent his trusted servant John Davy back to Woking to his wife with his hurriedly drafted will. It was a moving document, naming Margaret 'my most entire belovyd wyff' chief executrix, and revealing his fears that he would not survive the conflict. He bequeathed his soul to the Lady Mary and the blessed company of heaven 'and my body to be buried wher it shall best ples god that I dye'. Stafford had divided his small retinue, stationing ten of his men at Kingston to cover his line of retreat should he have to flee the battlefield.[61]

Meanwhile Somerset was attempting to gather men at Salisbury for the Lancastrian cause. On 14 April (the day of Warwick's death at Barnet) he had shown John Hall, the mayor's deputy, his powers of commission to recruit for Henry VI. The city had agreed to supply forty men. Messages were sent by Somerset to Southampton and other towns. But as the duke left for Weymouth, where Margaret of Anjou had landed, news reached the town of Edward's momentous victory at Barnet. Immediately the men of Salisbury resolved to send their forces to Edward instead. As was so often the case during the civil war, political expediency demanded a delicate balancing act from its

---

[59] WAM, 12183, fol. 40v. [60] *Ibid.*, fol. 50.
[61] SJC, D56.186; WAM, 12183, fol. 50.

participants. As Somerset's servants returned for the city's contingent, a stream of gifts and excuses were sent off to the duke, while messengers were urgently despatched in the opposite direction to assure Edward IV of their loyalty.[62]

Edward had won a decisive victory at Barnet on 14 April. This chaotic battle, fought in a swirling mist, had at first gone badly for him. Messages began to reach London that his cause was lost. But the king's personal courage, and confusion in the enemy line, where the earl of Oxford's contingent mistakenly swung back and was engaged by its own side, turned the struggle into an unexpected Yorkist triumph. Warwick and his brother, John Marquis Montagu, were slain and a number of the Lancastrian lords badly wounded, including the duke of Exeter and the earl of Oxford. But Edward too had lost many men, and needed to replenish his forces before marching against Margaret of Anjou's army. Stafford did not return with Edward's troops to London for this last decisive venture. On 17 April Lady Margaret hurried from Woking to the capital and sent out a rider to Barnet to ascertain the health of her husband. Stafford had been wounded and took no further part in the campaign.[63] But it was to prove a calamity for the remaining male members of the Beaufort family.

When the news of Edward's victory had reached Margaret's forces on 16 April, many of the Lancastrians reacted to the news with extreme pessimism. Somerset, however, argued for an aggressive strategy. They were better off without Warwick anyway, and Edward's forces would be weakened and in no condition to undertake another major engagement. Accordingly, they should be prepared to offer battle as soon as they had sufficient strength. These tactics were to prove disastrous. The immediate requirement was the levying of troops in the west country. John Courtenay, earl of Devon, who had fought with Somerset in Flanders in 1468, raised men in Devon, while the duke did so in the county of Somerset. On 25 April he was at Hindon, 9 miles south-east of Warminster. He then proceeded to Glastonbury and Wells, where his troops broke open the prison and a nervous Chapter gave him £30. At the end of the month Somerset and his brother rode into Bristol at the head of their forces, where they gained fresh men,

[62] Wiltshire RO, G23/1/2, fols. 97v–9; Southampton RO, SC5/1/13, fol. 31v (we owe the latter reference to Dr Rosemary Horrox).

[63] WAM, 12183, fol. 51; L. Visser-Fuchs, 'The casualty list of the battle of Barnet', *The Ricardian*, 8 (1988), 10.

artillery and money.[64] The campaign was now reaching its climax. On 4 May the Lancastrian and Yorkist armies faced each other at Tewkesbury. A damaging division occurred in the Lancastrian council of war. The majority of their commanders favoured adopting a defensive position and awaiting the arrival of Jasper Tudor, who was marching from Chepstow with reinforcements. But Somerset argued for an immediate engagement, and his military reputation and standing ensured that his counsel prevailed. His decision to launch an attack on the Yorkist position was not supported by Lord Wenlock, an indication of the unhappiness of many with his plan of battle.[65] His men were rolled back into the main Lancastrian position after fierce fighting and a rout developed. Somerset's brother John, marquis of Dorset, was killed in the hand-to-hand combat and the Lancastrian prince of Wales, Edward, was cut down attempting to flee the battlefield.

Somerset and a number of other Lancastrians had managed to reach the sanctuary of Tewkesbury Abbey. Edward IV granted a free pardon to those within consecrated ground. It was another promise the king did not intend to keep. Two days later his soldiers broke into the abbey. Somerset was hauled out and executed on 6 May.[66] The motive for Edward's perjury was a desire to extirpate the house of Lancaster. The hapless Henry VI, who died in the Tower on 21 May, was almost certainly murdered on Edward IV's orders. If Somerset had survived he might have become the Lancastrian claimant to the throne.

During the confused politics of the period 1469–71 Stafford and Margaret had looked to their own interests. Yet Stafford had joined Edward IV's army at Barnet and had been wounded in the Yorkist cause. As the king consolidated his authority after Tewkesbury, and began to punish those who had supported his enemies, Margaret was able to use this influence to safeguard some of her family. Her mother, Margaret duchess of Somerset, had received a pardon by the end of the year for her role in the Lincolnshire rebellion, along with John Welles, her son by her third marriage and John Eltonhede, a loyal Beaufort

[64] Wiltshire RO, G23/1/2, fol. 99; *HMC, 12th Report*, II (MSS of the dean and chapter of Wells), 93; A. E. Hudd, 'Two Bristol Calendars', *TBGAS*, 19 (1894–5), 140.

[65] The criticism of Somerset's conduct by Polydore Vergil is significant, namely that he 'drew his men forth into battaile array, muche against the advise of the other captains, who thought best to tarry til the erle of Pembroughe should coome': Vergil, *English History*, 151.

[66] Warkworth, *Chronicle*, 18; 'A chronicle of Tewkesbury Abbey', in *English Historical Literature*, 376–8.

servant from Northamptonshire.[67] The position of Margaret's own son was to prove more difficult. Early in September 1471 Henry and his uncle Jasper Tudor were still holding out in Pembroke castle against the Yorkists. According to the later testimony of the Tudor court poet, the blind Frenchman Bernard André, Margaret warned her son against accepting any offer of a pardon from Edward IV and advised him to flee abroad.[68] André had based his account on his conversations with Henry and Margaret, and there is no reason to doubt its basic authenticity. Lady Margaret knew only too well of Edward's breaches of faith towards her own kinsmen and his present mood of vindictiveness against any possible Lancastrian claimant, and must have feared for her son. Henry and Jasper heeded her advice. They escaped from Pembroke to the small port of Tenby, from where they set sail for France. Storms blew them off course and they were to land in Brittany towards the end of September. It was the start of Henry Tudor's long exile and a considerable question-mark hung over his political future. But more immediate concerns were to confront Margaret over the next few months. On 4 October 1471 her husband had died. Stafford, who had suffered periodic bouts of illness over the last two years, never really recovered from wounds inflicted at the battle of Barnet. It was a considerable blow for Margaret. At this difficult time her receiver Reginald Bray took care of the details of Stafford's burial at Pleshey.[69] But Margaret's widowhood was to be brief, for within the prescribed year of mourning she had re-married. Her new husband was Thomas Lord Stanley.

The Stanley family had risen to prominence in the fifteenth century through a combination of local influence (in Cheshire and southern Lancashire) and activity at court. Thomas, second Lord Stanley, was entrusted with the office of steward of the royal household during the second decade of Edward IV's reign, despite his somewhat equivocal political record. But Stanley repaid Edward's trust, serving his master loyally in a variety of government business, and the king in return delegated to him considerable power in the north-west. Marriage with such a magnate offered Margaret protection and an enhanced influence at the Yorkist court. A carefully worked marriage contract guaranteed

---

[67] PRO, C67/49, m. 32; *CPR, 1467–77*, 294.
[68] *Memorials of King Henry VII*, 15–16. André allows a rhetorical flourish. Margaret was not at Tenby, but she certainly was in communication with her son, through his chaplain: WAM, 12183, fol. 80.   [69] WAM, 5479.

her a yearly income of 500 marks from Stanley's estates in Cheshire
and north Wales. The marriage took place at one of Stanley's
Lancashire residences, possibly Knowsley, early in June 1472.[70] There
was something unseemly in the haste of these proceedings. A letter of
Edward IV in 1477 referred to the fact that 'after the old usages of this
our royaume none estate, ne person honourable, communeth of
marriage within the year of their doole'.[71] Despite the deep affection
Margaret felt for Stafford, she was willing to re-marry before the
arrangements for his burial had been completed.

For Stanley the marriage with Margaret Beaufort expanded his
territorial influence. He was given a life-interest in her considerable
estates, providing a foothold in the midlands and south of England.
Knowsley Hall, near Liverpool, was enlarged to provide Margaret's
household officers with a permanent place of residence. In practice the
couple were constantly on the move, attending court in London,
staying at Woking (where a 'new lodging' was constructed) or
travelling north to Lathom or Knowsley. Stanley allowed Margaret a
certain amount of influence in his Lancashire heartland. A property
dispute in Liverpool in November 1473 was delegated to a panel
comprising Stanley's son George, his brother James and his wife. In
August 1474 a dispute between Thomas Ashton and Richard Dalton
was referred to Margaret's own council learned.[72] She was also a
frequent visitor to the capital. Early in 1475 she witnessed the
preparations for Edward IV's expedition to France. Stanley was one of
Edward's captains. In a flurry of activity London craftsmen were paid
for the garnishing of his sallet and the crimson and blue sarsnet of
his standards. Other servants went further afield. Edward Fleetwood
received £50 to buy horses for Stanley in Flanders.[73] The gathering of
this great army, comprising almost half the English aristocracy, must
have left a considerable impression on her.

Margaret's marriage with Stanley was to strengthen her links with
the powerful and grasping Woodville family. By the end of the 1470s
Stanleys and Woodvilles worked in close co-operation in the administration of Cheshire and north Wales. Their partnership was cemented

---

[70] The marriage had taken place between the drawing up of Margaret's will, on 2 June
1472, and the arranging of the marriage settlement on 12 June (SJC, D56.195, 200). The
couple's relationship is discussed in greater detail in Chapter 5, 144–60.

[71] *Original Letters*, ed. Ellis, 2nd series, I, 132.

[72] Liverpool City Library, 920/MOO/574; Lancs RO, DDX/13/3.

[73] WAM, 32407, fols. 8–9.

by family connections. Sir James Molyneux, chancellor to Anthony Earl Rivers, was Lord Stanley's nephew. Stanley's son and heir George had married Joan, daughter of John, Lord Strange, and his first wife Jacquetta, the queen's elder sister. These contacts were reflected in court ceremony. Margaret played a prominent part in the reburial of Richard, duke of York, at Fotheringhay in July 1476, in attendance on the queen and her daughters. In November 1480 Margaret was particularly honoured in the celebration of the birth of the seventh princess, Bridget, at the new royal palace at Eltham, carrying the child, with the marquis of Dorset in attendance.[74]

Margaret's position within the Yorkist polity gave her an opportunity to negotiate the return of her son from exile. Her efforts were to culminate in an attempt, in 1482, to secure his rehabilitation at the Yorkist court. Her concern for his landed future had been indicated many years earlier. In May 1472 her west-country estates had been granted to trustees to perform the uses of her first will. When these obligations were discharged the trustees were to make an estate of the lands for Henry Tudor's inheritance. The will indicated Margaret's hope that one day her son might be restored to favour.[75] It was to take on a more significant form in a document of major political importance, drawn up in the king's presence at Westminster on 3 June 1482. The document described 'certain appointments and agreements made in the highe presens of oure soveraigne Lorde'. First Stanley explicitly promised not to interfere with the settlement of Margaret's west-country estates, made before their marriage. Then arrangements were made for the disposal of the estates of Margaret's mother, the duchess of Somerset, who had died a month earlier. Henry Tudor, 'called earl of Richmond', was to receive a larger portion of these (of a value of 600 marks a year) upon certain conditions. The principal was that Henry returned from exile, 'to be in the grace and favour of the king's highness'. Edward IV added his own seal to the indenture in confirmation of the agreement.[76]

This remarkable arrangement was the fruit of negotiations between the king, Stanley and Margaret. More was hoped for. Stanley was to

---

[74] F. Sandford, *Genealogical History of the Kings and Queens of England* (London, 1707), 391–2, where the reburial is given under the erroneous date of 1466; D. MacGibbon, *Elizabeth Woodville (1437–92)* (London, 1938), 131. For the contacts between the Stanleys and the Woodvilles, D. E. Lowe, 'Patronage and politics: Edward IV, the Wydevills and the council of the Prince of Wales, 1471–83', *Bulletin of the Board of Celtic Studies*, 29 (1981), 560.   [75] SJC, D56.195.   [76] SJC, D56.158.

recall, in 1486, that during Edward IV's reign his wife and many others had discussed the fact that Henry Tudor and Elizabeth of York were related in the fourth and fifth degree of kindred. The other parties to the discussion included the bishops of Ely and Worcester, an emissary from the pope, and the king himself.[77] But if a York–Tudor marriage had taken place, it was inconceivable that a major restoration of title and dignity would not have followed, for the alternative would have been the disparagement of the royal family. After the death of George duke of Clarence in 1478 the honour of Richmond estates were once more at the disposal of the crown. A draft pardon (undated) from Edward IV to Henry Tudor, written on the dorse of the patent of creation of Edmund Tudor as earl of Richmond on 23 November 1452, is suggestive of what was envisaged.[78]

In fact these plans were never to materialize. Edward IV's attitude towards Henry Tudor was now conciliatory. Yet it was hard to put aside the legacy of many years of suspicion and distrust. Bernard André described an earlier occasion, in 1476, when Henry had been warned by his mother not to come back to England if the king offered him one of his daughters in marriage.[79] Margaret's doubts were well founded. At this stage Edward IV had other plans for all his daughters. In November 1476 Henry narrowly avoided such a return, when he slipped away from the English embassy and sought sanctuary in a church in St-Malo. Even though Margaret was now vouching for Edward's good faith, the 1482 indenture also made provision, if Henry did not return to England, for an alternative division of the duchess of Somerset's property. Clearly there was some doubt as to how he would react to the agreement. Henry Tudor was bitterly to tell the chronicler Commynes that most of his life had been spent as a captive or fugitive. The legacy was an almost pathological suspicion.

However, a new and unexpected opportunity for encouraging Henry to end his exile was to arise. On 9 April 1483 Edward IV died. The protectorate of his brother, Richard, duke of Gloucester, came to an abrupt end when Richard announced that the sons of Edward IV were in fact illegitimate. Richard accepted the crown by proclamation on 26 June and was crowned on 6 July. The circumstances of the usurpation

---

[77] *Cal. Papal Registers, 1484–92*, XIV, 18–21.
[78] The draft of the pardon is on the dorse of WAM, 32378 (the patent of the creation of Edmund Tudor as earl of Richmond 23 November 1452).
[79] *Memorials of King Henry VII*, 23.

were bloody and confused. Edward's two sons were confined to the Tower and Queen Elizabeth Woodville had withdrawn into sanctuary at Westminster Abbey with her daughters. Lord Hastings had been executed and Stanley himself may have briefly been placed under arrest, though both he and Margaret were free to attend the coronation.

At this stage Margaret's intentions were to seek an alliance with Richard III and thus safeguard the arrangements made in 1482 for her son's return. She had opened negotiations with Richard in June, using the duke of Buckingham as an intermediary, and again the prospect of a marriage alliance between Henry Tudor and a daughter of Edward IV was mooted.[80] On 5 July Stanley and Margaret met Richard III and his chief justice William Hussey at Westminster and secured their support over a ransom debt Margaret was attempting to extract from the Orléans family. The next day Margaret played a prominent part in the coronation ceremony, bearing Queen Anne's train in the procession to Westminster Abbey and serving at the banquet afterwards with Katherine, duchess of Norfolk.[81] But the political atmosphere remained highly charged. It was clear that Richard did not completely trust Stanley, who after all had close links with the Woodville family (Stanley's heir, Lord Strange, had married a niece of Queen Elizabeth Woodville) and commanded him to attend his coronation progress through the realm as a political precaution rather than a mark of honour.

Lady Margaret, who had remained in London, quickly realized the extent of the opposition to the new Yorkist king. In a matter of weeks she took a calculated but highly dangerous step, abandoning her allegiance to Richard III and throwing in her lot with the plotters. At the end of July 1483 she participated in an attempt to rescue the princes, in which a newly restored Edward V would be supported by an invasion force led by Jasper and Henry Tudor.[82] However, an attempt to storm the Tower failed and about fifty of the conspirators were arrested. The young princes were withdrawn into the inner recesses of the Tower, and were not to be seen again. By September many people

[80] *Hall's Chronicle*, ed. H. Ellis (London, 1809), 388–9. Margaret submitted that the marriage arrangements would be entirely in Richard's hands, 'without any thing to be taken or demaunded for the same espousals but only the kynges favour'.

[81] WAM, 12320; *The Coronation of Richard III. The Extant Documents*, ed. A. F. Sutton and P. W. Hammond (Gloucester, 1983), 167, 169, 278–81.

[82] Details on this conspiracy were extracted by J. Stow, *The Annals or General Chronicle of England* (London, 1615), 460, from a now missing ancient indictment file.

believed them to be dead. Under these dramatic circumstances an entirely new strategy was formed, with Margaret Beaufort and the Woodvilles at its centre. Henry Tudor was to claim the throne of England, united with the Woodville faction through a proposed marriage alliance with Elizabeth of York. Negotiations with Elizabeth Woodville were carried out by Margaret's physician, Lewis Caerleon, whilst her communication with Henry Tudor in Brittany was undertaken by her servant Hugh Conway.[83] A number of her kinsmen and servants were to be found amongst the rebels of autumn 1483, including John Cheyney, Thomas Lewkenor, John Welles and John Heron. Yet the claim of Polydore Vergil that Margaret was the chief mover of the conspiracy deliberately underplayed the role of the Woodvilles. Thomas, marquis of Dorset, and Lionel, bishop of Salisbury, both played a crucial part in co-ordinating the revolt.[84]

If Margaret's plans for a York–Tudor marriage in the last days of Edward IV's reign were easily adjusted to the dramatic political situation of 1483, the nature of her communication with the duke of Buckingham must remain far more ambiguous. Tudor commentators glossed this incident, describing the duke as a willing supporter of Henry Tudor's claim to the throne. Buckingham was a proud and ambitious magnate, acutely conscious of his royal ancestry. In 1474 he had obtained a heraldic decree allowing him to display the arms of Edward III's youngest son, Thomas of Woodstock, duke of Gloucester, 'a coate neire to the king and of his royall bloude'.[85] In the early days of Richard III's reign he had been granted unprecedented power in north and south Wales. If the duke's motives for rebelling against a man who had shown him so much favour will always remain mysterious, it is difficult to countenance a situation in which Buckingham would have taken the colossal risk of rebellion to support the claim of a political unknown. If Henry Tudor had gained the throne Woodville pre-eminence would have been restored in Wales, at Buckingham's expense, and they, not he, would have held the dominant position at court. When Buckingham wrote to Henry on 24 September 1483 he informed him of his rebellion and invited him to

[83] Vergil, *English History*, 195–8; Griffiths and Thomas, *Tudor Dynasty*, 95–6.
[84] See for example J. A. F. Thomson, 'Bishop Lionel Woodville and Richard III', *BIHR*, 59 (1986), 130–5.
[85] R. A. Griffiths, 'The crown and the royal family in later medieval England', in *Kings and Nobles in the Later Middle Ages*, ed. R. A. Griffiths and J. Sherborne (Gloucester, 1986), 19–20.

join it. He did not acknowledge Henry as the next king of England. Serious consideration must be given to the possibility that Margaret duped Buckingham, encouraging him to claim the throne himself.[86]

All these plans came to nothing. The separate risings were badly co-ordinated and the Kentish rebellion was promptly crushed by the duke of Norfolk. Buckingham's tenantry deserted him in large numbers and Richard was able to move down to the south-west sector of the revolt in considerable force. By the time Henry Tudor's small fleet appeared off the coast of Dorset, Buckingham's cause was already lost and Tudor prudently beat a hasty retreat. The failure of the rebellion placed Margaret in considerable personal danger. She was only saved by the fact that her husband Lord Stanley had remained loyal to Richard during the crisis. In the parliament of 1484 she was spared attainder, 'remembryng the good and feithful service that Thomas Lord Stanley hath doon...and for his sake'.[87] Yet she was to forfeit her right to all titles and estates. The income in trust that she enjoyed from her husband was declared void, and the intended enfeoffment of west-country estates for the use of her son was dissolved. The properties were regranted to Stanley. Her right to inherit the lands of her mother was also cancelled, and lands that might have been conserved for the use of Henry Tudor were now dispersed among others. There can be no doubt of the punitive nature of these measures. Richard's treatment of Margaret was not, as some commentators have suggested, 'remarkably lenient'.[88] Richard could not have done more without alienating Lord Stanley, who was instructed to keep his wife confined in some secret place without her household servants.

Richard's decision to trust and reward the Stanley family formed a crucial plank in his policy of patronage over the next year. Thomas Lord Stanley was granted new lands and offices, and by 1484 held the posts of steward of the household and constable of England. It proved a fatal miscalculation. Stanley's loyalty in October 1483 probably owed more to his resentment of Buckingham's pre-eminence in north Wales than any new-found allegiance to Richard's cause. He allowed

---

[86] Buckingham's role is already undergoing a reappraisal: R. Horrox, *Richard III. A Study in Service* (Cambridge, 1989), 163; Griffiths and Thomas, *Tudor Dynasty*, 96. When the duke summoned the local gentry to come before him at Weobley, it may have been with the intention of declaring himself king (Owen and Blakeway, *A History of Shrewsbury*, I, 241).

[87] *RP*, VI, 250.

[88] For the earliest criticisms of Richard's 'leniency' towards Margaret see Buck, *Richard III*, cv; for a more recent view, S. B. Chrimes, *Henry VII* (London, 1977), 28.

his wife to continue communicating with her son and on his landing in Wales in August 1485, the support of the wider Stanley family network was a major factor in enabling Henry to gain the throne.[89]

Margaret's astonishing role in the conspiracy of 1483 was the culmination of her long period of political education during the Wars of the Roses. She had displayed considerable skill and bravery. The later recollections of Henry Parker, Lord Morley, who had served as a cupbearer in her household, made a pointed reference to the danger she had faced: 'albeyt that in King Richardes daies she was oft in jeopardy of her lyfe, yet she bore paciently all trouble in such wyse that it ys wonder to think it'. The Tudor tradition respected her prominent role in the revolt. In the words of the court historian Polydore Vergil, she 'was commonly caulyd the head of that conspiracy'.[90] But their version of events was deliberately propagandist. In view of the dynastic importance of Margaret's Beaufort lineage, she was assigned the part of a Lancastrian plotter. Bernard André ascribed to her foresight the warning that Henry Tudor should flee after Tewkesbury, and disdain Edward IV's offers of reconciliation. Yet he made no mention of her close connections with the Yorkist court, her efforts to negotiate her son's return from exile in 1482 or her initial loyalty to Richard III. The reality was more subtle. If Margaret's efforts on her son's behalf had an heroic quality, they were not forged out of a blind adherence to dynastic loyalty but the ruthless practice of realpolitik. Her calculating temperament and natural astuteness allowed the organization of an alliance with the Woodvilles in the autumn of 1483. This image, of a consummate and unprincipled plotter, reappeared in the works of Cornwallis and Buck and formed the basis of Shakespeare's portrayal of her. Margaret's tears at the coronation of her son, Henry VII, two years later reflected a fear that fortune's wheel might turn again. It was a reaction borne from the political turmoil of the period, but also a sign of her own essential pragmatism.

[89] M. K. Jones, 'Sir William Stanley of Holt: politics and family allegiance in the late fifteenth century', *Welsh History Review*, 14 (1988), 19–22.

[90] BL, Add. MS 12060, fol. 22v; Vergil, *English History*, 204.

3

THE REIGN OF HENRY VII

The month of September 1485 saw an emotional reunion of mother and son. Henry VII's victorious army had reached the capital by 7 September. After spending a fortnight in Baynard's Castle Henry travelled south to Guildford, which he had last visited nearly fifteen years ago. As far as the king's itinerary can be reconstructed he remained based in this area until 11 October, and almost certainly he spent most of the time at Woking in the company of his mother.[1] Here was an opportunity for relaxation, hunting in the nearby park and long conversation. It was a conscious recreation of their last meeting, the brief but happy time spent together in the autumn of 1470, before high politics had once again driven them apart. In the intimacy of his mother's sprawling manor house, set amidst the orchards and parkland of the Surrey countryside, plans could be laid for the future. It was here, in one of his earliest grants, that Henry provided his mother with a suitably splendid London residence. On royal orders a rush of repairs and alterations were made to the fine house of Coldharbour, overlooking the Thames, on behalf of 'my lady the Kynges moder'. Thomas Littley, the new clerk of the works, supervised the rapid schedule. He had been a servant of Margaret's and owed his post to her recommendation. Carpenters, joiners and glaziers worked hurriedly to refit windows, partition and furnish chambers and renovate the outbuildings. A scutcheon of Margaret's arms was set in a window by the water-side where it could easily be viewed from the river.[2]

---

[1] These details have been drawn from Miss Condon's unpublished itinerary of Henry VII.

[2] The document, PRO, E101/473/3, is discussed and fully transcribed in C. L. Kingsford, 'On some London houses of the early Tudor period', *Archaeologia*, 71 (1920–1), 21–50, from which all references will be taken.

Henry's gift to his mother was a token of his respect and gratitude. His disposal to Margaret of a number of politically important wards offers some insight into the topics of their discussions together. At Coldharbour rooms were made ready for Henry's intended bride, Elizabeth of York. Entrusting her to his mother reflected correct etiquette. Henry had little experience of the English court and had never met his prospective partner. Since Margaret had played a key role in negotiating the match two years earlier it was natural enough to rely on her advice and experience in the arrangements leading up to the marriage. Accommodation was also prepared at Coldharbour for the young Edward Stafford, duke of Buckingham. This was the wealthiest wardship at the disposal of the crown and Margaret's custody of Stafford anticipated by almost a year the formal grant. Henry's wish that his mother administer the affairs of the young duke again echoed her role in the conspiracy of 1483, when Margaret had worked to bring the Stafford affinity behind her son's cause. It was also a recognition that Buckingham himself had a viable right to the crown and thus needed to be carefully watched over. Most interesting was Margaret's custody of the ten-year-old Edward Plantagenet, earl of Warwick, the son of George duke of Clarence. Dynastically the young Plantagenet offered the greatest threat to Henry's claim to the throne, and may have been nominated as Richard III's successor after the death of Edward prince of Wales in 1484. One of Henry VII's first acts after Bosworth was to fetch the earl of Warwick from Sheriff Hutton, and keep him securely guarded. Margaret was equally aware of the political danger, and in the first year of the reign acted as a jailor on behalf of her son.[3]

The arrangements made between Margaret and Henry in the few weeks before the coronation indicated that her role as king's mother was as important and influential as that enjoyed by Cecily, duchess of York, in the early years of Edward IV's reign, of whom it had been said that she could 'rule the king as she pleases'. The coronation of Henry

---

[3] Information on the wardships is found in *Materials for a History of the Reign of Henry VII*, ed. W. Campbell, 2 vols., Rolls Series (London, 1873–7), I, 311; Kingsford, 'London houses', 44, 46. For the dynastic significance of Buckingham and Warwick see C. Rawcliffe, *The Staffords, Earls of Stafford and Dukes of Buckingham, 1394–1521* (Cambridge, 1978), 36–7; K. Mertes, *The English Noble Household, 1250–1600* (London, 1988), 148 (for Edward Stafford's pilgrimage to the burial place of Edward of Lancaster at Tewkesbury Abbey); *CP*, XII, ii, 395–6.

VII on 30 October 1485 demonstrated their sense of common cause. Bishop Fisher later recalled a revealing moment: 'when the kynge her son was crowned in all that grete tryumphe and glorye, she wept mervaylously'.[4] Despite the magnificence of the ceremony, with Henry clad in a long gown of purple velvet under a royal canopy, both he and his mother were only too aware of the transience of political fortune. The dramatic events of Richard III's reign left a lasting impression on Margaret. The Stanleys had received the spoils of the battlefield from a grateful Henry Tudor and hangings from Richard's tent were proudly displayed in their Lancashire residence at Knowsley.[5] Margaret had taken a personal interest in the division of this booty and had acquired the late king's book of hours, with its moving prayer composed for Richard's own use, offering an insight into his troubled state of mind in the last months of his reign. It contained an appeal to Christ to 'free me, thy servant King Richard from all the tribulation, grief and anguish in which I am held, and from all the snares of my enemies'.[6] Margaret had also found a place in her household for members of Richard's retinue. One of these, Ralph Bigod, a former knight of the body, revealed to her the confused scene in Richard's camp on the morning of Bosworth, with mass unable to be celebrated: 'when his chappelyns had one thing ready, evermore they wanted another; when they had wyne, they lacked bread, and ever one thing was myssing. In the meane season King Henry comyng on a pace, King Rychard was constrained to go to battle.'[7] The events of the previous two years had deeply affected Margaret, not only because of the danger and duress that she had experienced, but also as an exemplar of the sudden turns and twists in the pattern of loyalty and allegiance.

The parliament that assembled at Westminster on 7 November reflected the diverse strands that had carried Henry to the throne. For many it was a forum for redress for family losses suffered in the Lancastrian cause at the battle of Towton over twenty-four years

---

[4] Scofield, *Edward IV*, I, 170; *Mornynge Remembraunce*, 306.

[5] A seventeenth-century inventory records the display of a suite of hangings 'taken in Richard the thirdes tent in Bosworth field': O. Miller, 'Stafford and Van Dyck', in *For Veronica Wedgwood These: Studies in Seventeenth Century History*, ed. R. Ollard and P. Tudor-Craig (London, 1986), 123 (which we owe to Pamela Tudor-Craig).

[6] A. F. Sutton and L. Visser-Fuchs, *The Hours of Richard III* (Gloucester, 1990), 39–40.

[7] BL, Add. MS 12060, fol. 20; R. M. Warnicke, 'Sir Ralph Bigod: a loyal servant to King Richard III', *The Ricardian*, 6 (1984), 299–301.

earlier. For these petitioners Bosworth represented a Lancastrian triumph, and they were careful to stress the new king's blood-link with Henry VI. There was no doubting the importance of the Beaufort lineage. Parliament re-enacted the statute of 1397 that had declared the Beaufort family legitimate and significantly omitted the clause of 1407 that had barred them from the succession. The family's badge of the portcullis was adopted as the new royal emblem, alongside the red rose associated with Henry IV, in an effort to stress both the Lancastrian right of succession and the legitimacy of the Beauforts. Yet other parliamentary business involved restoration of lands or compensation to those who had suffered during the reign of Richard III. The majority of these were staunch Yorkists: a reminder of the loyalties of many of the exiles of 1483 who were to join Henry's invasion two years later. No appeal to the king was more powerful than that of support for his cause before 1485. Thus the overriding political concern was pragmatism. In his struggle to keep the throne Henry chose to portray himself as a symbol of continuity, a rightful successor to Edward IV, as well as legal heir of Henry VI. Both through the weaknesses of the Beaufort claim and the need to appeal to a broader basis of support, Henry chose not to justify his right and title through his mother's links to the Lancastrian house, but by 'verum Dei judicium', revealed in his victory at Bosworth.

Nevertheless, Margaret's status at the new royal court and the precedence and honour accorded to her were semi-regal. At the coronation of Henry's queen, Elizabeth of York, she accompanied her at the procession and sat at her right hand in the parliament chamber. In 1488 both she and Elizabeth were issued with liveries of the Order of the Garter, a sign of special standing, and a song was composed for the feast to celebrate their wearing of robes together. The daughter born to the royal couple in 1489 was named after her. It was an aura of regality that Margaret deliberately cultivated. In the Christmas celebrations of 1487 she was observed wearing 'like mantell and surcott as the quene, with a rich corrownall on her hede'. Again at the garter ceremony of 1488, she wore identical costume as the queen; robes of sanguine cloth furred with minever and woven with garter letters of gold.[8] In her heraldic insignia she made use of the royal

---

[8] J. Leland, *De Rebus Brittanicis Collectanea*, ed. T. Hearne, 6 vols. (London, 1774), III, 236; IV, 238, 254.

coronet with its fleurs-de-lys. The theme was strongly emphasized in the window portraying the royal family, commissioned for the church of Grey Friars, Greenwich, in 1503. The image of Margaret showed her with 'robes like a pryncess, corynell on head and rodde of gold in her hand'. Her cloth of estate was powdered with the portcullis and red rose.[9] Her role bore striking similarities to, and indeed may have been modelled on, that of Cecily duchess of York at the court of her son, Edward IV. A miniature from the Luton Guild Book (c. 1475) showed Thomas Rotherham, archbishop of York, Edward IV and his queen, Elizabeth Woodville, kneeling before an image of the Trinity. Cecily, in royal robes, displaying the quarterings of England and France, enjoyed particular precedence, being placed immediately behind the queen. The difference, and it was an important one, was that Cecily had by then been posthumously recognized as 'queen of right': her late husband honoured as 'rightful king of England'.[10]

Beneath the ostentation of court ceremony lay the demands of politics. The court poet Bernard André likened the first twelve years of Henry's reign to the labours of Hercules. A succession of risings and intrigues threw constant challenges to the Tudor dynasty's survival. Celebrations were interspersed with constant alarms. In May 1487 Henry heard that the adherents of Lambert Simnel had landed in Ireland. Realizing that an invasion was imminent, he sent for the queen's chamberlain, the earl of Ormonde, 'forasmoche as we have sent for our derrest wif and for our derrest moder to come unto us...we pray you that, yeving your due attendaunce uppon our said derrest wif and lady moder, ye come with thaym unto us; not failing herof as ye purpose to doo us plaisir'.[11] In November 1487 elaborate river pageants marked the queen's coronation. Yet danger was never far away. A new rash of conspiracies in 1494 implicated no less a person than the king's chamberlain, Sir William Stanley. The banquets, dances and jousts which followed the creation of Prince Henry as duke of York, in October 1494, had a political rationale. Through public ceremony it was asserted that Richard, the previous duke of York, was dead and Perkin Warbeck an imposter. Margaret played a prominent

---

[9] BL, Egerton MS 2341 (which we owe to Margaret Condon).

[10] *The Register of the Guild of the Holy Trinity in the Parish Church of Luton*, ed. H. Gough (London, 1906), 16–17, with Cecily described as 'veri et indubitati heredis corone Anglie'; C. A. J. Armstrong, 'The piety of Cicely, Duchess of York', in *England, France and Burgundy in the Fifteenth Century* (London, 1983), 138.

[11] Printed in Cooper, 38.

part in the creation procession, following behind the queen, again wearing her coronet. She stayed to watch the jousting afterwards and was among the ladies who advised on the giving of prizes.[12]

The Milanese ambassador met the royal family at Woodstock at a moment of particular crisis, early in September 1497. Two months earlier a dangerous Cornish revolt had been defeated at Blackheath. Now Perkin Warbeck was stirring up fresh unrest in the west country. The ambassador saw only the trappings of display, the richness of the king's collar 'full of great pearls'. He failed to notice the frantic military preparations as the Tudor regime was once again under threat.[13] Everyday government had ground to a halt in the process. Robert Pilkington, engaged in a property dispute over the Derbyshire manor of Mellor, found all legal activity suspended a few days into the Trinity term. It was, he recorded, a time of 'grete trowbull in the lond'.[14] The entries in Lady Margaret's book of hours, unusual in the extent of their political detail, bring across strongly the image of an embattled dynasty. The dates of Henry VII's victories at Bosworth, Stoke and Blackheath are all carefully recorded.[15]

Contemporaries noted the frequency with which Margaret accompanied the king and queen on royal visits or progresses. These tours of the country offered an opportunity to display the majesty of kingship and to cement political allegiance. In 1492 Henry and his mother travelled to Windsor to see work recommence on St George's Chapel. As scaffolding and ladders went up in the north transept Margaret made a personal contribution of 100 marks to John Shaw, the paymaster.[16] Four years later the royal party toured Margaret's Dorset estates of Canford, Poole and Corfe, reaching the imposing fortress on 30 July 1496. The progress occurred at a time when there were renewed fears of an invasion by Perkin Warbeck. The king's visit to Corfe made a propagandist point. Corfe castle had been the chief residence of the Beaufort family. Their re-building of the nearby parish church early in the fifteenth century demonstrated their new-found status. The coats-of-arms at the side of the north doorway reflected

---

[12] S. Anglo, *Spectacle, Pageantry and Early Tudor Policy* (Oxford, 1969), 53; *L and P*, I, 395.

[13] *Calendar of State Papers, Milan, I, 1385–1618*, ed. A. B. Hinds (London, 1912), 322.

[14] *Report on MSS in HMC, Various Collections*, II, 39.

[15] 'Notes from ancient calendars', 278–9.

[16] For the building of the 'new chapell', WAM, 32364; H. M. Colvin, D. R. Ransome and J. Summerson, eds., *The History of the King's Works*, 6 vols. (London, 1963–82), III, 311.

through heraldry the importance of the family's legitimization. On the left the shield lay on its side, indicating a bastard line, whilst on the right it was placed upright. The new tower, built through their patronage, emphasized their royal lineage, its roundels depicting the heads of John of Gaunt and Edward III. Such an environment served to emphasize Henry's own regality. He had restored Corfe to his mother and encouraged her to re-build the castle in even more splendid fashion. In 1488 large amounts of lead had been made available to her for the 'Byeldyng and repairing'. Improvements were made to the keep and new residential quarters, with greatly enlarged windows, were installed: appropriate to the demands of a royal visit.[17]

The progress represented the culmination of a consistent policy of rehabilitation of the Beaufort family. In December 1488 Edmund Beaufort, the last duke of Somerset (d. 1471), and his brother John, had been ceremonially reburied in Tewkesbury Abbey.[18] Charles Somerset, the bastard son of Henry Beaufort, duke of Somerset, had been brought up among the small group of Lancastrian exiles who had sheltered in Flanders after Tewkesbury. He had supported Henry Tudor in 1485 and risen rapidly in royal favour. Interestingly, he had originally been named Charles Beaufort, and his surname was changed to Somerset in the first year of the new reign, presumably so that Henry VII could portray himself as true heir of the Beaufort family. In 1493, in a nice touch, the king rewarded Somerset by granting an annuity of 10 marks to his mother (Henry Beaufort's mistress, Joan Hill).[19] The tour of 1496 allowed the royal entourage to halt at Wimborne Minster, resting place of Margaret's parents. Here was a memorial window to John Beaufort duke of Somerset and his wife Margaret (the remains of the glass were later transferred to the parish church of Landbeach, Cambridgeshire), and a fine alabaster tomb. The churchwardens' accounts of the Minster record an offering made by 'my lady the kyngs moder' and torches placed around the tomb. Hurried payments had also been made for the 'redying and makyng clene the churche yard' when news arrived of the king's 'comyng'.[20]

Comparison of the itineraries of Henry and Margaret for another year, 1498, reveals the regularity with which they joined company. In

[17] Margaret's work at Corfe is reconstructed from *Materials*, II, 364; WAM, 32350; Colvin, Ransome and Summerson, eds., *King's Works*, II, 623. [18] *Materials*, II, 380.
[19] *CPR, 1485–94*, 426.
[20] References kindly supplied by Patricia Hairsine from DRO, MI 23.

July they were together at London, Westminster, Sheen and Windsor, where Margaret ordered brooches from a local goldsmith for her grandchildren, Princess Margaret and Prince Henry. At the end of the month they left the capital for a tour of the eastern counties. At Castle Hedingham they were entertained by the earl of Oxford. The combined entourage then passed through Bury St Edmunds, Thetford, Norwich, Walsingham and King's Lynn. By early September they had reached Cambridge, from whence they travelled through Huntingdon and Peterborough before arriving at Margaret's residence of Collyweston on 7 September. The strain of such travelling during the hot summer months was beginning to tell. At Castle Hedingham Margaret exchanged her carriage for the greater comfort of a litter, carried by relays of servants, whose thirst would be quenched at frequent wayside stops.[21]

If the travels of the royal entourage often had a political purpose, they also offered an opportunity for relaxation. Henry was a keen huntsman. A royal warrant to Richard Anstey, 'yeoman of our stirrup', from the palace of Greenwich gives a vignette of one such excursion. Eight horses were to be prepared in the Tudor livery colours, cloth of white and green, lined with canvas, and other grooming materials included broad reins of red leather, three horsecombs, sponges, bags and halters and 'dusting cloth'.[22] Margaret clearly saw the residences under her care as adjuncts for the king's recreation. At Collyweston the park was enclosed and substantially enlarged. At Madeley (Staffs) her keeper of the park was sternly reprimanded for letting the stock run down. He was told in no uncertain terms that Margaret intended 'the saide deer and game to be reserved and kept for the kinges pleasur and oures ayenst such season as we shal repaire unto these partes'.[23]

Royal household ordinances made provision for Margaret's accommodation, along with other members of the immediate family, at all the palaces and other residences used by the crown. At Woodstock, Margaret's lodgings were placed close to her son the king's linked by a 'drawt' (withdrawing) chamber 'that belongs to the kings chamber and my lady his mothers'. Here was a place for the two to be together in utmost privacy, whether to discuss affairs of state or relax at cards

[21] For full details of the progress see Appendix 1 below, 260–1.
[22] The manuscript is displayed at Sudeley Castle.
[23] Staffs RO, D593/A/1/29/5 (which we owe to Dr Colin Richmond).

or chess. In the Tower Margaret's rooms were to be found next to the king's own bedchamber and the council chamber.[24] Their proximity is suggestive of a role of discreet but constant surveillance, similar to her observation of the queen's coronation 'secretly in a house', and foreign observers were quick to perceive Margaret's pervasive influence at court. An illustration of this is found in Margaret's self-appointed role as guardian of regulation and protocol. When Princess Margaret left Collyweston for Scotland, in July 1503, Margaret allowed only those with a blood-link with the royal family into the great hall for the farewell ceremony. Her concern for the order and detail of both household and court is very much a theme of Henry Parker's recollections: suggesting a vigorous and possibly rather intimidating presence.

The public profile Margaret enjoyed at the early Tudor court was a visible sign of the respect accorded by her son. The strength of their emotional bond is better shown by the presents they regularly sent each other (Margaret's New Year's gift to Henry in 1507 was a magnificent cup of gold worth £104) and the tone of their correspondence. Henry would refer to his 'grete and singular moderly love and affection', Margaret to her 'derest and only desyred joy yn thys world'. The fact that Henry was an only child gave a particular focus to their feelings. In a letter written in 1501, on the anniversary of Henry's birth, Margaret movingly referred to 'thys day of Seynt Annes, that y dyd bryng ynto thys world my good and gracyous prynce, kynge and only beloved son'.[25] The difficult circumstances of the birth, in which the lives of both were in danger, were mirrored in the political adversities that they had faced. It was the dimension of struggle and survival that gave their relationship its considerable power.

Yet familial affection did not in itself guarantee political influence. If observers had been struck by the dominant role of the king's mother, Cecily Neville, in the first year of Edward IV's reign, it quickly became more circumspect as the young Yorkist monarch asserted his own personality. Similarly, if Lady Margaret's advice and guidance were vital to her son in the early months of his rule, Henry was soon to take the initiative in matters of government and statecraft. Within a couple of years the new monarch, enjoying a deep and loving relationship

---

[24] Colvin, Ransome and Summerson, eds., *King's Works*, III, 266; IV, 351.
[25] Cooper, 66–7.

with his wife Elizabeth of York and the blessing of a male heir, had renegotiated the terms of the Stafford wardship (securing a substantial income for the crown) and removed Edward Plantagenet from Margaret's custody to the greater security of the Tower. As Henry VII's own confidence grew the influence of the broader royal family lessened, in part by accident, in part by design. The king's uncle, Jasper duke of Bedford, was now well over fifty. After the tribulations of his exile he was content with commissions in Wales and Ireland, which removed him from the centre of the political stage. The early deaths of two of Elizabeth of York's uncles (Sir Edward Woodville, killed in Brittany in 1488, and Richard Earl Rivers, who died in March 1491 leaving the earldom extinct) helped relegate the remaining members of the Woodville family to a minor role in policy making. A partial exception was made for Margaret's husband Thomas Stanley. Stanley was created earl of Derby and his office of constable of England was confirmed by Henry. He sat regularly on council meetings and was allowed to extend his regional power into the midlands. These honours were both a mark of Stanley's status as the king's step-father and a recognition of Henry's sense of debt to the family for their assistance in 1485. Sir William Stanley, whose intervention at Bosworth decided the outcome of the battle, received confirmation of the grants he had gained in Richard III's reign and was elevated to the office of king's chamberlain. Yet here Henry VII was more cautious. William received little in the way of fresh territorial reward and significantly was not promoted to the peerage. A sense of dissatisfaction with his treatment, heightened by concern over his right of title to the most important of his properties, the lordship of Bromfield and Yale, may have led to his involvement in Yorkist conspiracies.[26]

Henry was a shrewd and often chronically suspicious monarch. Always guarded in his dealings with others, he rarely intimated the true direction of his plans and strategies. Francis Bacon, alert to the king's control and manipulation of even his closest councillors, suggested that as the reign progressed Henry reverenced his mother greatly but heard her little. It was not a view shared by the Spanish ambassador. In 1498 he observed how 'the king is much influenced by his mother', placing her authority as greater than the king's chamberlain, Sir Giles Daubeney, his chancellor, Cardinal Morton, or

---

[26] Jones, 'Sir William Stanley', 12–13, 20–2.

Richard Fox, keeper of the privy seal.[27] Nor is it borne out by the evidence of their correspondence. A letter to Margaret of July 1504 provides an example of the calculating nature of the king's thought. The occasion was his negotiation with the French crown over a debt owed by Louis XII to Lady Margaret. The king opined:

> hit will be ryght hard to recover hit without hit be dryven by compulsion and force, rather than by any true justice whiche is not yet as we thynke any conveniant tyme to put into execution. Nevertheless it hath pleased you to gyve us a good interest and meane, if they woule not conforme thayme to rayson and good justice, to diffende or offende at a convenyant tyme, when the caas shall so require herafter. For such a chaunce may fall that thys your graunte might stande in grete stead for the recovery of our right and make us free, wheras we be now bounde.[28]

Both Henry and his mother shared an appreciation for the need of spies and informants and Margaret's castles and residences formed a chain of watchtowers, vigilantly guarding against treasonable activity. On one occasion her agents at Tattershall castle apprehended persons being shipped up the Witham in suspicious circumstances.[29] Although Margaret's role may have been redefined at certain stages of her son's reign the constant threat to the Tudor dynasty ensured their continuing political partnership.

In the 1490s the king had undertaken a vigorous building programme, designed to emphasize the prestige of the dynasty. In 1495 Henry decided on a proper burial and tomb for the corpse of Richard III in the church of the Grey Friars, Leicester. A contract was drawn up with the Nottingham alabasterman Walter Hilton. The decision is suggestive, after the exposure of the conspiracy of 1494, of a hope that Yorkist plotting would soon come to an end.[30] After fire destroyed the royal residence at Sheen in 1497 Henry built a magnificent new palace on the site, which he was to rename Richmond: its dramatic roof-line with its high chimney-tops was to set a new fashion in court building. Henry's spending on the magnificence of kingship, precious jewels, tapestries and furnishings, led to the contemporary pun on his new palace, 'Rich Mount'. By 1501 such optimism seemed to be justified. Perkin Warbeck had been captured and executed along with the earl of Warwick. A prestigious marriage had been arranged for Henry's eldest son Arthur with Catherine of Aragon; another was soon to be

[27] Bacon, *History of the Reign of King Henry the Seventh*, 230; *Cal. State Papers, Spanish*, I, 163, 178.   [28] Cooper, 92.   [29] KRO, U1475/M169, m. 2.
[30] R. Edwards, 'King Richard's tomb at Leicester', *The Ricardian*, 3 (1975), 8–9.

formalized with Scotland whereby the Princess Margaret would marry James IV. The celebrations planned for Catherine's arrival in England were to emphasize a sense of dynastic strength and optimism. The Tudor dynasty had gained international acceptance. The fruit of the union between Arthur and Catherine would, it was hoped, soon ensure a stable succession.

The festivities were on a scale of exceptional splendour and Henry took an unusually active interest in their planning. In June 1500 Richard Pynson was commissioned to circulate advertisements of the decorations and pageants throughout the city of London. The wedding would take place at St Paul's, transformed by a sea of tapestries. At Westminster and Richmond spectacular banquets would be held. Disguisings and pageants would be prepared to entertain the guests. The king appointed two of his councillors, Sir Reginald Bray and Lord Abergavenny, to liaise with the city guilds. Henry displayed his customary attention to detail. On 24 August 1501 Garter Herald took barge to Richmond 'to have the kinges mynde' on the appropriate colours for the prince's trumpets. The arrival of Arthur and Catherine in London at the beginning of November prompted a month of festivities. On 14 November the king, queen and Margaret stood with others 'in secret maner' in St Paul's for the marriage ceremony 'in a closet latised'.[31] There followed a series of sumptuous joustings and disguisings, court and capital awash with colour. Margaret had followed these events with keen anticipation: her book of hours noting the dates of Catherine's departure from Spain (27 September) and her landing at Plymouth (2 October). She was now to play her part in the mood of celebration. Her residence at Coldharbour was refurbished, with no less than £666 being spent on cloth of gold, silks and velvets and other sundries, so that the couple could be entertained there in style. Wages and liveries were paid out to the household men attending upon the marriage.[32] For both Margaret and her son the occasion represented the high-point of the reign and an occasion of real and mutual happiness.

Yet tragically the hopes that underlay these displays were to be undermined by an atmosphere of fear and uncertainty that once again eddied around the court. In April 1502 disaster struck when the king's

[31] *Chronicles of London*, ed. C. Kingsford (Oxford, 1905), 248; G. Kipling, *The Triumph of Honour* (Leiden, 1977), 72–95.
[32] PRO, SC6/Eliz./3368; SJC, D102.2, pp. 17–18.

eldest son Arthur suddenly died at Ludlow. The news came as a horrific
shock. The messenger arrived at Greenwich late on 4 April and a
nervous council deliberated on how best to inform the king, before
delegating the task to his confessor, who broke the news to him in the
early hours of the following morning.[33] Since Henry's third son
Edmund had perished two years earlier, and the health of Prince Henry
was not robust, the dynasty's future was once more plunged into
uncertainty. Henry's intimate circle shrank further with the loss of his
wife (who died on 11 February 1503) and also his trusted councillor
Reginald Bray. Both had exercised a stabilizing influence on a king
whose sense of inner stability and perspective may have been
irretrievably damaged. The unfortunate court astrologer William
Parron, who a few months earlier had forecast that Henry's queen
would live to be at least eighty, wisely left the country. The exiled de
la Poles became the focus for a fresh rash of conspiracies. In 1503
Margaret drew up a series of ordinances for mourning apparel. The
careful detail of the funeral ordinances, specifying with minute
exactness the size and form of hoods, trains and surcoats, hints at the
sense of tragedy that had overtaken the Tudor court.[34] Margaret and
her son faced the growing danger of a new rising aiming to restore a
Yorkist successor.

A growing shadow was cast over the last years of Henry VII's reign,
a time of 'sorrows darke'. As the king's health became increasingly
uncertain Margaret took up residence in the palaces of the south-east
to remain close to her son. Light briefly shone through the clouds at the
beginning of 1506 when Henry and his court fêted Philip of Habsburg,
king of Castile, and his Queen Joanna. Regal hospitality was accorded
to the travellers, driven by storm to take refuge on the English coast.
Again Margaret played a major part, entertaining her son and
members of the king of Castile's household at Croydon (a residence she
had borrowed from William Warham, archbishop of Canterbury). Her
interest in the event had a more pertinent justification. The price of the
festivities, culminating in a magnificent installation of Philip to the
Order of the Garter, was more than offset by Castile's agreement to
surrender the renegade Edmund de la Pole. Margaret had followed the
politics of the occasion closely: a detailed description being made for
her of the king of Castile's arrival in England, his entertainment and the

[33] Leland, *Collectanea*, V, 373.
[34] BL, Add MS 45133, fol. 141v, also discussed below, p. 187.

decision to give up Edmund de la Pole, the Yorkist claimant.[35] However, de la Pole's youngest brother Richard remained at large, and
was to cause further trouble for the Tudors. Longer-term diplomatic
benefits were also hoped for. In April 1506 Margaret's servants had
travelled to Richmond to escort her granddaughter, the Princess Mary,
to Croydon, where both were serenaded by King Philip's lutenists.[36]
Later that year the Emperor Maximilian was to propose a marriage
between Mary and Philip's son Charles. He doubtless had the benefit of
the reports of the Castilian suite, which had seen Mary in the intimate
setting of her grandmother's household.

Yet for the most part the king became an increasingly introverted
figure. The zest that had characterized the celebrations of 1501 had
largely disappeared from the scene. His policies were becoming
increasingly harsh and unpopular. However, his sole surviving son
Henry shook off the frailties of health and developed into an athletic
teenager. Summer tournaments, encouraged by the presence of the
young prince, were held annually by the court. Here at least was hope
for the future. Margaret attended the first of these occasions, in June
1507, and watched the performance of her grandson with considerable
pride. She had ordered and paid for the saddle and harness that marked
his first joust. The following summer she showed her appreciation of
his 'running at the ring' by sending him a small gift.[37] Margaret at
least had this consolation when her son the king, after months of ill-
health, passed away in April 1509.

If Henry VII and his mother had been united in their efforts to protect
the fledgling Tudor dynasty, the mechanics of their co-operation
deserve careful scrutiny. One important aspect of their relationship was
found in the personnel of government and administration. Margaret's
trusted household and estate officials formed a useful reservoir for the
king to draw on in his appointments to royal service. Margaret's
receiver Reginald Bray became chancellor of the duchy of Lancaster
and one of Henry's most influential councillors. William Smith became
clerk of the hanaper; another of Margaret's agents, William Cope,
became the king's cofferer. Contemporaries recognized that service to
the king's mother formed a useful pre-requisite for a royal appointment,
and that this was to remain the case throughout the reign. William
Bolton, prior of St Bartholomew's, Smithfield, was a skilled architect.

---

[35] SJC, D91.21, pp. 103, 108. [36] *Ibid.*, pp. 99, 110.
[37] SJC, D91.19, pp. 34, 93.

The grace of his building work is exemplified in the oriel window, looking onto the choir of St Bartholomew the Great, which bears his arms. Margaret had employed him in 1501 to oversee the improvement of her London mansion of Coldharbour. She was impressed with his performance and several years later secured for him the post of master of the works for Henry VII's chapel at Westminster.[38] Yet such a trend, while real, should not be exaggerated. Richard Fox, keeper of the privy seal, was on occasions to co-operate closely with Margaret in matters of government and shared her interest in education. However the oft-repeated assumption that he was a protégé of Margaret's, owing his initial preferment to her patronage, is not supported by any concrete evidence. All that is known is that Fox was a student at the university of Paris, which he left to join Henry's band of exiles in 1484. Sometimes an association with Margaret, however brief, was rehearsed as a means of appeasing the king. Henry recognized a service performed for his mother in much the same way as one rendered during his period of exile, as a debt of honour. In a deposition to Henry VII Sir John Hussey related how 'I came first to my lady your moders service which was in the second yeere of your most noble reigne'.[39] Hussey, accused of embezzling customs profits in the port of Boston, was anxiously trying to deflect a full-scale royal investigation.

As the reign progressed an overlap often existed between the councils of Margaret and her son. Both drew on the expertise of highly talented legal advisers, such as the serjeant-at-law Humphrey Coningsby. Decisions were sometimes passed from one to the other. In 1500 the detailed arrangements for the construction of a new sluice on the Witham at Boston were referred from the royal council to the deliberation of Margaret's own body. She enjoyed an ease of access to the machinery of royal government but equally was able to benefit from the lustre of a group of exceptionally able courtiers and counsellors. Margaret's support for a crusade against the Turk, given special emphasis by Fisher, took place at a time when Henry VII and his council were engaged in lengthy communications with the Knights of St John at Rhodes. Their extensive financial support culminated in Henry being nominated as Protector of the Order in 1506.[40]

---

[38] PRO, SC6/Eliz./3368; Colvin, Ransome and Summerson, eds., *King's Works*, III, 214.

[39] PRO, SC1/51/179.

[40] *Mornynge Remembraunce*, 308; C. Tyerman, *England and the Crusades, 1095–1588* (Chicago, 1988), 350–1. Margaret's close interest in these proceedings is shown by her entertaining of papal agents at Croydon and Hatfield, 1505–6: SJC, D91.21, p. 47.

On an official level, Margaret had her own licence to retain under fee (the only woman able to do so), the king wishing 'her specially in our name to accept and take into our service' those men she thought fit and to receive their oaths. The Beaufort livery of the red rose or portcullis was issued and in February 1502 a small book was compiled 'for names of such persons to be retained with my lady'.[41] The arrangements were to the advantage of Henry VII, and Margaret actively desired that this should be the case. Early in 1508 her agent Edward Heven sat on commissions to decide which of her servants in the county of Lincolnshire could serve the king. Messengers were despatched to Alford, Louth and Lincoln with Margaret's instructions 'to calle in her reteyned servauntes afore therein to doe the kynges grace service'. A meeting of retainers assembled at Horncastle early in April: paper and parchment were brought up to record those willing to enter royal service.[42]

In the realm of foreign affairs the interests of the two were again united. Margaret was always concerned to gain the latest news of the diplomatic machinations facing her son. A postcript to a letter of March 1488, to Richard Fox, requested the latest news from Flanders. At the time of the king's expedition to France in 1492 it was Margaret who made the greatest financial contribution (1,000 marks) and also donated large supplies of grain (the only person to do so).[43] In April 1497 the return of an embassy that had at last succeeded in normalizing relations with the Burgundians occasioned a typically sardonic remark. Margaret had written to one of the English delegation, the earl of Ormonde, acknowledging a gift. She was unable to resist a weighted jibe against the pretensions of her great rival, Richard III's youngest sister, Margaret of York, dowager-duchess of Burgundy, whose glittering court had supported a host of plotters against her son's regime. 'I thank you heartily that ye list so soon remember me with my gloves', she commented, 'the which were right good, save they were too much for my hand. I think the ladies in that parts be great ladies all, and according to their great estate they have great personages.'[44] Beneath the mockery one senses the bitterness felt towards the duchess, who had sheltered the pretenders Lambert Simnel and Perkin Warbeck and encouraged their plots against the Tudor dynasty.

[41] PRO, KB27/926, rex rot. 3; SJC, D91.20, pp. 11, 19.
[42] SJC, D91.19, pp. 91–2.   [43] WAM, 32364.
[44] PRO, SC1/51/189 (holograph letter), see Plate 13.

Starkly materialist motives underlay some of the diplomacy. Henry put all his resources behind his mother's attempts to pressurize the French over a long-standing debt owed by the Orléans family. She was able to use freely royal heralds and ambassadors, legal advisers, and the king's French secretary John Meautis to help her present her case. Henry was also prepared to intervene directly, appealing to Charles VIII to secure a favourable verdict in the Paris *parlement*. The action was opportunist, reviving a long-dormant case, and revealed one of the more unattractive aspects of their relationship. Margaret and her son were well acquainted with the records of the dispute, which clearly showed the amount of money that remained outstanding. Yet their demands grossly inflated the residue of the debt. This 'great matter', a constantly recurring theme of their correspondence, carries all the hallmarks of the avarice that was to taint both their reputations. The beneficiary of this combined pressure was Henry VIII, who was finally able to secure recognition of the debt by treaty in 1514.[45]

However, it would be naive to imagine someone as strong-willed and acquisitive as Margaret always selflessly sublimating her concerns beneath those of her son's. Her overriding ambition to promote her family of the half-blood, the St Johns, was on occasions damaging or contrary to royal interests. The most dramatic example occurred in 1494, when Margaret used her influence to procure an extraordinarily advantageous match for her nephew of the half-blood Richard Pole (the son of Margaret's half-sister Edith St John) with Margaret Plantagenet, daughter of George duke of Clarence.[46] The arrangement carried a huge danger, and if Clarence's daughter had been left unmarried – the dynastically prudent course – a lot of trouble would have been avoided. In the event the Poles were to prove almost as great a danger to Henry VIII as the de la Poles had to Henry VII. Margaret's determination had prevailed over the king's wishes and interests. It was without doubt her most serious political misjudgement.

On another occasion Henry VII decided to transform Margaret's manor house of Woking into a royal palace, and use it for his own political and diplomatic purposes. In June 1503 a rather peremptory arrangement was imposed on his mother, making her give up Woking

---

[45] M. K. Jones 'Henry VII, Lady Margaret Beaufort and the Orléans ransom', in *Kings and Nobles in the Later Middle Ages*, ed. R. A. Griffiths and J. Sherborne (Gloucester, 1986), 254–69.   [46] 'Pedigrees of noble families', 295.

in return for a life-interest in Hunsdon (Herts). Margaret acceded to this with extremely bad grace. Reluctant to lose one of her favourite residences she continued to haggle over the agreement. In October 1505 a compromise was reached, allowing her the right to appoint to certain offices within the manor and occasional use of the palace on payment of a fixed rent. She remained dissatisfied and took care to recover Woking as soon as she could, in May 1509, within weeks of her son's death.[47]

Nevertheless, their partnership was for the most part a harmonious one, and the degree of influence Margaret enjoyed with her son gave her a dominating position within the realm. As the venerable lady made her progresses through the midlands and the south-east suitors would flock to her to gain favour or support, such as the 'poor man that sued to my lady...coming out of Lancashire', attracted less by any reputation for piety than the trappings of wealth and power.[48] Her own 'good lordship' was effective and much sought after. In 1504 an action was taken, with the support of Sir Richard Empson, against the abbey of Peterborough over its possession of the manor of Thornhaugh. An alarmed abbot immediately sent a messenger to London with an appeal to the king. But he turned to Lady Margaret for advice and assistance. The abbot journeyed to Collyweston laden with gifts 'pro consilio habendo in dicta materia'. During the course of the litigation he was able to consult regularly with Margaret's own council. Payments were also made to members of the royal council, legal advisers and the vice-chamberlain of Margaret's household Richard Lynne.[49]

The various dimensions of Margaret's political role in the early Tudor period were to focus on her principal residence of Collyweston, a manor house 4 miles west of Stamford, transformed by her into a palace. On one level her building activity reflected her concern to assist and promulgate court ceremony. The major improvements carried out to the house between 1502 and 1503 were a response to the demands of a full-scale royal visit. New foundations were laid along the inner court running adjacent to the middle gate. The old walls were removed and a new lodging put up. The purpose of this work was to provide

---

[47] *CCR*, 1500–9, no. 250; *Calendar of Ancient Deeds*, III, 18 (A3989); SJC, D91.19, p. 32; Cooper, 215.   [48] SJC, D91.17, p. 25.

[49] *Account Rolls of the Obedientaries of Peterborough*, ed. J. Greatrex (N'hants Record Society, 1984), 175, 185–6.

both accommodation and display: four great bay windows were fitted with the Beaufort arms and new battlements were constructed around the middle gate. One unfortunate local craftsman, working on the armorial glass, represented the Beaufort supporter (the mythological beast the Yale) as an antelope. One can almost sense the eruption as Lady Margaret inspected the great chamber window. The accounts record that 20d was given to William Hollmer for 'a draght of the said Ivell at London' and 7s to John Delyon of Peterborough for 'changing of Antelope into an Ivell'.[50]

The entourage that accompanied Princess Margaret from Richmond to Collyweston in the summer of 1503 formed one of the last great court progresses. At Collyweston the party halted for three weeks of celebrations before the formal farewell to the young princess, who then was to travel to Edinburgh for her marriage with James IV. Margaret was there to oversee the entertainments. Her choristers, who sang, acted and performed various disguisings, were swelled by additional recruits from the college of Tattershall and, further afield, from Cambridge and Westminster. It would have been an attractive outdoor setting, with the newly enlarged gardens, with their ponds and summer-houses, sloping down to the water-meadows of the Welland. An entry in Margaret's book of hours recorded the arrival of the king and Princess Margaret on 5 July, accompanied by 'a grete multitude of lordis and other noble persones'.[51] The scale of the occasion, with the entire royal court present, was a source of particular pride, marked by gift-giving and rewards to courtiers and servants. The festivities had an important political point. They represented the culmination of years of negotiation with Scotland, the marriage alliance setting the seal on a new peace treaty. Another marriage, actually celebrated at Collyweston, followed a similar theme. On 16 July the union of Gerald Fitzgerald and Elizabeth Zouche took place in Lady Margaret's chapel with the single publication of banns. Elizabeth was Margaret's kinswoman (her grandmother was Margaret's half-sister) and had been brought up in her household. The marriage was politically important and would have represented the fruits of discussion between the king and his mother. Gerald was son and heir of the earl of Kildare and had long been in England as hostage for his father. Now Henry

---

[50] SJC, D91.14, pp. 97, 99; M. K. Jones, 'Collyweston – an early Tudor palace', in *England in the Fifteenth Century*, ed. D. Williams (London, 1987), 134–6.
[51] 'Notes from ancient calendars', 279.

chose to be more conciliatory. After the marriage Gerald was allowed home, carrying rich gifts of clothing from the king. The next year he was appointed treasurer of Ireland.[52]

The festivities and celebrations during this July sojourn reflected Margaret's influence on the ceremony of the early Tudor court. Collyweston also represented a separate court establishment in its own right, particularly for the numerous aristocrat and gentry women who boarded there, along with members of Margaret's household. There was a 'presence chamber' for the visits of members of the local gentry and ecclesiastics and scholars. Matters were of course conducted at a slightly lower level than Henry VII's own court. An interesting comparison can be made with the establishment of the queen, Elizabeth of York, over a similar period. Elizabeth maintained her nephews and nieces, the Courtenay children and provided financial support for her sister Catherine. Her expenses in matters of charity reveal her conciliatory role. Payments were made to an old servant of Edward IV and to a man who had helped her uncle, Anthony Woodville Earl Rivers in 1483, in the last days before his execution. In matters of politics, although she was rarely separated from her husband, her own household and court could also be significant. When a Welsh tenant appealed to her over an injustice involving the king's uncle, Jasper Tudor, duke of Bedford, Elizabeth intervened personally and her letter to Jasper was firm and authoritative.[53] Similarly, Margaret's court offered an opportunity to mitigate some aspects of royal policy. The queen's sister, Cecily of York was able to stay at Collyweston after the king's disapproval of a disparaging third marriage to Thomas Kyme, a Lincolnshire esquire.[54] Margaret and Elizabeth of York, both participants in the conspiracy of 1483, were able to facilitate the rapprochement with former Yorkists.

Yet if Margaret's ménage accommodated Yorkist ladies, wards, suitors and scholars, it had a stronger political profile, maintaining regular contact with the local aristocracy and particular bishops. Here the enlargement of her manor house into a palace had broader implications. Between 1499 and 1501 over £100 was spent on a new

---

[52] *CCR, 1500–9*, 89; J. Lydon, *Ireland in the Later Middle Ages* (Dublin, 1973), 179–80.

[53] For Margaret's 'chamber of presence', see SJC, D102.9, p. 13. Information on Queen Elizabeth drawn from *Privy Purse Expenses of Elizabeth of York*, ed. N. H. Nicolas (London, 1830), 17, 20, 23, 78. The details of her intercession in the matter involving Jasper Tudor have been kindly supplied by Mr Pugh.

[54] The issue is discussed fully below, pp. 134–5.

series of buildings 'standing ayenst the great gates of the maner'. These included a new council house, with adjoining chamber (positioned by the gates for those involved in legal suits), and a prison.[55] The building work was co-incident with the creation of a political role for Margaret in the administration of the midlands. On 17 January 1499 Margaret despatched a letter from Collyweston to the mayor and common council of Leicester. She had received an appeal from Roger Tryg, a citizen of the town, that he had been unjustly slandered by one Robert Croft over his allegiance to the king. Tryg had complained that municipal ordinances against malicious slander had not been put into effect. Margaret's intervention was brisk. The mayor was informed 'we therefore counsail you in avoyding further inconveniences, all favour and partialite without any further delay sette apart, to execute the said statutes and ordenaunces, so as the said Roger have no cause reasonable to make further compleynt for his remedy herein'.[56] Two points are of particular interest. First, that Margaret's council was acting as a forum for redress, with judicial powers similar to those enjoyed by the prince of Wales's council on the marches. Secondly, that the case involved an impugning of loyalty to the Tudor monarchy.

This governmental role may have been the reason for an unusual and quite striking change in Margaret's sign manual. In 1499 she abandoned 'M Richmond', the form she had used since the 1460s, for 'Margaret R'. The new signature was distinctly regal, mirroring the king's 'HR', employed since August 1492, and the queen's 'Elizabeth R'. The precise significance of 'Margaret R', whether it now stood for 'Richmond' or 'Regina', remains unclear. It no longer resembled an aristocratic sign manual, where the Christian name was always abbreviated and followed by the full title.[57] An illustration of this delegation of royal authority, combining with the new signature, can be seen in letters of Margaret to the city of Coventry. They referred to a complaint of Owen Birch that the master of the town's Trinity guild owed him money. The mayor was directed, in Margaret's name, to settle the matter in 'acorde with right good conscience and all the

---

[55] SJC, D102.9, pp. 118–45.

[56] *Records of the Borough of Leicester*, ed. M. Bateson, 3 vols. (London, 1899–1905), III, 356 (drawn to our attention by Dr Ian Arthurson).

[57] The first example of the signature 'M Richmond' that we have found dates from November 1468 (WAM, 12182, fol. 34), the last April 1497 (PRO, SC1/51/189). The first example of the new style 'Margaret R' dates from Collyweston January 1499 (Cooper, 64).

equitie of the kings laws...as you tende the kinges pleasure and ours and use due ministracion of justice'. When no immediate action was taken a further summons was despatched, repeating the instructions and adding 'we wol and in the kinges name commande you'.[58]

Margaret's own council was also empowered to settle disputes with its procedure, as of the court of chancery, different in a number of respects from that of the king's court. Pleading was informal, usually by the litigants themselves and the council's decision applied only to the cases before it: they were not regarded as precedents and each was judged on its own facts. In May 1502 Margaret's council learned was empowered by a privy seal writ, 'by virtue of the kynges commaunde-ment', to examine a bill of complaint between William Fermour of Fotheringhay and Elizabeth Elmes. Both parties were called before Lady Margaret and their depositions recorded by William Merbury, the controller of her household. Earlier evidences, which had been submitted to the king's council, were sent to Collyweston. The next step was the appointment of arbitrators, chosen by Margaret from her own officers, who were to decide the case and deliver their judgement, in writing, to the two litigants.[59] The case clearly shows that a court of equity was in operation at Collyweston.

One consequence of this disposal of justice was that Margaret's concern to protect the new dynasty was given a firm legal footing. In January 1500 two Warwickshire men were brought before Margaret at Collyweston over treasonable words spoken on the matter of Blackheath Field. This battle had dispersed the Cornish rising, though rebellion had then been renewed in the west country by Perkin Warbeck. In view of the claims of successive Yorkist conspirators, it is not hard to sympathize with words perhaps more representative of bewilderment than treachery: 'for why tys hard to know who is Ryghtwys kyng'.[60] Nevertheless, such utterances touched on a raw nerve end. So too did the scurrilous tales concerning Henry Tudor's ancestry. One of these, emanating from a Colchester tavern, was also brought to Margaret's personal attention.[61]

Margaret's authority extended into the northern counties. In May 1502 the sheriff of York had arrested a number of persons and brought

---

[58] CUL, Add. MS 7592; Coventry City RO, A79/12.   [59] PRO, Req. 2/4/246.

[60] WAM, 12245.

[61] BL, Stowe MS 144, fols. 100–2, headed 'depositions concerning Margaret countess of Richmond'.

them before the royal council. One of these, a certain William Parker
esquire, was then entrusted to Margaret's custody. Her servant Richard
Aderton (who was regularly employed moving felons from Collyweston
to the London prisons of the Marshalsea, Ludgate and Newgate)
escorted him to the jail at Lincoln. Payment was made for cord, to bind
him down, and for the expenses of Aderton and two others watching
over him. Margaret had evidently satisfied herself of his 'good
demeanour', for in June 1505 she secured for him a general pardon,
which was duly authorized under letters patent three months later.[62]
In September 1503 her council dealt with a Yorkshire property
dispute, and the proctor of the guild of St Christopher and St George in
York sued for a pardon for an infringement against a local statute.[63]
She was also to intervene in matters involving the duchy of Lancaster,
and again the scope of her powers was considerable. Sir Robert
Southwell was later to appeal for compensation for losing a wardship,
adjudged to be of a fee held of the duchy of Lancaster. The decision had
been taken subsequent to letters of the king addressed to Lady
Margaret.[64] The sudden arrival of this new orbit of authority superseded
processes of appeal that would normally have been taken to the royal
courts and occasioned surprise and a certain measure of resentment.
Many years later, in the reign of Henry VIII, Lord Darcy drew up a
petition against the duke of Richmond's council in the north, noting
how 'the like commission that my lady the kings grandam had was
tried and approved greatly to the kings disadvantage in stopping of the
many lawful processes and course of his laws at Westminster Hall'.[65]

The decision to set up what in effect was an unofficial council of the
midlands was a novel one. It was a response in part to the existence of
a power vacuum in the midland counties. In Edward IV's reign the
region had been dominated by powerful magnates such as Richard
Neville, earl of Warwick, and William, Lord Hastings. Although Henry
VII was prepared to trust certain members of the nobility in more
limited spheres of influence, allowing John de Vere, earl of Oxford, a
measure of local autonomy in Essex and East Anglia, he had no wish
to return to the delegation of regional authority that had characterized
the Yorkist period. At first the king had been content to allow the
Stanley family to build up a certain amount of power in the midlands.

[62] *CPR, 1494–1509*, 291, 444; SJC, D91.21, pp. 33, 35.
[63] SJC, D91.20, p. 182.   [64] SJC, D94.397.
[65] R. R. Reid, *The King's Council in the North* (London, 1921), 87.

Margaret's last husband Thomas earl of Derby began settling local disputes in Derbyshire. Yet the violent activities of other members of the family, acting as though they were above the law in matters affecting the royal prerogative, began to give Henry cause for concern.[66] After the execution of Sir William Stanley in 1495 the king kept a close watch on them, and their political role was strictly limited. Yet Henry's decision to delegate power was also a response to the vigorous programme of enlarging the crown's fiscal authority that was to become a feature of the last decade of the reign. The king's view of the turmoil that had afflicted the English monarchy over the preceding thirty years was that political problems had stemmed from the crown's financial weaknesses. He saw stability resting on a solvent and secure king. An acceleration of earlier trends led to more ruthless and thorough exploitation: from 1500 extensions of the royal prerogative were investigated by the council learned and moribund feudal levies examined as sources of income. In conjunction with this Henry extended his use of bonds and recognizances. The growing fiscal severity of the last years of the reign created an enormous burden of work for the king's councillors: a delegation of power to Margaret's own council represented a way of spreading the load.

A woman presiding over such a regional court broke new ground. Margaret's role stimulated a remarkable discussion in the Inner Temple. Thomas Marowe, in a treatise of 1503, implied that a *femme sole* could be made a justice of peace through royal commission, a view shared by two lawyers closely connected with Lady Margaret, Humphrey Coningsby and Robert Brudenell. The possibility soon became a remote one. In a similar debate at Lincoln's Inn in the early seventeenth century Margaret Beaufort offered the only concrete precedent. The king's attorney declared that he had seen 'many arbitraments' made by her.[67] For a brief period, from 1499 to 1505,

---

[66] Henry VII's concern stemmed from Stanley involvement in the murder of William Chetwynd of Alspeth in 1494: PRO, KB9/402/7. This reference and much background information have been kindly provided by Dr Christine Carpenter.

[67] B. H. Putnam, *Early Treatises on the Practice of Justices of the Peace in the Fifteenth and Sixteenth Centuries* (Oxford, 1924), 194–6. Olga Horner is preparing an article which argues that the playwright Henry Medwall (who was in the service of Morton and then the king) used Lady Margaret as a role model for his heroine in his version of Buonaccorso's *Fulgens and Lucres*. Medwall transforms Buonaccorso's meek, submissive Lucres into a self-confident, independent heroine, who has no predecessor in English drama and no successor until the Elizabethan dramatists. In Medwall's version the two suitors (Cornelius and Gayus) appeal to Lucres, who is portrayed as a model judge and

Collyweston had become a seat of justice in the midlands. Messengers regularly arrived from the royal palaces of the south-east, or passed on to other administrative centres at Ludlow and Lancaster. Margaret's agents left the palace on royal business, to collect fines for knighthood or to act on bonds and obligations.[68] In this context Margaret was supporting and participating in an increasingly unpopular regime. For the members of her council it was a time of constant activity. One of her councillors, Christopher Browne, was an alderman of Stamford. The growing demands on his time meant that by 1502 he had to exercise his municipal office by deputy and a year later fellow town councillors were actually concerned about his legitimately remaining on their own body.[69]

While Collyweston was a focus for Margaret's territorial and political interests it also provided a natural spring-board for her increasing patronage of the university of Cambridge. Margaret's interest in Cambridge was to a certain extent directed through the influence of men of her household, in particular her confessor John Fisher. Yet her standing in the region gave her an added authority. Thus the king and council were happy to allow a complex dispute between the town and the university to be settled through her own arbitration. In the summer of 1501 the town of Cambridge had prosecuted the university before the king's council, in a 'new controversy' which had arisen following the wounding of Hugh Rankyn, a former town treasurer. It was only the latest in a series of town versus gown incidents, dating back to 1495, to come before the royal justices. Lady Margaret was now empowered to intervene. Arbitrators were chosen in her presence, at the petition of both parties, and a series of informal sessions were held under her presidency.[70] Between 1501 and 1503 members of her council regularly visited Cambridge and a constant stream of messengers passed from the town to Collyweston. The master of God's

diplomat. She hears each side, consults witnesses and prepares a written statement with a copy to each suitor. Her decision is not to be taken for a 'generall precedent'. Olga Horner has analysed the legal terminology of the debate and shown that it is based on the proceedings of a court of equity. There is no hard evidence for the first performance of Medwall's play, though it is normally placed in the late 1490s. It is a stimulating argument. We are grateful to Ms Horner for making her work available to us, and look forward to seeing it in print. [68] SJC, D56.213.

[69] A. Rogers, 'Late medieval Stamford: a study of the town council, 1465–92', in *Perspectives in English Urban History*, ed. A. Everitt (London, 1973), 29.

[70] M. G. Underwood, 'The Lady Margaret and her Cambridge connections' *Sixteenth Century Journal*, 13 (1982), 67–8.

House, summoned to Collyweston in May 1503, recalled an impressive display of conciliar authority. No less than fourteen councillors were present, including serjeants-at-law, household officers and Cambridge men. On 12 May 1503 a long and detailed agreement was hammered out, covering a range of contentious issues: tolls and stall rents, definitions of scholarly privilege and controls of university taxes.[71] The agreement also established what might be described as a 'machinery of arbitration'. Margaret, and after her death the lord chancellor and two chief justices, were given power to deal with any future problems that might arise. The first of these occasions was in 1508, when Margaret and her chancellor Henry Hornby were involved in the framing of a new composition.[72] The arbitration award set the seal on Margaret's influence in Cambridge. Her visit to the town in 1505 was accorded the honours of regality. She was met by a delegation from the town as far west as Caxton and her arrival was greeted with the joyous ringing of bells.[73] Margaret's increasing interest in Cambridge, culminating in her foundation of Christ's in 1505, provided a broader tableau for the interests of mother and son to be united. She had departed from Collyweston in 1505 and lived in a succession of 'borrowed residences' around the Thames valley, at Hatfield and Croydon, in order to be closer to her son. Yet her interest in Cambridge affairs continued unabated, and encouraged a more positive role for king and court. In April 1506 the king celebrated the feast of St George in the magnificent setting of the chapel of King's College. Later in the year, at the hallowing of Christ's, Margaret was joined by a number of Henry's courtiers. It was probably in August 1507 that Fisher gave his oration at Cambridge to Henry VII and his mother. Both were congratulated for their support of the university and the successful establishment of the new dynasty was welcomed.[74]

Yet all the time the king's health was seriously weakening. In the spring of 1507 and again in February 1508 his life had been despaired of. At this moment of crisis Margaret was in almost constant attendance: in March 1508 makeshift lodgings were hurriedly erected at Richmond to house her servants as she watched over her son.[75] At the end of March 1509 he was again very ill and 'utterly without hope

---

[71] A. H. Lloyd, *The Early History of Christ's College, Cambridge* (Cambridge, 1934), 284; C. H. Cooper, *Annals of Cambridge*, 2 vols. (Cambridge, 1842), I, 260–70.

[72] Underwood, 'Cambridge connections', 68.   [73] Cooper, *Annals*, I, 275.

[74] See Chapter 7 below, pp. 229–30.   [75] SJC, D91.19, pp. 75–8.

of recovery'. Margaret, now based in her London house of Coldharbour, made regular journeys by barge along the Thames to the palace of Richmond. Henry VII passed away on 21 April. The dying king had designated his mother chief executrix of his will. Her authority was such that she took the major part in organizing the funeral and the preparations for her grandson's coronation. One contemporary description of Henry's death listed the composition of the council which met to arrange details for the interment. It was headed by 'the moder of the said late king', the culmination of her ceremonial role within the early Tudor court.[76] Her political status was also enhanced and she may have chosen the composition of the interim council, to govern until her grandson's coronation. One of its first acts was to authorize the arrest of Empson and Dudley and the indications are that Lady Margaret supported if not actively encouraged such an action.[77] It is possible that she felt royal policy had become too harsh in the last years of her son's rule, and, like many others, saw Empson and Dudley as culprits if not scapegoats. Yet Margaret had herself participated in the most vigorous and ruthless aspects of Henry VII's government. A more plausible explanation is that Margaret resented their influence, regarding them as intrusive on her own special relationship with her son.

At the beginning of May bargemen conveyed Margaret and her goods from Richmond, where she had remained during the last days of her son's illness, to the Tower, where her grandson was in residence. Black cloth was delivered to Margaret and her servants from the royal wardrobe. In the funeral ceremony of 11 May 1509 Lady Margaret was given precedence above all other women of the royal family in attendance: a tribute to her redoubtable efforts during Henry VII's reign.[78] She had assisted in every aspect of Tudor ceremony, government and administration and fought for the safeguarding of the dynasty. It was a formidable achievement.

[76] BL, Add. MS 45131, fols. 52v–3 (which we owe to Dr Steven Gunn). Margaret's gift for torches carried at the king's burial is recorded in *Medieval Records of a London City Church* (St Mary Hill), EETS, o.s., 125, part 1 (1904), 268. Her role is discussed in more detail in Chapter 8 below, pp. 235–6.

[77] E. W. Ives, *The Common Lawyers of Pre-Reformation England* (Cambridge, 1983), 235–6. In July 1507, when Margaret acquired Creek Abbey for Christ's, she was forced to pay heavily for it. Dudley, acting as intermediary, secured a handsome profit on the transaction. It was an incident Margaret was not likely to forget. See below, p. 222.

[78] San Marino, California, Henry Huntington Library, HM 745 (book of expenses of those attending Henry VII's funeral), 5–6, 61–3.

4

THE COUNTESS AND HER PROPERTY

At the head of one of Margaret's receiver's accounts a scribe had penned a device symbolizing the wealth and power of a great landlord. It showed a rose set in a decorated circle, attracting many sources of profit: lands, deodands, pastures and 'secula', the fruits of worldly office. Long before the end of her life, Margaret's estates had become a major source of income, underpinning her religious patronage and educational foundations. They represented bastions of power in the localities, carrying the hallmark of her enhanced prestige and status. At the beginning of another account a Beaufort portcullis was inscribed, adorned with roses, around which entwined a canticle of praise to Lady Margaret.[1] It is in the administration of her properties that one finds the complete range of Margaret's activities, from the expression of responsibilities to kinsmen and dependants to a rigorous and harsh fiscal exploitation coupled with the purposeful maintenance of loyalty to her son's regime.

The story of Margaret's properties begins with her fortunes in the marriage market. The marriage of a young woman was in itself a financial asset to the crown, if she was an only child and heiress and her father had died whilst she was still a minor (i.e. under fourteen years of age). She and her marriage then became an extremely valuable piece of patronage. As Margaret's father, John Beaufort duke of Somerset, had held land of the crown, her wardship and marriage had passed to the king, who had then given it to the highly favoured earl of Suffolk (as the equivalent of a substantial cash gift). The

---

[1] The inscriptions are found in PRO, SC6/Hen. VII/1771 (see Plate 5) and Sizergh Castle, Strickland MSS, V.

background to these transactions is clouded by the confusion over the disposition of John Beaufort's landed estate.

John Beaufort's paternal inheritance consisted of a group of manors concentrated largely in Somerset, Devon, Northamptonshire and the Welsh marches, of a yearly value of a little under £600. His landed position was substantially increased in 1439 on the death of his mother, Margaret duchess of Clarence, which brought him a quarter share of the Holland estates worth some £618 a year. The demands of John's large ransom encouraged him to undertake a vigorous programme of estate administration and further enlarge his landed position. In 1443, before his embarkation for France, he received a royal grant of properties worth £400 p.a. including a two-thirds share of the Richmond fee of the lordship of Kendal.[2] His sudden death a year later led to complications over the division of this property. The manors of Woking and Sutton and the family residence at Corfe castle descended to his only surviving younger brother Edmund. The portion of the lordship of Kendal reverted to the crown. The remainder of the properties were divided between the widowed duchess of Somerset, whose jointure had only been partially completed at the time of her husband's death, and their daughter Margaret Beaufort, whose wardship had been acquired by the duke of Suffolk.

The extent of this division was at first unclear, and during Suffolk's brief period of wardship the duke challenged the rights of the duchess of Somerset and other feoffees to some of the estates. Suffolk wished to extract as much profit from Margaret Beaufort's lands as possible. The de la Pole estates (with an annual income of around £670) were barely adequate to support a ducal title.[3] After the death of Suffolk the hastily arranged match between Margaret and John de la Pole was dissolved. Margaret Beaufort's wardship and marriage was now to serve royal policy by buttressing the estate of the recently ennobled Edmund Tudor, earl of Richmond. The dramatic elevation of the king's half-brothers Edmund and Jasper Tudor, one of the few decisions that Henry VI took of his own accord, took them from penniless obscurity to the upper echelons of the Lancastrian peerage. Between November 1452 and the summer of 1453 a stream of royal grants provided them with territorial endowment. The grant of the wardship of Margaret Beaufort to both brothers on 24 March 1453, and the subsequent marriage of

[2] *PPC*, V, 253, 288.
[3] Information drawn from BL, Egerton Roll 8779 (kindly supplied by Mr Pugh).

Margaret and Edmund some time in 1455, formed a significant part of this policy. The passage of time and Henry VI's own patronage had now clarified Margaret's landed position. Her estates in the south and midlands and her share of further outlying properties in Yorkshire and in Wales represented an annual income of well over £800. The likely reversion of lands held in jointure by her mother and enfeoffed before her third marriage to Lionel Lord Welles in 1447 brought the potential value of Margaret Beaufort's landed wealth to over £1,000 p.a.[4]

Thus at the time of her marriage to Edmund Tudor the twelve-year-old Margaret was a great heiress. It was normal practice to wait until the woman was fourteen before consummating the marriage, indeed this was often specified in the contract. Yet Margaret's territorial position gave the twenty-six-year-old Edmund a brutal and exploitative motive for immediately making her pregnant. By this he ensured a life-interest in his wife's inheritance, for once a living child was produced (no matter how short its life) the father became tenant by courtesy of England, and was legally entitled to enjoy his wife's estates until his death. A comparison can be made with Henry Bolingbroke (afterwards Henry IV), whose marriage to another major heiress, Mary Bohun, followed a similar pattern. Within little more than a year of the match (on 16 April 1382) the thirteen-year-old Mary had given birth to a son, who was to live for only a short period of time.[5] Margaret's experience was traumatic. Her child's birth was a difficult one, and at one point mother and son were close to death. Tudor's behaviour was ruthless and inconsiderate: he was more concerned about being materially well provided for himself than in founding an aristocratic dynasty. Yet ironically his death in south Wales in November 1456 was to strengthen further Margaret's landed position.

Margaret's third marriage, to Henry Stafford, in 1458, brought to her new husband not only her share of the Beaufort and Holland estates, but also a substantial dower from the earldom of Richmond. This consisted of lands of a nominal value of £200 p.a., though in reality their worth seems to have been much higher: two parts of the Richmond fee of the lordship of Kendal and the manor of Bassingbourn

---

[4] Comments based on the enfeoffment made by the duchess of Somerset in April 1447 (Stamford, Burghley House, unclassified fifteenth-century deeds) and the valor of Margaret Beaufort's estates drawn up in 1455 (PRO, DL29/651/10533–4). For a breakdown of these properties see Appendix 2 below, pp. 262–4.

[5] K. B. McFarlane, *Lancastrian Kings and Lollard Knights* (Oxford, 1972), 17.

(Camb.). The royal letters patent confirming the grant were couched in extremely wide terms: their intention seems to have been to award Margaret a worthy dower beyond an exact share of the late Edmund Tudor's property (assessed at £600 p.a.).[6] The timing of these letters patent, of April and July 1459, was significant. The duke of Buckingham's eldest son had died during the previous year, and the bulk of the Stafford estates would now descend to Duke Humphrey's infant grandson. Buckingham was to settle 400 marks worth of property on the couple, including the manors of Colston Bassett (N'hants.), Rugby and Whatcote (Wark.) and Norton-in-the-Moors (Staffs.).[7] Beyond this Henry Stafford was largely dependent on his wife's income. Margaret's inheritance and her dower provided him with a comital lifestyle. The favour shown in this grant was an indication of the importance of the Beaufort and the Stafford families to a beleaguered Lancastrian dynasty.

The Yorkist victory at Towton in March 1461 forced the couple to move cautiously in reckoning with a new regime. Stafford, concerned to protect his wife's properties, quickly made his peace with Edward IV. Edward in his turn chose to assist Stafford and Margaret. In 1461 Margaret's inheritance and dower were protected from resumption; similar clauses of exemption were obtained in 1464.[8] Edward IV's safeguarding of Margaret's dower rights was particularly important. These were the most vulnerable of the properties for they represented part of the endowment of Edmund Tudor as earl of Richmond. The earldom had lapsed in 1461 and the honour of Richmond had been granted to the king's brother George duke of Clarence. Edward had few scruples in overturning the rights of dowagers when it suited his political purposes: his respect for Margaret's position was a clear sign of his goodwill.

In the first few years of the new reign Stafford and Margaret further augmented their properties. The manor of Dartford was acquired from Margaret's mother, and the Beaufort estates in Woking and Sutton were regained with the co-operation of the king. In 1467 the couple toured their west-country estates, holding a great court at the Somerset manor of Martock. Stafford also made efforts to secure his rights of presentment to Thornton church and purchased new lands around

---

[6] *CPR*, 1452–61, 368, 504.
[7] PRO, Prob. 11/4, 21 Stockton; Staffs RO, D641/1/2/181, 251–2.
[8] Scofield, *Edward IV*, I, 203.

Windsor.[9] This territorial expansion was threatened by a collision of interests with the powerful magnate Richard Neville, earl of Warwick. Letters were sent to Sir John Stanley about the fee-farm due from Walsall, a manor that had been incorporated into the possessions of Warwick. Neville's promotion of his supporters the Parrs in Westmorland led to a legal challenge being mounted to Margaret Beaufort's portion of the lordship of Kendal. It was during this anxious period that Stafford's servant Reginald Bray established his standing in the eyes of his mistress. He had acted as a receiver-general in 1467, making a circuit of the southern territories and receiving revenues from Kendal. The following year enquiries about Walsall and Kendal were made through Bray. On Passion Sunday 1469 he had dealt directly with the auditor during Stafford's period of sickness, and as both financial and legal adviser the young countess relied heavily on him.[10]

Stafford's death in October 1471 left Margaret potentially an even wealthier widow. In his last will Stafford had settled on Margaret the midland properties made over to him by his father in 1460, and the Berkshire manors he had purchased in 1467. However the will was contested and not proved until over a decade later.[11] In the immediate aftermath Bray assisted Margaret over the arrangements for Stafford's burial and accompanied her in June 1472 into the household of her fourth husband Thomas, Lord Stanley. Margaret's new husband enjoyed great estates and regional power in Lancashire, Cheshire and north Wales. His office of steward of the royal household afforded Margaret a powerful protector, with valuable influence at Edward IV's court. The marriage settlement guaranteed Margaret a yearly income of 500 marks. The sum was to be drawn from Stanley's estates in Cheshire and north Wales, and Margaret's agent Gilbert Gilpyn took seisin of the properties on behalf of the countess. Later in the decade Stanley repossessed these lands and assigned his wife a pension from his receiver-general.[12] Stanley also recognized the enfeoffment of Margaret's estates in the west country made in May 1472. The lands were set aside for the eventual use of Henry Tudor, should he return from exile. When Margaret and Stanley left Woking for the Lancashire fortress of Lathom, Bray accompanied them, placing money from the

---

[9] WAM, 5472, fol. 23v. The court at Martock is referred to retrospectively in Lancs RO, DDK/1746/17.　　　　[10] WAM, 5472, fols. 32, 41.

[11] PRO, Prob. 11/6, 5 Wattys (2 October 1471).

[12] SJC, D56.200; Liverpool City Library, 920/MOO/1091; Clwyd RO, D/DM/426.

enfeoffed properties in her own hands. Stanley's role lay in protecting these estates, although they lay far outside his own sphere of regional power; we find him prosecuting cattle thieves at Curry Rivel in 1472, and taking legal action against an unlicensed hunter in Queen Camel park two years later.[13]

For Stanley the marriage expanded his territorial influence. For Margaret there was a guaranteed annual income and an influential guardian of west-country lands held in trust for her son. She was to take an active supporting role in the affairs of her husband, acting as arbiter in some of the Lancashire property disputes coming before Stanley's court at Lathom. She helped to draw up arrangements for a further landed endowment for her son. In an indenture of June 1482, drawn up in the king's presence at Westminster, it was agreed that if Henry returned from exile he would receive most of the lands of Margaret's recently deceased mother, the dowager-duchess of Somerset (worth around 600 marks a year). If he failed to come back the income from the lands was to be divided evenly between Stanley and Margaret.[14] The violent political events of the next few years were to overshadow this agreement. Margaret's role in the conspiracy of 1483 against Richard III brought her to the nadir of her fortunes. She was only spared attainder through the influence of her husband. She was to forfeit her rights to all titles and estates and the income in trust that she enjoyed from her husband was declared void. The main body of her estates, which had been assigned to her husband for life, were to revert to the king on Stanley's death. Stanley was charged to keep his wife a virtual prisoner, separate from her own household.

It was Henry VII's accession in 1485 that transformed Margaret's landed position. The first parliament of the reign had reconfirmed her marriage settlement with Stanley, effectively reversing the punitive measures of Richard III. Of much greater long term significance was the declaration of Margaret as a *femme sole*. The recital, formally enrolled during the same parliament, made clear Margaret's prominence as matriarch of the new Tudor dynasty. Henceforth, for the term of her life, she could sue in any manner of legal actions, and have for her own use lawful title and property as 'sole persone not covert of anie husband'. She could take and receive feoffments, deeds, presentments and sales and draw up or revise her will at regular intervals.[15] From the fourteenth century onwards married women had on occasions declared

[13] PRO, CP40/844, m. 286; WAM, 32407, fol. 5v.   [14] SJC, D56.158.
[15] *RP*, VI, 284, 311–12.

themselves *femme sole* for the purpose of trade, to run a business and train apprentices. Their status allowed the financial advantage of being able to shift goods or cash from one partner to the other. The possibilities of this legal device had been entirely economic.[16] For a married aristocratic woman to declare herself *femme sole* was quite unprecedented. This clear statement of intent, the product of high quality legal advice, was almost certainly on Margaret's own initiative. It redefined her relationship with Stanley. From now on the king's mother was to be a major landowner in her own right, entrusted with important wardships and acting as arbiter in local disputes. Her further accumulation of property and the style of her estate administration form an essential backdrop to any understanding of her character or motivation.

The period 1485–7 witnessed the development of Margaret's own system of estate management, completely separate from that of her husband. The financial arrangements, no doubt the result of negotiations between Margaret, Stanley and the king, were as follows: the profits of lands of Margaret's heritage and jointure, as held while her mother was still living, were divided with a third retained by Margaret, two-thirds delivered to her husband; the revenues from estates formerly held by Margaret's mother were split evenly between the two; all properties granted to Margaret after 1485 were for her sole use. Henry VII did not intend to enrich the new earl of Derby by means of grants to Lady Margaret. Margaret was responsible for the administration of all these estates, and Stanley's share of the receipts was brought to him by her own officers. She also held an annual pension from Stanley, reduced to £200.[17] The redefinition was in the interests both of Margaret and her son, since her properties and those subsequently granted to her would now effectively be held in trust for the crown. This represented a material blow to Stanley but the steady flow of royal patronage he enjoyed between 1487 and 1489, with its rich harvest of lands in northern Lancashire, provided generous compensation elsewhere, effectively buttressing his newly acquired comital status.[18]

Lady Margaret's enhanced territorial position was provided for in the

---

[16] C. M. Barron, 'The "golden age" of women in medieval London', *Reading Medieval Studies*, 15 (1989), 40.

[17] Information on this division is taken from WAM, 32355.

[18] B. Coward, *The Stanleys, Lords Stanley and Earls of Derby, 1385–1672, the Origins, Wealth and Power of a Landowning Family* (Manchester, 1983), 13–14.

so-called 'great grant' of 22 March 1487. Here she received from the
king substantial estates that offered an annual income of over £1,000,
unencumbered by any interest to Stanley. The bulk of the properties
were concentrated in the midlands and west country and represented
a formidable addition to her inheritance and jointure.[19] The total
income, including Stanley's pension, for the year 1487–8 amounted to
£1,960. It was a substantial revenue, comparable to that enjoyed by
one of the leading magnates in the early Tudor period, John de Vere,
earl of Oxford.[20] The lands included in the grant reveal a great deal
about Margaret's sense of identity and the methods behind her pursuit
of wealth and power.

    The first group of properties in the grant were the so-called 'Exeter
lands', a large group of Devonshire manors and more scattered estates
in Derbyshire, Northamptonshire and south Wales. They represented
the lion's share of the forfeited estates of Henry Holland, duke of Exeter:
the Devonshire estates alone were worth nearly £600 p.a. Margaret's
wish to possess these properties was evident from the first few months
of the reign. The Holland mansion of Coldharbour, situated on the
Thames within the city of London, was acquired by her in September
1485, although her possession was only formally confirmed in the
grant of March 1487. Its speedy renovation and the prominent display
of Margaret's coat-of-arms formed an emphatic reminder of the
importance of the Holland estates to the Beauforts. Yet although
Margaret was heiress to the rights of her paternal grandmother
Margaret Holland, duchess of Clarence, which had augmented the
Beaufort inheritance between 1439 and 1442, she had no lawful claim
to the Exeter estates. On the attainder of Henry Holland, the last duke
of Exeter, in 1461 all these properties had been made over to his wife
Anne, the eldest sister of Edward IV. In 1472 the Duchess Anne had
divorced Exeter and remarried Thomas St Leger and their infant
daughter had been contracted in marriage to the son and heir of
Thomas Grey, marquis of Dorset. At the beginning of 1483 an act of
parliament had declared the young girl heiress to the Exeter estates, for
which marriage the queen was to pay Edward IV 5,000 marks.[21]

[19] *Materials*, II, 130–2.
[20] R. Virgoe, 'The recovery of the Howards in East Anglia, 1485–1529', in *Wealth and
     Power in Tudor England*, ed. E. W. Ives, R. J. Knecht and J. J. Scarisbrick (London, 1978),
     8.
[21] Discussed in Ross, *Edward IV*, 336–7. The valuation of the lands, compiled for Lady
     Margaret, is WAM, 32390.

This arrangement, which would have provided a major landed endowment for the Greys, was overturned in the aftermath of Richard III's accession as a plank in the king's policy of dismantling Woodville influence. Dorset fled to France to join Henry Tudor's band of exiles. Richard's long-term intentions for the lands are not completely clear, but it is highly probable that he planned to restore the properties to the heir general, his close ally Ralph Lord Neville, who succeeded to the earldom of Westmorland in 1484. After Bosworth Margaret's own designs on the estates pre-empted Greys and Nevilles alike. The intended match between Dorset's son, Thomas Grey, and Anne St Leger was allowed to lapse. Instead Margaret intervened to arrange a fresh marriage for Grey with her family of the half-blood, the St Johns: Thomas Grey marrying Eleanor, the daughter of Oliver St John of Lydiard Tregoze.[22] The Nevilles were politically muzzled. The earl of Westmorland was placed in Margaret's custody in September 1485. In December he entered into a number of bonds with the king and made over to Henry the 'rule, keeping and marriage' of his eldest son Ralph. These obligations were then passed over by Henry to his mother. Margaret's agents collected revenues from Westmorland's estates as security for the arrangement. His son passed into her custody and was maintained by her kinsmen the Cheyneys on a payment of a fee from Margaret's receiver. Before 1489 she had arranged his marriage, which took place in the presence of Henry VII, with another of her kin: Mary, first daughter of William Paston by Anne, daughter of Edmund Beaufort, duke of Somerset.[23]

Margaret had used her influence with her son, the king, to the detriment of those still to gain his trust. The marquis of Dorset's attempt to escape back to England from his French exile in the summer of 1485 had left a question mark over his absolute loyalty to his new sovereign in the first years of the reign. Westmorland's support for Richard III had left him politically vulnerable. Years later Margaret was to use similar means to acquire lands for the foundation of Christ's College, exploiting the difficulties of families who had been associated with rebellion against the new dynasty.[24] The Holland estates were important to her and she made full use of her authority within the new

---

[22] *DNB*, XXIII, 204.
[23] *CP*, XII, ii, 552; *Materials*, I, 191, 311; WAM, 32364, 32389.
[24] See below, pp. 220–1.

regime to pursue her interests. The rich manor of Ware (Herts) had
formed part of the Holland earldom of Kent, but had descended through
the earls of Salisbury to Edward Plantagenet, earl of Warwick and
Salisbury. On coming of age in 1496 Edward would have been legally
entitled to inherit Ware as part of the moiety formerly held by his
mother Isabel. Margaret had shown an immediate interest in Ware, on
22 September 1485 securing the right to appoint a steward there. The
young earl of Warwick was held in her custody: the grant of Ware in
March 1487 pre-empted any possibility of the unfortunate captive
succeeding to the property. The injustice of this action was recognized
early in the reign of Henry VIII. In 1513 Margaret Pole, the sister and
heir of Edward, earl of Warwick, was created countess of Salisbury and
Ware was restored to her as part of that honour.[25]

Similar tactics were used to regain Beaufort properties formerly held
by Margaret's uncle, Edmund duke of Somerset, or great-uncle,
Cardinal Beaufort. The lordship of Canford in Dorset offered a yearly
income of over £80. It had passed from the Beauforts to Alice Montagu,
countess of Salisbury, and again Edward, earl of Warwick and
Salisbury, would have a right to the property on coming of age.
Margaret received the manor in the great grant of 1487. In 1492 she
acquired further properties where the heir was rightfully Edward
Plantagenet. Margaret submitted a bill to parliament claiming
Amesbury, Winterbourne Earls (Wilts) and Henstridge and Charlton
(Som.) as heir of Cardinal Beaufort. The petition revealed her sense of
grievance. The lands should have come to her but for Alice late
countess of Salisbury, who 'by the great help and favour of Edward IV
and Richard earl of Warwick her son' had secured the estates in
1461.[26] The claim was notable for its technical detail, referring to
patents and evidences dating back to the reign of Edward III. It was also
a sign of unprincipled greed. Margaret's bill was based on her position
as heir of Cardinal Beaufort. It was a very wide view of the law.
Margaret would have had a right to the properties only if the cardinal
had inherited them from her own ancestors. In fact the estate had been
purchased, and thus could be willed out. The cardinal had made the
properties over to the hospital of St Cross in Winchester, to form the
major part of its endowment. From the documents supporting her own

[25] *Materials*, I, 81; *VCH, Herts*, III, 387.
[26] *RP*, VI, 446–7. Margaret ingratiating herself with the king as 'your most loving and lowly
    Modre'.

petition Margaret would have been only too aware of the rights of this charitable institution, and of the pious wishes of her great-uncle. Yet the lands were not to be restored to the hospital, which was quite ruthlessly abandoned. Instead Margaret used the properties to secure her own landed rights, returning them to the crown in 1506 in exchange for the confirmation of a life-interest in Canford. Again Henry VIII was later to recognize that the lordship of Canford belonged to the earldom of Salisbury, and it was included in the grant to Edward Plantagenet's sister, Margaret Pole, in 1513.[27]

These instances showed Margaret was able and willing to exploit her newly found political pre-eminence, just as she felt others had done, to her disadvantage, in the Yorkist period. In the parliament of 1487 the great grant was confirmed, Margaret to possess her properties 'in as ample a manner as any others have enjoyed them, any gift or grant of Edward IV or Richard III notwithstanding'. In July 1504 she obtained a pardon for all purchases, alienations or intrusions relating to the inheritance of Henry duke of Exeter or any similar transactions that had occurred during the minority of Edward earl of Warwick and Salisbury, son and heir of Isabel, duchess of Clarence.[28]

The other major element of the grant of March 1487 was the acquisition of honour of Richmond estates in both Lincolnshire and Kendal. The main body of these, situated in the Fens in the region around Boston, had been held by George duke of Clarence until his death in 1478, and afterwards had been retained by the crown. Margaret's concern to gain these lands, along with the nearby castle and lordship of Tattershall, signified an intention of building a powerful territorial presence in this part of the midlands. Similarly her wish to obtain the third part of the Richmond fee in the lordship of Kendal marked a concern to re-establish direct estate administration and commence an active exploitation of its resources. Both the concentration of properties in Lincolnshire and the Richmond portion of the lordship of Kendal had a particular importance for Margaret, and each will be the subject of a specific study.

The great grant furnished Lady Margaret with a substantial landed income and provided the spur for an overhaul of the administration of her west-country estates. In February 1488 an exemplification was

[27] M. A. Hicks, 'The Neville earldom of Salisbury, 1429–71', *Wiltshire Archaeological Magazine*, 73 (1980), 146–7.   [28] *RP*, VI, 387; SJC, D4.16.

made at Margaret's request of a late fourteenth-century commission touching the liberties of Corfe. Corfe had a symbolic importance for Margaret. She had acquired it in the grant of 1487 because it had long been the chief residence of her family, and shortly afterwards she had commenced major rebuilding within the castle. Her assertion of lordship, ranging from the rights of her constable and lieutenant to wreck of the sea to pleas of vert and fiscal demands on the town, was thorough enough to stir up local resentment.[29]

During this period of re-organization Margaret briefly took up residence in Sampford Peverell (Dev.), where a new rectory house was built for her use. It was a two-storied, L-shaped stone building, with a hall and large parlour, above which Margaret's personal chambers were situated. In 1488, during her stay at Sampford, she supervised work on a major improvement scheme, the diversion of a large watercourse, Morleigh Water, to a water mill within her manor.[30] It was an interest in engineering and harnessing the power of water that foreshadowed a much greater project, the construction of a tidal sluice at Boston in 1500. She also contributed to the rebuilding of an aisle of Sampford's church of St John the Baptist, part of a broader sweep of patronage, encompassing the churches of her Somerset manors of Langport and Curry Rivel. These projects reflected a more civilizing influence, but were also vehicles for an impressive demonstration of family and dynastic achievement. The arms of England and Derby were displayed in a window at Sampford's church; the exterior of Curry Rivel was decorated with roses and the portcullis. The most dramatic opportunity was offered at Langport. Langport's church, on a hill or 'isle', dominated its surrounds, the low-lying marshland of Athelney. The new tower, built to an extraordinary height, could be seen for miles around. Its turrets carried four massive portcullises, facing north, south, east and west.[31] These were the visible signs of a network of patronage, in which the right of presentment was used to reward servants and consolidate local influence. In pursuit of these objectives Lady Margaret used her undoubted standing to gain turns to livings of which others were patron, such as in September 1492, when her

---

[29] CPR, 1485–94, 201; BL, Add. MS 29976, fol. 64v; *Materials*, II, 364.

[30] For the house see W. A. Pantin, 'Medieval priests' houses in South-West England', *Medieval Archaeology*, I (1957), 139; for the diversion of water, *Materials*, II, 132.

[31] W. Bond Paul, 'The church, Langport Eastover, county of Somerset', *SANHS*, 40 (1894), 68.

negotiations led to Thomas Harsnape's presentation to the rectory of Binfield, by the gift of the abbot of Cirencester.[32]

The expansion of Margaret's landed wealth allowed her servants and officers greater scope for developing their own competence. Reginald Bray remained receiver-general as late as 1497, when he was succeeded by his assistant of the 1480s Nicholas Compton. Compton had risen to prominence under Bray's guidance, and in the period 1488–93 regularly delivered money to William Bedell, the treasurer of Margaret's household. Bedell himself participated in the estate administration. From 1488 to 1492 he had received the proceeds from the wardship of the young duke of Buckingham from the old Stafford servant Richard Harpur. After Harpur's death in 1492 Bedell assumed responsibility for the lands himself, remaining receiver until the duke entered his inheritance in 1498. Bedell, who was later to note in his will that he owed 'all that I ever had' to Margaret, was apart from Bray her longest serving major officer.[33] The receiver for the 'Exeter lands' was originally a former servant of the duke of Clarence, John Hayes. In 1492 he was convicted of treason, and his place was taken by his deputy, Hugh Oldham. Oldham had been a servant of William Smith, keeper of the hanaper, at the beginning of the reign, and continued to receive royal advancement as well as prospering in Lady Margaret's household. In 1490–2 Oldham, whose place of origin suggests an initial link with the Stanleys, received revenues of the earl of Westmorland in Devon and those of the lordships of Canford and Poole. After Hayes's attainder Oldham replaced him as receiver under Bray's general supervision. When Bray was promoted to full-time royal service Oldham became responsible for all Margaret's west-country holdings. Before being made a bishop in 1504 he had become Margaret's chancellor.[34]

---

[32] *Register of Thomas Langton, bishop of Salisbury, 1485–93*, ed. D. P. Wright (Canterbury and York Society, LXXIV, 1985), 42; a letter of Thomas Hunton, prior of St Swithun, Winchester, informed the abbot of Cerne that a certain brother John was to remain there until 'the most noble lady mother of King Henry VII...shall make provision for him': *The Register of the Common Seal of the Priory of St Swithun, Winchester, 1345–1495*, ed. J. Greatrex (Hampshire Record Series, II, 1978). We are grateful to Dr J. A. F. Thomson for discussing this material with us. Margaret's ecclesiastical patronage is discussed in greater detail below, pp. 195–7.

[33] Bedell's will is PRO, Prob. 11/19, 8 Ayloffe (4 September 1513). The background to the careers of Compton and Bedell is drawn from WAM, 32348, 32389.

[34] WAM, 32364, 32390; SJC, D102.10. Hayes' treason left him 'in great danger of his life'. Margaret's former servant William Cope intervened on his behalf with the king, though

The growing efficiency of Lady Margaret's estate management had brought the clear annual revenue from her lands to over £2,200 in 1495–6. After 1500 her administration became even more centralized with Compton giving place to Hugh Ashton in 1501–2, and Ashton receiving for all the estates, including those in the west country, after Oldham's promotion to Exeter.[35] Ashton, like Oldham a Lancashire man, ended his life as archdeacon of York and a benefactor of St John's College, Cambridge. His recruitment to a major office was a sign of the increasing clericalization of Lady Margaret's household in the last decade of her life and her growing association with Cambridge graduates, or those cultivating a connection with the university. However, it was the death of her husband, Thomas Stanley, in 1504 that was to increase dramatically her landed income. Stanley's death freed the substantial charges on her inheritance and jointure. Since Margaret was already administering the properties and paying wages of officials and extraordinary or foreign expenses, the sums liberated were clear profit. After the deduction of Stanley's pension, they represented over £600 in annual revenue. This fresh income was to be used for the substantial building work at Margaret's foundation at Christ's College, which commenced in 1505.

Lady Margaret's land management was founded on a meticulous sense of what was legally due to her. Charges on her receipt were inspected vigilantly. A quit rent from Tidburst (Herts.) was respited but not fully allowed because the abbot of St Albans had not properly demonstrated the evidences before Margaret's council. It was subsequently allowed in May 1501 after Reginald Bray and other councillors had inspected the required proofs.[36] Feudal dues were rigorously exploited, in a fashion that at times appears harsh and obtrusive to us. William Hedley of Frampton (Lincs.) had a cart and horse confiscated by Margaret's officers because they were the instruments which had accidentally killed a sixteen-year-old boy. Margaret's actions reveal that she was well informed at a local level. In 1495, for example, she brought an action at common law against a sub-tenant, John Aclane of Little Bray (Dev.). He had inherited his father's lands and was denying the right of Lady Margaret to 'maritagium', the right to dispose of him in marriage. She had based her claim not on direct

Hayes was forced to pay 500 marks for his pardon. He was kept in Cope's custody at Exeter and it was Cope who gained a substantial share of his estates: PRO, C1/279/47 (which we owe to Margaret Condon).   [35] SJC, D102.10.
[36] BL, Harleian MS 602, fol. 1.

lordship, but on the fact that his land formed part of a manor whose lord was himself a minor and ward of Margaret's. Here she was standing on the very letter of her feudal right, and she pursued the case as far as distraint on Aclane's goods for his non-appearance at court.[37] Informers were sometimes employed to gain 'inside information'. A certain John King was well paid for bringing tenants of Medecroft (Beds.) 'afore my ladys council' in an action against the bailiff there. On another occasion King was rewarded for bringing Margaret information concerning the parsonage at Wrestlingworth.[38]

In her land transactions Margaret had the backing of a highly skilled council, including many men who were rising high in royal service. All through her life she had sought out legal counsel of particular quality. William Hody, a regular adviser to Margaret and Henry Stafford in the 1460s, had become chief baron of the exchequer by the beginning of Henry VII's reign. Humphrey Coningsby, an exceptionally able serjeant-at-law, was regularly employed by Lady Margaret, and after her death referred to his service with her 'of counsell and of fee for many years'.[39] Margaret also retained Robert Brudenell, another legal officer of considerable merit. Lady Margaret was prepared to use the law frequently to protect her properties (with many suits of trespass and theft) and to pursue arrears of rent. When Richard Walters carried across the fen goods of his that had been distrained by Margaret's bailiff, her agents returned and confiscated his boat as well.[40] She regularly brought actions against her own officers for debt. James Clarell (Margaret's cofferer in 1494 and 1498–9) owed £59, 'for whiche he should have been imprisoned'. Thomas Haselwode stood as surety only to be sued himself. John Knight was a long-standing auditor, in Margaret's service from 1487, who had performed many useful services. On John Hayes's treason in 1492 he had toured the Devonshire estates gathering the rents. Yet Margaret was prepared to present his widow for debt in 1502.[41] The most striking example concerns Roger Ormeston, Lady Margaret's chamberlain and one of her most loyal officers. In his will he had bequeathed Margaret a standing cup with a gilt cover. This gift did not prevent Margaret suing his widow and other executors for a debt of £22 in 1506.[42]

Margaret's legal actions derived from a strong sense of rightful

---

[37] PRO, SC6/Hen. VII/1772; CP40/931, fol. 221v; CP40/932, fol. 37.
[38] SJC, D91.20, pp. 40, 78.   [39] See Appendix 3 below, p. 271.
[40] PRO, KB27/902, m. 8; /908, m. 57v.   [41] PRO, C1/205/71.
[42] See Appendix 3 below, p. 280.

obligation. When she complained that her presentation at Cheshunt (Hugh Oldham) was being hindered, Humphrey Coningsby (acting as her proctor) traced her title back to John de Montfort, duke of Brittany.[43] Shortly before her death a book of her suits was drawn up, listing the actions she had initiated and recording the money she had received. The sums being pursued included small amounts owed to her paternal grandfather, John earl of Somerset, nearly a hundred years earlier. Her readiness to bring to court the widows of loyal servants, and her concern over even the smallest of debts, carries the taint of avarice, more strongly echoed in the punitive fiscal policy of her son in the last years of his reign. Close to death, Margaret may have regretted the harshness of some of her legal actions, settling the costs of many of her prisoners and thus releasing them from her custody.[44]

Margaret's influence with her son and the vigour of her estate administration made her a dominating figure at a local level of lordship. In 1503 Sir John Saville of Thornhill (Yorks.) saw Lady Margaret as the most powerful protector that he could have for his six-year-old son and heir. A year earlier a remarkable contract had been drawn up between Margaret and Roger Horton of Catton in Derbyshire. Horton had agreed that his son should be married to such 'gentilwoman' as Margaret was to think fit, and was to be educated 'by the advice of the said princess' at school or inn of court. In return Margaret promised to support Horton's title to recover any manors or lands within the realm of England, by 'petition, accion, sewte, entre or otherwyse'.[45]

In many respects Margaret was willing to act as an agent for her son rather than simply as a self-interested landowner. This was seen most clearly in her stewardship of politically important wardships for the crown. On 3 August 1486 Margaret was formally granted custody of the lands of the young Edward Stafford, duke of Buckingham, her kinsman; the grant was to take effect retrospectively, with a right to revenues from September 1485. The extent of Margaret's wardship was, however, limited, because of the generous assignment to the late duke's widow Katherine Woodville (a dower and very substantial jointure), who had married Jasper Tudor, newly created duke of Bedford. Katherine's jointure included the lordships of Newport,

[43] WAM, 4683.   [44] SJC, D91.19, p. 10.
[45] *Calendar of Inquisitions Post Mortem, Henry VII*, II, *1497–1505*, 512; *Descriptive Catalogue of Derbyshire Charters*, ed. I. H. Jeayes (London, 1906), 77.

Thornbury and Tonbridge. Among the lands that came under Margaret's direct control were the Welsh lordships of Brecon and Caurs, and English estates centred around Maxstoke, Stafford and Holderness. Apart from revenues owing to Jasper Tudor in respect of his wife's dower, the properties were burdened with further charges. These included 500 marks a year to contribute towards the maintenance of the Stafford brothers and £1,000 a year payable towards the costs of the royal household. These expenses ensured the wardship would not be a major source of fiscal profit, indeed in the first three years of her custody of the estates Margaret made an overall loss. In the period 1485–8, the net receipts totalled £4,232 6s, whilst the charges amounted to £4,480 7s; involving a loss of around £248.[46]

In the English estates Margaret reformed the system of accounting. Receipts were centralized, with fees and wages subject to her final sanction. The appointment of a receiver-general (Richard Harpur from 1485 to 1493; William Bedell from 1493 to 1498) curtailed unnecessary local expenditure. Foreign expenses were cut to a minimum. The bailiff feodary of Staffordshire, which incurred a financial loss, was dispensed with entirely.[47] These measures were efficient and successful, with delivered income increasing from each receivership, and they were to provide the young duke with a model for his own reforms. The problem that Margaret faced was in the collection of revenue from the Welsh lordships.

In Brecon Lady Margaret's authority was much weaker than in the English lordships. In part this reflected the general difficulties of administration in the Welsh marches. However, there were more specific problems. The region had shown strong support for Richard III. In October 1483 Buckingham's castle of Brecon had been sacked by those angered by his decision to throw in his lot with the supporters of Henry Tudor. Richard had rewarded the local inhabitants by remitting farms and reducing rents. There was as a result considerable unrest early in the reign of Henry VII. An attempt by 'various rebels moving against the king' to take the castle and town had narrowly failed. Brecon castle had been garrisoned with 140 soldiers to withstand any future attack. Fines had been levied against those who had supported the rebels, including the porter of the castle gate who had allowed the escape of those held for being sympathetic to the late king.[48] Amidst

---

[46] T. B. Pugh, *The Marcher Lordships of South Wales, 1415–1536* (Cardiff, 1963), 241–2.
[47] Staffs RO, D641/1/2/76; Rawcliffe, *Staffords*, 55.   [48] BL, Egerton Roll 2192.

this disorder and uncertainty, Margaret's officers faced massive problems in trying to collect revenue. As Richard III had substantially reduced rents, 'no man would take an increment above the old rent or would pay it'. Similarly, nobody wished to claim the office for the 'great farm'. No income was received from the agistment of the forest because Richard had granted the inhabitants free passage. Overall receipts from the lordship were vastly reduced. The great sessions in Brecon, where tenants customarily paid a fine to be excused the duty of attendance, faced in 1488 a drop in receipts from 2,060 marks to 760 marks. By 1496 the income from the sessions had risen to 1,100 marks, still little more than half the anticipated charge, and the lion's share of this (some 800 marks) was delivered by Margaret's agents to the king.[49] Attempts to regain rents fared even worse. By 1494 the income from the lordship stood at £300, little more than a third of its nominal value. In that year William Bedell, Lady Margaret's new receiver for the Stafford lands, David Philip, one of her most trusted servants, and John Gunter, an experienced royal auditor were sent to Brecon with specific instructions for the collection of debts. They had little success. Faced with considerable opposition at the local level Margaret was forced to write off a long standing deficit of £2,095.[50]

Margaret's overall administration of the Stafford wardship was efficient and responsible. In 1488 she used her influence with Richard Fox to get a privy seal warrant issued against the receiver of Holderness, John Dalkyns, who had not rendered account but had 'sodenly departed from hens otherwise than according to the trust that was put in him'. Dalkyns was summoned to appear before Lady Margaret's council within fifteen days of his receipt of the writ. In 1495 she was still pursuing him at law for a debt of £94 in Holderness, and continued to recover arrears as late as 1504.[51] Upon hearing news of unlicensed hunting in the park of Madeley near Stafford, the keeper, Thomas Chattok, was sent a sharp reprimand. Chattok was informed that Margaret 'be not contented' by reports of the wastage of the park. No man was to be allowed to hunt without her licence, and 'yf any persones of wilfulness attempt to brek this our comaundement we then wol that ye do certifie us of thair names to the entent we may provide for thair sharp punishment in example of other like offenders herafter'.

[49] PRO, E101/414/6, fol. 103v.
[50] PRO, SC6/Hen. VII/1652. m. 5v; Rawcliffe, *Staffords*, 128.
[51] PRO, C82/329/103 and 104; CP40/931, m. 212; /933, m. 14v; SJC, D102.10, p. 26.

Two years later, as palings were being repaired and strengthened around the park, action at law was commenced against Walter Cony, Roger Bagnell and others for breaking into Madeley.[52]

A different side of Margaret's personality was shown in her repairing and rebuilding of Maxstoke castle (Wark.). Maxstoke, one of the principal Stafford residences, had been deliberately slighted by Richard III after the rebellion of 1483. Part of the castle was demolished and its stone used for the king's improvements to Nottingham castle. After taking possession of the Stafford estates Margaret initiated an extensive programme of rebuilding. Between 1487 and 1496 all the issues from the estate 'were expendyd in reparacions'. These included a new north range, work on the great hall and banqueting hall, and a connecting range around the inner courtyard.[53] Rather than exploit the revenues from Maxstoke, Margaret recognized the destruction caused by Buckingham's participation in the 1483 rebellion as a moral obligation, which she was to honour fully.

In the year 1497–8 Lady Margaret brought no less than twenty-eight suits for debt in a final attempt to recover her losses before the new heir came of age.[54] The problems in Brecon had ensured that Margaret would derive little financial profit from the wardship. Despite this, her improvements in accounting procedure and rigorous use of the law were to have a strong influence on the young duke when he entered his estates. Yet Margaret's sense of responsibility lay with the king, not Buckingham. It is significant that she made no effort to intercede with Henry VII over the excessive fines levied on Stafford for the remarriage of his mother (in 1496) and for allegedly entering his properties before coming fully of age.

Margaret's income from the major wardships served in many ways as an extension to the royal treasury. William Bedell's accounts over the period 1488–93 show money from the Stafford wardship subsidising the young prince of Wales's household, contributing to the new works at Windsor and on one occasion paying the staff of the royal chapel. Hugh Oldham and Sir Robert Willoughby were held responsible to the countess's treasurer for the collection of £100 a year from the earl of Westmorland's lands, to support the upkeep of Ralph Lord Neville. Henry VII subjected the inheritance of Westmorland's infant

[52] Staffs RO, D593/A/1/29/5; D641/1/2/78; PRO, CP40/931, fol. 57.
[53] N. W. Alcock, 'Maxstoke castle, Warwickshire', *Archaeological Journal*, 135 (1978), 216–18.   [54] Rawcliffe, *Staffords*, 179–80.

grandson (who became heir in 1499) to fierce financial exploitation. In 1506 a fine from Edward Sutton Lord Dudley passed through Margaret's treasury. In 1494 Dudley had bought the wardship and marriage of John son and heir of Lord Grey of Powis. He had to pay heavily for the grant. Margaret's servant Robert Fremingham delivered £20 from Dudley for the use of Grey's widow, Lady Powis. Once again Margaret was helping to administer royal fiscal policy.[55]

However, in one important area Lady Margaret placed a particular interest above her service to her son's regime: her concern for her family of the half-blood, the St Johns. Oliver St John, head of the younger branch of the family, had married Elizabeth Bigod. To his manor and house at Lydiard Tregoze (Wilts.) had been added by royal grant Deptford (Kent), Garsington (Oxon.) and Hatfield Peverell (Ess.). Oliver had benefited from his close connection with the king's mother, gaining the office of sheriff of Lincolnshire, a county where she had considerable influence. His memorial was to record with pride how he had been a 'squire unto Lady Margaret'. But on his death in 1497, with his son John not yet of age, the estates were vulnerable to exploitation from the crown. Oliver had willed to his wife his lands of Lydiard Tregoze and of the king's grant, at her death returning to their son and his heirs. This transaction was not secure, and Margaret stepped in to protect the properties from the king, for the use of the family. Her accounts record her treasurer, William Bedell, receiving money from Garsington in 1500, described as 'master St John's lands'. Her chamberlain also received money from Hatfield Peverell and Deptford, balanced against his outlay for Prince Arthur's wedding in 1501. In March 1502 the household paid £20 to John St John 'of the lands of the king's gift for Lady Bigod's dower'. Receipts from Lydiard itself came into Margaret's coffers 'for the use of master St John in 1503. St John and his wife were both being paid exhibitions at this period and in 1502 legal expenses for suits at the exchequer were also being met by Margaret's treasury.[56] Although Margaret had been given no office as guardian under Oliver's will, and without any recorded arrangement for a wardship, she had retained a powerful interest: receiving profits of lands not her own, protecting the inheritance from her son's avaricious designs and making it secure for John St John.

[55] WAM, 32389; SJC, D102.10, 141; BL, Add. MS 59899, fos. 120v, 126.

[56] *Lincs Rec. Soc.*, 1497–1505, I, 204; PRO, Prob. 11/11, 13 Horne; *Calendar of Inquisitions Post Mortem, Henry VII*, II, 472; SJC, D102.2; D102.10, pp. 55–8, 177.

Oliver St John's widow died in 1503, naming Margaret the overseer of her will. Further payments to John were made from Margaret's treasury in 1504 and additional legal expenses were met the following year.[57]

In two other instances Lady Margaret acted to alleviate the harshness of her son's policy and protect those connected with the St Johns. The Zouches of Haringworth were related to Margaret through William Lord Zouche's second marriage (*c*. 1450) with Elizabeth St John. Zouche's grandson and heir from his first marriage, with Alice St Maur, had been forced to pay heavily for his support of Richard III. John Lord Zouche had been taken prisoner at Bosworth and attainted in the first parliament of Henry VII's reign. He received a general pardon in July 1486, restoration of goods and chattels and a small annuity. His landed estate proved far harder to recover. In 1489 his attainder was reversed, but only in respect of the inheritance of his grandmother through William, Lord Zouche's third and final marriage, to Anne Lady Scrope of Bolton. His landed income was insufficient to support his dignity, and he was styled as a knight. After serving in the French expedition of 1492, three years later Zouche's attainder was fully reversed, though his lands remained heavily burdened with life-interests. Lady Margaret had exerted her influence in Zouche's favour, helping to secure a pension of 100 marks for his wife and children and bringing some of his offspring up in her own household.[58] She intervened more directly to assist the junior branch of the family, the Zouches of Bulwick (N'hants.) who were the lineal descendants of William, Lord Zouche's second marriage with Elizabeth St John. Their grandson John had married into the Willoughby family. His efforts to acquire the lordship of Codnor were assisted by John St John of Bletsoe and Sir Henry Willoughby. In 1500 the childless Lord Grey had agreed for Zouche to purchase Codnor, and to have seisin of other properties in Essex and Lincolnshire, for the payment of 600 marks. To secure his own title Zouche had enfeoffed the property on St John and Willoughby. Here, however, Henry VII had intervened, pressuring Grey to revise his intentions, and to sell Codnor to the crown for the use of the king's son Henry duke of York, for more favourable financial terms.[59] Remarkably, Lady Margaret was able to regain Codnor for the Zouches. In July 1507

---

[57] PRO, Prob. 11/13, 23 Blamyr; SJC, D91.20, pp. 20, 64; D91.21, pp. 75, 77.

[58] *RP*, VI, 424; *CP*, XII, ii, 945; *CPR*, 1485–94, 223; *Materials*, II, 85.

[59] *Cal. Ancient Deeds*, I, 64–5 (A547); V, 42 (A10747) and 522 (A13484).

Henry VII indented with Sir Henry Willoughby and John Zouche esquire for the return of Codnor to Zouche, though they had to pay more heavily for it. Margaret was active behind the scenes, her accounts recording a loan of £200 to Willoughby to pay the crown for the redeeming of Codnor to 'Master Zouche that hath married his daughter'. The estate was reconveyed to Willoughby, for the ultimate use of John Zouche and his heirs, in 1508.[60] The Zouches' marriage link with the St Johns had afforded them a powerful protectress. Zouches were brought up in Lady Margaret's household and the marriages of Elizabeth and Eleanor Zouche were celebrated in her chapel at Collyweston, Eleanor receiving a gift of £16 from the countess.[61] The landed prospects of the family had been safeguarded, and in the case of the junior line augmented.

The second instance concerns the Parker family. William Parker had been one of Richard III's closest followers. He had received his Suffolk residence of Pentlow Hall for his loyal service against the rebels of 1483 and was the king's standard bearer at Bosworth. Parker's fortunes in Henry VII's reign were chequered. He had married Alice Lovell, sister and heir of Henry Lord Morley, but in the late 1480s had suffered the oppressions of the duke of Suffolk while trying to buy lands for her jointure. He fell into bouts of insanity in 1493 and 1502; on the latter occasion the king noted courses to be taken for the discharge of his debts. However, his son Henry Parker was to enter the household of Lady Margaret and became her cupbearer and personal attendant. He was to marry Alice, daughter of John St John of Bletsoe. Between 1499 and 1503 Lady Margaret received from the estates of William Parker £120 for Alice's jointure. On William Parker's death Margaret took steps to protect her servant's inheritance. Parker's widow, who had inherited Lady Morley's lands as well as her brother's, subsequently married Sir Edward Howard. In 1507 Lady Margaret paid Howard 500 marks 'to redeem master Parkers lands'.[62] Henry Parker was to recall the society of his mistress with affection. To her he also owed the security of his landed estate and title.

Margaret Beaufort's support for the St Johns showed her prepared to temper or even defy the policies of her son. Her supervision of the landed fortunes of her adopted family was constant: deeds and evidences of their property settlements were stored in a cupboard close

[60] SJC, D91.21, p. 79; *CPR, 1494–1509*, 583–4.   [61] SJC, D91.21, p. 79.
[62] SJC, D102.10, pp. 31, 144; D91.19, p. 59.

to her bedchamber, where she could easily inspect them. That, when she chose to, she could disregard Henry VII's wishes or moderate his demands, was proof of the overwhelming authority she held with the king throughout his reign.

Lady Margaret's influence in the reign of Henry VII rested on the wealth she enjoyed from her properties. These funded her household and allowed her acts of religious or educational patronage. The sudden release of capital after the death of her husband Thomas Stanley, earl of Derby, boosted her landed income to some £3,000 a year and provided a psychological and material incentive for her foundation of Christ's College, Cambridge. As a great landowner Margaret was well aware of obligations of charity towards dependants and was capable of acts of great sensitivity and kindness, seen in her concern to provide board, lodging and clothing for poor children found at the Lincolnshire village of Doddington or her gift of the manor house at Torrington (Dev.) to an old priest forced to walk many miles to his church.[63] Yet her estate administration, always efficient and thorough, was also harsh and severe, and her territorial ambitions unprincipled and ruthless. These themes are thrown into sharper relief by a detailed survey of two concentrations of lands particularly closely managed by Margaret: the lordship of Kendal and her Lincolnshire properties.

THE LORDSHIP OF KENDAL

Margaret Beaufort's property rights in the lordship of Kendal provide a strong illustration of the themes of acquisitive legal action and active and purposeful estate management. During the political turmoil of the Wars of the Roses Margaret's role was defensive: she was struggling to protect her title to far-flung but important lands. In the reign of her son she took the initiative, extending her control in the area and vigorously pursuing her interests. The progression from a defensive to an aggressive stance as a landowner mirrored the enhancement of Margaret's political status after 1485.

The disposition of interests in Kendal in the later middle ages is a complex story. The original barony had been partitioned between two coheiresses in 1246: a division of title that was to remain up to the sixteenth century. One portion became known as the Marquess fee. It

---

[63] SJC, D91.21, p. 39; Cooper, 42.

included the castle of Kendal and properties and rents in the town itself, and nearby Strickland Roger, Staveley and Underbarrow. By the late fourteenth century it had been acquired by the Parr family through the marriage in 1383 between Sir William Parr and Elizabeth, grand-daughter and heiress of Thomas de Ros. The Parrs were originally from Lancashire but during the first part of the fifteenth century they had built up a powerful presence in Westmorland, and Kendal was to become their chief residence. The second portion was known as the Richmond fee. It also included rents in Kendal and its surrounding area, as well as in Kirkby Lonsdale. But the bulk of the fee was centred further north around Grasmere and Windermere, and the lands of Ambleside, Troutbeck, Crosthwaite, Rydal and Loughrigg. In the fifteenth century it had been used as part of the endowment for two earls of Kendal, John duke of Bedford and Margaret's own father John Beaufort duke of Somerset.

John Beaufort had died with his arrangements for his wife's jointure still incomplete. His property in the Richmond fee of Kendal had been held in tail male and now reverted to the crown. His widow, Margaret, duchess of Somerset, lost her dower portion in an act of resumption in 1450. A year later Thomas Harrington was granted a twenty-four-year farm.[64] The remaining third of the Richmond fee was held by Bedford's widow, Jacquetta of Luxembourg. Jacquetta had re-married Richard Woodville, who by the 1450s had received the title of Lord Rivers and had become an important member of the Lancastrian establishment. Respect for her position and the influence enjoyed by her husband ensured that her dower rights in Kendal were not prejudiced.

Margaret Beaufort was to gain her interest in Kendal through a different route. On 6 March 1453 Edmund Tudor was granted the remaining two-thirds of the Richmond fee. A rental from March 1453 to Michaelmas 1454 showed Edmund Tudor in possession of the estates, appointing a receiver, Robert Duket. He enjoyed the profits of agistment in the largely forested areas around Windermere and Grasmere and the farm of fulling mills situated on the fast-flowing streams running into the lake. Fishing rights on Windermere and its islands were also farmed. Some £200 was received by Edmund in this first year of account.[65] But his period of possession was destined to be brief. On 3 November 1456 he died in south Wales. However, Margaret, as his widow, was granted the fee as surety for her dower. These estates provided a substantial part of her landed income at the time of her third marriage to Sir Henry Stafford and Edward IV's decision to confirm these dower rights was a notable mark of favour.

Thus in the first half of Edward IV's reign the Kendal lands were a remunerative if distant group of Margaret's properties. They offered her husband, a younger son with little in the way of territorial endowment, an annual income of around £200. There is no evidence that she or Stafford ever visited them personally but the lands were not leased out en bloc and the couple's receiver, Reginald Bray, and other servants made regular journeys to the north to collect rents. However, in the late 1460s a threat to these estates suddenly materialized. It arose from the powerful Neville family and their efforts to promote the interests of their supporter and retainer Sir William Parr in Westmorland. On 20 July 1468 Richard Neville earl of Warwick had participated in an enfeoffment of the castle of Kendal and surrounding lands designed to secure the succession of Parr's heirs to these estates.[66] At the same time a challenge was made to Stafford's and Margaret's right of title to the Richmond fee. The motive seems to have been Neville self-interest, an opportunist desire to install one of their followers in a newly recreated barony of Kendal that would enhance their own position in the north.

The line of legal attack was a claim that Edmund Tudor had been retrospectively attainted and that Margaret's dower rights were thus void. It was an action that exploited a real measure of uncertainty, for in the Yorkist parliament of November 1461 Edmund's brother Jasper had indeed been attainted and the lands of both Tudors had been parcelled out to supporters of the new regime. Henry Tudor, a minor, had been degraded from the earldom of Richmond. In the summer of 1468 local opposition prevented the collection of rents in the lordship. The result was a flurry of activity in Stafford's and Margaret's camp. Payments were made to clerks and solicitors and on 1 August 1468 the couple secured a privy seal writ confirming their present possession of the lands: 'understanding that the said Sir Henry Stafford and Margaret his wyff, Countesse of Richmond, be occupiers of the said parts...to have and accompte the same withoute any exaction of dettes or demandes'.[67] However, this confirmation specifically refrained from

---

[66] CPR, 1467–77, 106.　　　　　[67] PRO, E159/245.

any guarantee of title. As the couple's servants attempted to resume their collection of rents and fees Stafford and Margaret determined to gain proper acknowledgement of their right title, by entering a plea in the court of the exchequer.

Between the end of May and early July 1469 evidences were amassed and scrutinized. On 31 May Robert Bardsey, a clerk of the pleas, was retained to help draw up their case. Searches were made for inquisitions, accounts and acts of resumption. On 13 June the serjeant-at-law William Jenney was paid to oversee the Kendal matter. He was to be assisted by two other lawyers, Humphrey Starky and William Comberford, and the auditor, Robert Wattno. On 8 July the plea was enrolled at the exchequer.[68] The importance of safeguarding the title to Kendal was re-emphasized as political conditions entered a period of turbulence. In July 1469 Sir William Parr was one of the Neville company who moved against royal forces at the battle of Edgecote. The king was temporarily confined in Neville custody at Warwick and revenge was taken against William Herbert, earl of Pembroke and Lord Rivers; Herbert was executed on 27 July and Rivers on 12 August. However, Edward soon regained his liberty and by the beginning of October was back in London. Although open hostilities had died down, it was in an atmosphere of considerable tension that the legal proceedings were resumed. At the start of the Michaelmas term, Stafford's counsel reiterated the claim to the original two-thirds of the fee granted to Edmund Tudor and the rights in reversion to the remaining third, at present held by the king's mother-in-law Jacquetta of Luxembourg. On 23 October they met at the Bell in Fleet Street to go over the plea 'and the dowtes of the same' and three days later a douceur was paid to the king's attorney, Henry Sotehill, 'to be friendly'. A search was made for the proviso to the act of resumption of 1464 which allowed Margaret's dower rights to the endowment of her late husband Edmund Tudor. Stafford's lawyers were to advance their case that Edmund was never attainted. Henry Sotehill, the royal attorney, using the customary legal formula did not answer this: the court was not willing to come to judgement and the matter was suspended for a number of months.[69] In the interim Stafford and Margaret did their best to assert lordship at the local level. In November 1469 Reginald Bray rode to Kendal accompanied by a new receiver

---

[68] WAM, 5472, fols. 36v–40v.
[69] *Ibid.*, fols. 46–8v; PRO, E368/242, mm. 118–19.

(the trusted Stafford servant William Fleming), yeomen and a page. A court was held at Calgarth on 17 November, 'rewle' was set on tenants and some £71 of rents and farms collected.[70]

In the Trinity term 1470 the judges delivered an ambiguous verdict, leaving the situation unclear. They were willing to accept the validity of the privy seal writ of 1 August 1468, but did not confirm the couple's title to the estates.[71] However, the weathercock of political fortune swung again. Richard Neville, forced into exile in the spring, returned to oust Edward IV, and the readeption of Henry VI commenced in October, 1470. A period of intensive negotiation began in London between Stafford and Margaret and Warwick's chief supporter George duke of Clarence over the honour of Richmond. Clearly, Stafford's support was seen as worth courting. Although the discussions ended in a compromise agreement, a by-product was that the couple were granted the keeping of Jacquetta's third for seven years at a rate of farm to be agreed.[72] The political situation was outstripping any legal settlement. Here was a clear indication that the Readeption government, anxious to recruit support, was prepared both to recognize and enhance Stafford's and Margaret's position in Kendal. The disregard of Jacquetta's undisputed right of dower was a ruthless act. She was an elderly lady, and the violent death of her second husband in the disturbances of 1469 had left her with no one to protect her interests. Stafford and Margaret showed themselves willing to exploit her vulnerability for their own advantage. This volte-face seemed to remove the threat to the lordship. In fact a new phase of uncertainty was to commence.

The arrangements for the Richmond fee may have contributed to Sir William Parr's disillusion with the Neville faction. Along with the Harringtons he hastened to Nottingham to support Edward IV on his return from Holland in March 1471. His desertion of Warwick and return to Edward's allegiance was substantially rewarded. He became controller of the household and one of the king's closest followers. His brother Sir John Parr, who had also fought for Edward at Barnet and Tewkesbury, became a king's knight and master of the horse. After Lancastrian resistance had been crushed Edward delegated regional power to trusted courtiers and household men. Sir William Parr's

---

[70] WAM, 5472, fol. 48v.
[71] PRO, E368/242, m. 120v.
[72] Hicks, *Clarence*, 97.

influence in the north was deliberately built up. He was knight of the shire for Westmorland from 1472 and sheriff from 1475. He was to become one of the government's chief supporters in the north-west, given considerable diplomatic and military responsibilities on the border with Scotland. Significantly he was one of the two household men to be elected as knight of the garter in the second half of the reign.[73]

Once Edward had decided to entrust the Parrs with a large amount of local authority, it was natural that he would augment their landed position. It was likely that he intended an eventual reunification of the barony of Kendal as part of that process. Yet since Stafford had also fought for Edward at Barnet a compromise was required. In July 1471 an agreement was reached, almost certainly at the king's prompting, whereby Stafford and Margaret demised the two parts of the Richmond fee to Parr and his descendants, in return for a yearly cash fee of £190. Although they had received financial compensation it was the price of recognizing a right of reversion to the Parrs of the two-thirds of the Richmond fee on Margaret's death. The third part, at present farmed by Margaret and Stafford, was also to revert to the Parrs on the death of Jacquetta of Luxembourg.[74] It was a bitter pill for Margaret to swallow. At a time when she was concerned about the long-term landed prospects of her son substantial properties were to be detached from her inheritance. Yet in political terms it was inevitable. Henry Tudor had fled with his uncle Jasper to Brittany. Edward IV could hardly be expected to allow the claim of a self-styled traitor.

Margaret accepted the compromise. After the death of her husband Sir Henry Stafford, in October 1471 she returned to the court of the exchequer, now with a much reduced demand and significantly making no plea for her long-term possession of Kendal. On 2 November she was able to secure her right of title to other honour of Richmond lands. On 25 November she conceded the demise of the previous July, with new provisions for the distraint.[75] Edward IV had executed a skilful settlement. Margaret was left to safeguard her cash fee. On 27 November she drew up an indenture with Sir William and Sir John Parr and Sir Thomas Strickland. The Parrs were bound over to the countess for 2,000 marks: surety for their regular payment of the

---

[73] Ross, *Edward IV*, 326.
[74] Guildford Muniment Room, 3242/19/1; *CPR, 1467–77*, 334.
[75] PRO, E368/242, m. 121v–2; Guildford Muniment Room, 3242/19/2.

annuity in quarterly instalments. Their right to the issues and commercial revenues of the lordship was fully recognized. In March 1472 an exemplification of the arrangements was issued.[76] The death of Jacquetta in the same year left Sir William Parr master of both Kendal fees, secure in the knowledge that when Margaret died the entire inheritance would descend to his family.

The fluctuating events of 1468–72 reveal the constant interweaving of expediency and legal process that was so typical of the times. For Margaret it was a proving ground for an aggressive use of the law and political dominance. Despite her marriage in the summer of 1472 to the king's steward Thomas, Lord Stanley, the Parrs' hegemony in Westmorland remained undisturbed. Before departing with the king on the French expedition of 1475 Sir William Parr ensured the succession of his heirs of the body by a new enfeoffment of some of the Kendal properties. The preparations for the campaign had afforded Edward IV the opportunity to resolve some of the territorial disputes in the north-west, most notably that between the Stanley and Harrington families over Hornby in northern Lancashire. The royal licence for Parr's enfeoffment coincided with the grant to him of the office of sheriff of Westmorland for life. The two together represented the king's determination to promote the Parrs' interests. Sir William was given a major role in the Anglo-Scottish negotiations in 1481 and was appointed warden of the west march.[77]

Thus despite the influence of her husband, Lord Stanley, at court, Margaret was forced to accept the Parrs' pre-eminence in Kendal. Their hegemony had been continuous in the second half of Edward IV's reign and had climaxed with the grant of one of the major offices in the region, the wardenship of the west march. In these circumstances there was little hope of a restoration of Margaret's interests in Kendal. The political situation was fundamentally changed after the accession of Henry VII. Sir William Parr had died in 1483. His family's interest in the Richmond fee was drastically curtailed by the crown. The first parliament of the reign restored Margaret's possession of the original two-thirds while in March 1487 the remaining third was also granted to her. Margaret now took on a presiding role in the lordship and helped arrange a marriage between William Parr's widow, Katherine,

---

[76] Guildford Muniment Room, 3242/20.
[77] *CPR, 1467–77*, 531–2; Ross, *Edward IV*, 326.

and Nicholas Vaux of Harrowden (N'hants.). Vaux had been brought up in Margaret's household and the match had taken place by 1487. The younger Parrs were to become her agents and servants in the region.[78] The lordship of Kendal had a strong symbolic value to her. It was after all the endowment that had supported the creation of Margaret's father as duke of Somerset and had been the core of her dower lands as countess of Richmond. The mythical beast the Yale, adopted by Margaret in her heraldic insignia after 1485, was a supporter strongly associated with the barons and earls of Kendal.

The purposeful restoration and extension of Margaret's rights in the lordship coincided with parliament conferring on her the legal status of *femme sole*. This measure transformed Margaret's position within her marriage. Stanley was allowed the larger share of the revenues (two-thirds of Margaret's original inheritance) and his financial rights were scrupulously respected. However, Margaret now held the initiative in the practical arena of estate management, permitting Stanley's younger son Edward to keep his posts in the lordship and agreeing to the appointment of William Wall (Thomas Stanley's chaplain) as receiver, perhaps to soothe her husband's feelings. In practice Wall's duties were extremely limited. Responsibility for the collection of the receipts was held by Margaret's trusted servant, Sir Reginald Bray, acting as Wall's deputy. Wall's function was to deliver Stanley's share of the income to him, and occasionally to carry cash sums to Margaret's receiver-general. She did not have a high opinion of his abilities. In 1501, with Bray engaged in royal service, the unfortunate chaplain rendered account unsatisfactorily. Annuities and other obligations had been left uncollected. Margaret roundly dismissed him and sent one of her own servants to Kendal to put matters to right. She also took the opportunity to allay the fears of her son, the king. Edward Stanley's pursuit of 'maintenance' within the lordship over the last few years had given Henry cause for anxiety. Margaret suggested a subterfuge. A royal letter would be sent to her, commanding her to employ in Kendal only those retained in the name of the king's son, Henry duke of York: in Margaret's own words 'it shall be a good excuse for me to my lord and hosbond'.[79]

---

[78] G. Anstruther, *Vaux of Harrowden* (London, 1953), 7; WAM, 16019. For the Kendal yale see Appendix 5 below, p. 291.

[79] The letter is printed in Cooper, 66–7. Background information drawn from Sizergh Castle, Strickland MSS, IV–VI.

There were sound economic reasons for Margaret's renewed interest in Kendal. After a period of depression in the first half of the fifteenth century, the region's prosperity had undergone a remarkable revival. This was chiefly due to the flourishing of a cloth-manufacturing industry, which drew its advantages from the power of the cascading mountain becks of Langdale and Grasmere. The area's population was steadily expanding as a result. The rapid increase in the number of fulling mills provided an obvious source of material gain. In Grasmere there had been six mills in 1453; by the early sixteenth century, the figure had trebled. A rental of 1493–4 showed new mills in Grasmere, Langdale and Ambleside being let out on the instructions of Margaret's council. In 1506 payments were made to Margaret for two new fulling mills which had been built at Loughrigg.[80] But a broader area of profit was to be derived from the growing pressure on cultivatable land as the population rose. There was a steady increase in rents accruing from new holdings. The growth in the communities of Grasmere, Langdale and Loughrigg led to the clearing of low-lying woodland. The process was rigorously supervised. Charges were made by the auditor and receiver for 'approvements, intakes and wastelands' enclosed by Margaret's licence. New rentals were negotiated with tenants, such as Thomas Grygge, whose 'three intakes in diverse places' had been enclosed from waste belonging to Lady Margaret. From 1505 onwards new holdings in Grasmere and Langdale were classed as five- and ten-cattle tenements: the smaller paying a yearly rent of 6s 8d, the larger 13s 4d.[81]

Commercial revenues were encouraged, Margaret instructing that eight new shops be built in Kendal in 1505, including a chamber for leatherworkers and a bakery with its oven. A further source of income was provided by the salmon fisheries. Here a substantial yield accrued from more thorough management. In the rental of 1453–4 the fisheries had been in a state of decline. In Grasmere the 'defect of fishery in several waters' was noted and other areas frequently referred to the general decay. Improvements undertaken on Margaret's orders included the construction of lock-gates and the building of a large 'piscarium' at Kirkby-Kendal. But the exploitation had a harsher side. A walk-mill set up under the chapel at Troutbeck was pulled down by

[80] A. J. L. Winchester, *Landscape and Society in Medieval Cumbria* (Edinburgh, 1987), 118; M. L. Armitt, 'Fullers and freeholders of Grasmere', *TCWAS*, n.s., 8 (1908), 140, and *Rydal* (Kendal, 1916), 201.   [81] Armitt, *Rydal*, 96–7, 200–1.

Margaret's agents, lest damage be done to the fish breeding in Windermere.[82] Ruthless exploitation of lordship could cause resentment. Fines imposed by the manorial court for encroachment were unpopular and in one case led to a violent affray. The construction of a new brick prison in Kendal, the 'Tolbooth', served as a reminder of the darker aspects of Lady Margaret's concern to exploit her rights.

The decision to build a prison can be traced back to an incident in 1502. A thief had been taken in Margaret's franchise and as there was no 'common geylle', her servant Thomas Philip had sent him to Walter Strickland's house, to be imprisoned in a strong tower. Unfortunately, the malefactor had managed to break out. This matter had occurred at a time when Henry VII was fining heavily for escapes for jail and Strickland was summoned before king and council to answer for it. Margaret had conducted her own enquiries and after interviewing Strickland at her palace of Collyweston interceded on his behalf: he was 'nowe of good rule and demeanour', willing to see 'good order and peax be kept in his cuntrie which moveth us the more to tender his furtherance'.[83] Nevertheless, it was an embarrassing incident, for the security of prisons had become a political issue in the eyes of the king. The episode no doubt prompted Margaret to build a 'tolbooth', for the 'imprisoning of felons and other transgressors'. It was sited on the west side of Stricklandgate, a gloomy structure 18 feet by 13 feet, with one small window but without chimney, courtyard or sewer. It was completed in 1506.[84]

The financial yield from Kendal rose steadily under Margaret's administration, reaching an annual figure of around £380, a sum further swollen by efficient collection of long-standing arrears of rent. Her careful scrutiny of her rights remained the hallmark of her ownership. Often respites were only granted pending more detailed examination of the evidences. The clerk of her court was constantly in the saddle, consulting with justices of Lancaster or Margaret herself at Hatfield or Cambridge. The account for 1505–6 conveys her highly personal and continuous interest in the lordship. Expenses were recorded for Hugh Ashton, riding from Croydon to Kendal with Margaret's instructions concerning arrears. The receiver had travelled to a meeting with Humphrey Coningsby and Robert Brudenell,

[82] Comments based on Sizergh Castle, Strickland MSS, IV; PRO, SC6/Hen. VII/877; Armitt, 'Fullers and freeholders', 141.   [83] WAM, 16016, 16019.
[84] PRO, SC6/Hen. VII/877, fol. 16v; J. F. Curwen, *Kirkbie-Kendal* (Kendal, 1900), 336–7.

Margaret's legal counsel, to discuss the exploitation of a wardship. The auditor, riding to Hatfield to render his account, stopped off for five days at Cambridge, for further discussions with the countess.[85] The overwhelming impression is one of vigilant and at times ruthless efficiency. It was a style of management that closely resembled her son's vigorous administration of royal lands.

THE LINCOLNSHIRE CONNECTION

Lincolnshire had been an area of political instability in the Yorkist period, with Edward IV facing a number of serious risings in the county. On the accession of Henry VII a family settlement was envisaged in which the region would fall under the effective control of Margaret Beaufort and her half-brother John Welles. The elevation of Welles's status and responsibilities was a key part of this scheme. John Welles had been a virtual unknown in the second half of Edward IV's reign. Deprived of his own inheritance, he had resided with Margaret's mother, the duchess of Somerset, at her castle of Maxey in the 1470s. In 1483, almost certainly at Margaret's prompting, he had taken part in the rebellion against Richard III, and after its failure had gone into exile with Henry Tudor in Brittany. Margaret felt great affection and respect for the Welles family. Lionel Lord Welles, who had married the widowed duchess of Somerset in 1447, had been a father-figure to her. He had enjoyed great local influence in Lincolnshire in the early 1450s, when he had resided in splendour at Maxey along with Margaret and members of the St John family. In 1470 Edward IV's execution of Richard Lord Welles and his son Sir Robert had almost extinguished the male line. Thus the restoration of Welles influence in Lincolnshire had a strong psychological importance to her.

To achieve this she and her son worked in partnership to build up the humble interests of her kinsman. In the first parliament of the reign John Welles's attainder of 1484 was reversed. More importantly, the retrospective attainders of 1475, which had barred him from his family inheritance, were also overturned.[86] The Welles barony had undergone a fluctuating course under the Yorkist regime. In 1461 Lionel Lord Welles had died fighting for the Lancastrian cause at Towton. He had

---

[85] PRO, SC6/Hen. VII/877, fol. 16v.
[86] *RP*, VI, 273, 286–9. For details of the Welles family see Genealogical table 4, p. xxiii.

been attainted posthumously. However, Richard Welles, his son by his first marriage to Joan Waterton of Methley (Yorks), had gradually worked his way back into royal favour. He had fought alongside John Neville against the Lancastrian rebels at Hexham, and was rewarded with a partial restoration of property in 1465. In 1467 he regained the use of his title and full body of estates. But he and his son and heir Sir Robert were to become embroiled in the Lincolnshire rebellion of 1470, after which both were executed. However, neither Richard nor Robert were attainted and the barony was allowed to pass to Robert's sister Joan. On Joan's death the barony should have passed to John Welles, Lionel's son by his second marriage, to Margaret Beauchamp, duchess of Somerset. Here Edward IV had intervened. A retrospective attainder had been passed on Richard and Robert Welles in the parliament of 1475 to enable the king to grant the lands to Joan's husband, the trusted Yorkist Sir Richard Hastings (brother of Edward's chamberlain William Lord Hastings). This political manoeuvre had deprived John Welles of his estates.[87]

John's restoration to the barony of Welles in 1485 gave him possession of a group of manors centred around Alford, Cumberworth and Theddlethorpe in the parts of Lindsey, Lincolnshire. This area of authority was further enhanced by the appointment of Welles on 10 October 1485 as steward for life of the Bolingbroke honour (all the duchy of Lancaster lands in Lincolnshire) and constable of Bolingbroke castle. A further land grant in May 1488, 'for services beyond the seas and in England', provided additional estates in the county.[88] By this time Welles had made a spectacular marriage with Cecily of York. Cecily had been in the keeping of Margaret from September 1485. She was the second surviving daughter of Edward IV, and the heiress-apparent of the House of York, after the queen herself, and thus from January 1486 Henry VII's eldest sister-in-law. Her marriage to Ralph Scrope (brother of Richard III's ally Thomas Lord Scrope of Upsall) was dissolved in 1486, enabling her to marry Welles (elevated to the rank of viscount in September 1487) sometime late in 1487.[89] It was a relatively undistinguished match for a daughter of Edward IV, likely to have been brought about only through Margaret's concern to honour a kinsman. Welles was to remain in political terms a minor if loyal figure up to his death in 1499. In Lincolnshire he sat regularly on

[87] *CP*, XII, ii, 445–8.   [88] *CPR*, 1485–94, 236.
[89] Horrox, *Richard III*, 295 n. 109.

commissions of the peace and *de valliis et fossatis* alongside such trusted servants of Lady Margaret as Oliver St John and David Philip.[90]

Margaret's own position in Lincolnshire was founded on her family estates, grouped around the manors of Billingborough, Bourne and East and West Deeping. The focus for these properties was the castle of Maxey, crenellated in the late fourteenth century, with its small central tower, inner court and fortified gatehouse. Stanley and Margaret had taken possession after the death of the duchess of Somerset in 1482 and had immediately set about improving the site. A small dam was erected by the water mill on the nearby Welland, and an aqueduct built to carry water to scour the moat. The range of buildings was extended by Margaret early in Henry VII's reign, with new houses constructed around an outer court.[91] The castle was used by Margaret as a residence and was to be the administrative centre for all her Lincolnshire properties.

To the north-east of Maxey was a vast tract of marshland known as Deeping Fen. Across the fen lay settlements at Spalding, Cowbit and Crowland. Here Margaret was to inherit a long-standing and violent dispute between the lords of Deeping and Crowland Abbey over reclaimed land in Goggisland marsh. Margaret's father had extended Deeping's boundary rights, leaving a legacy of local unrest and disorder. The accounts of Deeping for 1482–3 (the year that Stanley and Margaret took full possession) record incursions from Crowland. An embankment was deliberately breached causing the flooding of several acres. Marker stones and boundary turf were hauled down. Twenty-four men had to be employed to repair the damage and another eight stood guard against any further attempt to cut the banks.[92] Margaret was later to adopt a conciliatory approach towards Crowland and its tenants. At the time of the incident she and her husband were deeply angered and the abbot was fined heavily for failing to maintain the embankments properly. Margaret's concern for proper drainage and reclamation of the fen was to be a feature of her lordship. On her instructions a 'view' or survey of the 'defaultes of sewers' on the perimeter of the marsh was compiled. Fines were

---

[90] *CPR, 1485–94*, 491–2; M. M. Condon, 'Ruling elites in the reign of Henry VII', in *Patronage, Pedigree and Power in Later Medieval England*, ed. C. D. Ross (Gloucester, 1979), 113.

[91] The description of Maxey is based on an early sixteenth-century drawing: PRO, MP1/251 (which we owe to Margaret Condon).   [92] PRO, SC6/909/16.

imposed on the inhabitants of Cowbit and Moulton, on the eastern edge
of the fen, for their inadequate repair of drains. Her own tenants were
kept busy. In 1507 bread, ale and cheese were distributed by her
servants to the large team working on the South Eau dyke.[93]

Margaret's properties in and around Deeping were of an annual
value of around £125. The honour of Richmond estates incorporated
in the grant of 1487 were potentially of far greater worth. In addition
to rents and commercial revenues in Boston, the estates comprised the
manors of Frampton, Kirton, Wykes, Skirbeck, Gayton and Washingborough: valued at around £280 a year. In practice the income from
these lands was far less. Boston was in a state of economic decline. In
the surrounding countryside considerable revenue was being lost
through increasing flood damage. The bulk of Margaret's properties
were situated below sea-level, east of the great causeway that ran
through Donnington and Sutterton to Boston. They were protected by
a massive range of sea defences and embankments. The principal of
these commenced south of Wyberton, where it ran parallel with the
river Witham as a guard against river flooding from the heavily silted
outfall. It then swung westwards past Frampton and Kirton, little more
than half a mile from the sea, before turning again, to offer protection
from the outfalls of the Welland and Bicker. According to local
tradition Margaret may have come herself to view the great line of embankments, afterwards being entertained at Cressy Hall in Surfleet.[94]
She would have travelled along the Holland causeway, linking
Donnington, Gosberton and Spalding. The approach to Donnington
alone contained no less than thirty bridges, each 10 feet broad and 8
feet high; and it was wide enough for two carts to meet and pass. From
Gosberton the sea defences could be surveyed, rising high above the
opposite bank of the Bicker.

In the latter part of the fifteenth century the regularity of flooding in
this region had become a major problem. In 1483–4 payment of over
a half of the revenues from Frampton was respited because the water
level had once again risen and inundated the lands. Margaret's officers
were regularly employed maintaining the drainage systems. Hugh
Ashton and a large workforce had serviced the sewer at Spalding:
waterways were cleared and banks and causeways repaired. However,
the problems being experienced extended far beyond the scope of these
measures. One of the chief difficulties was from the flooding of the lower

[93] PRO, SC6/Hen. VII/357, m. 3.   [94] Cooper, 50.

reaches of the Witham. The river had become increasingly silted, allowing the strong tidal flow to force the river water back through the partially blocked outfall. Embankments were breached and the water overflowed into the surrounding countryside. In Boston itself the problem had become chronic by the turn of the century. In October 1499 Sir John Hussey had received £40 from Margaret for new works erected in the town against the incoming water. The silting of the haven in Boston had exacerbated the economic difficulties of the port. In 1493–4 Margaret's income from fees for the use of the crane in the harbour had dwindled to a paltry 10 s. Her rented income from honour of Richmond properties along the quayside, leased to merchants and traders, had also declined substantially.[95]

Margaret had a strong interest in the town's fortunes. Merchants such as Hugh Ward and Thomas Robertson were regular suppliers of her household, Robertson arranging for Flemish tapestries and Bruges satin for the countess's residences to be delivered to the port via London. Christopher Browne, appointed mayor of the staple in 1500, was one of her chief councillors. Her clerk of the works, James Morice, became controller of the customs from 1504. Other household men were prominent in the administration of her properties within the town: her summoner Edward Heven acting as bailiff in 1502–3.[96] Her role was one of responsible stewardship. In Kendal her concern had been to harness the growing prosperity of the community and its hinterland; in Boston it was to arrest its decline. In 1502, £70 was spent on the 'newe makyng' of six tenements. Four years later thirty-two oaks were brought down river from Tattershall for the repair of further tenements.[97] Her sense of identification with the community is seen most strongly in her active membership of the town's Corpus Christi guild, together with her servant and constable at Maxey David Philip and her half-brother John Lord Welles. After the death of Thomas Welby of Moulton Margaret intervened personally to ensure that lands he had purchased for the guild were properly delivered.[98]

Lady Margaret's sense of responsibility for her honour of Richmond properties was deeply felt. She regarded them as a form of trust for the crown. When on one occasion her liberties were infringed her plea to the king's council reminded it that the rights were part of Henry's

[95] S. Rigby, '"Sore decay" and "fair dwelling": Boston and urban decline in the later middle ages', *Midland History*, 10 (1985), 54–5.
[96] SJC, D91.20, p. 91; *CPR, 1494–1509*, 204, 308, 386, 414.
[97] PRO, SC6/Eliz./3368; /Hen. VII/1773.   [98] WAM, 16017.

legacy.[99] An action had been taken 'contrarie to right and consciens and to the disinheritance of your said most humble moder and of your highnes in time coming if it should thus rest unformed'. In 1500 she worked in close partnership with her son in a scheme designed to improve the condition of Boston's harbour and lessen the danger of flooding within the region. In February 1500 an indenture was sealed in London with a Flemish engineer, Matthew Hake, for the construction of a tidal sluice on the Witham at Boston; this was a major initiative designed both to scour the silted harbour and lessen the likelihood of inland flooding. The project was to be funded through a levy on the parts of Holland, but in the interim Henry VII and Margaret made most of the cash payments to Hake and his workforce. Royal commissioners and Margaret's own agents gathered in Boston in the middle of March to prepare for their arrival and bricks and stones were assembled at St Botolph's churchyard close by the river side. Margaret's council took responsibility for the practical arrangements, deciding on where the sluice was to be sited, requisitioning raw materials and acquiring a large storage area. The plan was ambitious but well conceived. A stone pier was to be built in the middle of the river, some 13 feet wide and 44 feet long. Doors were hung at each side, which closed against piers erected at the side of the river. James Morice, Margaret's clerk of the works, acted as overseer and the sluice had been completed by the summer of 1502, when Hugh Ashton made a grand tour to inspect 'the conveyance of the water'.[100] In July 1502 Margaret travelled to Boston to view the work, pausing to admire the skills of some fenland fishermen, crossing the marshland on their stilts. She was given a triumphal reception, with all the town guilds turning out in her honour.[101] Margaret's determination to seek a remedy to the port's difficulties through a complex work of engineering stands as testament to her sense of responsibility as a landowner. She drew little direct profit from the mercantile activity in the town, although she was entitled to a duty on goods, including wool, which passed through the port. Her income lay principally in rents rather than trade. Yet she was concerned for the town's well-being, witnessed in her extensive rebuilding of tenements along the quayside.

---

[99] PRO, DL1/2, no. 23.

[100] M. K. Jones, 'Lady Margaret Beaufort, the royal council and an early Fenland drainage scheme', *Lincolnshire History and Archaeology*, 21 (1986), 11–18.

[101] SJC, D91.20, pp. 30–2.

Margaret's interest in Tattershall, also acquired in the grant of March 1487, revealed a different aspect of her lordship. Repairs and small alterations were made to the impressive brick castle built by Ralph Lord Cromwell. Watch was kept on the crossing point of the Witham, navigable upriver as far as Lincoln and in 1505 a certain Thomas Borell was fined for using the waterway to ferry suspicious persons.[102] But Margaret's energies were largely directed towards the nearby collegiate church, founded by Cromwell in 1439. The new church was nearing completion as Margaret took possession. Glass had been set in the windows in 1482 and in 1486 a bedehouse had been completed. Margaret's servant and steward of Tattershall Edward Heven was the benefactor of a chapel in the north transept. The original statutes of the college had provided not only for almsfolk, but also six choristers and, should revenues permit, four poor boys to be taught song and grammar. A grammar school was in existence in 1492, and in 1498 three children were brought to Margaret's household from Tattershall, probably for her own chapel. When the king stayed at Collyweston in 1503 a chorister of the college joined her choir. In 1504 John Mason, a youth of her chapel, was sent to be taught by the schoolmaster at Tattershall. He returned to her household, now at Hatfield, in 1507 where he sang his first mass. The college was encouraged to augment its music books and other manuscripts: the accounts for 1495–6 record payments to Robert Lound, the provost of the choir, for the notation of chants and for the writing, noting and illuminating of a 'Historia Transfigurationis' and the binding of a further seven copies of the same.[103]

A residual interest in Tattershall had been held by Maud, Dowager-Lady Willoughby, one of Cromwell's two nieces and a Stanhope relative of Margaret's through the marriage of Joan Willoughby to Richard, son of Lionel Lord Welles. It was only after Maud's death that Margaret fully took over the role of patron of the college. In 1501 she undertook a revision of the statutes and submitted them to the pope for his approval. Her new code paid respect to the deceased Lady Willoughby, associating her as co-founder with her uncle, Lord Cromwell. Margaret's statutes provided for a higher rank of warden,

[102] KRO, U1475, M169, m. 2.
[103] KRO, U1475/Q19/2; SJC, D91.17, p. 47; D91.20, p. 105; D91.21, p. 117; R. Done, *A Guide to the Collegiate Church of the Holy Trinity, Tattershall* (Coningsby, 1983).

one who would be able to leave the college in the service of a king or prince. He would be able to hold any ecclesiastical preferment below the rank of a bishop, have an increased commons allowance and a greater number of servants. The only services where compulsory attendance was required of him were the obits of Lady Willoughby and Lady Margaret herself.[104] Shortly after the revised statutes were approved by Pope Alexander VI, Henry Hornby, a leading member of her household, became warden. In 1508 he was succeeded by Edmund Hanson, who had previously been responsible for distributing Margaret's exhibitions to scholars. During Hornby's tenure the college enjoyed the protection of the most powerful of Lady Margaret's servants: among those retained in 1508 was Sir John Hussey, 'recently one of the Lady's council'.[105] Margaret took her own position of patron seriously enough to write a strong letter to the king's auditor warning him against the oppression of the college's tenants at Waddington. He was urged to support their suit before the royal council, 'wherin in our opynyon ye shall do a right godly and meritorous deed'.[106]

Margaret's care for the college of Tattershall brought together different strands of her outlook: her piety, charity, concern for education, and sense of familial responsibility. She was capable of charitable acts of great kindness, as was seen in her endowment for an anchoress at Stamford. Margaret's interest in the town may have been encouraged by the Browne family, who had been closely connected with the household of her mother. Margaret Browne had been a regular visitor at Maxey. Her husband, the wealthy wool merchant William Browne, had founded a hospital in Stamford and contributed generously to the rebuilding of the church of All Saints. Browne's son Christopher was a leading member of Lady Margaret's council and may have encouraged her to join the town's guild of St Katherine. Margaret made generous provision for the anchoress, Margaret White, with grants from her paternal estates. She also made personal visits to the convent at Stamford where the anchoress lived and left the nuns there money in her will. In 1504 she had a small house built for her adjoining the church of St Paul and provided its furnishings, wall-hangings and bed-linen. Lady Margaret delighted in such projects. In November 1504, with the anchoress installed in her new lodging,

[104] KRO, U1475/Q21/4.
[105] KRO, U1475, Tattershall receiver's account 1507–8.   [106] PRO, DL12/1/5.

Margaret paid her an afternoon visit bringing apples and wine for a little refreshment.[107]

Through her effective administration of her Lincolnshire estates Margaret was steadily to increase her income. In 1493–4 these lands had yielded only £266. In 1502–3 revenues collected reached the sum of £350 and three years later these had climbed to £399.[108] The construction of the sluice at Boston had halted financial losses through flood damage, though many of the worst-affected properties only recovered slowly. A more efficient system of accountancy was instituted and unnecessary offices dispensed with. Richard Bothe, a relative of Edward Bothe the keeper of Margaret's jewel house, replaced in a single post a number of different ministers within the honour, the fees payable to whom were thereby saved. Feudal resources were exploited with increasing vigour, the value of such shown by the sale of two wards in 1505–6, realizing £50. Her accumulation of wards had reached such an extent that her servant David Philip was rumoured to keep a house at Thorney to accommodate the overflow.[109] Margaret was adept in detecting fraud by any of her financial officers. A tenant of hers in Boston was rewarded for travelling several times to Collyweston to inform her of sums concealed by the feodary Richard Galee. Her lordship became more severe in the last years of the reign, as she lent support to her son's policy of 'good rule'. Special courts were held in Boston in 1507 'pro bono regimine' in her lands and felons escorted from Donnington to the jail at Lincoln. Her officials were in regular attendance at the county sessions and another body of servants was sent to Bourne to seek out felons and robbers. Threats and assaults on her agents, 'so that business remained undone', indicated the unpopularity of these measures.[110]

Where her own family were concerned Margaret was both an intermediary and protectress. This was to be demonstrated in her involvement in the settlement of the Welles family estates. Margaret had used her influence with her son, the king, to promote the interests of her half-brother John, Lord Welles, who had been restored to the barony in 1485. About to cross over to France with the royal expedition in 1492, Welles had drawn up his first will, in which his

[107] SJC, D91.20, p. 155.
[108] Comments drawn from PRO, SC6/Hen. VII/1771–3.
[109] *The Itinerary of John Leland, 1535–43*, ed. L. T. Smith, 5 vols. (London, 1906–10), IV, 291.   [110] PRO, SC6/Hen. VII/1772, 1773.

estate was to descend to his wife, Cecily, and the heirs of their body. His title to the lands of his father Lionel was confirmed by act of parliament. At the time of this will, Welles had two young daughters, Elizabeth and Anne, whose position and rights as coheiresses were being safeguarded. As Henry VII was commencing major new building work at St George's Chapel, and Margaret was making financial contributions to the project, Welles also asked that he be buried at Windsor.[111] On 8 February 1499, when he drew up his final will, the situation had changed. He had no male heir and both his daughters had died. His main concern was that his wife retain a life-interest in his estates. This provision was to the disadvantage of those who held claims on the barony descended from the daughters of Lionel Lord Welles by his first marriage to Joan Waterton of Methley: they were represented in 1499 by William, Lord Willoughby, Sir Robert Dymoke, Sir Thomas Lawrence and Katherine, the sole surviving coheiress. Welles's arrangements depended on the co-operation of the crown, and not surprisingly he had named the king and Lady Margaret as overseers.[112]

Henry was happy to respect the position of Cecily of York, who was of course his own sister-in-law. Cecily remitted the place of Welles's burial to the king's will, and he was laid to rest in the Lady Chapel at Westminster. The arrangements were to be threatened in 1502 when Cecily remarried a mere esquire, Thomas Kyme of Friskney, without royal permission. It was a disparaging match that had pre-empted Henry's rights to the remarriage and thus insulted and angered the king. Cecily was banished from court and Henry took action to re-occupy the entire Welles estate. Here Margaret intervened. She was very fond of Cecily, who during a visit by John Lord Welles in the 1490s was remembered by Henry Parker as sitting at Margaret's board under the same canopy of estate. She now sheltered Cecily and Kyme at Collyweston and attempted to negotiate a compromise that would retain at least some of the estates for Cecily and her new husband. Lady Margaret's accounts record a rush of activity between 1502 and 1503, with her servants riding to inspect the evidences of some of the manors concerned and agreements being drawn up between Margaret and Cecily. In 1503 a settlement was achieved. Certain of the Lincolnshire manors (the so-called Scottney fee) were to be surrendered by Cecily to the king. The remainder of the estates would be held by Cecily for life,

[111] SJC, D15.49.
[112] *North Country Wills* (Surtees Society, 116, 1908), 68–9; *RP*, VI, 542–4.

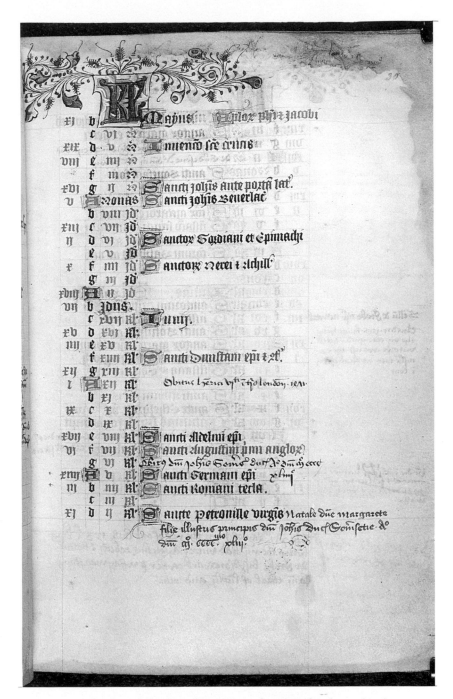

1   Calendar of the Beaufort Hours, showing the date of Lady
Margaret's birth, 31 May 1443

2   Portrait of Lady Margaret in the master's lodge at Christ's
College

3 Portrait of Lady Margaret by Roland Lockey, in the hall at
St John's College, Cambridge

4   Miniature of Lady Margaret by Lucas Hornbolte

5   Rose emblem at head of PRO, SC6/Hen. VII/1771

6 Aerial photograph of the site of gardens at Collyweston palace

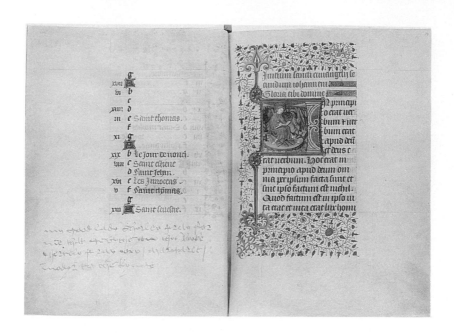

7 Presentation inscription in the book of hours given by Lady Margaret to Lady Shirley

8 The badge of Thomas Stanley and arms of Lady Margaret in their book of prayers

9 The mass of St Gregory

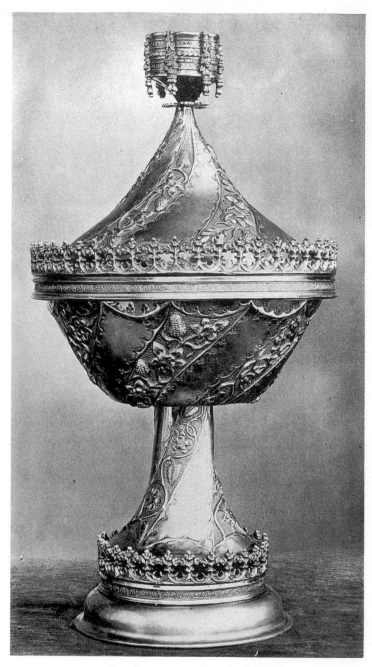

10   Standing cup at Christ's College

11 Beaker at Christ's College

12 Pair of salts at
Christ's College

13 Letter of Lady Margaret to the earl of Ormonde, 1497

14 John de Gigli's dedication to Lady Margaret

15 The oriel of the master's lodge at Christ's College

16 The great gate of Christ's College

17 The great gate of St John's College
18 Bust of John Fisher by Pietro Torrigiano

revert to the crown for ten years, and then be distributed among the coheirs to the Welles barony. Finally Thomas Kyme was to be discharged from all actions or fines resulting from his occupation of the Welles estates.[113] It was a remarkable juggling act. Margaret had managed to appease the king, safeguard the rights of the Welles coheirs, and protect Cecily, who avoided the fine for marrying without royal licence and had a parcel of the properties secured for her own use.

As the reign entered its last decade Margaret was at the plenitude of her power in Lincolnshire. In 1500 she had secured a royal writ enabling her to empanel a commission consisting of the leading landowners within the county, in an attempt to resolve the boundary dispute between the parts of Holland and Kesteven. The commissioners included Robert, Lord Willoughby, Thomas, Lord Roos, George, Lord Hastings, Sir Robert Dymoke and Sir Edward Stanley. After a four-day perambulation of some of the more difficult stretches of the fenland they assembled before Lady Margaret, 'whose special and private interest was considerable', at her castle of Maxey on 8 September to report their findings. After deliberations between Margaret and her own councillors the results were sealed and despatched to the royal chancery.[114] The delineation, which restored a measure of order to the area, also returned to Crowland the disputed lands of Goggisland marsh (which ran along part of the Holland–Kesteven boundary) held by Margaret as lady of Deeping. The decision was taken on Margaret's prompting, less out of sympathy for the abbot (whose tenants had deliberately damaged her properties) than as a result of an incident that had deeply angered her. Certain of her tenants of Deeping had torn down a sacred marker cross, erected to the honour of St Guthlac above a holy well. Margaret, whose husband Thomas Stanley was patron of another holy well (at the shrine of St Winifrid of Flintshire), had pursued the culprits, causing them 'deserved punishment both ecclesiastical and secular' and to be 'for ever interdicted from certain boundaries of both the Deepings'.[115]

Margaret's dominating presence throughout the county found expression in 1508 in the measures taken to gather men from among

---

[113] Information taken from SJC, D91.20, p. 126; D102.10, p. 143; PRO, SC6/Hen. VII/1772; C47/9/52/7.

[114] Lincs Archives Office, SP.S.503/101, transcribed in *Fenland Notes and Queries*, 2 (1892–4), 143–7, 209–11, 294–6.

[115] *Ibid*. For Margaret's interest in this hermit saint see SJC, D91.19, p. 35 (donation to the building of St Guthlac's chapel. 1507).

her servants and tenants for the king's service. Messengers rode out to Lincoln, Alford, Louth, Boston and the remoter parts of the fens with instructions for all to meet at Horncastle before Margaret's commissioners.[116] Her achievements in the region, particularly the construction of the Boston sluice, impressed contemporaries. Her range of interests encompassed a strong sense of responsibility, whether towards the welfare of communities under her protection or the education and care of the young or aged, that stemmed from a worldly but deeply felt piety. Yet her style of lordship, always thorough, could at times be intimidating, a sentiment caught well by Lincolnshire lawyer James Harrington. Harrington described how no man dared do wrong through fear of her authority: 'All controversyes were pacified...nor there was none of the nobility nor any of the gentry that durst attempt to doo anything that was injurious or wicked least that this Noble lady should either chide them to their faces or complain of them to the King.'[117] Her estate administration in Lincolnshire, efficient and at times ruthless, bore similarities to Henry VII's vigilant and acquisitive fiscal practices. Her ability to protect her own kin from Henry's territorial ambitions serves as a reminder both of her strong sense of family obligation and the measure of authority her wishes held with her son.

[116] SJC, D91.19, pp. 91–2.
[117] The Harrington MS was compiled in 1509 and copied and translated by Sir Thomas Lambarde in 1607: Spalding Gentlemen's Society, Strong Room, book 79.

5

HOUSEHOLD LIFE

Lady Margaret's estates fed her household. Their revenues contributed towards the food and clothing of her successive establishments. These provided a focus for patronage and politics, charity and piety: the foundation stones upon which lay the nobility's existence. The convergence of influences and personalities in the last decade of her life would generate a lasting impact, through the academic clerics that were her officers, on the world of education. Margaret Beaufort's household expanded throughout her life, as her status rose from that of a marriageable heiress to the king's mother, when numerous links were maintained between her own and the royal household. We have already seen how the acquisition of property determined the way her estates were administered; we must now consider what life was like at the centre of this complex of inherited and granted land which was eventually to become her legacy to the crown.

The earliest household of which we have any details was that maintained by Margaret and her third husband Sir Henry Stafford at Bourne in Lincolnshire. The property was part of Margaret's estate, conveniently close to her mother's residence at Maxey. Bourne castle had been a favourite dwelling-place of the Holland family at the end of the fourteenth century and the nearby abbey had been enlarged through their patronage. The choice reflected Margaret's strong identification with the Holland inheritance that had descended to her from her grandmother, Margaret, duchess of Clarence. It was a spacious site: the castle, with its two courts and numerous towers, was set in parkland bound by the water of St Peter's Pool and Bourne Eau, its roof-gardens offering a commanding view over the Fens. Margaret's fondness for Bourne was shown in her first will of 1472, when she

made provision for her burial in the abbey and set aside money for
Edmund Tudor's remains to be moved from Carmarthen to a tomb
beside her.[1]

It was a small, highly mobile establishment. The staff was not large,
wages being paid to thirty male servants and two female. John Burton,
the steward, and his companion John Manchester bought provisions
from the markets of Bourne, Stamford and Oakham. Beer, ale and
staple salt fish were supplied by Bourne traders; woolfells and hides
sold back to merchants.[2] If the household was to some extent a force
in the local economy, its essential feature was one of tranquil
domesticity. This early establishment showed Margaret's need to be
close to her mother and her relations of the half-blood the St John
family. Margaret Beauchamp, dowager-duchess of Somerset, was a
strong-willed and determined landowner, who paid close attention to
the authentication of her rights. She had renegotiated a ransom
agreement made with the captive count of Angoulême, ordering a
comprehensive survey of the evidences and meticulously checking the
financial calculation.[3] Her alertness to archival detail would be passed
on to her daughter. She enjoyed considerable influence in this area of
the Fens and in 1465 had encouraged their joint admittance to the
confraternity of the nearby abbey of Crowland. Close contact was
maintained with the St Johns: Henry Stafford and Oliver St John
serving together on a boundary commission at Stamford. A more
intimate picture is glimpsed during the Christmas festivities in 1466.
Stafford and Margaret, accompanied by Elizabeth St John and a
handful of servants, were entertained at Maxey castle for no less than
six weeks.[4]

At the time of this Christmas celebration preparations were being
made for an important move south, to the substantial manor house of
Woking in Surrey. The manor had also come into Margaret's possession
as part of the inheritance of her grandmother Margaret Holland. It lay
in an attractive setting on the river Wey, a mile south of the small town
of Woking, screened by a copse and surrounded by parkland. A survey
of 1327 showed a moated manor house with outbuildings, including

---

[1] E. Venables, 'Bourne: its abbey and castle', *Associated Architectural Societies, Reports and
Papers*, 20 (1889), 2–18; SJC, D56.195.

[2] The period at Bourne is reconstructed from WAM, 12181, fols. 1–52. For an excellent
general discussion of household consumption see C. Dyer, *Standards of Living in the Later
Middle Ages* (Cambridge, 1989), 49–70.   [3] BL, Add. MS 35814.

[4] WAM, 12181, fol. 52.

a poultry house, and a second moat surrounding a garden, reservoir and orchard. Beyond the moat were sheds for horses, sheep and cattle, granges and a deer-park. Entrance was commanded by a gatehouse and drawbridge, leading into an outer court, with its lodgings and stables. A second gate opened out onto the great hall, with adjoining pantry and buttery, the chapel and the private chambers of lord and lady. Beyond these were the gardens, bordered by the fruit trees of the orchard, which ran down to a large fishpond and the winding river. Again there were visible reminders of the Holland legacy. The great north window of Woking parish church had been donated by Thomas Holland, earl of Kent, at the end of the fourteenth century. The duchess of Clarence had expanded the site: a receiver's account for 1420–1 recorded almost £250 spent on the new works.[5] It was an impressive complex, suitable for use as a centre of estate administration and conveniently close to the capital. The manor had been held by Edward IV after the second attainder of Henry Beaufort, duke of Somerset, in 1465. The king's decision to restore the property to Stafford and Margaret two years later was a significant mark of favour, that brought the couple and their household into the orbit of Yorkist court politics.

A flurry of improvements took place before Stafford and Margaret moved into their new residence at the end of March 1467. The counting-house was re-roofed, stables repaired and a new larder built. Carts and extra staff were hired from the abbot of Bourne to speed the transfer south.[6] Their establishment was enlarged; an influx of Stafford servants bringing up the total strength to between forty and fifty. These included men of particular quality: William Wisetowe (who was to become the steward), Thomas Rogers (their auditor), Reginald Bray (their receiver-general) and John Harpur. They were officials with a pedigree of service, personally recommended to the young couple by the duchess of Buckingham. It was an indication of enhanced status and a more active political role.

Woking's proximity to the capital transformed the activities of the household. Supplies were regularly bought in London. The grocer Thomas Hill provided spices and fresh fish were bought from William

---

[5] The description of Woking is based on R. A. C. Goodwin-Austen, 'Woking manor', *Surrey Archaeological Collections*, 7 (1874), 44–9; D. J. Haggard, 'The ruins of Old Woking Palace', *ibid.*, 55 (1958), 124–6. The rebuilding of 1420–1 is found in WAM, 12163, fols. 6, 20v.   [6] WAM, 12181, fol. 50.

Rodley, to supplement those obtained from the large fishpond, fed by a watercourse from the river Wey, west of the manor house. Goods were transported along the Thames to the nearest wharf and then overland to Woking.[7] The household now received visits from those members of Stafford's family involved in business in the capital. Guests included his younger brother John, his nephew, Henry duke of Buckingham and his Bourchier relatives Henry earl of Essex and Thomas archbishop of Canterbury. A close connection was built up with the nearby town of Guildford. Local merchants such as John Clement provided goods on a regular basis. Stafford and Margaret paid frequent visits to the town; Henry Stafford was the most important magnate in the area; his presence acted as a focus for courtiers and kinsmen. The young duke of Buckingham was entertained at Guildford over Christmas 1469; John Lord Berners, chamberlain of the queen's household, lunched with Stafford there in July 1470. Margaret's interest in Guildford was to last long after her third husband's death. On 6 February 1486 Margaret, Reginald Bray and William Smith supported two local merchants (Henry Norbrigge and Thomas Kingston) in the foundation of a chantry in the church of the Holy Trinity.[8] A similar, enduring connection was made at Woking. A local trader, Richard Machom, dealt with the household so often that in 1469 he received livery. Gilbert Gilpyn, steward of the household, came originally from Westmorland and had come into Stafford's service through his wife's properties in Kendal. Gilpyn chose to settle in Woking, and supervised affairs there until his death in 1505, when he was buried in Woking parish church.[9]

The co-operation necessary between suppliers and members of the household to cater for important occasions was seen most clearly in the entertainment of Edward IV at the hunting lodge of Brookwood, 2 miles west of Woking, on 20 December 1468. A pewter dinner service and glass 'galoners' were bought at London and servants carefully transported the five dozen dishes and four dozen saucers to Brookwood. Stafford's chaplain John Bush, who often took a hand in arranging provisions, was sent to Guildford to help John Clement with further purchases. Stafford rode to meet the king at Guildford and after hunting

[7] *Ibid.*, fol. 83v; 12189, fol. 56v.
[8] O. Manning and W. Bray, *The History and Antiquities of Surrey*, 3 vols. (London, 1804–14), I, 48–9.   [9] *Ibid.*, 138.

with him in Woking park escorted him to Brookwood. Wildfowl and a variety of fish were consumed, including pike, 'half a great conger for the king's dinner', thirteen lampreys and seven hundred oysters, washed down with five barrels of ale. The king, Stafford and Margaret dined under a magnificent canopy of purple sarsenet specially made for the occasion whilst music was provided by the royal minstrels.[10] Beneath the celebration lay the reality of politics. Faced with a threat against their share of the lordship of Kendal, Stafford and Margaret were seeking to conciliate the king.

The household's everyday routine centred on the close and happy relationship that the couple enjoyed. They were almost always in each other's company, and on the rare occasions when they were apart sent each other frequent messages. When Stafford travelled up to London at the time of the parliament Margaret accompanied him. They also toured their estates together. In the summer of 1467 they both began a circuit of Margaret's west-country properties. In August they stopped off at the Somerset manors of Curry Rivel and Langport, purchasing provisions from William Lord Zouche, with Stafford and Margaret riding off together to inspect the outlying estates. In October they put up at their Devonshire manor of Sampford Peverell accompanied by a riding household of forty-four. John Manchester was despatched to Exeter to collect provisions and firewood was carried into the inner court. Beds were hired and rushes collected for the lord's and lady's chambers.[11] Even in the most harmonious of marriages it was unusual for the wife to travel so much with her husband rather than supervise affairs at home. Margaret was not encumbered with the responsibility of raising children. But it was also a sign of her personal activity, her close identification with her inheritance and wish to be involved in the management of her own estates.

Although Margaret was allowed an annuity of 100 marks a year there was in practice little distinction between her affairs and her husband's. They always worked together on business matters. Reginald Bray received a 'bill of reckoning between them taken'. Margaret would often sign receipts on Stafford's behalf. When cash was in her hands and debts fell due she paid them. Both were to share the task of

---

[10] WAM, 12186, fol. 42.

[11] WAM, 12185, fols. 21v–3v, 31–47, 50–63. The accounting problems that arose from such a mobile household are discussed in Mertes, *Noble Household*, 85.

disbursing rewards to their household servants. Stafford provided John Dey and his bride with clothing for their wedding and when William Barnes left the establishment he received 10s 'above his wage' as a golden handshake. Margaret rewarded the chamberer Christopher before his wedding and presented a gift to William Wisetowe, the steward.[12]

In the summer season the two would hunt together. In August 1468 they toured the great parks of Hampshire: Gifford, Odiham, Warbleton and Bentley. The following year John Stafford joined them on a trip to Windsor; William Norris to Henley, where a buck was slain 'by my lord and lady', after which all dined on bread and ale in the hunting lodge. In August 1470 they enjoyed the Surrey parks of Midhurst and Farnham.[13] At Christmas they would be entertained by players from Tonbridge, Staines and Kingston. They were clearly very happy together. On one occasion Stafford made his wife a handsome New Year's gift of £5 in gold farthings. Their wedding anniversary (3 January) was always celebrated: for that of 1471 a servant was sent to London to purchase luxury items, lamb, curlew, plover, snipe and larks.[14]

After the move south links were maintained with the household of Margaret's mother. Stafford and Margaret stayed in 'the duchess of Somerset's place' in London (the tower house 'Le Ryall') in January 1467 and November 1468. Servants of the duchess were entertained at Woking: David Philip (later one of Margaret's most trusted officers) at Christmas 1469.[15] However the role of Stafford's mother, the dowager-duchess of Buckingham, who had recommended many of the newly recruited staff, became more important. Anne Neville, duchess of Buckingham, was a vigorous and determined administrator. After the death of her first husband, in June 1460, she maintained a small, highly centralized household and channelled most of her substantial income (over £2,000 p.a.) into improving and expanding her favourite residences at Writtle (Ess.) and Kimbolton (Hunts.). A forceful personality, with great political influence, she had been chosen by the anxious aldermen of London to lead a delegation to treat with the Lancastrian army in February 1461, 'with other wytty men with

[12] WAM, 5472, fols. 3v, 37v, 40v, 57, 58.
[13] *Ibid.*, fols. 12, 41v–3v; 12183, fol. 6.
[14] WAM, 5472, fol. 58; 12189, fol. 46v.
[15] WAM, 12182, fol. 34; 12186, fol. 26.

her'.[16] But she was also a cultivated lady, who possessed her own library and encouraged Margaret's literary interests. In April 1469 some of her books, which she seems to have lent to Margaret, were brought back from Woking to her residence in London. In her will she left her daughter-in-law works in English and French and her own book of hours, decorated with Stafford knots and the Lancastrian badges of the chained swan and antelope.[17] She was an active landowner and severe in the use of the law, against tenants and servants alike. For the young couple, whom she took very much under her wing, she became a powerful protectress. In the autumn of 1468 she commanded Reginald Bray to come to London in all haste 'for a great matter' touching Stafford and his wife. When Sir Henry Stafford fell seriously ill early in 1469 his mother, the dowager-duchess Anne, took responsibility for his treatment, hiring doctors and apothecaries. There was regular contact with the duchess's officers.[18] One of these, William Knyvett, would eventually become steward of Margaret's own household and one of her most important counsellors.

The latter years of the marriage were overshadowed by the fears aroused by Stafford's deteriorating health and the growing political uncertainty, occasioned by the estrangement of Richard Neville, earl of Warwick, from the Yorkist regime. It was a time when the trusted members of the small household proved their mettle. Reginald Bray took over much of the responsibility. In November he rewarded those accompanying him on the dangerous journey to Kendal, to protect the estates of his lord and lady, on account of the 'trowble in the world'. Others were caught up in the perils of the times. On 13 April 1471 a horse was purchased for Gilbert Gilpyn, the steward of the household, as he prepared to ride with his master to do battle for Edward IV at Barnet. John Dey rode back to Woking on the eve of the combat, carrying Stafford's message to his wife and hastily drawn up will.[19]

The nature of Stafford's recurrent bouts of illness is difficult to determine. It may have been the skin complaint erysipelas, known commonly as St Anthony's fire, and regarded as a mild form of leprosy. Stafford and his wife had been admitted into the confraternity of Burton Lazars in 1467. In March 1470, as Stafford and his retinue

[16] *English Chronicle*, ed. Davies, 109.
[17] For the return of books, WAM, 5472, fol. 33; the bequest is printed in Cooper, 17. We owe the detailed information on the book of hours to Nicholas Rogers.
[18] WAM, 5472, fols. 21v, 23v, 30.   [19] *Ibid.*, fol. 63.

were travelling northwards with the royal army, his chaplain John Bush distributed alms 'at places of the lepers' between Pontefract and York.[20] Such an affliction might explain Margaret's extraordinary devotion to St Anthony, the patron of leper houses. Fisher recalled her particular fasting on this saint's day. Statues of St Anthony adorned her chapel. However, the evidence is at best inconclusive. What does emerge, both from Stafford's earlier testament and his final will, is his complete trust in Bray, charged to settle his outstanding debts, and also his closeness to his wife, who was named as sole executrix.[21]

After Stafford's death on 4 October 1471 Margaret maintained a reduced household of sixteen, headed by three of her ladies-in-waiting (Elizabeth Johnson, Jane Atkins and Elizabeth Denman), and based at her mother's residence, 'Le Ryall', in London. At this time of vulnerability Reginald Bray again took charge of most of the practical matters, receiving £30 for the distribution of 'my ladys lyverys'. Broader affairs were dealt with in consultation with her mother and provided a telling demonstration of the lasting importance of her maternal lineage. As Margaret drew up her first will in May 1472 she relied heavily on the support of her mother's relatives, the Stourton family of Mere in Wiltshire. John Lord Stourton had been a principal feoffee and executor for her father in 1444. His sons William and Reginald were to be the chief witnesses to Margaret's arrangements for enfeoffing her west country estates. It was also to the Stourton family nexus that Margaret turned for business and legal advice: William Carant and the lawyer William Hody, who provided assistance, had both married into that family. Additional support was provided through the Stafford connection: Henry's brother, John, earl of Wiltshire, and Walter, Lord Mountjoy (who had married the widowed Anne, duchess of Buckingham, as her second husband in 1467).[22]

Early in June 1472 Margaret married Thomas, Lord Stanley, the king's household steward, moving to the very centre of an aristocratic household. This new establishment has left only fragmentary records. As a result, her final marriage is without doubt the best known and least understood. It began as a marriage of convenience, entered into solely for pragmatic reasons. One recent historian has gone so far as to declare that Margaret 'never identified herself as a Stanley'.[23] Her first vow of chastity, undertaken whilst Thomas Stanley was still alive, is

---

[20] WAM, 12184, fol. 52.   [21] SJC, D56.186; D91.15.   [22] SJC, D56.205.
[23] J. J. Bagley, *The Earls of Derby, 1485–1985* (London, 1985), 15–16.

seen as evidence of her personal distaste for the arrangement. It is a misguided view that begins with almost every authority misdating the match by some ten years, and consequently underplaying the significance of this new alliance for more than a decade before 1485. In the Stanleys' own circle the match was seen as a manifestation of the initiative and patronage of Edward IV, 'that king royall...Who married you to the Margaret Richmond'. Yet the marriage was not in the king's gift. Edward may have played a part in arranging the match, but Lady Margaret negotiated the settlement very much on her own terms and secured a generous annual allowance charged on Stanley's properties in north Wales.[24] She had allied herself with another great noble house, giving her closer ties with the victorious Yorkist court circle. With Stafford she had sought to conciliate the king and their partnership was also the living out of a difficult balancing act; her marriage to Stanley, whether or not it was at first personally agreeable to her, was the fruit of its success.

Continuity between the Stafford and Stanley households was provided as some of Margaret's most trusted servants moved to the new establishment: William Cope, John Heron, William Hody and of course Reginald Bray. Margaret had insisted on bringing these men with her as part of the terms of her agreement with Stanley. During 1473 Bray was involved in the sensitive legal discussions between Stanleys and Woodvilles over the territorial endowment of Edward, prince of Wales.[25] After some hard bargaining the Woodvilles accepted Stanley predominance in Cheshire and agreed to provide Stanley's eldest son George, Lord Strange, with preferment within the prince of Wales's council. Bray, who had dealt with the expenses of Lord Strange's legal counsel in London, speedily occupied a position of trust within the Stanley household. He was to view this new period of service with considerable pride. When he became armigerous in 1485, the eagle's foot of the house of Stanley became the most prominent charge on his surcoat. Yet his close relationship with Lady Margaret was maintained. He was to account for clothing and other goods ordered for Margaret and her daughter-in-law, Lady Strange, who was presumably staying with her. He and his mistress drew up indentures settling arrangements made for Stafford's burial, paying for the costs of his tomb and the chaplain singing for his soul.[26]

---

[24] *RP*, VI, 311.   [25] WAM, 32407, fol. 5v.   [26] *Ibid.*, fols. 5, 11v.

Although Margaret had brought some of her favourite servants with her they did not form a separate establishment (as Stanley was to claim in the aftermath of Buckingham's rebellion) but were employed within the Stanley household. Margaret's time was now divided between her new husband's principal residences at Lathom and Knowsley, his castle of Hawarden in north Wales, and the demands of court activity in the capital. Woking was maintained as a convenient base near London, the park enclosed and new lodgings added to the manor house. Most of her time seems to have been spent at Lathom, a formidable place whose machicolated battlements were girded with nine towers, rising above an outer, walled circuit. Here velvet cloth was sent to her, tawney chamlet for a kirtle and fur for a gown. Her favourite horse was equipped with a new harness, a sign of the constant travelling Margaret was to undertake. The couple were frequently in each other's company. In September 1472 Margaret accompanied her husband and his three younger brothers as they travelled from Lathom to Chester and then Hawarden, where the party stayed for four days. During the following month she joined her husband in the capital. On her departure for the north Woking was left in good order: the new lodging was glazed and palers and ditchers were busy securing the park.[27] Over the next two years her routine alternated between Lathom, where she assisted Stanley in local arbitration awards, and the king's court, where her husband held responsibility for supervising the 'below-stairs' departments of the household. In 1474 Stanley and Margaret spent Christmas at Baynard's castle in London. Whilst Bray gave out rewards to royal household officers on his master's behalf, a green gown and striped and plain black damask were bought for her. Stanley's own henchmen were clad in cloth of silver.[28] His marriage with Margaret gave him a social standing which confirmed the political reality of his importance to the king. In these terms, at the very least, his bride meant a lot to him: traces of the extensions made to Knowsley Hall to accommodate her household still survive, along with a beautifully ornamented fire-back (a finely worked iron slab used to protect the wall of the fire-place) containing Margaret's heraldic insignia as countess of Richmond.[29]

[27] *Ibid.*, fol. 12; Liverpool City Library, 920/MOO/1091.
[28] WAM, 32407, fol. 5v.
[29] J. Hoult, *The Vill, Manor and Township of Knowsley* (Liverpool, 1930), 32.

The personal affection that existed between Margaret and her last husband is much harder to gauge. Her admission to confraternity with the Carthusians in 1478, along with Stanley and other members of his family, shows a shared interest in the order. A similar vein of piety is revealed by the prayers of the Passion and the Holy Name in a book that Margaret commissioned for her husband, with its four charm-like formulae (versions of the Charlemagne legend), found in the middle of the prayer book. Whoever recited these prayers would not perish in battle, was assured immunity from the plague and in the case of women, protection during pregnancy.[30] Stanley's reluctance to commit his forces during the Wars of the Roses was to give him a reputation for political guile that was to last for centuries. A fear of uncertain or reckless military adventure dominated his outlook, and was seen most strongly in his cautious tactics before Bosworth in 1485. Margaret's own fears were also reflected in these prayers. Her dread of the pestilence that had struck down her second husband, Edmund Tudor, was vividly recalled by Fisher. In an age where periodic outbursts of the plague added to other uncertainties, Margaret was later to acquire a manuscript book (*c.* 1500) compiling precautions that could be taken against the pestilence. This work, decorated with the Beaufort arms, gave advice on medicines, diet and interestingly enough a list of prayers and anthems that could be used preventively, including suffrages to St Sebastian and St Anthony.[31]

A shared apprehension, underlying a somewhat ruthless pragmatism, perhaps best characterizes the couple's sense of common cause. It was given depth and force by the dangers of Richard III's reign. Henry Parker was to recall Margaret's patience and fortitude after the failure of the 1483 rebellion, when her estates were confiscated and she was placed in virtual confinement. It was her husband who was able to protect her from the full rigours of attainder. 'The most pleasant song of Lady Bessy' portrayed Margaret giving her blessing to the renewed invasion attempt in 1485, whilst Stanley was to wrestle with his conscience over his oath of allegiance to Richard III.[32] In the event, Henry Tudor's successful campaign proved a triumphant vindication of the Stanleys' concerted family strategy.

The accession of Henry VII was to alter Margaret and Stanley's relationship. As Henry's mother, Margaret now had a special role in

[30] Westminster Abbey MS 39.   [31] Cambridge, Fitzwilliam Museum, MS 261.
[32] 'The most pleasant song of Lady Bessy', ed. J. O. Halliwell, *Percy Society*, 20 (1877).

court ceremonial and royal progresses. The frequency with which Margaret attended on the king suggests that to him his mother's presence was often as important as his wife's. The household ordinances devised by the king in December 1493 contained arrangements for enhancing the dignity of the royal family as well as for that of the king himself. When the king comes from evensong to take spice and wine, it shall be served to him, his mother and his sons with equal state, they having 'squires of their own to bear the cups'. In his mother's own house, if a bishop be her guest, 'he must sit at the upper end of her board and so be served as he is served in the king's presence', and at the lower end of the board will be 'a messe of earles or counts, barons or baronesses'. In church, when the king's mother is in the presence of the king and queen, she may have her own cloth of estate, 'travers' and 'carpet'. Provision must always be made for her in the royal palaces, as would be for the king, queen and their children.[33]

Margaret's importance within the court is fully borne out by the evidence of formal and more relaxed occasions. At Easter 1488 she and the queen received livery of the Garter, and took part in the procession at Windsor. In February 1490 she joined the king and queen in attending a play at Westminster.[34] A letter of William Paston of 10 September 1493 brings out this constant sense of proximity, referring to the king, queen and 'my lady the kinges moder' residing together in the midlands, they 'lye at Northampton and will tary ther till Michelmas'.[35] Margaret's role demonstrated not only her close relationship with her son, but also that of matriarch of the emerging Tudor dynasty. On 30 November 1489 she acted as one of the godmothers of the Princess Margaret (named after her), who was to become her favourite grandchild. The well-being of the queen and royal children were never far from her thoughts. 'Blessed be god', she wrote to the earl of Ormonde in April 1497, 'the kyng the quene and alle oure swet chyldren be yn good hele, the quen hath be a lytyll crased, but now she ys well, god be thankyd.'[36] On 24 February 1499

---

[33] BL, Add. MS 4712, fols. 3–22.   [34] Leland, *Collectanea*, IV, 254.

[35] N'hants RO, Fitzwilliam MS 370 (which we owe to Margaret Condon). William Paston, who had married Anne, daughter of Edmund Beaufort, duke of Somerset, was one of Lady Margaret's estate officials and was to name her as chief executrix of his will: *Paston Letters*, VI, 158.

[36] PRO, SC1/51/189. After Princess Margaret's departure for Scotland in 1503 Lady Margaret regularly sent her gifts and during her illness in 1507 despatched one of her

she acted as godmother to Henry VII's third son Edmund. Her accounts record her considerable expenses: the rewards to the midwife and nurses and the christening gift worth £100. Her book of hours noted not only the date of birth of all Henry VII's children, but in the case of Arthur and Margaret, the hour of their birth, and her accounts record a number of payments and rewards to the queen's midwife.[37]

Margaret's newly found status was combined with a separate landed estate and income. This allowed her to recruit her own mobile establishment whilst remaining based at her husband's residences of Lathom and Knowsley. As Margaret attended the king, at court or on progress, or visited her own properties, she was accompanied by her riding household. The move of a number of her officers into royal service bridged the gap between her own establishment and her son's. Her unique position subordinated her relationship with her husband, although Stanley was now honoured as the king's stepfather. During the magnificent court ceremonies of 1487 he was announced by the heralds as 'beauper de roy notre souveraigne', and the 'rich corrownall' worn by Margaret on that occasion was carefully depicted, on Stanley's instructions, on her effigy at Burscough Priory. This, rather than his office of king's constable, enabled him to maintain a high profile at court, where he was to be one of Prince Arthur's godfathers. The marriage had become a partnership of equals: Margaret as the king's mother and substantial landowner, Stanley as the head of a great aristocratic house. Stanley adorned the windows at Lathom with his wife's arms and the inscription 'our lady the kinges mother'.[38] Margaret used her title of countess of Derby with as much pride as she did that of Richmond.

From 1485 was forged a new alliance of interests, where Margaret drew on her husband's territorial connection and affinity in the

waiting-women to help care for her: SJC, D91.19, p. 115; D91.21, p. 24; N. Macdougall, *James IV* (Edinburgh, 1989), 196–7.

[37] SJC, D91.20, p. 190. However, there is no evidence that Margaret, rather than the queen, oversaw the education of the royal children, or was responsible for the appointment of John Skelton as their tutor; R. M. Warnicke, 'The Lady Margaret, Countess of Richmond; a noblewoman of independent wealth and status', *Fifteenth-Century Studies*, 9 (1984), 227.

[38] Cooper, 57 n. 1. For the memorial to Margaret at Burscough see the instructions in Stanley's will, printed in P. Draper, *The House of Stanley* (Ormskirk, 1864), 42–3. It was transferred to the church at Ormskirk after the Reformation: J. Bromley, 'The heraldry of Ormskirk church', *THSLC*, 58 (1906), 88–9.

creation of her own household and expression of her political, educational and charitable enterprises. There is a tendency to overplay Margaret's role and underestimate that of her husband; a reflection of the hagiographical treatment of her piety, which has generated its own mythology. The 'Stanley churches' in north Wales are commonly attributed to her munificence, or at least her initiative. The well-chapel at the shrine of St Winefride's, Holywell, dates from the late 1480s. A profile of what is believed to be the couple is to be found high in the ceiling of the crypt. This could be seen as reflecting a common sense of cause. The cult was being deliberately encouraged by Henry VII and it has been argued (without any specific evidence) that Margaret may have influenced Caxton in his decision to print a life of St Winefride. Yet study of the emblems adorning the crypt reveals the benefactors were all members of the Stanley family. Interestingly Sir William Stanley, the king's chamberlain, seems to have been the chief donor, assisted by Thomas Lord Stanley. His badges of the wolf's head and the rebus of his wife Elizabeth Hopton (a barrel with a hop plant issuing out of it) are surrounded by other Stanley emblems of the legs of Man, the eagle's foot and stag's head.[39] The emblematic evidence points to an alternative identification, that the couple represented were in fact Sir William Stanley and his wife, and their generosity was played down in any local tradition after Stanley's execution on charges of treason in 1495. There is no record of Margaret ever making any donation. In the summer of 1502, when both were staying at Collyweston, it was Thomas Stanley, not his wife, who sent an offering to Holywell on the feast day of St Winefride (22 June).[40] At Mold the church of St Mary was rebuilt with a profusion of Stanley emblems displayed along the spandrels of the barrel-vaulted roof. At All Saints, Gresford, Stanley is known to have donated the east window in 1500.[41] Nowhere are Margaret's own badges or coat-of-arms to be found.

These examples provide a warning against superimposing a role for Lady Margaret where no clear evidence exists. It was at Manchester, the linchpin of the Stanley hegemony in Lancashire and Cheshire, that Margaret brought her own wealth and status to enhance the profile of her husband's family. The Stanleys' interest in the collegiate church,

---

[39] C. David, *St Winefride's Well: An Illustrated Description* (Kildare, 1971). The view that Margaret was the active force behind the cult has been most recently expressed in M. J. C. Lowry, 'Caxton, St Winifred and the Lady Margaret Beaufort', *The Library*, 6th series, 5 (1983), 101–17.   [40] SJC, D91.20, p. 22.

[41] E. Hubbard, *The Buildings of Wales: Clwyd* (London, 1986), 168, 390.

founded in 1422, had resulted in the election of Thomas's brother James as warden in 1481. On his death in 1485 he was succeeded by his nephew James Stanley, the future bishop of Ely. Under James Stanley a vigorous phase of patronage was initiated, including the rebuilding of the north aisle of the church and part of the choir. Stanley also encouraged the benefactions of Hugh Beswick, who was to found a guild chapel in the church and directed that one of the priests in his own chantry there should teach grammar.[42] Margaret's support for this renewal is revealed from the one surviving memorial of the rebuilding, the wainscotting now preserved in the Chetham Library. Here the Stanley emblem of the eagle's foot is surrounded by Margaret's own badges, the portcullis and the rose. She was able to encourage her son's interest in the project. Shortly before Stanley's preferment to Ely in 1506, the newly appointed bishop despatched a messenger to Richmond and to Croydon for discussions with the king and Lady Margaret on the choice of his successor.[43] The next nominee was Robert Cliff, formerly of Clement's hostel, Cambridge, to be followed by Stanley's own chaplain Richard Alday. On James Stanley's death in 1515 Alday supervised the building of his tomb: to be placed in the chapel that Stanley had founded within the collegiate church.

Manchester provided a focus for Margaret's patronage. It also became a reservoir from which she drew her own substantial household and affinity. Ranulph Pole (of a Cheshire family closely linked to the Stanleys) had served as an officer within the collegiate church. Margaret presented him to the rectorship of Hawarden in succession to James Stanley. His brother William Pole was later to be an usher of her chamber. Hugh Ashton, employed by the church as early as 1464, was to become Margaret's receiver and controller of her household. Christopher Urswicke, a chaplain at Manchester, was chosen by Margaret as her confessor. Another man with strong Manchester ties was Hugh Oldham, whose family had been based in the area from the early fifteenth century. Oldham was to become Margaret's receiver and chancellor, a connection that secured his preferment to the bishopric of Exeter. Yet it was to Manchester that he

---

[42] F. R. Raines, *The Rectors of Manchester and the Wardens of the Collegiate Church of that Town*, part I, Chetham Society, n.s., 5 (1885), 46; P. Hosker, 'The Stanleys of Lathom and ecclesiastical patronage in the north-west of England during the fifteenth century', *Northern History*, 18 (1982), 226; M. G. Underwood, 'Politics and piety in the household of Lady Margaret Beaufort', *Journal of Ecclesiastical History*, 38 (1987), 46–7.

[43] SJC, D91.21, p. 115.

devoted his benefactions, developing Beswick's chantry into a larger foundation which eventually became Manchester grammar school. Oldham made the warden of Manchester the first visitor of his foundation, and, when a schoolmaster was nominated in 1515, it was stipulated that the warden and fellows were to have future powers of appointment.[44]

Oldham was to become one of Lady Margaret's most important officers. His cousin Roger Ormeston (who left Oldham a fine ring in his will) was to serve as her chamberlain until his death in 1504. Hugh Ashton, Oldham, Ormeston and Miles Worsley (Margaret's cofferer from 1499 to 1509) all came from the same part of Lancashire, on the outskirts of present-day Manchester. This north-western element was to form the core of Margaret's household in the 1490's, when she chose to retain Lathom and Knowsley as her chief residences. In his foundation of Manchester grammar school Oldham had spoken of the need to establish learning in Lancashire. Such concerns were widely felt and the sentiments were repeated in Thomas Butler's foundation deed for Warrington school.[45] Yet they struck a chord with Margaret, who determined to promote these aspirations on a broader stage. Bernard Oldham, Hugh's brother, was found preferment as rector of Crewkerne (Som.) through Margaret negotiating a turn of the presentation with Sir William and Joan Knyvett. He was to support John Combe, the previous rector, in establishing a grammar school there.[46] Again, it is important not to overplay her role. There is no evidence that Lathom in the 1470s was a 'northern academy' where Hugh Ashton, Thomas Butler and William Smith, the future bishop of Lincoln, were all educated side by side at Lady Margaret's expense. Maurice Westbury of Oxford, summoned by Margaret to teach 'certayn yong gentilmen at our findyng', is usually thought to have been their tutor, but the chronology is all wrong.[47] Westbury was summoned in 1494 by which time Smith was well beneficed, Butler had marched to Bosworth at Stanley's side and Ashton was a fellow of Manchester

---

[44] Raines, *Rectors of Manchester*, 37–8, and see in general A. A. Mumford, *Hugh Oldham* (London, 1936).

[45] *Annals of the Lords of Warrington, part 2*, ed. W. Beamont, Chetham Society, o.s., 87 (1873), 419.

[46] N. Orme, *English Schools in the Middle Ages* (London, 1973), 201.

[47] *Epistolae Academicae Oxonienses*, ed. H. Anstey, 2 vols., Oxford Historical Society, XXXV–VI (Oxford, 1898), II, 614.

college. Tempting as it is to suggest that Smith, Oldham and the others issued from an 'academy' at Lathom burning with a common cause, its existence has been inferred from their later performance. The motivation for Margaret's patronage evolved over many years through her experience of a great aristocratic household and its territorial connections. It did not suddenly and miraculously appear fully formed.

During the first part of Henry VII's reign Margaret and Stanley worked in unison. When Henry VII travelled north to visit his mother in the summer of 1495, it was at Lathom and Knowsley that he was entertained. Their mutual interest is shown in the plans for a marriage that never in fact materialized. The death of George Lord Strange in 1497 had left Stanley's young grandson, also named Thomas, as heir to the earldom of Derby. In 1498 his marriage was being arranged with Elizabeth, the elder daughter of Margaret's half-brother John Viscount Welles and papal dispensation had already been secured.[48] For Margaret, an alliance with a major aristocratic house furthered her ambition of elevating the Welles family. On Stanley's side the match offered his line a close blood-link with the Tudor dynasty. Elizabeth's sudden death later that year meant these hopes were never to be realized.

However the couple's relationship was to undergo a further change at the beginning of 1499, when Margaret undertook a vow of chastity, with Thomas Stanley's permission, and set up her own establishment at Collyweston.[49] Taking such a step during the husband's lifetime was unprecedented. Margaret was able to evade the canonical issue by only giving an intention ('the whiche thing I had before purposed in my lord husband's days') though Fisher's own recollection clearly shows that the vow had taken place, in the presence of Richard FitzJames, bishop of London. Her reasons for this move deserve detailed consideration. The accession of Henry VII had already vested in her an exceptional degree of independence. In her mid-fifties Margaret evidently now preferred a more separate and chaste lifestyle. This was not intended as a deliberate slight to her husband, indeed Thomas Stanley was to be a regular guest at Collyweston, where rooms were reserved for his use. However, it was a characteristically assertive decision, carrying an edge of ruthlessness. Margaret was never to return to Lathom, and

---

[48] Lancs RO, DDK 2/14.
[49] *Mornynge Remembraunce*, 294; Cooper, 97–8. See below, pp. 187–8.

however brave a face Stanley kept up publicly, he cannot have found his new position easy to come to terms with. For Margaret the recruitment of an independent household provided an ideal forum for her own concerns. James Clarell, the cofferer of her riding household in the 1490s, was dismissed and an entire body of officers appointed. Henry Hornby became her secretary and dean of chapel, James Morice her clerk of works, William Merbury her controller and Miles Worsley her new cofferer. It represented a final phase in a steadily evolving education, allowing her the freedom to develop fully her own interests. It was to be a revealing reflector of her mature personality.

Political reasons underlay this decision. The accession of Henry Tudor allowed Margaret a degree of freedom quite unparalleled in a late medieval aristocratic marriage. It also resulted in a higher and more compelling loyalty, that of a mother to her son. Thomas Stanley's role at court and in the localities had been enhanced after 1485, and the king accorded his step-father honour and respect. Yet a more subtle tension had now come into being. In the latter part of the 1490s Henry had become increasingly suspicious of the Staffordshire branch of the family, the Stanleys of Elford, and also some of Thomas's own offspring, particularly Edward Stanley. Margaret's decision had been taken after accompanying her son on the progress through the eastern counties in the autumn of 1498 and was doubtless a measure that the two had carefully discussed. One suspects that Stanley was presented with very much of a *fait accompli*. The king was planning to delegate considerable political power to his mother and probably advised her to distance herself from their activities.

It was at Collyweston, four miles west of Stamford overlooking the Welland valley, that Margaret set up her own establishment. Here was an attractive manor house, built by Sir William Porter in the early fifteenth century and considerably enlarged by Ralph Lord Cromwell, that Lady Margaret was to transform into a palace. It was to be her place of longest continuous residence upon which she lavished special attention. By 1506 the two courts contained a great hall, parlour and domestic offices off which was a woodyard; a chapel and its adjoining revestry connecting with Margaret's own chambers along a gallery; a library equipped with desks, a chamber of presence and various rooms allotted to members of her household. The children of the chapel had a chamber furnished with desks and presses, and in 1506 grammar books were bought for them. It was a choir of considerable size: an inventory of chapel vestments mentions nineteen surplices for children and twenty-four for men. The almsfolk, whose house was in the kitchen yard, had a common hall, a garden and running water pumped from a nearby well. There was also a 'frey loge', where messengers and guests could be put up. A secure jewel house and counting-house catered for the assets of the household, while at the gates, its point of interaction with the village and world beyond, stood a council house and a prison. Two clockhouses, one set in a great tower overlooking the whole complex, kept the household to a regular timetable.[50]

Further work was undertaken extending the garden and park. An orchard was planted, new ponds created and a number of summer houses built. Weeds and nettles were cleared and ponds scoured. Supervising these projects gave Lady Margaret considerable pleasure, as she busied herself planning a garden walk, to be laid out from the lodge to one of the new ponds, and discussing one of her new herb gardens with a local expert, William Love. Love was rewarded for his travels to gather herbs for the orchard and garden, as was another, guided by 'the sight' of Love and his wife. The parson of nearby Blatherwycke, Robert Louthe, was called in to advise on the planting of apple trees in the orchard. The rush of frenetic activity was too much for Collyweston's elderly gardener, who was laid off for five weeks with an attack of 'the ague'.[51] Typical of Margaret's thoroughness were the measures taken to prevent the flooding of the watermeadows. Dykes were laid out from the lower fishpond with water-gates built in at regular intervals. A specialist, James Matley of Bourton (Yorks), was recruited for the task, his contract stipulating that if further flooding occurred repairs would be at his own expense. Near the house a small fenced herb garden was set out, for the use of William Elmer, one of Margaret's physicians. A door connected it with one of the palace courts. Gardens were both productive and a source of refuge from the communal bustle of the courtyards: one of the chambers reserved for the queen's use was next to a garden and led into it.[52] The overall effect of these improvements was to harmonize the palace with its surroundings, particularly the watermeadows running down to the Welland valley, and provide an expanded arena for household

[50] The details are taken from SJC, D102.9; D91.22.
[51] Material on the gardens is drawn from SJC, D91.14; D91.22. Jones, 'Collyweston', 136. See Plate 6. [52] SJC, D91.21, pp. 74, 92.

entertainment and recreation. On one occasion the children of the chapel were to perform 'ballets' for Lady Margaret in the open 'by the woodside'.[53]

If Collyweston was the focal point for Margaret's household activities, Coldharbour, the London house granted to her by the king, was not neglected. Its river frontage, which boasted 'a summer parlour by the waterside', was carefully repaired after gales in 1505. In April 1508 the keeper of the little park was rewarded for making a 'house of boughs' for Margaret to sup in.[54] Modifications and alterations were also made to those 'borrowed residences' that Margaret was loaned whilst in transit from the midlands to the capital. The period between 1505 and 1506 was one of particular mobility. During the summer of 1505 Margaret's household left Collyweston for Fotheringhay, where the castle was cleaned thoroughly and the court levelled clear of accumulated rubbish. The countess's chamber was made secure with locks and bars, and locks were delivered for thirty-nine chambers for the household. Wainscot and board were carried from Collyweston and supplies of timber commissioned from the bailiff at Fotheringhay.[55] In the autumn Margaret and some of her household met the king at the manor of Haling in Surrey. Various repairs were made and a stair was constructed so that Margaret could descend from an inner chamber to the garden. From there she moved first to the manor of Croydon, made available by the archbishop of Canterbury, and then Hatfield (Herts), lent by James Stanley, bishop of Ely. At Croydon Peter, a joiner of Southwark, made a door of wainscot for her closet, next to the high altar in the chapel. He provided a lockable cupboard in her inner chamber where she could keep sugar and spices, doubtless for the possets and spiced wines taken of an evening. The episcopal manor had also to accommodate Margaret's almsfolk: bedsteads were mended for them, partitions erected and shutters fitted to the windows. On the move to Hatfield Margaret had alterations made to the almshouse, chapel and presence chamber with the co-operation of the bishop's bricklayer, who came to inspect the works.[56]

Margaret's residence at Hatfield coincides with the only extant treasurer's account showing the provisioning of the household. Substantial demands were made upon the local economy. Pasture had

[53] SJC, D91.20, p. 100.
[54] SJC, D91.22, pp. 201, 203, 223, and for the 'house of boughs' SJC, D91.19, p. 17.
[55] SJC, D91.22, pp. 41–6.   [56] *Ibid.*, pp. 57,75.

to be enclosed at Hatfield, Cheshunt and Ware; a slaughterhouse was also hired. A great volume of traffic converged on the household, provisions or gifts in kind: oxen, sheep, cygnets, small game birds and cartloads of hay donated by John Fisher, bishop of Rochester. Margaret wrote to her bailiff of Ware concerning the 'devising of vitailles', to ensure the speedy delivery of market produce to Hatfield. The biggest single expense apart from consumption of cattle and sheep was on ale and beer (215 tuns of it) with 17 tuns of red and white claret and 5 gallons of the rarer muscadel. Fish consumed included salmon, two barrels of sturgeon and sixty lampreys; fruits included 'lymons in pickell', oranges in syrup, apples and prunes. Yet the presence of a large household also provided a catalyst for trade. Animal products were sold off to local merchants and millers purchased the residue of corn.[57]

The surviving household records for the last decade of Margaret's life reveal her at the plenitude of her power, and show her servants and messengers, pack horses and wagons criss-crossing the eastern counties on her behalf. What were the social activities of her establishment? Fisher was to praise the sobriety of Margaret's habits, claiming that there was no place in her household for 'entrements', 'jonquies and reresoupers' or 'bankettes'. All these were forms of entertainment centred around meals; the last three involved feasting outside the main meal times and reresoupers could last well into the night.[58] Margaret's careful temperament as estate manager may have been offended by the waste involved, just as her sense of order would have sanctioned great feasts but not informal late-night revels. Yet Fisher's recollections become more fragmented as he moves away from the chapel and inner chambers of the household and into the great hall. There is plenty of evidence that Margaret liked to entertain and amuse herself. She had a fool named Skyp, whom she provided with a pair of 'startups' or high-heeled shoes reaching above the ankle and in her last years was accompanied to her various residences by 'Reginald the idiot'. Privately she enjoyed a game of chess, and played for stakes, as did her son the king. She sent a man of Buckden to go on pilgrimage

---

[57] SJC, D91.16. See also the substantial outlay on foodstuffs when Margaret of Brotherton's household was based at Framlingham in the late fourteenth century: R. E. Archer, 'The estates and finances of Margaret of Brotherton, *c.* 1320–1399', *Historical Research*, 60 (1987), 274–5.

[58] E. K. Chambers, *The Medieval Stage*, 2 vols. (Oxford, 1903), II, 181.

on her behalf whilst she gambled at blank or cards.[59] Publicly, festivities abounded. At the feast of St Nicholas boy bishops were sponsored at Collyweston, and 'clerks of St Nicholas', funded by Lady Margaret, celebrated in the town of Croydon. An abbot of misrule and his sports held sway one Christmas, while John Harrison arranged the 'disguisings'. Players would set up a scaffold stage and visiting Spaniards 'who danced the Morice' were suitably rewarded. Such entertainment was mixed with more decorous forms: the recitals of the children of her chapel. When she departed from her palace it was ceremonially, to the singing of an anthem of Gaude flore, a hymn to the Virgin.[60]

Henry Parker's description of Lady Margaret's establishment struck a different emphasis. It showed Margaret's great-granddaughter, Queen Mary, for whom it was intended as an exemplar of public and private virtue, an ordered regime embracing both pomp and charity. He recalled a New Year's Day when he served his mistress's table with a retinue of no less than twenty-five knights. Below them was a continuous round of festivity: in her hall 'as fast as one table was up another was set'. He testified to Margaret's methodical care, her visits to her servants when they were sick and her feeding of the poor during the Christmas season. Yet these charitable acts took place within the liberality of a great and powerful household, in which Lady Margaret could afford to dispense a New Year's gift worth £100 to the duke of Buckingham. According to Parker her 'checker role' tallying her dependents amounted to some 400 persons.[61] Here was a sense of wealth and grandeur without going to the extremes of ostentation.

It has to be recognized that Parker was putting across an ideal picture. The magnificence of the New Year's Day festivities that he so vividly remembered was no ordinary occasion. It was Margaret's way of honouring a close personal friend, William Smith, on his elevation to the bishopric of Lincoln. She may have employed over 400 people at

[59] SJC, D91.21, p. 41 (Skyp); D91.19, p. 7 ('playing at the blanke'); D91.21, p. 30 (chessmen for Margaret and the king at Richmond).

[60] The information has been drawn from SJC, D91.20, pp. 126, 190; D91.21, p. 61; D91.20, p. 121, and the 'gaude flore' from D91.20, p. 97. 'Gaude flore virginali' was a votive antiphon, and might have been intended as an offering to the Virgin as Margaret set out to travel: F. L. Harrison, *Music in Medieval Britain* (London, 1963), 315.

[61] BL, Add. MS 12060, fos. 21v–2: 'she had in her cheker roule contynually two and twenty score of ladies, gentylmen, yeomen and offycers'; R. M. Warnicke, 'The Lady Margaret Beaufort, Countess of Richmond (d. 1509) as seen by John Fisher and by Lord Morley', *Moreana*, 19 (1982), 47–55.

times of particular importance, such as her entertaining of king and courtiers in the summer of 1503. Yet when estimates of her funeral costs were drawn up in 1509, it was envisaged that a total of 228 officers and servants would accompany her body to its last resting place, and this gives a surer idea of the size of her establishment.[62] To this extent Parker's account must be treated with an element of caution.

Nevertheless, the broader impression is borne out by the document evidence. For the year 1506–7 no less than £1,542 was spent on the upkeep of the household. Expenses on pious objects such as almsgiving and offering at shrines (£94) were outstripped by those on rich cloths, jewels and plate (£117) and on rewards (New Year's gifts totalled £115, the overall amount was £211). This was not an indicator of extravagance for Margaret, unlike her former ward Edward, duke of Buckingham, never fell into debt. Rather it was the sign of largesse, the outward demonstration so necessary in a major aristocratic household. By this period Margaret's expenditure had outstripped that of the wealthiest English peers, the duke of Buckingham and John de Vere, earl of Oxford.[63] Her establishment was now the greatest in the realm after the king's. Forty years ago she had helped manage a small household of thirty. Now she presided over a hierarchy of officers and departments. That she took a close personal interest in its day-to-day disbursements is evident from the fact that her signature is on every page of the surviving accounts. When her household transferred to Richmond at the time of the king's illness in March 1507 she supervised the payment of rewards to servants in the pantry, buttery, kitchen and wardrobe; the gifts to the gentlemen ushers and gardeners.

Henry Parker chose to emphasize Margaret's concern for her dependants. His portrayal is supported by the records, which show her clothing and housing her almsfolk, providing education for her servants' children and providing allowances for christenings, marriages and burials. The good lord or lady was expected to exercise responsibility for their servants' rites of passage through life. Mistress Windsor, who received a reward on Relic Sunday (15 July) 1498, was Margaret's goddaughter. Both she and her husband were found places

---

[62] SJC, D4.7.
[63] SJC, D91.21. For the comparative expenditure of Buckingham, Oxford and Northumberland see J. M. Thurgood, 'The diet and domestic household of the English lay nobility, 1265–1531' (London MPhil, 1982), 66.

in her establishment. The marriage of a member of the household needed careful attention. When Elizabeth Webb, one of Margaret's gentlewomen, married Fulk Woodhall he entered into an agreement with Lady Margaret to settle lands in Northamptonshire and Oxfordshire on his bride. He was to die only a few years later. The arrangement Margaret had negotiated ensured provision for his widow.[64] The marriage between Margaret's servant Sir Ralph Shirley and Anne, daughter of Sir Henry Vernon was also drawn up within the household. Feoffees for Anne's jointure included Sir John St John, Henry Hornby and John St John. Indentures of the marriage had been laid out for Lady Margaret's inspection on 10 April 1502. Her gift to Lady Shirley still survives, an attractive book of hours that was acquired by Margaret's father during his campaigns in France. It contains her own inscription, giving Anne Shirley her blessing and asking to be remembered in her prayers.[65]

Margaret's move to Collyweston in 1499 did not mark a complete break with her husband. He was a regular visitor at the palace and enjoyed hunting in the surrounding park. On one occasion Margaret provided the stake money when he gambled at cards with his grandson. However, she was not present at Lathom when Stanley, close to death, drew up his last will on 28 July 1504, nor was she named an executrix. Margaret's public reaction gave no hint of estrangement. Full mourning was observed in the household when news of Stanley's death reached Collyweston on 3 August. The accounts record sums paid to the Greyfriars of Stamford for a dirge and mass for him and to other religious orders for their intercessions. On 23 August Stanley's grandson and heir arrived from Lathom, escorted by forty-seven riders, and he and Margaret attended a requiem mass at Stamford.[66] Nevertheless, Margaret's first vow of chastity, taken most unusually during her husband's own lifetime, marked a form of separation from Stanley and lent a distinct tone to her own household, reminiscent of the 'viduata', the order of widowhood bound by a common dedication to pious and educational enterprises.

[64] SJC, D91.17, p. 24 ('Mistress Windsor'); D56.187 and G. Baker, *History and Antiquities of the County of Northampton*, 2 vols. (London, 1822–30), I, 712 (Webb and Woodhall).

[65] SJC, D91.19, p. 70; D91.20, p. 19; S. M. Wright, *The Derbyshire Gentry in the Fifteenth Century* (Derbyshire Record Society, 1983), 232. The book of hours is SJC Library, MS N.24; the inscription is on fol. 12v (see Plate 7).

[66] SJC, D91.20, pp. 165, 168. Stanley had died on 29 July. For his will see Draper, *House of Stanley*, 42–3.

The women who surrounded Lady Margaret, as guests or as her personal attendants, to some extent occupied the place normally taken by the 'familia' of a male peer or gentleman. Margaret's relationship with Elizabeth of York, for whom rooms were reserved at Collyweston, is tinged with ambiguity. The 'subjection' of the queen to the king's mother was noted by the Spanish ambassador in 1498, who formed the impression that little love was lost between them. On one occasion Margaret peremptorily dismissed a man who was seeking to enter Queen Elizabeth's service. On the other hand Margaret had actively worked for the king's marriage and was seen, publicly at any rate, to act jointly with the queen as a patron of devotional literature. She and the queen both made the request that Catherine of Aragon should learn French, so that they might converse more easily with her when the bride came to England.[67]

Margaret's role reflected the interplay of patronage. Just as her male servants were able to achieve rapid placement within the royal household, so their wives often gained access to the queen's establishment. Yet her influence was more direct. At the time of the marriage festivities of 1501, Margaret had a list made for her convenience of some of Queen Elizabeth's officers, and of those, both Spanish and English, attending Princess Catherine. Amongst those attending the queen were Margaret's kinsmen John St John and Alexander Frogenhall and one of her most trusted servants, Richard Aderton. Some of the names on the list were blank. The posts were evidently awaiting further discussion between Margaret and the queen.[68] Again, the public profile is one of co-operation and support on a major state occasion but one is left to wonder if in private Elizabeth of York resented this interference in her own affairs. Shortly before Margaret's death there was considerable overlap between the ambit of her own household and that of Princess Catherine. Griffith Richards became clerk of the signet to both. Robert Merbury served Margaret and Catherine as usher of the chamber, Robert Bekinsall as almoner.[69]

Lady Margaret was to entertain a number of other women of high rank as guests within her own household. Elizabeth of York's sister

[67] M. Dowling, *Humanism in the Age of Henry VIII* (New York, 1986), 17. Margaret's abrupt dismissal of a Nottinghamshire yeoman, John Hewyk, who was seeking to enter the queen's service, is recorded in *Records of the Borough of Nottingham*, ed. W. H. Stevenson, 5 vols. (London, 1882–1900), III, 301.   [68] SJC, D102.11.
[69] *L and P Henry VIII*, I, i, 41, 48, 67.

Cecily was the widow of Margaret's half-brother, John, Viscount Welles. She was a regular visitor to Collyweston, and among Margaret's records was the dispensation of 1499 which enabled Cecily, like herself, to maintain a regular pattern of worship in her household. Cecily's remarriage to a humble esquire Thomas Kyme, in 1502, had angered the king but Margaret sheltered the couple and presented Cecily with a gift of 'a fine image'. The two ladies clearly enjoyed each other's company and shared common interests. Margaret had among her books 'a printed legend bought of my lady Cecil'. Cecily had a chamber reserved for her use at Croydon in 1506, and when she died a year later Margaret paid some of the expenses of her funeral.[70]

Anne Lady Powis, a daughter of William Herbert earl of Pembroke, also spent much of her time at Collyweston, where she had a chamber reserved for her. Her presence served as a reminder of the gratitude felt both by Margaret and her son to Herbert's wife Anne Devereux, who had supervised the young Henry's education at Raglan in the 1460s. Lady Powis, who had shared Henry's childhood days at Raglan, provided a living link between the new dynasty and the turbulent politics of the Wars of the Roses. She was to be a constant companion in the last years of her life. When she died in 1506 Margaret provided for priests, clerks and nine children of the chapel to attend to her obsequies. Lady Powis's own daughter was to be remembered in Lady Margaret's last will: she was to receive 'a heart of gold with a fair sapphire' from the jewels of the chapel.[71]

Another aristocratic lady linked with Margaret through personal ties was Elizabeth Talbot, dowager-duchess of Norfolk, widow of the last Mowbray duke. The earliest evidence of their relationship hints at political manipulation. In 1486 the duchess was persuaded, at Margaret's 'speciall desire, instance and requeste' to sell to Reginald Bray the attractive manor of Chelsea. However, a genuine friendship was to emerge, largely through their shared interest in academic endowments. The Norfolk dowager-duchess was a generous benefactor in the rebuilding of Corpus Christi College, Cambridge, enabling the buttressing of its old court. She was also the patron of its master

[70] BL, Add. MS 12060, fol. 21v; SJC, D91.19, p. 30; Underwood, 'Politics and piety', 44, 49.
[71] Underwood, 'Politics and piety', 48–9. The heart of gold was probably a symbol of devotion to the heart of Christ. James Leyson, presented to Blackdon by Thomas Stanley, left a similar heart in 1513 to the dean of Wells: *Somerset Medieval Wills, 1501–30*, ed. F. W. Weaver (Somerset Record Society, 19, 1903), 174.

Thomas Cosyn. In 1497 Margaret granted her a turn of presentation to the chaplaincy of the hospital at Bedminster so that she could advance his prospects. Cosyn was to matriculate as doctor of divinity in 1501 and went on to further university distinctions, serving as Fisher's successor as Lady Margaret Professor of Theology from 1504 to 1506.[72] Margaret and the duchess seem to have been on close terms at this time. Towards the end of 1505 one of the duchess's servants brought Margaret a gift of a pair of spectacles. In April 1506 Margaret paid her a personal visit. Elizabeth Talbot was to make her will in November 1506, appointing Cosyn one of her executors and stating that besides gifts to him and others she had given the king £100 and 'such parcels as in my life I have given to my ladys grace the kings mother for a poor token of my remembrance'.[73]

Among the gifts which Margaret distributed during her lifetime were a primer and psalter, valued sufficiently to be mentioned in the will of Elizabeth, Lady Scrope, a daughter of John Neville, marquis of Montagu.[74] Lady Scrope, another who had rooms reserved for her at Collyweston, sought Margaret's assistance in a property dispute that had arisen after the death of her second husband Sir Henry Wentworth. Wentworth's son and heir Richard had disputed the terms of the marriage settlement and prevented Lady Scrope taking possession of the lands. In 1502 an arbitration panel was set up headed by Margaret's chamberlain Sir Roger Ormeston, and Richard Wentworth was bound by heavy financial obligations to accept its findings.[75]

The hospitality afforded to these ladies also revealed Margaret's strong sense of family obligation. Anne, Lady Clifford, who was put up with two of her daughters, was the daughter of Margaret's half-brother John St John. In 1493 she had married the eccentric Henry Lord Clifford, the so-called 'shepherd-lord', who had avoided political retribution in the Yorkist period by adopting the disguise of a peasant-

---

[72] M. M. Condon, 'From caitiff and villain to pater patriae: Reynold Bray and the profits of office', in *Profit, Piety and the Professions in Later Medieval England*, ed. M. A. Hicks (Gloucester, 1990), 141; *Cambridge University Grace Book B, part I*, ed. M. Bateson, Luard Memorial Series II, Cambridge Antiquarian Society (Cambridge, 1903), 162. Their friendship is reminiscent of that of Mary de Sancto Paulo and Elizabeth de Burgh in the fourteenth century: H. Jenkinson, 'Mary de Sancto Paulo, foundress of Pembroke College, Cambridge', *Archaeologia*, 66 (1914–15), 402–46.

[73] SJC, D91.21, p. 60; D56.3.

[74] *Testamenta Vetusta*, ed. N. H. Nicolas, 2 vols. (London, 1826), II, 588.

[75] SJC, D56.156, 161.

farmer. Restored to his estates by Henry VII he seldom came to court but led a strange, reclusive existence in his tower of Bardon, near Bolton, where he devoted his energies to a study of astronomy. The marriage was evidently not a success. Anne's chaplain explored the possibility of a separation, travelling to court to discuss the matter with the king and Lady Margaret. Margaret offered placement within her household. The chaplain then appealed to Richard Fox, bishop of Durham, for his assistance in the matter, 'that nowe with your help I trust she shall come up and attend upon my Lady'.[76] A room was also appointed for Margaret's kinswoman Mary, Lady Rivers (a grand-daughter of Edmund Beaufort, duke of Somerset). Lady Rivers's sister, a nun at the house of minoresses near the Tower of London, also received occasional payments.[77] Noblewomen, veterans of politics and marriage, were assured of finding a comfortable reception within Margaret's own mature household. They were not in constant attendance but sojourned, paying for their board and bringing servants with them. They provided a variety of company and a means of sharing a common sense of piety. They offered a bridge between present affairs and the turbulent past, made relevant by Margaret's continuing apprehension at the uncertain future of the dynasty.

However, Margaret's constant companions, closer to her in that they shared her daily movements between chambers, board and chapel, were her own attendant women. One of them was Perrot Doryn or 'Perrot the Frenchwoman', who was perhaps originally hired to help with Margaret's translations or to tutor Catherine of Aragon. A French priest was paid as her confessor in 1503. In August 1509 Perrot was listed as one of three female chamberers. In her will Margaret left her 5 marks in ready money and the grant of an annuity should she remain in England. Her position clearly depended entirely on her relations with Margaret; although the annuity was granted in October 1509 she later complained to the executors that she had not received it, although others had got theirs.[78]

Edith Fowler had a better pedigree of service for her husband Thomas had served as an esquire of the body to Edward IV. Edith handled the expenses for clothing and other personal needs of

[76] SJC, D102.10, p. 138, 142–3; *CP*, III, 294; *Letters of Richard Fox, 1486–1527*, ed. P. S. and H. M. Allen (Oxford, 1929), 18.   [77] SJC, D102.10, p. 138.
[78] SJC, D3.78; Cooper, 135.

Margaret's almsfolk. She later purchased an estate near the manor of Roydon, which was used to endow a chantry for the Fowlers in their mistress's chapel at Christ's College.[79] Lady Jane Guildford, 'my lady Jane', was another of Margaret's close attendants and headed the list of her staff present at the funeral of Henry VII. She was the widow of Sir Richard Guildford, controller of the royal household, and had also served the queen and her two daughters Margaret and Mary. Her services to the royal family were recognized in 1514 when she received an annuity of £20.[80]

These women accompanied Margaret in the regimen of a meticulously ordered establishment. Fisher was to describe how her ordinances were read out four times a year, and remembered Margaret's authoritative style of management. So too did Henry Parker, a member of Margaret's inner circle, and thus particularly well placed to describe the running of the household. The strength of Margaret's affection for him is clear. She had paid for his schooling at Oxford and arranged for him an advantageous marriage. The expenses of his wife and two children were also met: bonnets and ribbons being provided for the young offspring, and their 'diet' of bread, milk, butter and spices whilst Parker completed his education. In 1507 she gave him money to go and see a joust in London and two years later found placement for him in Henry VIII's own household.[81]

It was Parker's marriage to Alice, daughter of Sir John St John of Bletsoe, that set the seal on his rapid rise in favour. The St Johns, as Margaret's second or adopted family, enjoyed a place in the household as if they were her own. Oliver St John of Lydiard Tregoze was a member of her riding household. In 1498 Margaret had made an offering at the marriage of his son, John St John, and had presented him with an embroidered carpet or hanging of her own work, executed in gold thread, showing the various branches of the St John family.[82] John St John was to record in a later deposition how he had remained in the household for many years, until the time of Margaret's death. Care was lavished on the various members of the family brought up within her establishment. When Maurice St John prepared to enter royal service as a member of Henry VII's elite bodyguard, Margaret paid for his

[79] SJC, D91.19, p. 27; A. H. Lloyd, 'Two monumental brasses in the chapel of Christ's College', *Proceedings of the Cambridge Antiquarian Society*, 33 (1933), 66, 72.

[80] *L and P Henry VIII*, I, i, 713; Chrimes, *Henry VII*, 112.

[81] SJC, D91.19, pp. 80, 92.   [82] See above, p. 31.

equipment.[83] Provision was also made for their cousins, Richard and Alexander Frogenhall and Anne and Lionel Zouche. Margaret's concern for the St Johns had been a consistent feature in all her establishments. Elizabeth St John had often stayed with Margaret and Stafford in the 1460s and on one occasion they looked after her when she was sick. Members of the Frogenhall family had accompanied Margaret and Stanley in the 1470s. In her own mature household they were exalted to the highest position. Sir John St John of Bletsoe was to become chamberlain after Ormeston's death in 1504, and was named as one of her executors in her last will.

Henry Parker's account was written many years after his service to Lady Margaret had ended. It was a nostalgic evocation of the great estate of the foundress of the Tudor dynasty that glossed over the harsher aspects of her establishment. The prison built by the gatehouse at Collyweston and the movement of felons from jail to jail found no place in his description. Nevertheless, Parker captured, in his recreation of ritual and ceremonial, the mood of the greatest household in England, apart from that of the king and queen. Like so many other establishments, Margaret's was at its finest *en fête*. At Coldharbour in November 1501 servants scurried back and forth preparing for the reception of Catherine of Aragon. The house was refurbished, windows glazed and new ovens installed in the kitchen. Margaret's own parlour was laid with a new carpet of 'imagery work' and a fresh litter was constructed for her, decorated with a silken fringe. Ermine, mink and two furs of 'calaber' (grey squirrel) were bought for her own use and her gown trimmed with lace. Tawney medley cloth for her servants' livery cost £160 and a copper-smith hammered out over two dozen badges of the Beaufort portcullis. When the day of Catherine's arrival came Margaret's waiting-women were rowed down the Thames from Westminster to attend 'the first music'. A thousand gold rings supported the 'riche cloths of arras' hanging about the banqueting chamber, which glittered with the plate displayed on a great cupboard. Care was taken by the hostess as to the placing of guests, so that each Spanish lady and gentleman had an English companion. Entertainment was provided by the minstrels of the queen and the earl of Northumberland, two companies of actors and Matthew, the earl of Oxford's juggler.[84]

[83] For Maurice St John see SJC, D91.20, 162.
[84] SJC, D102.2, pp. 13–18, 25–32; PRO, SC6/Eliz./3368.

Through her obligations as great lady of the household to those maintained in it, whether kindred, wards or servants, Margaret developed an interest in their education and careers. This is revealed in casual ways, such as a payment for the schooling of three almschildren or the purchase of grammar books for the chapel children. More specifically, it was seen in dealings with those individuals put out to apprenticeships or maintained as scholars. During 1504 a daughter of John Walters was bound as an apprentice in London, on Margaret's order, at a cost of £2 13s 4d. Similar arrangements were made in 1506 for an almschild, Nicholas Davy, and for Randall Sant, whom Boniface Stanley (a surgeon) 'took to his prentis for twelve years to learn his syens'. The falconer's son was put to school at St Albans in the spring of 1508, payments included the taking of his Easter rites.[85]

Most schooling arrangements concerned the children of the chapel. Service there was well rewarded, with leaving gifts and loans, and from the chapel the boys went to school at other institutions. Scholars from Lady Margaret's chapel were supported at Eton, the London Charterhouse, Oxford and Cambridge. Through such means the arm of the household reached into the centres of education, and connections were made between its officials and tutors and fellows of colleges. Lady Margaret's patronage of education, therefore, was not merely a product of her own interest in learning or her personal devotion : it had a social context in the needs of people living with her, for whom provision was necessary. The household would continue to support individual scholars. Roger Collingwood of Queens' Cambridge received an exhibition, delivered by Henry Parker, when he was licensed to study abroad even though an income had already been reserved by his college.[86] Margaret's patronage may have been crowned by the foundation of colleges but these were not the result of abstract schemes developed in isolation from other forms of involvement.

Conversely, it was from Margaret's establishment that an increasing interest in Cambridge was generated. John Fisher, Margaret's spiritual director, was its catalyst and it was to fall to him to superintend the

[85] SJC, D91.20, pp. 173, 196; D91.21, pp. 39, 91, 117. For further details see Appendix 3 below, p. 283. The scale of the support for individual scholars is comparable with that of the household of Elizabeth de Burgh in the fourteenth century: C. A. Musgrave, 'Household administration in the fourteenth century with special reference to the household of Elizabeth de Burgh, Lady of Clare' (London MA, 1923), 14.

[86] CUL, Queens' College Archives, QC Bk76, fols. 23, 25; SJC, D91.19, pp. 34, 115.

birth and endowment of St John's College. Yet Fisher held many responsibilities elsewhere. His colleague in that enterprise, and a man more involved in some of its practical details was Henry Hornby. Hornby had served as Margaret's secretary, dean of chapel, and after 1504 chancellor. Hornby left a far greater mark than Fisher on the running of the household and his career illustrates, more effectively than Fisher's, the varied interests of Margaret's academic administrators.

The Hornbys, from Deeping in Lincolnshire, had originally been recruited into the service of Margaret's mother, the dowager-duchess of Somerset. When Stanley and Margaret took over the late dowager's estates in 1482 they appointed George Hornby, Henry's father, to take charge of their horses within the manor. Henry's early career is obscure. He was presented by Thorney Abbey to the living of Deeping St James, which he vacated in July 1481, shortly after incepting as a master of the arts. He had entered into the study of theology in 1489, and at that time contributed towards drawing up an office for the feast of the Name of Jesus.[87] It was this notable achievement which drew him to the attention of Margaret. In September 1494, the year that Margaret was recognized patron of the feast by the pope, she presented him to the living of Trefdreyr in Cardigan. By 1499 Hornby was serving as her secretary and dean of her chapel, and the details of his own informal account book reveal he had become one of her closest officers.[88]   In addition to many other preferments he succeeded Margaret's physician Thomas Denman as master of Peterhouse in 1501, crowning his Cambridge career. His influence in Lincolnshire was not neglected. Margaret revised the statutes of Tattershall College to enable him to hold the wardenship in plurality.[89] He was also elected as alderman to the guild of the Virgin Mary in Boston. His will reflected both his Cambridge connections (with an endowment for his anniversary at Clare and bequests to Peterhouse and St John's) and his standing in his native county. Bequests were made for the upkeep of bridges and roads at Boston, Stow and West Deeping. Altar cloths were left to East Deeping church and vestments to the guild of the Virgin in Boston. More significantly, he was to found a grammar school at Boston, arranging for the stipend of its master to be paid by

[87] R. W. Pfaff, *New Liturgical Feasts in Later Medieval England*, Oxford Theological Monographs (Oxford, 1970), 82–3. For Hornby's background: PRO, SC6/909/16.
[88] SJC, D102.10.   [89] KRO, U1475/Q21/4.

Peterhouse.[90] His local position was enhanced by personal ties: his sister had married into the Pulvertoft family and her son was to become the bailiff of Margaret's Tattershall estate.

Hornby's importance reflected the crucial role of the chapel within Margaret's establishment. Payments to London printers for mass books and primers 'in nomine Jesu' show that under his deanship it had become a centre for the devotion and that the household was using both mass and office. Hornby superintended the children of the chapel, and in the autumn of 1504 journeyed to London, Windsor and the west country searching for new recruits.[91] He also disbursed money for Margaret's charitable enterprises, accompanying her on a visit to an anchoress at Stamford and giving a gift to a poor man that his mistress had seen walking on crutches.[92] His account book was not a comprehensive financial record. The audit of domestic expenditure was carried out by the cofferer Miles Worsley. Yet the fact that it offers an overview of affairs (dealing with most of the major officers of the household) as well as handling special receipts, such as the board payments of the sojourners, is testimony to his position of special trust.

Hornby had a number of academic colleagues within the household. Hugh Oldham, a student of arts and both laws at Oxford, who migrated to Cambridge in 1493, was the most seasoned in high office having served as Margaret's chancellor. John Fothede, fellow and master of Michaelhouse, acted more briefly as Margaret's controller between 1504 and 1506, at the time of the endowment of Christ's. Robert Bekinsall, also a Michaelhouse fellow and Fisher's successor as head of Queens', was to become her almoner. Hugh Ashton, the receiver-general, was the least academic within the group. He held no degree except a Bachelorship in Canon Law, granted with a dispensation from study in 1508, obviously at the instance of Lady Margaret. Yet he was closely involved with the establishment of St John's and contributed personally towards its endowment. Although he later became an archdeacon of York, Cambridge retained his affection and his chantry chapel and effigy were set up at St John's.[93]

The presence of this contingent of university men made it all the more likely that Margaret's generosity would turn towards Cambridge in the last years of her life. The break with her husband's establishments

[90] PRO, Prob. 11/19, 6 Ayloffe. For the Corpus Christi school see *VCH, Lincs*, II, 451.
[91] SJC, D91.20, p. 178.   [92] *Ibid.*, p. 182.
[93] For further details see Appendix 3 below.

at Lathom and Knowsley and the development of her own fully separate household, with all its varied activities, allowed a forceful expression of her own personality. It was the culmination of a long period of education, through the households of her mother, the Staffords and the Stanleys, to a mature appraisal of her concerns and interests. Her educational charities reflected the preoccupations of the higher ranks of her own independent household. Fisher made a great impression on Margaret, both in his ability and piety, but he did not labour in isolation: the obligations of a great and powerful establishment provided both the opportunity and the justification.

6

A PORTRAIT OF THE COUNTESS

Lady Margaret used her resources, both in land and personnel, in a determined way to uphold her own rights and those of both lines of her family, and made some wise choices of men for her service. She worked in partnership with, and complement to, her son in the realms of justice and politics. The repercussions of this partnership added to the sinister aspects of the last years of the reign. The dominant past perception of her as a pious but passive figure isolated in a brutal age must give place to a more complex one. Her life, like those of her contemporaries, was a mixture of rights and duties, of power and obligation, of aggression and compassion. She was no recluse, but a veteran of bruising political battles. A powerful figure in her age, she shared its cultural preoccupations, not only as has often been stressed, in the expression of a strong personal piety and interest in the advancement of learning, but in the fascination of the time with history and chivalry. These were not passive concepts, but part of the dynamic of political life. Like the possession of land and retinues, interest in them helped to define an individual's social importance.

In the realms of piety and patronage of learning the higher nobility to which Margaret belonged were moved by much the same tastes and interests as were the wealthier bourgeois. The two groups were bound by commercial and financial ties through the wide-ranging activities of individual merchants such as John Shaw and John Mundy and by the king's and nobles' dependence on the city of London. John Knight, of the parish of St Andrew in Holborn, London, left directions in his will for the safe custody of records which he held as auditor to a host of great men including the king and William Berkeley, earl of Nottingham, and Thomas Stanley, earl of Derby. His bequests included a primer

bound in velvet and unnamed books.[1] Lady Margaret may not herself
have owned a merchant fleet like John Howard, but she had her tolls
and markets at Boston and in the west country and she acted as a
moneylender though within a restricted court and family circle.[2]
Gentry and merchants as well as nobles could support scholars at
university and found chantries and colleges for priests. They also could
own books of hours for their devotions and be instructed in ways of
leading a prayerful daily life.[3]

The historical and chivalric aspects of this culture were celebrated on
a grand scale. The production of histories and romances usually took
place under the patronage of nobility or royalty. Spectacles and
tournaments, organized and backed financially by wealthy citizens,
starred the nobles as chief participants and accompanied major
political events. Edward IV was himself strongly influenced by the
chivalric revival propagated by the court of Burgundy under Philip the
Good and Charles the Bold. These dukes ruled territories approximating
to modern Belgium and Holland as well as Burgundy itself. They
conducted a foreign policy independent of France and the Empire, in
which relations with England had an important place. Edward IV's
youngest sister Margaret married Charles the Bold in 1468 amid a
blaze of elaborately staged pageantry, an event celebrated in Molinet's
poem *Le Trosne d'Honneur*. The theme of honour as portrayed in the
same poem inspired another pageant which accompanied the wedding
of Prince Arthur, son of Henry VII, to Catherine of Aragon in 1501.[4]
Lady Margaret had acted as hostess to part of the Spanish retinue on
that occasion and prepared for them a spectacular feast.[5] It was all part
of a spectrum of entertainment – disguisings, processions, jousts – with
scenery and props full of biblical and dynastic symbols designed to
cement the royal alliance.

The mixture of sacred and secular common in such events also

---

[1] Will of John Knight, 8 Sept. 1496, PRO, Prob. 11/11, 1 and 7 Horne.
[2] A. Crawford, 'The private life of John Howard', in *Loyalty, Lordship and Law*, ed. P. W.
Hammond (London, 1986), 9–10.
[3] See for the social range of patronage of learning and piety, J. R. Lander, 'Education and
the arts', in *Government and Community, England, 1450–1509* (London, 1980), 152–72;
P. Heath, 'Urban piety in the later middle ages', in *The Church, Politics and Patronage in
the Fifteenth Century*, ed. R. B. Dobson (Gloucester, 1984), 209–23. For ownership of
devotional books and training in devotional methods see C. de Hamel, *A History of
Illuminated Manuscripts* (London, 1986), 159–85; W. A. Pantin, 'Instructions for a
devout and literate layman', in *Medieval Learning and Literature: Essays Presented to
Richard William Hunt*, ed. J. J. G. Alexander and M. T. Gibson (Oxford, 1976), 399–422.
[4] Kipling, *The Triumph of Honour*, 75.   [5] Above, p. 166.

figured in the different kinds of literature familiar to Margaret and other nobles of her time. Her mother-in-law, Anne Neville, duchess of Buckingham, bequeathed her the *Legenda Sanctorum*, a book of saints' lives, translated into English; a lectionary in French; and a primer bound in red velvet and clasped in silver-gilt. These were books commonly used to aid the devotions of laypeople during the Latin mass. She left her besides, however, 'a book of French called Lucun', a French version of the works of the silver-age Latin poet Lucan, as Margaret herself was to leave not only mass books, but classical epics and the *Canterbury Tales*.[6]

Family attachments influenced deeply the ways in which piety was expressed. Margaret's own mother had inherited part of a psalter originally commissioned by her father-in-law, John earl of Somerset. She took care to have this incorporated in a new book of hours illustrated by the London painter William Abell. The book was passed on to Margaret and treasured as a place in which to enter details of family history and public events.[7] It was at her mother's suggestion that Margaret became a confrater of Crowland Abbey. The monks valued her good offices, as they had her mother's, in their quarrels with the men of Deeping, of which both women were successively ladies of the manor.

Lady Margaret honoured her mother and father with a chantry at Wimborne, the place of her father's death. Nor did she neglect her duty towards her grandmother, Margaret Holland. Margaret Holland's ancestors had founded Bourne Abbey in Lincolnshire and were buried there. Thomas Holland, earl of Kent, got licence from Richard II in 1397 to hold Wilsford Priory, a cell of the French abbey of Bec, and assign it to Bourne. This licence had remained unexecuted, and Bourne was still trying to assert its title to Wilsford in 1442.[8] One of Lady Margaret's first acts after her son's accession was to ask him to grant Wilsford and its possessions to the abbey. In doing so she honoured the name of the Hollands and righted what she must have considered an ancient injustice.[9] She and Stafford resided at Bourne Park near the abbey during the earlier part of their marriage and Margaret continued to visit it later and left it a mass book in her will.

---

[6] W. E. Axon, 'The Lady Margaret as a lover of literature', *The Library*, n.s., 8 (Jan. 1907), 34–41.   [7] BL, Royal MS 2A XVIII; above p. 32.

[8] *CPR*, 1396–9, 144; PRO, E135/22/90.

[9] Royal grant, 12 March 1486, *Materials*, I, 386–7.

These public acts of piety were supported by a pattern of private
devotions. Practices which in earlier times had largely been the
preserve of ascetics set apart from the world were during the fourteenth
and fifteenth centuries beginning to involve laity who were neither
hermits nor members of religious communities. The daily regime of
Joan, Lady Cobham (d. 1344), was marked by such devotions, but the
number and intricacy of them increased as time went on. The growth
and diffusion of cults such as that of the Holy Name of Jesus and the
Five Wounds of Christ is evidence of the importance placed on the
believer's personal attachment to Jesus and the emblems of his Passion.
The greater number of vernacular spiritual writings, in both French
and English, from the end of the fourteenth century onwards gave the
laity guides by which private attitudes could be more searchingly
examined. Prayer became a discipline not reserved to holy men or
places, but permeating the whole of life.[10] This gave an added edge to
the traditional problem of how to combine a good Christian life with
one lived amid the pressures of the world. Walter Hilton, the great
English mystic, was addressing this problem at the end of the
fourteenth century in his treatise of Mixed or Medled Life. This was
written for a temporal lord to guide him in combining private worship
and meditation with the demands of tenants, his household, and the
general litigious bustle which made up the busy world of his
contemporaries. Hilton's combination of practicality and orthodoxy
had a particular appeal for Lady Margaret, on whom such lessons were
not lost. She had commissioned the printing of his *Scala Perfectionis* by
Wynkyn de Worde in 1494, but bought another copy in 1507, when
Julian the notary printed an edition which also contained Hilton's
treatise on Mixed Life. Part of Wynkyn de Worde's verse colophon of
1494 was appended at the end of the volume.[11]

The devotions of the great and noble, of which there are detailed
accounts, need to be set in the context of more general expectations
about personal piety in the fifteenth century. The child, whether
wealthy bourgeois, gentle or noble, was brought up to say religious
offices and attend mass, as part of the wider social obligations

[10] Pantin, 'Instructions', 408–9; C. Richmond, 'Religion and the fifteenth century
  gentleman', in *Church, Politics and Patronage in the Fifteenth Century*, ed. R. B. Dobson
  (Gloucester, 1984), 194–208.
[11] H. M. Gardner, 'Walter Hilton and the mystical tradition in England', *Essays and Studies*,
  22 (1936), 108; SJC, D91.19, p. 9, March 1507.

attendant on being part of a household.[12] Sir John Heveningham, a
moderately wealthy gentleman, used to hear three masses by 9 a.m.,
before going into his garden 'to say a little devotion'.[13] Fisher recalled
that Lady Margaret herself rose at 5 a.m. to hear 'four or five masses'
before breakfast. Cecily Neville, duchess of York, rose slightly later, at
7 a.m., and heard matins and low mass in her chamber. The rest of
both Margaret's and Cecily's devotional day was apportioned between
private prayers, reading and meditation, and the more public service of
their chapels.[14]

Privacy in devotion, whether alone or in the presence of a confessor,
spiritual director or waiting woman, seems to have been expected in
the fifteenth century. A merchant could be advised to go to 'his secret
chamber' for prayer and serious conversation with chosen friends and
advisers. The oratories and private chapels of wealthy laymen, inspired
perhaps by the rich chapels of some bishops and abbots, were patently
designed to assist this seclusion. Even more striking were the chambers
with windows looking onto the interiors of the chapels, such as Lady
Margaret had at Christ's College.[15] In a household book printed by
Wynkyn de Worde the chamberlain is told 'at morn' to go to the
church or chapel 'to your soverayne's closet and laye carpentes and
cuysshons and lay downe his boke of prayers, than drawe the
curtynes'.[16] One is reminded of Roland Lockey's portrait of Margaret in
which she is shown at prayer, in front of a luxurious heraldically
decorated hanging, shielded by a canopy and resting on a prie-dieu. In
a wider sense such withdrawal was part of the privacy and comfort
available to those who built lodges, pavilions and belvederes, and
increasingly complex living quarters behind their great halls, as did
Margaret at Maxstoke and Collyweston.

[12] Caxton's *Book of Courtesy*, first printed at Westminster 1477–8, ed. F. J. Furnivall, EETS,
o.s., 3 (1868), 5, 12, 35.

[13] Richmond, 'Religion', 199. The hearing of a number of masses was partly a consequence
of a rather mechanical view of their effect on the plight of souls in purgatory, but prayers
at mass were said for many other personal needs. For a recent survey of the social
implications of the doctrine see C. Burgess, 'A fond thing vainly invented: an essay on
Purgatory and pious motive in late medieval England', in *Parish, Church and people*, ed. S.
J. Wright (London, 1988), 56–84.

[14] Armstrong, 'The piety of Cicely', 135–56.

[15] For Christ's see p. 225. Mention of conversation with friends as well as spiritual advisers
in the 'Instructions' suggests a secular parallel: those 'secret households' of the fifteenth
century which formed inner cabinets to run the greater household; M. Girouard, *Life in
The English Country House* (Harmondsworth, 1980), 76–8.

[16] *The Lay Folks Mass Book*, ed. T. F. Simmons, EETS, o.s., 71 (1879), xxxviii n. 7.

Just as the glazed windows of the oratories looked onto the chapels, and the parlours adjoined the great halls, so the thread of private devotion and meditative reading, alone or with companions, was linked to the more public worship of the great chapels of the nobility, and to the conviviality of tables overspread by canopies and laden with plate. Henry Parker recalled of Margaret that at the beginning of dinner her conversation was 'joyous' because she liked 'merry tales' (and indeed included Boccaccio and Chaucer in her library); later in the meal her almoner or Parker himself would read her 'a virtuous story'. Just before rising high seriousness was reached, when she would talk of 'godly matters' with the bishop near her.[17] Cecily duchess of York's lunch-hour was filled with the reading of such works as Walter Hilton's tract on Mixed Life, Bonaventure's *Life of Christ*, and accounts of visions of the mystics. After lunch she would spend a busy hour receiving petitions and attending to suits, and at supper she would repeat to those about her some of the things she had heard at lunch. One gets the impression that the duchess's taste in reading, as in tapestries and hangings, was if anything more overtly pious than Lady Margaret's.[18] To judge from their horaria Margaret made slightly more use of her chapel, for visiting altars and for private devotions. Parker remembered it as a notable liturgical centre, 'in no way inferior to the king's'.

Chapels and colleges were the settings for cults and patterns of worship which particularly appealed to their owners. Lady Hungerford had a striking attachment to the use of the Bridgettines of Syon Abbey. Combined with the use of Sarum it influenced the order of services in her mortuary chapel at Salisbury.[19] Margaret Beaufort had an especial devotion to the Holy Name of Jesus, of whose feast she was recognized patron by the pope, and the office and mass of the Name of Jesus were certainly used in her chapel. John de Gigli, papal collector in England (1485–90) and bishop of Worcester (1497–8), dedicated to Margaret a manuscript of the office and proper of the mass attached to the feast. Its elaborate introits rehearsing the names and virtues of Christ evoke a splendid liturgy such as could certainly have been conducted before her. The dedicatory verses in the manuscript hail her as the king's

---

[17] Warnicke, 'The Lady Margaret', 47–55.

[18] Armstrong, 'The piety of Cicely', 143–53, and the duchess's will in *Wills from Doctors' Commons, 1495–1695* ed. J. G. Nichols and J. Bruce, Camden Society, o.s., 83 (1863), 2; cf. the discussion of Lady Margaret's tapestries, below p. 189.

[19] M. A. Hicks, 'The piety of Margaret Lady Hungerford', *Journal of Ecclesiastical History*, 38 (1987), 1–38.

mother 'tanti dignissima mater regis' and ask her to accept this witness of her sacred praises (no doubt a reference to her celebration of the Name in her worship), humble though it is and not suitably bound in jewels and gold as it ought to be. Margaret is prayed to remember the donor, Gigli, and she and her son are wished long life, and he as great success in war as he has in peace. Finally Jesus 'who gave his name to this little book' is asked to give greater heed to Margaret's prayers. Gigli was close to another object of Margaret's affection, for he dedicated to Cardinal Morton a work on the canonization of saints relevant to the contemporary cause of Henry VI.[20]

Lady Margaret's chapel housed not only the books and furnishings necessary to sing mass, but the images of various saints. Statues of St Mary Magdalene, holding her box of the ointment with which she anointed the head of Christ, of St John the Baptist and of St George were presented after her death to Christ's College. From her executors St John's College got those of St Margaret, her patron, St Anne, St Peter, St Anthony and another statue of St George. In her chapel were also altar cloths worked with the figures of St Margaret and St Mary Magdalene, their backgrounds sprinkled with embroidered flowers; while others represented the Trinity, which also figured on a communion chalice, and the Passion of Christ. One altar cloth featured St Leonard, the French hermit saint who was the patron of prisoners and the sick. Copes were worked with the figures of St Katherine, St Mary Magdalene and St George.[21] Fisher recalled in his month-mind sermon that Margaret's 'peculiar fasts of devotion' were on the days of 'St Anthony, St Mary Maudeleyne, St Katheryn, with other'. The saints he named, also represented in her chapel furnishings, were all commonly associated with works of mercy and were frequently patrons of hospitals. St John the Baptist, St Anthony and St Leonard led the life of hermits, while St Mary Magdalene typified compassion and penitence. St Katherine touched an aspect of charity especially important to Margaret, for the saint was recognized as the special patron of scholars, and had been adopted by a new Cambridge college,

---

[20] Underwood, 'Politics and piety', 47–8. Gigli's manuscript is BL, Add. MS 33772; see Plate 14. For his dedication to Morton see C. Harper Bill, 'The familia of Archbishop Morton', *Journal of Religious History*, 10 (1979), 248 n. 74.

[21] Inventory of chapel stuff, n.d., c. 1509, SJC, D102.13.

St Catharine's, as recently as 1473.[22] Asceticism, or at least austerity, and almsgiving seem therefore to have figured largely with her, although she never showed a marked respect for the claims of hospitals: she neglected to pursue her great-uncle's interest in St Cross at Winchester, and transformed the hospital of St John at Cambridge into a college.

Rather different is the note struck by the presence of St George, warrior, symbol of the nation and patron of the Order of the Garter whose robes Margaret on occasion wore. The statue transferred to Christ's showed the saint on a green mount; under his feet writhed the diabolical dragon which he was treading down. The dragon in a different context, however, represented Cadwallader, Wales and the Welshness of the Tudor dynasty. Among her plate were twelve flagons 'wreathen with chains issuing from dragons' necks and swans' necks'. There was a constant intrusion of her family and dynasty into sacred themes: on the vestments of her chapel the sign for Jesus, IHS, was often coupled with her own Beaufort emblem of the portcullis, while 'margaretts' (marguerites), the large daisies which represented her own name, were frequently worked into both vestments and plate.[23] The dynastic dimension was never far from any aspect of her life.

In a society in which death was expected to occur early, and a long life therefore regarded as a reprieve, a good deal of attention was lavished on family monuments, chantries, chapels and charitable works, as a preparation for the afterlife. Lady Hungerford actually carried out a financial obligation which she might have escaped – discharging her son's debts – out of a desire for the salvation of her own and her husband's souls.[24] Margaret Beaufort gradually constructed her complex will between 1472 and 1509 inspired by successive family and religious obligations, until the final product was to benefit both her family's souls and the cause of education, in the chantries of Christ's and St John's Colleges and at Wimborne Minster. Such monuments, however, were only half the picture for attention had also to be paid to corporal works of mercy, and the increasingly well-mapped life of prayer. Walter Hilton had understood very well that

[22] S. C. Aston, 'Ad honorem Sancte Katerinae Virginis', in *St. Catharine's College 1473–1973*, ed. E. E. Rich (Cambridge, 1973), 33–58.

[23] R. F. Scott, 'On a list of the plate, books and vestments bequeathed by the Lady Margaret to Christ's College', *Communications of the Cambridge Antiquarian Society*, 9 (1899), 355–61; inventory of plate, SJC, D91.1, pp. 5–6.

[24] Hicks, 'The piety of Lady Hungerford', 25.

a layperson immersed in worldly business had a duty to his or her dependants. According to him, tending them was to be like tending the feet of Christ.[25]

Lady Margaret's solicitude for her dependants was vouched for by both Parker and Fisher. Her household accounts bear witness to daily expenditure on her almsfolk, with characteristic personal touches such as primers bought for two poor children, and arrangements for boarding out and caring for the children of poor women.[26] Fisher paints a portrait of her occupying all her senses in different aspects of piety:

> her ears hearing the word of God and the divine service, which daily was kept in her chapel with great number of priests, clerks and children, to her great charge and cost; her tongue occupied in prayer much of the day; her legges and feet in visiting the altars and other holy places, going her stations customably when she was not let; her hands in giving alms to the poor and needy, and dressing them also when they were sick, and ministering unto them meat and drink.[27]

These acts of compassion are made more poignant by what follows, when Fisher describes her own, probably arthritic, pain: 'these mercyfull and lyberall handes to endure the moost paynfull crampes soo grevously vexynge her and compellynge her to crye, "O blessyd Ihesu helpe me. O blessyd lady socoure me."' The fragility of life, the vulnerability of even the great and noble to suffering, was thus borne in upon her servants, who were moved to pray for her, while at the same time being set an example of charity.

The Shepherd's Calendar, another popular devotional work bought by Margaret towards the end of her life, sets such works of mercy in the wider context of social and moral obligations.[28] Man is seen as a moral and physical unit: abstaining from certain foods is one facet of the 'governance of health'; other aspects are not taking sudden vengeance, doing no violence to the poor and suffering no detraction at table. Within the household no division is to be suffered, and this increases personal prosperity. Parker related how Margaret praised to her servants one of their number, Ralph Bigod, a former knight of the body to Richard III, for not allowing detraction of his erstwhile master. He

---

[25] Gardner, 'Walter Hilton and the mystical tradition', 107.
[26] SJC, D91.20, pp. 171–2, 180–2; D91.21, pp. 39, 100; D91.19, p. 22; Underwood, 'Politics and piety', 41.　　　　[27] *Mornynge Remembraunce*, 300.
[28] SJC, D91.19, p. 13; *The Shepherd's Calendar*, ed. G. C. Heseltine (London, 1930), 118–20.

was thus held up as an example of a loyalty which transcended personal and political enmities, and the unity of the household was subtly enhanced. Fisher stressed this skill of hers in 'bolting out', or exposing, causes of friction between her officers. In his eyes and those of other contemporaries it was a consequence of the pious and sober conduct of her own life.

It is therefore in the domain of social duty as well as private motivation that we have to consider Lady Margaret's piety, and this leads us always back to the court, the royal family, and her impact on national life. The elderly lady who needed spectacles to read her 'French books', sacred and secular, also enjoyed a unique status, supplying the place usually occupied by a queen dowager.[29] Her devotion to the reformed Franciscans, the Observants, who granted her confraternity in 1497, was also shared by Edward IV and Henry VII. Henry had confirmed Edward's reception of them into England and granted them the use of the chapel of Holy Cross, Greenwich, in 1494. In 1498 he persuaded the conventual Franciscans to make over three houses to the Observants and founded a house for them at Richmond in about 1500.[30] She was interested enough in the king's affection for the order to contribute through his confessor towards building an Observant house in France.[31]

Royal and family connections, as well as personal interest, dictated her enthusiasm for the Carthusians, an order encouraged by the crown through its important foundation at Sheen in 1414, and for the Bridgettines. Margaret visited the Sheen charterhouse and the Bridgettines at Syon, offering at the rood of the charterhouse in 1498. A papal licence granted her leave in 1504 to visit, converse and dine with the inmates of enclosed houses.[32] Margaret's grandmother, the duchess of Clarence, had likewise received papal permission to visit and enlist the prayers of the Bridgettines of Syon. She had encouraged their piety by disseminating copies of the Life of Jerome, composed by a male member of that double community and dedicated to her. The work was printed by Wynkyn de Worde in 1499. In her own relations with these communities, both through personal contact with their members and

---

[29] Spectacles and spectacle cases are mentioned in inventories of her goods, SJC, D91.5, pp. 24–5.

[30] A. G. Little, 'The introduction of the Observant Friars into England', *Proceedings of the British Academy*, 10 (1921–3), 461–3.   [31] SJC, D91.20, p. 80.

[32] SJC, D56.20; E. M. Thompson, *The Carthusian Order in England* (London, 1930), 340–1.

in encouraging wider circulation of devotional texts, Lady Margaret was to follow in the footsteps of the duchess.[33]

There had also been enthusiasm for the Carthusians in the Beaufort family: Cardinal Beaufort had a Carthusian confessor and was a benefactor to the order. It is quite likely that Margaret communicated her own interest to her last husband, Thomas Stanley: when the Chartreuse extended confraternity to them both in 1478 the grant included Stanley's first wife, Eleanor Neville, and other members of his family.[34] Margaret maintained a scholar, Richard Moyne, at the charterhouse of London, and received a gift of books from a monk there.[35] The prior of the charterhouse at Coventry, the only one officially to maintain a school, brought to her in 1507 news of a bequest by a widow of the town to Christ's College. It may be that the testatrix, who had already provided for the Coventry house and made Lady Margaret supervisor of her will, wished to ensure a route for the charterhouse's scholars to Cambridge.[36]

As one would expect from a patron of education, Lady Margaret's interest in contemporary piety extended to its dissemination. The nature of her involvement, however, needs careful examination. She was not simply a pious laywoman lending the London printers her name to grace the devotional works which left their presses. It has been convincingly suggested that she and other royal ladies were also, with their households, a market for books of devotion and meditation which became increasingly common products of the presses of Caxton towards the end of his life and of his successor Wynkyn de Worde. It was not so much the personal taste of the printers which dominated the market, as their response to an existing demand. The demand was produced by a cultural milieu in which the great nobles played the leading part.[37]

It was not piety, however, but politics which had drawn Caxton and Lady Margaret together. The first book whose printing she is known to have commissioned was a romance, originally from a thirteenth-century French source, called *Blanchardin and Eglantine*. When Caxton

---

[33] G. Keiser, 'Patronage and piety in fifteenth century England: Margaret duchess of Clarence, Symon Wynter, and Beinecke MS 317', *Yale University Library Gazette* (October, 1985), 32–46. [34] SJC, D56.185.

[35] July 1502, household accounts SJC, D91.20, p. 30; Underwood, 'Politics and piety', 48.

[36] Below, p. 229, and Underwood, 'Politics and piety', 51.

[37] G. Keiser, 'The mystics and the early English printers', in *Exeter Symposium IV, Papers read at Dartington Hall* ed. M. Glasscoe (July, 1987), 9–25.

first sold it to her the action of the romance mirrored some of the
political events of the time. In 1483 Lady Margaret's envoy Lewis, her
physician, had come to negotiate secretly with Queen Elizabeth
Woodville in sanctuary from Richard III at Westminster, near Caxton's
shop. The subject of negotiation was the marriage of Margaret's son
Henry and Woodville's daughter, Elizabeth of York. Like the heroine of
the story, Princess Elizabeth was to be a damsel constant 'to the man
she had promysed and agreed to' and Henry the plighted husband who
had put his life 'oft in jeopardy' for her.[38] Like Blanchardin, Henry was
exiled from his intended bride, and the situation of the romance, with
Eglantine besieged by her enemies, was not unlike that of the confined
queen and her daughter, surrounded by the threat of Richard's regime.
Margaret kept the book which Caxton had sold her for six years,
returning it to him in 1489 with a command to translate and print it.
That same year Caxton established himself in Henry VII's patronage
with his edition of the *Faytes of Armes*, and in 1490 his *Eneydos* was
dedicated to Prince Arthur. His last book for named patrons was of a
different kind: he printed for Queen Elizabeth and Lady Margaret an
edition of *The Fifteen Oes*, prayers attributed to St Bridget of Sweden.[39]

If Caxton thus came into the king's favour through that of Lady
Margaret, his successor de Worde continued to find a ready market in
the countess and her protégee the queen. The circumstances of his
printing Hilton's *Scala Perfectionis* in 1494 show the close relations
between monastic editors, the printing trade and the personal standing
of a noble patron. We know from the dedicatory verses that Margaret
was well acquainted with the text: 'This hevenly boke, more precyous
than golde, / Was late dyrect, with great humylyte, / For godly plesur
thereon to beholde, / Unto the right noble Margaret, as ye see, / The
kyngis moder, of excellente bounte, / ...This mythty pryncesse hath
commaunded me / T'emprynt this boke, her grace for to deserve.' The
text was beloved of the Carthusians, and members of the Sheen and
London charterhouses were in the 1490s instrumental in disseminating the version of the manuscript from which de Worde's edition
was made.[40] Carthusians and Bridgettines established a version of the
text, which included a long passage about the Name of Jesus probably

---

[38] *Blanchardin and Eglantine* ed. L. Kellner, EETS, e.s., 58 (London, 1890), 1.

[39] G. D. Painter, *William Caxton* (London, 1976), 166–9, 183–4.

[40] H. M. Gardner, 'The text of the Scale of Perfection' *Medium Aevum*, 22 (1936), 11–30;
The Scale of Perfection, ed. G. Sitwell (London, 1953), v.

in Hilton's original. They also made various interpolations elsewhere which dwelt upon and invoked the Name, sometimes substituting 'Jesus' for 'God'. The same year the work was printed the pope recognized Lady Margaret as promoter of the feast of the Name in England. The marks of her personal devotion – her hearts of precious metal and collars of gold on which IHS was inscribed, the celebration of the Name in the liturgy of her chapel, her alteration of the name of 'God's House' Cambridge to 'Christ's' – were thus paralleled by efforts to publicize the feast of which she was patron. She was herself concerned to circulate de Worde's book: a copy was presented by her and the queen to Lady Margery Roos, their lady-in-waiting.[41]

Lady Margaret's efforts on behalf of devotional literature extended much further, however. She encouraged book purchase and production, undertook translations herself and bought up many copies when they were printed. Richard Pynson was paid for a hundred books in 1505, and in 1506 for fifty books 'the whiche my lady's grace translatyd oute of French into Englysshe'.[42] She provided Ingelbert de la Haghe, a Rouen printer, with money to spend for her on books at Paris. Ingelbert printed at her expense an edition of the Hereford breviary, and she bought from him two mass books printed on vellum.[43] Her chapel was furnished with printed books of the office for the Holy Name, and a servant who worked there, Leonard of the Vestry, acted on occasion as a bookbinder. Another servant, Peter Baldwyn, who worked at her London mansion of Coldharbour, was referred to as binder and illuminator.[44] John Fisher himself expounded before her the penitential psalms, a necessary part of books of hours at this period, and his sermons were printed by de Worde in 1509. At least five copies were bound and circulated in the household, and de Worde was paid for six copies in 1509.[45]

---

[41] P. J. Crofts, 'A copy of Walter Hylton's Scala Perfectionis', *Sale Catalogue, Bernard Quaritch Ltd* (London, 1958). Lady Margaret also disseminated a number of images on parchment in her household, Underwood, 'Politics and piety', 49.

[42] SJC, D91.21, pp. 27, 142. The fifty were no doubt copies of the *Mirror of Gold for the Sinful Soul*.

[43] SJC, D91.21, pp. 43, 164; H. Plomer, *Wynkyn de Worde and his Contemporaries* (London, 1925), 30.

[44] Books for the office, 1504, SJC, D91.20, p. 171; Inglebert, 1505, D91.21, p. 43; Leonard, 1503, D91.20, p. 111; Peter, 1502, D91.20, p. 25, 1507, D91.19, p. 17.

[45] SJC, D91.19, p. 112; D102.1, fol. 5v; *The English Works of John Fisher*, ed. Mayor, 1–2, 267.

Margaret's own activity as a translator singles her out among English women aristocrats of the period. She confined herself to translating from French, for her knowledge of Latin was sufficient only to read the headings of her service books. She confided to Fisher that she regretted not having paid more attention to the study of the language when she was young.[46] Consequently, she had to rely on the expertise of the learned: in her translation of the *Mirror of Gold for the Sinful Soul* she relied on the French edition issued at Paris and corrected 'de plus clercs, maistres et docteurs en theologie'. This spiritual treatise, aimed at providing insights about the world and about holiness, by which the sinner could be led towards repentance, was afterwards printed for Margaret by Richard Pynson, *c.* 1506.[47]

Her most famous work of translation was that of the fourth book of the *Imitation of Christ* by Thomas à Kempis. This book, 'exhortatio ad sacram communionem', was an encouragement to the faithful to receive the sacrament frequently and an exposition of the importance of the mass in the Christian life. The fourth book had formed part of the *Imitation* as preserved in the finished original work of à Kempis (1441), but was scarcely known in England. The first English translation of the *Imitation*, written in the mid-fifteenth century, had a very restricted circulation.[48] Margaret commissioned William Atkinson, a fellow of Jesus College, Cambridge, to provide a new English translation of the first three books of the *Imitation*. It was far more rhetorical, indeed freer, in style than the old version and Atkinson modified the discourse on monastic life so as to make it appeal to laity in the world who sought guidance in their daily devotional life. Margaret herself, unable to match Atkinson in working from the Latin, translated the fourth book from a French version. Their combined work was published by Pynson in 1504.[49] The appearance of the complete text in a new English version marked a landmark in the history of the book in England.

---

[46] *Mornynge Remembraunce*, 292; but there are signs that she had not given up, even in old age: SJC, D91.21, p. 9, 'to sir Christopher clerk of the closet for a book bought for my lady grace called Vergil, 6s 8d'.   [47] Brunet, III, col. 1751, *STC*, I, 6894.5.

[48] *De Imitatione Christi*, ed. J. K. Ingrams, EETS, e.s., 63 (1893), xxiv. For the background to the *Imitatio* in England, see R. Lovett, 'The Imitation of Christ in late medieval England', *Transactions of the Royal Historical Society*, 18 (1968), 97–121.

[49] *STC*, II, 23954.7. Leonard of the Vestry bound seventy-six copies 'of John Gerson's printing' during 1503, SJC, D91.20, p. 122. The reference is to the *Imitatio*, the authorship of which was sometimes ascribed to Jean Gerson, the early fifteenth-century chancellor of Paris university. A London printer was also paid for 'printing my lady's books', *ibid.*, p. 104.

Another edition of the combined translations was issued in 1517 by Pynson and in 1518 or 1519 by Wynkyn de Worde. De Worde published another edition of the first three books only in 1528, by which time perhaps the need was felt for a fresh translation of the whole from the original Latin. The need was met by an anonymous translator in about 1531. Such was still the standing of Atkinson's and Margaret's work, however, that the translator explained that his own respected the 'substance and effect' of theirs.[50]

It is as well not to underrate the commercial aspects of the relations between Margaret and the printers. She provided both inspiration and the opportunity for competition between the rivals Pynson and de Worde, and in the process helped to popularize English translations of continental works. Her undoubted personal zest for translating fitted well with the notions of Pynson himself. In his preface to the *Shepherd's Calendar* he makes the 'corrupt' language of an earlier edition, which in fact had merely been written in a Scottish dialect, an excuse for issuing his own.[51] Her household was a market for these leading printers, and the use of her name as a sign of royal approval was as important to them as her personal interest. The background to the edition of *The Ship of Fools* which de Worde published on 6 July 1509, after her death, bears witness to the commercial elements at work in patronage.

The *Ship of Fools* by Sebastian Brandt was one of the most popular works of the early sixteenth century. It was a satire on the mores of the time, composed by a stern German moralist who yet claimed to be successor to Horace and Lucilius. It became the vehicle in various Latin, French and English versions for a variety of interpolations apposite to contemporary personalities and events, the subjects varying according to national taste. Pynson and de Worde competed to bring out an English version of the work, employing different translators.

---

[50] H. S. Bennett, *English Books and Readers, 1475–1557* (Cambridge, 1969), 170. Serious doubt has been cast on the identity of Richard Whitford as the translator. See Glanmor Williams, 'Two neglected London Welsh clerics, Richard Whitford and Richard Gwent', *Transactions of the Honourable Society of Cymmrodorion*, 1 (1961), 23–44, especially 30–1. We are grateful to Veronica Lawrence for this reference.

[51] The earlier edition was the *Kalendar of Shyppars*, printed at Paris in 1503; *The Shepherd's Calendar*, ed. Heseltine, foreword. Margaret acquired one unnamed edition of the work, in March 1507 (accounts, SJC, D91.19, p. 13), and de Worde's edition, translated by Robert Copeland, in February 1509 (D102.1, fol. 5v). For Copeland's work see Bennett, *English Books*, 116, 162.

Pynson's was Alexander Barclay, a learned priest, who worked away under the patronage of the bishop of Bath and Wells at the college of Ottery St Mary, Devon. During 1508 and 1509 he translated a French verse paraphrase of *The Ship* published at Paris in 1497, itself made from a Latin translation. In 1499 a prose paraphrase of the French verse one had appeared, this time published at Lyons. The competitiveness of the French printers was to be mirrored in their English colleagues. In 1509 Wynkyn de Worde asked his apprentice, Henry Watson, to produce a prose translation (shorter and more accessible than the verse) of the prose Lyons paraphrase. Although de Worde credited Lady Margaret with having 'enticed and exhorted' Watson to do the work, his own market sense was the prime mover. In the event his edition came out first, in July, while the more cumbrous verse translation by Barclay, textually far superior, appeared from Pynson's press in December. The story serves as a warning not to overestimate Margaret's personal commitment to all projects associated with her.[52]

We should also consider the immediate circumstances of *The Ship*'s publication, for here again the dynastic associations in Margaret's piety appear. De Worde had printed Fisher's sermons on the penitential psalms in 1508, with a second edition in 1509. At Margaret's desire he also printed Fisher's sermon at Henry VII's funeral, and shortly afterwards his 'mornynge remembraunce' of Margaret herself, the new king's 'grandame' as she was called on its title page. After all his work de Worde could fairly justly be termed Lady Margaret's printer. If her connection with the publication of *The Ship* was largely imputed by him after her death, he still could find useful the publicity of having worked for the grandmother of the reigning monarch.

The Ship lent itself gloriously to the celebration of the new reign: Brandt's original work had included panegyrics of the Holy Roman Empire, but both Pynson and de Worde now interpolated glowing references to England and her rulers. Barclay adjusted verses in praise of the Red Rose to include a reference to the new young king, and Watson made similar adjustments in his prologue. Since Barclay's references to Henry VIII and the Red Rose are much more frequent and passionate than those of Watson, the pre-emption of Pynson's edition by de Worde's must have been the more galling for him. Unlike Caxton before him, however, de Worde was not to find his way into royal

[52] A. Pompen, *The English Versions of the Ship of Fools* (London, 1925), 283.

favour through having served Margaret: perhaps her death forestalled his success, but Pynson became the king's printer instead.[53]

The importance of Lady Margaret's name for the printers, through whom she helped to popularize devotional literature, was but one expression of her independent public standing. Within the royal court she seems to have been accorded a role as guardian of certain aspects of protocol. Numerous copies of a set of ordinances made by her for clothes to be worn in time of mourning have survived; the immediate occasion, in 1503, was Queen Elizabeth's death. Ordinances for royal christenings have also been attributed to her, and her willingness to draw up regulations was characteristic: Fisher records the reading of her household statutes four times a year.[54] Margaret's association with the court and its culture entailed an extrovert existence not often associated with her, it having been overshadowed by her reputation for personal austerity. Yet a court life she certainly had, regularly appearing with the king during the early 1490s at Christmas, Easter and at Garter feasts. Her wardrobe at the end of her life contained relics of those days. During her last decade she kept her own court at Collyweston but she occasionally visited her son, and her last public appearance was at the feast for her grandson's coronation.

Margaret had enjoyed since her son's accession a degree of legal and social independence not achieved by many contemporaries until widowhood.[55] Her right to hold property 'as anie other sole person not covert to anie husband' was recognized in her son's first parliament. She also obtained permission from Stanley to adopt the chaste state of the widow in advance of his death, a concession appropriate to her independent standing. The vow before John Fisher by which she

---

[53] *Ibid*, 283, 286.

[54] The most authentic copy of the mourning ordinances is that in BL, Add. MS 45133, fol. 141v, lacking some of the elaborations of Harley MS 6072. In 1507 money was paid from the household to the Garter herald 'for making a book to wear mourning clothes by', perhaps a revision of the ordinances of 1502–3 (SJC, D91.19, p. 8). The christening ordinances are printed by Leland, III, 179–84, from Harley MS 6079. Recently, however, doubts have been raised about their authenticity; K. Staniland, 'Royal entry into the world', in *England in the Fifteenth Century*, ed. D. Williams (London, 1987). For Fisher's remarks on her statutes, see *Mornynge Remembraunce*, 296.

[55] This was often assumed as a formal state with its own dress, disciplines of prayer and charitable works, and many women took a canonical form of oath in church to dedicate themselves to the life. It also, however, meant freedom from suitors and sole possession of land and income. For these oaths, and the role of the *viduata* see *Documents of the Diocese of Lincoln, 1450–1544*, ed. A. Clark, EETS, o.s., 149 (1914), 19–21.

confirmed her state of chastity after 1504 was also remarkable in that it did not follow an established canonical form, making no mention of the rule of St Paul, or of any biblical authority. Margaret merely invoked God the Father, Jesus, Mary and the company of heaven as witnesses, and committed herself to Fisher's spiritual guidance.[56]

Lady Margaret's presence as a royal personage is conveyed strongly in the half-length portrait of *c.* 1530 in the master's lodge at Christ's College, possibly based on the miniature of her by Lucas Hornbolte. Unlike the Lockey portrait, it does not show her at prayer, although she clasps an open book of devotions, but portrays a woman of regal pose looking out of her picture. Lady Margaret was physically slight, but the alertness of these eyes beneath high-arched brows would rapidly have commanded attention. The style of the portrait is the same as that of a series of likenesses of the late Plantagenet kings.[57]

The apparently sombre dress of her portraits should not mislead us into envisaging a withdrawn and subdued person. It was indeed a dress appropriate to the order of widowhood, with a wimple overlaid by a transparent white barb worn over the chin. These, with the black or dark brown dress, give her the appearance of a nun, especially when set starkly against an embroidered canopy. Yet barbs were a feature of court dress and figure in her mourning ordinances, while a gabled coif was in fashion at the time. The ordinances themselves drew back from excess in this respect: no widow's peak which overshadowed the face was to be worn 'for the deformity of the same'. Margaret's own peaked headdress left her face open and visible, and was in no sense a veil over the features. Black itself was as much a shade of wealth as of austerity, and was favoured as princely attire by René of Anjou and Philip the Good.[58] In Margaret's wardrobe at her death were seven gowns of black velvet set off with ermine trimmings, and a mantle of tawny. Along with these there remained an old scarlet gown with a long train, ornamented with badges of the Garter and evidently to be worn on St George's day. In another inventory we find a crimson gown to be worn with her 'circuit', not a diadem but a surcoat, such as she had worn at Christmas 1487. At the royal marriage of 1501 her men's livery was of medled tawny (a cloth of more than one colour), while her chariot

---

[56] Fisher's comment on the vow, *Mornynge Remembraunce*, 294; the text is given in Cooper, 97, from SJC, C7.11, fol. 47.   [57] Plates 2–4; Appendix 6 below.
[58] J. Huizinga, *The Waning of the Middle Ages* (London, 1924), 249.

men wore scarlet. The very buttons of the horse harness were of gold of Venice.[59]

The splendid furnishings by which she was surrounded sounded no deeply pietistic note. The themes of her tapestries at Hatfield and Croydon at the end of her life were predominantly those of epic heroism: the fates of kings and heroes. Some were legends beloved in Burgundy and at her son's court: the labours of Hercules, the tales of Alexander, and of Hannibal to whom Henry VII was once compared by Oxford university. One was a story of modern heroism: that of Matthew Gough one of her father's war captains. With these were epics of the Old Testament, King Saul, Sampson, Nebuchadnezzar and, in the tapestry of 'Parys, Helen and Moyses', classical and biblical themes combined. Among the verdours recently made at her death were ten pieces illustrating the theme of the Red Rose and the White, while roses and portcullises abounded among the hangings.

An inventory of the closet next her bedchamber, made at her death, gives a fascinating glimpse of the variety of objects by which she was surrounded in her inner chambers. It was a hoard which combined her personal needs with the extravagant allurement of precious metals. Images of piety took their place beside the evidences of legal bargains and struggles which absorbed much of her life. Here, among items in a 'litell blak cofre' were silver pots for medicinal powders, 'a lytell goblet of golde havinge on the kever [cover] a portcullis', silver candlesticks and spoons, 'a smal shryne gilt with reliques and glased', a 'litell bag conteyning a hert of reliques', 'a plate sylver and gylt with the ymage of the salutacion of our lady'. There were also two pairs of gold spectacles, ivory combs and purses, one of gold chequered with 'trewluffs of grene': the love-knots of fidelity, whether to Christ or earthly lovers. Another purse held 'cramp rings' of gold and silver. These were remedies against the stiffness of her joints lamented by Fisher in his month-mind sermon. Nearby, in an inner cupboard within a locker, were stored bonds, indentures of marriage and annuities arranged for her dependants, and title deeds of her own, such as the jointure made to her by her husband, Thomas Stanley, and the king's patent for founding the Cambridge preachership. In another chest, or 'standard', pieces of linen were folded with two primers, or service books, bound in velvet, one of which was to find its way to

---

[59] Inventories, 1509, SJC, D91.2, pp. 1, 3, 5, D91.3, p. 11, 14, D91.6, p. 6; dress at the marriage, D102.2, fol. 26v, D102.6, p. 6.

William Smith the bishop of Lincoln, the other to the future Henry VIII, her grandson.[60]

In the keeping of Margaret's gentlewoman, Edith Fowler, yet more lavish items were found. They included plenty of pure jewels and jewellery: twelve great pearls, five little rubies, three stones set in gold with a sapphire and three rubies, three gold rings, one embellished with the device of the Garter, whose robes Margaret wore, another with a diamond, the third with a turquoise. There were obscure curiosities: pieces of 'unicorn's horn' (narwhal horn) and 'a serpent's tonge sett in golde garnished with perlis'. There were also curiosities of piety: 'a rose with an image of oure lorde and in every naile [of the cross] a pointede diamonde, and four perles with tokens of the passion on the bake side'. A note records that all the diamonds were afterwards, in the general pillage of her goods, set in the king's Garter badge. Two 'books of gold' had golden leaves as mounts for images: a portable compendium of saints made from precious metal. Images were frequently set in gold in this way like icons, sometimes in isolated 'tablets': one such was modelled on the rood, the crucifix with Mary and St John in attendance, St John the Baptist being on the back.[61]

The named religious images in this shimmering display were those of St John the Baptist, St Katherine, St Jerome, the Nativity, and Our Lady of Pity. The last was a pieta, and it was popularly reproduced in woodcuts surrounded by the emblems of the Passion. Lady Margaret maintained a chaplain to sing before the image of our Lady of Pity, at Westminster Abbey, further evidence that she shared this common devotion.[62] Other items reflected her devotion to Christ and his sufferings: a piece of the holy cross set in gold, with pearls and precious stones, a 'bede' of gold with the arms of the Passion (that is a shield displaying the Five Wounds of Christ); a tablet of the vernacle, bearing an image of the handkerchief with which St Veronica was said to have wiped the face of Christ, which left an imprint upon it. Two collars of gold were decorated with the sign IHS, the abbreviation for Jesus, and would have appeared as sacred counterparts of the broad chains and pendants worn by the nobility and officers of the court.

These inventories reveal something of Margaret's personal preoccupations, for the items were not stored in her jewel house but kept close by in her chambers or with her chief female attendant, mistress Fowler.

---

[60] Tapestries recorded in inventories SJC, D91.12, D102.4; personal possessions in D91.5, pp. 24–5, D102.18.   [61] SJC, D91.10.   [62] *Excerpta Historica*, 99.

The things listed range from writings reaching back into the 1470s, to the relics of a gem-laden piety whose core was a devotion to Christ and his saints, and whose practical effect was the hoarding of solid gold and silver. Yet if we find some of this repellent, tending in our age to associate piety with austerity and worldliness with magnificence, the two were not so sharply antagonistic in hers. Her age displayed a fondness for the exotic and the austere in close conjunction: in romances the court and castle were never far from the forest and hermitage. Such an attitude is apparent in the story of Blanchardin and Eglantine itself. The princess Eglantine not only makes the stations of the cross within her citadel as her lover fights against the heathen without; she also takes a practical hand in affairs, garrisoning the city, and arranging a marriage so that she may achieve her own desires. If a knight's appearance at a tournament garbed in a hermit's gown could betoken his coming retirement from public life, it also showed how these two images of chivalry and piety could function together in the mind of actor and audience.[63]

The ideals of magnificent valour and pious discipline were perfectly embodied in the Crusades, enthusiasm for which persisted and even experienced a revival in the fifteenth century. Margaret herself was granted the pope's indulgence for her contributions towards raising a fleet against the Turks in 1476, and towards the end of her life Fisher recalled her remark that she would willingly go with the crusaders and 'wash their clothes, for the love of Jesus'. In 1507 she gave Fisher alms for the monks of St Catharine's Mount to ransom Christians captured 'in heathenesse'. The spur was the need, as then perceived, to unify Christendom against the Turkish danger, and it was a popular one: Brandt's *History of Jerusalem* had appeared in 1495. The spirit of pilgrimage, if not crusade, to the Holy City, had recently touched the life of one of the king's closest counsellors. Sir Richard Guildford, a companion of Henry before and at Bosworth, and controller of the royal household from 1492, turned from affairs of state in 1505 to make his pilgrimage. He died at Jerusalem the next year, and a journal of the trip was published by Pynson.[64]

United in their view of the duty of a militant Christian society under

[63] Anthony, Earl Rivers proclaimed his retirement in this way at the great royal tournament of 1477; Kipling, *The Triumph of Honour*, p. 123.

[64] Indulgence, SJC, D56.6; Caxton printed it in a more restricted form early the next year, PRO, E135/6/56, STC, II, 14077c.106. Fisher's recollections, *Mornynge Remembraunce*, 308; ransom, SJC, D91.21, p. 100. For Guildford, see Chrimes, *Henry VII*, 112.

attack, Margaret and Fisher also had similar views on the nature of the Church and its reform. For Sebastian Brandt, as for earlier moralists and later reformers, the chief evil lay in the decay of the moral leadership of the pope. Fisher, however, concentrated not on the head but on the body, seeking a renewal of spiritual discipline for clergy and laity. He tried to achieve this principally through providing training for the clergy in the universities, for which he gained Margaret's moral and financial support, and also by working diligently in his own diocese. They both used the system of church patronage and endowment, whether to benefit colleges or to reward individuals: their hope was to help the spiritual life of the Church through appointing men of good quality and endowing nurseries of good learning.

Neither Fisher nor Margaret, however, wanted to change the Church's structures, though they wished to see them revitalized. Both saw Rome as the centre of Christendom and the pope in consequence as its indispensable leader. Fisher recounted how Margaret knelt for long periods reciting the prayers known as the Crown of Our Lady, 'after the manner of Rome'. In 1505 a scholar went to Rome to pray there for her, and she received a gift of beads blessed by the pope.[65] This was not merely respect for a theoretical moral leadership, which indeed Fisher acknowledged Rome often lacked, but belief in aids to spiritual survival. For the pope at Rome held the keys to the spiritual treasury of Christendom. The logic of this belief, so hotly contested by the later Protestant reformers, made the indulgences for remitting penance for sins which issued from the curia part of the divine economy by which men and women would be saved. Successive popes granted ample indulgences to Henry, his queen and his mother. The indulgence of 1504, in which Margaret had been granted leave to visit enclosed religious houses, was exceptional in other ways. It was in the form of a confessional letter granted both to the king and his mother, and allowed them the extraordinary privilege of gaining full remission of their sins at the hands of their chosen confessors every six months. The normal privilege granted to royalty had been annual remission; that to Margaret's grandmother, the duchess of Clarence, was triennial. Frequent absolution was eagerly sought in an age when death struck so readily.[66]

[65] *Mornynge Remembraunce*, 295; scholar at Rome, and beads, SJC, D91.21, pp. 59, 66.
[66] William Lunt, *Studies in Anglo-Papal Relations during the Middle Ages, II: Financial Relations of the Papacy with England 1327–1534* (Cambridge, Mass., 1962), 450 nn. 26, 27.

As they affected the prestige and wealth of particular chapels and churches, and their shrines, indulgences also became part of the temporal economy. Lady Margaret, as she provided for her tomb at Westminster or visited each altar in her household chapel, must have viewed the benefits of indulgences with the same realism, and sometimes cupidity, with which she governed and improved her estates. Indulgences were a guarantee of God's good lordship, mediated through the pope and other bishops, in return for the perpetual service of pilgrimage, prayer and the maintenance of church endowments.

If Margaret's own piety was imbued with respect for Rome and its position in Christendom, her son, equally traditional in piety, exercised effective political control of the Church in England. His was a reign in which cardinal-protectors watched over the diplomatic relations of England and the papacy at the papal court, in which a non-resident Italian was appointed to an English see, and the English College in Rome fell under the direct management of the English crown.[67] Henry's relations with the pope were not always smooth, and on occasion he exercised a guardian's role in the English Church which in practical, though not theoretical, terms fell little short of his son's. When the pope wished to combine the Observant with the conventual Franciscans he retaliated by threatening the wholesale expulsion of the conventuals unless the independence of the newer order, which both he and his mother supported, were guaranteed.[68] Nevertheless, the relationship was always one of careful negotiation, and it never broke down, as happened under the impulsive Henry VIII.

The public side of Margaret's piety supported the prestige of the English Church and its links with the crown. Her chantry in Henry VII's chapel at Westminster was endowed with as great spiritual privileges as any that attached to the Scala Celi chapel at Rome.[69] She

---

[67] W. Wilkie, *The Cardinal Protectors of England: Rome and the Tudors before the Reformation* (Cambridge, 1974), *passim*; R. J. Knecht, 'The episcopate and the Wars of the Roses', *Birmingham Historical Journal*, 6 (1957–8), 126–31.

[68] Little, 'Observant Friars', 458.

[69] *CCR, 1509–9*, 289–93, no. 770, ii. The chapel of Scala Celi, where St Bernard was said to have beheld a ladder set up to heaven, was near Tre Fontane outside the walls of Rome on the Ostian Way. The bones of many martyrs were thought to rest beneath its altar. Masses were said there for the release of souls from purgatory through the merits of the Virgin Mary. Altars at English churches besides Westminster, including St Botolph's Boston, Lincolnshire, and various East Anglian churches, possessed similar indulgences. Devotion to the Scala Celi and its expiatory powers was growing in the late fifteenth and

took a personal hand in the finances of two bishops, Fisher (bishop of Rochester 1504–35), and William Smith (bishop of Lichfield 1493–6, of Lincoln 1496–1514), to ensure that they had sufficient to further the well-being of the Church: to Fisher she gave, by his own statement, a large sum of money which he eventually devoted to St John's College, Cambridge; to Smith she lent money to visit his diocese of Lichfield.[70] Her use of episcopal residences, establishing her household at both Hatfield (the bishop of Ely's manor) and Croydon (belonging to the archbishop of Canterbury), and staying at the bishop of Lincoln's palace at Buckden, also illustrates the intimacy between the royal family and the bishops. The royal family could make personal demands, sometimes onerous, upon the episcopate and other clerical dignitaries when need arose. William Smith and Richard Fox, both keen patrons of education and a reformed clergy, spent the majority of their episcopates busily engaged on royal service. Even Fisher, the model bishop, was dispensed by the pope to be absent at the great Christian festivals in order to act as confessor in residence to Lady Margaret. The fact that he obtained a specific dispensation to do this has been seen as evidence of his scrupulous observance of canon law.[71]

In her dealings with religious houses Margaret showed a similar willingness to use the Church to her own advantage, and to safeguard her own rights, but her attitude was moderated by a respect for the proper religious function of these communities. In 1501 her bailiff at Tidburst and Kendall (Herts), claimed an allowance for twenty-eight years arrears of quit rent due to St Albans Abbey. The claim was allowed only when Margaret's council had thoroughly investigated the rents in question, compelling the abbey to submit proofs of title.[72]

early sixteenth centuries and is especially evident in Northamptonshire wills. It is interesting that Margaret should have wished to attach to her chantry privileges common in the east of the country where her personal connections were strongest. See C. E. Woodruff, ed. *A Fifteenth Century Guidebook to the Principal Churches of Rome, c. 1470*, (London, 1933), 51–2; R. M. Serjeantson and H. I. London, 'The parish churches and religious houses of Northamptonshire: their dedications, altars, images and lights', *Archaeological Journal*, 70 (1913), 246–7; P. Thompson, *The History and Antiquities of Boston* (Boston, 1856), 134, 137, 183. We are indebted to Dr Nigel Morgan for these references.

70 *Early Statutes of St John's College, Cambridge*, ed. J. E. B. Mayor (Cambridge, 1859), 238–40; the loan to Smith, 1493, WAM, 32364.
71 E. E. Reynolds, 'John Fisher and the Lady Margaret Beaufort', note in *Moreana*, 6 (August, 1969), 32–3. We are grateful to Maria Dowling for supplying us with the text of the papal brief to Lady Margaret, 6 Jan. 1506, from Vatican Archives Armarium 39, vol. 22, fol. 442v.   72 Cooper, 65, BL, Harleian MS 602, fol. 1.

In another case she made concessions to an abbey with which, since it owned estates bordering her own, it was wise to be on good terms. The abbot of Peterborough petitioned her successfully for the right to extract rents and toll from her estates in Maxey and West Deeping, resolving a dispute which had lasted a century. The decision in the abbot's favour was made by Margaret 'of her vertueux and godly mynde intending the ministracion of justice and that the abbot and convent and their successors should the more quietly and devoutly attend the service of Almighty God'. Such firm phrases were intended not only to settle a troublesome question, but to remind the monks where their priorities lay: time spent in legal haggling was time lost to the service of God, and a disservice to those who had established and endowed the abbey. Margaret also granted to the priory of Deeping St James a mill at which to grind corn for its own domestic use, while carefully safeguarding her own rights at another Deeping mill which she commanded both her tenants and the priory's to use. The *quid pro quo* for this grant was prayers for herself and her son, to be said in the priory's mother house of Thorney Abbey.[73] Her shrewdness was combined with a real respect for the holiness of the abbeys. She was offended by the fact that consecrated boundary crosses belonging to Crowland Abbey had been tampered with by lay hands during disputes between the men of Kesteven and Holland: her arbitration was intended not only to settle a quarrel but to put an end to violation of sacred property.[74]

Margaret's sense of what was justly due to her, however, did not inevitably tally with the interests of the religious with whom she dealt. In 1494 she tried and failed to obtain from Durham cathedral priory the right to present to a prebend attached to the college of Howden. She remained on good terms, however, and was made a confrater of the priory, along with Oldham and Bray, in 1502. Two years later the prior sent her a gift of a pillow stuffed with feathers from 'St Cuthbert's fowls'. In 1507 she felt entitled to ask for the nomination of her candidate to another benefice in the priory's gift, but again was refused. The prior's letters to her agents made clear, courteously but firmly, that Durham resented such interference.[75] At law she could be aggressive as

---

[73] L. Gaches, 'Liberty of Peterborough', *Fenland Notes and Queries*, 6 (1904–6), 33; Cooper, 77–9. [74] *Fenland Notes and Queries*, 2 (1892–4), 143–7, 209–11, 294–6.
[75] Durham, Registrum Parvum IV, Prior's Letter Book, 1484–1519, fols. 33, 157–8 (kindly drawn to our attention by Dr J. A. F. Thomson).

well as concessionary. The prior of Tonbridge once tried to claim exemption from her jurisdiction in Kent, and himself brought her bailiff before another court for felling timber. Margaret considered that her officer's use of the wood 'not worth above two shillings' was fully justified. It was an obvious attempt to breach her jurisdiction and so she entered a plea to the king and his council setting out the details and warning that in future the rights of the king, her heir, would suffer.[76]

She could also sustain a difficult cause against one religious house in order eventually to benefit another, a process in which church livings were considered as pawns in a larger game rather than cures of souls. In 1487 Henry VII granted his mother, among many other properties, the manor of Cheshunt. In 1489 he further granted her the advowson (or right to present the incumbent) of Cheshunt church, which had originally been attached to the manor.[77] The advowson, however, had previously been granted separately by Edward IV to the dean and chapter of Windsor, as part of his provision for St George's chapel. Edward had granted with it a licence for Windsor to appropriate the income of the church. Lady Margaret affirmed her title to both the advowson and income, by virtue of the king's two grants, despite a counter-claim by Windsor. In 1492 she presented William Smith to both Cheshunt and Swineshead, Lincolnshire, the second rich living which she was to present to Westminster.[78] In 1494 in the face of continued opposition from Windsor, she presented Hugh Oldham to both livings. Windsor was dismayed at the prospect of the living of Cheshunt passing permanently out of its hands and contested the presentation. Margaret won her legal cause against Windsor, however, and once her former agent Christopher Urswick succeeded John Morgan as dean in 1495 he formally relinquished to her all rights in Cheshunt.[79] Despite this, the eventual fate of both rectories was unclear, for in 1497 Margaret gained licence to grant them both to Windsor to endow her own chantry there. This plan lasted until 1499, when the king finally decided to raise his new chapel at Westminster. Oldham resigned the livings and Westminster took possession of them in 1500, but in the meantime Margaret had held them in her

[76] PRO, DL1/2 no. 23.   [77] *CPR*, 1485–94, 155, 292.

[78] *VCH Herts*, III, 456. Margaret acquired the living of Swineshead (Lincs) and land there from Thomas West, Lord de la Warre, in 1492, WAM, 575.

[79] WAM, 4688, 4693.

patronage, disposing of them to men who, though deserving, were far too busy to have resided in their cures.[80]

To Lady Margaret such manoeuvrings were part of economic reality. She was not slow to take up rights even though she might have only a passing interest. Thus in 1488, while guardian of Edward duke of Buckingham, she had, in virtue of her wardship, presented a new incumbent to the church of Vaynor Wynho, Brecon. The previous incumbent had failed to produce letters from the king bearing Margaret's seal as patroness to show confirmation of his title. The same year another presentation by the king to the church of Trefdreyr in the archdeaconry of Cardigan was suppressed in favour of a new appointment, this time made jointly by the king and Lady Margaret acting as Lady of Yscoed. In 1494 Margaret preferred to the same Welsh church her clerk Henry Hornby, who was about to hold in plurality the rectories of Thrapston (N'hants) and Burton Bradstock (Dors.).[81]

Just as Lady Margaret combined devotion to God and the shrines of the saints with obligations to the dynasty, and with practical concern for her feudal rights, so she lived a rigorously disciplined religious life within the splendours of a household which was equipped for lavish hospitality. She did not avoid banquets and ceremonies on state occasions when hospitality or public necessity required it. Yet Fisher singled out her temperance as one of the signs of the strength of her interior discipline: 'eschewynge banketts, reresoupers, joncryes betwixt meles'.[82]

Compatible with this impression of personal sobriety is a certain intellectual austerity. Margaret's was a piety which, if it had its own form of credulity, avoided that associated with some forms of devotion to the saints and their relics. This was a subject treated in the fourth book of the *Imitation of Christ*, which Margaret translated. It stressed the central place of the eucharist in the life of worshippers and contrasted it with credulous running after relics whose wrappings of cloth of gold and gems obscure the truth of God's grace. Much was made of the importance of penitence in preparation for receiving grace through the sacrament, compared with the peep-show which an

---

[80] *CPR*, 1494–1509, 79; WAM, 574, 4681; pp. 207–8, for Margaret's changes of plan.
[81] *Episcopal Register of St. David's. 1397–1518*, ed. R. F. Isaacson, Cymmrodorion Record Series, 6, 2 vols. (London, 1917), II (1407–1518), 527, 529, 551.
[82] *Mornynge Remembraunce*, 294.

inattentive use of relics could become. In another of the books with which Margaret was familiar, Hilton's *Scale of Perfection*, the importance of the sacraments as a guide for people's experience of God's grace was stressed. Too much emphasis on feeling as a gauge of the quality of religious life was portrayed as untrustworthy and dangerous. Heresy, stemming from neglect of the discipline of the Church, was violently condemned, perhaps too violently to be consistent with the book's general exhortations to charity.[83]

Devotion to Christ, apparent in all her benefactions, in her attention to the cult of the Holy Name, and in her reverence for the eucharist, seems to have been her chief concern. It had, of course, its sacred foci and loci apart from the worship of the mass, just as did the devotion to any particular saint, for acknowledgement of concrete symbols was a normal part of medieval (as it is of much modern) Catholic piety. She commissioned one of the Bonshommes of Ashridge to provide her with an image of the Lord painted on a cloth.[84] The focus of the Ashridge community was a phial of the Blood of Christ. Ashridge also had a previous family connection: her great-uncle, Cardinal Beaufort, had left it £100 for building purposes.[85] This personal devotion was accommodated within the traditional forms of penitence and absolution administered by the Church. When the pope officially sanctioned the feast of the Name of Jesus at the petition of Margaret, he granted it the same indulgence as accompanied the feast of Corpus Christi. A generous indulgence was also granted to those who celebrated or heard the mass of the Name during thirty days.[86]

Attention to the fundamentals of orthodoxy and discipline, must not, in Lady Margaret's case, be confused with too great an aloofness from the variety of popular religion. It has lately been suggested that the 'privatizing' of fifteenth-century religion in oratories and patterns of devotion for individuals may have led to a tendency among the educated to despise not only relics but such social manifestations as 'boy bishops'. She, by contrast, went to the trouble of providing two

[83] *De Imitatione Christi*, ed. Ingrams, 261; *The Scale of Perfection*, ed. Sitwell, 91. There is a trace of her interest in another mystical writer. She acquired in 1507 a copy of Henry Suso's *Horologium Sapientiae* 'with the lyffe of St. Benet in the same book', a description of the work as printed by Caxton in 1490; SJC, D91.19, p. 13.

[84] SJC, D91.19, p. 102: probably a sepulchre cloth used in the Easter rites.

[85] Harriss, *Cardinal Beaufort*, 379.

[86] Papal letter, 4 Oct. 1494, SJC, D56.184; R. N. Swanson, *Church and Society in Late Medieval England* (Oxford, 1989), 293. The indulgence for thirty days remitted the pains of purgatory for the equivalent of three thousand years of temporal penance.

such boy bishops on the feast of St Nicholas, one for her own household and one for the town of Collyweston. She even sent her dean to Peterborough to borrow a real mitre from the monks. She also paid an abbot of misrule, and for dancing by children on Twelfth Night.[87]

Identification with popular beliefs extended to her own devotions. The text of the book of prayers at Westminster Abbey bearing her own and Stanley's arms, displays elements familiar outside the closed world of the noble's oratory. There are phrases included in the forms of popular printed indulgences purchasable by a wide range of ordinary people.[88] The holy names of Christ, according to legend vouchsafed by an angel to Pope Leo the Great, are written out and those who recite them are promised protection from sudden death, fire, water and fevers and from the penalty of dying without confession. These holy names include some with magical associations, and the whole list disclosed to Pope Leo, and by him transmitted to Charlemagne, was commonly used as a charm against various ills. The book as a whole is devoted to an appreciation of the effects of the Passion of Christ, and to prayers in honour of the names by which his holiness is revealed. It also stresses the same theme as the fourth book of the *Imitation* in the inclusion of prayers to Christ for grace to make a good confession and so receive the benefits of the eucharist. One miniature shows a scene commonly represented, the vision of Christ, surrounded by the emblems of his Passion, to St Gregory as he celebrated mass. This story of the vision was the basis for the many portrayals of Christ with these emblems, known as the Image of Pity. Margaret herself possessed such images, one with St Margaret and St Katherine standing on either side, set in a gold tablet, another in the variant form of a pieta also surrounded by the emblems.[89] In this prayer book devotion to the person and suffering of Christ is thus combined with an appeal to his power through the ritual invocation of special names. Similar invocations are found in the service book containing the office and mass for the Name of Jesus dedicated to Margaret by Gigli. Both there and in the office according to the Sarum use, however, they are set in a clearer order of worship: Christ is being asked to protect from ills those who 'devoutly venerate' his name through the liturgy of the feast.

In its diversity of attitude Margaret's religion reflected that of her

[87] Richmond, 'Religion', 203; accounts, 1503, SJC, D91.20, 52, 124, 126, 190.

[88] Westminster Abbey MS 39. We are grateful to Dr Eamon Duffy of Magdalene College, Cambridge, for drawing our attention to this point, and allowing us access to his work on late medieval popular religion, Plate 8.   [89] *Ibid.*, fol. 83; Plate 9.

age. Her natural curiosity and social position enabled her to develop some acquaintance with the devotional literature of the mystics and moralists. Her enthusiasm for the cult of Jesus reinforced respect for the mass and the sacraments of communion and confession. Fisher noted that she received communion twelve times a year, an unusual number when the Church only insisted that the faithful receive it once. In the indulgences she received there was also reliance on forms of number-magic, such as the added worth of celebrating a mass for a particular mystic number of days on end. The Stanley prayer book and some of the prayers in a book of tracts, which she later acquired, about remedies for plague, show a similar confidence in the power of reciting prayer-formulae to protect from worldly ills.[90] Margaret had the proprietary sense of her age and class in religion as in everything else: masses, prayers and endowments could reasonably be expected to confer spiritual and perhaps temporal benefits on her and on her friends and kindred.

In Margaret, the proprietary and acquisitive tendency was tempered by a concern for justice and worthy stewardship. According to Fisher her household provided a setting for the display of the traditional virtues and duty to God and one's neighbour, and these were integrated in the disciplined life of its mistress. The example of charity was not of course set by her alone. Margaret of York, besides being an active patron of Caxton, was renowned for her good works. Nicolas Finet's 'Benois seront les Misericordieux', at Brussels, contains an illumination showing her visiting the dying and attending funerals, and dispensing charity to prisoners and the poor.[91] In the case of Margaret Beaufort, Fisher's literary account of her charity is complemented by Parker's celebration of her good lordship displayed in the conviviality of her table. There were occasions when this was not so, and when people resented both the countess's acquisitiveness and her passion for dispensing justice.[92] Nevertheless, one sees in her works, whether she was providing for the comfort of her almsfolk,

---

[90] Cambridge, Fitzwilliam Museum, MS 261, described in F. Wormald, *A Descriptive Catalogue of the Additional Illuminated Manuscripts in the Fitzwilliam Museum, Acquired 1895–1979* (Cambridge, 1982), 194–6.

[91] Brussels, Bibliothèque Royale MS 9296, fol. i; Weightman, *Margaret of York, Duchess of Burgundy*, 203–4.

[92] The petition by Sir Robert Southwell to her executors about a wardship wrongly adjudged to her (SJC, D94.397), and her failure to carry out her great-uncle Cardinal Beaufort's bequest of land to St Cross hospital Winchester, support this impression.

extending the dwelling of the anchoress of Stamford and remembering her in her will, resolving disputes between Crowland Abbey and her tenants, or furthering the trade of the London printers, a constant blend of the practical and the pious which argues at least an active and disciplined will.

Such a blend of piety and practicality was also to be found in many of the men who surrounded her: in Hugh Ashton, a future archdeacon of York and benefactor of St John's; in her clerk of works James Morice who possessed a significant library of devotional literature;[93] in Henry Hornby and John Fisher, academics who were also active theologians and benefactors of their colleges. She herself set them an example in the range of her involvement. A watchful landlord, she was ready to chasten the king's auditor for rumour of a wrong to her tenants of Tattershall. Ever zealous of her family rights, she was at the same time sensitive to the wider needs of the community, as is shown by the respect engendered by her building of the great sluice at Boston. In short her behaviour, lacking the ineffective ostentation of Henry VI while it retained his core of piety, showed, despite its flaws, some acquaintance with how to live 'the medled life'.

[93] Keiser, 'The mystics', 23.

7

THE COUNTESS AND THE UNIVERSITIES

A mixed or 'medled' life was characteristic of those institutions on which Lady Margaret lavished greatest attention – the colleges and universities of Cambridge and Oxford. These varied communities of priests, and of clerks not in priestly orders, prayed like monks for the souls of their benefactors while pursuing religious and secular studies. They equipped themselves for various careers: to serve the Church as local clergy, members of the hierarchy or administrators, to serve the king as lawyers and civil servants and to staff the households of clerics and laity alike. The colleges, at this period primarily homes for university graduates studying for higher degrees, had long attracted noble patrons. Lady Margaret was the greatest in a line of female benefactors. In 1340 Robert de Eglesfield, chaplain to Philippa queen of Edward III, had gained her support as Fisher gained Margaret's to establish and endow Queen's College, Oxford. Elizabeth Lady Clare took over responsibility for University Hall in Cambridge and transformed it into her own well-endowed foundation, Clare College, in 1338. The interest and energy which she deployed, both in looking after its financial well-being and in personally ratifying its statutes, foreshadows Margaret's refoundation of God's House as Christ's College. Lady Clare's friend and distant relative, Marie de Valence countess of Pembroke, founded Pembroke College and set in motion, but did not bring to fulfilment, a project for founding another college at Paris. Like Lady Margaret, the countess of Pembroke had charitable interests other than academic ones: she was a benefactor to the Franciscans and foundress of a convent of Minoresses in Cambridgeshire, Denny Abbey.

The confidence of benefactors reflected in the many foundations of colleges during the fourteenth century was soon to be matched by causes for concern. By 1450 the universities of Oxford and Cambridge showed cracks in the impressive structure of scholasticism reared in the preceding two centuries. Their system of regent lectures, by which young university masters supplied the teaching needs of the university without receiving a regular salary from it, was rare in Europe at this date.[1] Their great faculties of theology, especially that at Cambridge, were suffering a decline through a falling off of the prestige and numbers of friars active in them. At Oxford orthodox theology had been disturbed both by the heresy of the early fifteenth century and by the invasion of academic freedom during Archbishop Arundel's repression of it. One college, Lincoln, had been founded in 1427 by a bishop himself once tainted with heretical leanings, in order to combat error in others.

Amid the strains, however, were many signs of vigour. New colleges continued to be founded. Four in particular, Magdalen at Oxford, and God's House, King's and Queens' at Cambridge, enabled the 'new learning' in Latin and later Greek classics to find homes in the libraries and lectures of these old universities. Cambridge, especially, apart from its theology faculty, entered a period of expansion.[2] Between 1400 and 1475 a new complex comprising university library, assembly room and lecture schools was built. In 1440–3 King Henry VI founded a royal college whose site adjoined this complex and whose scale was designed to mirror that of New College, Oxford. In 1448 Queen Margaret, inspired by Andrew Doket, followed suit with a foundation, Queens', which was later for a brief period to be the Cambridge home of Erasmus.[3]

Cambridge, like Oxford, had during its history been closely involved with the crown, first as appellant seeking settlement of the disputes endemic between the university and its host town, then as receiver of royal benefactions in the foundations of both the king and his servants. Finally, it began to receive eminent visitors – the king, his family or ambassadors from abroad – and to play a part in the pageant of royal diplomacy as it developed fully in the sixteenth and seventeenth centuries. The interest shown by Lady Margaret in Cambridge was, among other things, an important step in the development of this public profile of the university. We must remember that her

[1] A. B. Cobban, *The Medieval Universities* (London, 1975), 156–7.

[2] For the overall rise in numbers at Cambridge see T. H. Aston, G. D. Duncan and T. A. R. Evans, 'The medieval alumni of the university of Cambridge', *Past and Present*, 86 (1980), 26–7. For the various faculties there at this period see *ibid.*, 62–3, and D. R. Leader, *A History of the University of Cambridge*, I: *The University to 1546* (Cambridge, 1989), 89–210. [3] For Doket, see p. 212.

benefactions took place against a background of numerous royal visits and that she, through her constant concern, was herself the university's best advocate at court.

The scale on which Lady Margaret adopted Cambridge graduates into her service was remarkable, but increasing scope for university graduates, especially in higher church posts, was a feature of the times.[4] The higher rate of pay for graduates on the staff of the household of Henry Percy, fifth earl of Northumberland in 1510, is an example of the interest in academic qualifications in a noble household.[5] Some nobles themselves benefited from contacts with university men: Margaret's adopted family, the Stanleys, had members studying for short periods at Oxford and her husband received an ingratiating letter from the university shortly after Bosworth.[6] Her own family had an important earlier connection with Oxford and Cambridge: in 1426 Thomas Beaufort, duke of Exeter, had left £200 to be distributed between them as capital for loans to needy students.[7]

Margaret herself patronized both universities before finally concentrating on Cambridge. She endowed divinity professors in both, and in 1494, shortly before she first met John Fisher, she asked Oxford to release a master of arts, Maurice Westbury, to act as a tutor for young gentlemen being educated 'at our findyng'.[8] Her cofferer that year allowed sums to Dr Edmund Hanson of Oxford for loans to scholars, and she was maintaining John Jackson and one Burgon as her scholars at Oxford in 1498–9.[9] Hugh Oldham, her receiver, had studied at Oxford before incepting in canon law at Cambridge. The younger university would have found her favour worth soliciting even without the benefit of Fisher's influence. As the king's mother, she was known to exert a powerful influence on a monarch who otherwise refused to be swayed by factions of any kind. She also had a certain local presence near Cambridge, for the honour of Richmond included numerous appurtenances in Cambridgeshire villages, with jurisdiction which she occasionally enforced at common law. In Collyweston, in nearby Northamptonshire, she had after 1487 a substantial manor house which from 1499 was transformed into a palace, the centre for the transaction of most of her affairs.

[4] Aston, Duncan and Evans, 'The medieval alumni', 85 n. 183.
[5] *The Northumberland Household Book*, ed. T. Percy, (London, 1770), 51, 323.
[6] *Epistolae Academicae*, ed. Anstey, II, 484, 499.
[7] J. W. Clark, *Endowments of the University of Cambridge* (Cambridge, 1904), 556.
[8] *Epistolae Academicae*, ed. Anstey, II, 614.
[9] WAM, 22830; SJC, D91.17, pp. 20, 50.

The concentration of Lady Margaret's attention on Cambridge is nevertheless almost certainly due to her relationship with John Fisher, who held office both in the university and as her confessor.[10] Their first recorded meeting was in 1494 or 1495 at Greenwich, where they had lunch together.[11] He had gone to court as senior proctor on university business, though the precise nature of it, or of the cause of his meeting with Margaret, is uncertain. It could have been a university appeal for the rebuilding of Great St Mary's church, although Margaret's recorded contributions for that work came much later, between 1503 and 1505.[12] It could equally have been connected with the benefaction of Thomas Barowe in 1494, in whose chantry in Great St Mary's her name was linked with the king's and with that of Richard III. This benefaction endowed the university with a total of £240, which served not only to endow the chantry but as initial capital for rebuilding the church. It also had a symbolic value, as the bequest of a man who had served Richard III and been disabled from high office after Bosworth, but whose parting gesture was one of reconciliation between the Roses. Fisher and the king's mother may also have discussed other matters, such as the current controversy between the university and the mayor of Cambridge. The almost continuous town and gown quarrel at this period was to result in Margaret's famous composition of 1503, perhaps her most significant arbitration.[13] Whatever the subjects at that lunch, it transformed both their lives. She recalled, when confirming her vow of chastity before Fisher, that she resolved to make him her spiritual guide 'the first time I see you admitted'.

Lady Margaret's first major university benefaction was the foundation of an endowed lectureship in theology at each of the two universities, the modern Lady Margaret Professorships. There had been earlier attempts to provide lectures with a more secure financial basis. In 1432 Oxford had pleaded with John duke of Bedford to endow some masters to lecture in the arts and other faculties. Later in the century Cambridge arranged to give some direct support to regents lecturing for the university by a system of collections from colleges through the university bedells.[14] In 1481–2 an attempt was made to maintain a

---

[10] Just as John Langton's position as university chancellor as well as chaplain to Henry VI influenced the king's decision to begin the foundation of King's College. See Plate 18.

[11] *Grace Book B, part I*, 68. The proctors' accounts spanning 1494–5 lack some folios and the year cannot be established with certainty.

[12] For this, and her Cambridge benefactions in general, see also Underwood, 'Cambridge connections'. [13] Above, pp. 90–1.

[14] D. R. Leader, 'Teaching in Tudor Cambridge', *History of Education*, 13 (1984), 105.

theology lecturer out of a royal benefaction elsewhere. The bishop of Salisbury, Richard Beauchamp, had persuaded Edward IV to endow a chantry in St George's chapel at Windsor and grant the nomination of the priest who would serve it to Oxford university. The university petitioned that this priest should be allowed time to lecture in theology at Oxford, and actually presented a theology graduate for the post. His successor, however, was an arts graduate and therefore could not have lectured in the higher faculty. Although a scholar in theology was presented in 1486, the scheme to support a theology lecture through the chantry foundered.[15]

Lady Margaret and her son also took an interest in the endowment of Windsor, where St George's chapel continued to rise until 1508 and where Garter feasts were kept early in the reign. They transferred their grand plans for royal tombs and chantries to Westminster Abbey, however, and Margaret eventually made Westminster responsible for financing her university benefactions. The story of this change, bound up with the search for a fitting resting place for the body of Henry VI, and with his possible canonization, is also inseparable from that of the lectureships and preachership which Margaret founded.

Richard III had moved the body of the murdered king from Chertsey Abbey, where a statue of Henry had been venerated since 1473, to St George's chapel Windsor in 1484. Ten years later Henry VII made his petition to Pope Alexander VI which resulted in enquiries into the grounds for canonizing his Lancastrian predecessor. In 1496 Henry expanded the work of the rival dynasty by beginning a new Lady chapel on the site of Edward III's chapel of St Edward and St George: it was to house his own tomb and a shrine over the burial place of Henry VI.[16] Lady Margaret contributed towards the king's works at Windsor and she now drew up proposals for a chantry for herself on this site.[17] On 1 March 1497 letters patent were issued to her for three purposes. First, she was permitted to convey to St George's the rectories of Cheshunt and Swineshead and to endow the canons with lands to the value of £150, to support four chaplains in a chantry. Second, she

---

[15] *The History of the University of Oxford*, ed. T. H. Aston, III, *The Collegiate University*, ed. J. McConica (Oxford, 1986), p. 306; *Epistolae Academicae*, ed. Anstey II, 469, 479, 490, 502, 507.

[16] For the course of works at Windsor, Colvin, Ransome and Summerson, eds., *King's Works*, III, 305–13. For a brief summary of the attempts at canonization see B. P. Wolffe, *Henry VI* (London, 1981), 355–7.

[17] A contribution of £66 13s 4d was recorded in 1492–3, WAM, 32364.

gained licence to establish her lectureships in the universities, and to endow them to the value of £20. Third, she gained licence to set up a chantry for her own family at Wimborne Minster.[18] In July 1497 Christopher Urswicke, her former agent who was now dean of Windsor, officially accepted her proposal to found a chantry there near the king's.[19]

Unlike the previous scheme for supporting the university lectureships from Windsor, the grant of March 1497 treated them as distinct corporations, capable of holding land and of going to law. They were to be endowed posts in their own right, not posts to be occupied by a suitably qualified man whose official job was that of chaplain in the Windsor chantry. Indeed, an undated draft of the terms of foundation of the Oxford lectureship makes clear that at one stage the lecturer's salary was to be drawn direct from lands for which he must render the accounts and which would thus fall directly under his management.[20] The direct connection of Lady Margaret's scheme with Windsor at any stage is therefore questionable, but what is not in doubt is that the corporate status of the lectureships was never removed. This meant that even when their support was confined to estates granted to Westminster Abbey they had a specific power of legal redress: should the abbey default on its obligations, the lecturers could sue for distraint. Oxford spoke truly when it thanked the countess for having done what no benefactor had done before.[21]

Further progress on the Windsor chantry was halted by developments in the case of the royal candidate for sainthood. The likelihood of Windsor becoming one of the most prestigious places of pilgrimage provoked both Chertsey Abbey and Westminster Abbey to renew strongly claims to Henry VI's body. Despite the complex history of preparations, its removal to Westminster was never actually to take place, and it remains at Windsor to this day. The solemn translation, however, was still a possibility in 1504. The tug of war between great religious houses was important for an age whose sense of the sacred was consciously rooted in favoured locations. Westminster was already

[18] *CPR, 1494–1509*, 79.
[19] Windsor College MS XV.58.c.13, in *The Manuscripts of St. George's Chapel Windsor Castle*, ed. J. N. Dalton (Windsor, 1957), 104.
[20] *History of the University of Oxford*, III, 348. A foundation document of the Cambridge lecture was inspected by the vice-chancellor and doctors and taken to Lady Margaret in 1498–9, but we do not know what it contained; *Grace Book B, part I*, 120.
[21] *Epistolae Academicae*, ed. Anstey, II, 646.

distinguished by its galaxy of royal tombs and its connection with another royal saint, Edward the Confessor. Lady Margaret herself had already established a chantry in the chapel of Our Lady of the pewe nearby, in 1494, and at the end of 1496, at the same time as she was furthering her Windsor project, she established another chantry in St Edward's chapel.[22] In 1498 the royal council called a hearing at which witnesses on behalf of Westminster testified that Henry VI had himself wished to be buried there: one of them even indicated the spot in St Edward's chapel which the king was said to have marked out. We do not need to believe all the details of this story, and we may suspect that the weight of so much previous royal association with Westminster was enough to begin to convince Henry VII.[23] In July 1498 he made a new agreement for a chantry with Westminster, having petitioned the pope that it might receive the body. On 28 April 1499 Margaret cancelled her previous licence to endow Windsor. On 10 May she obtained licence for Westminster to appropriate Swineshead and Cheshunt rectories and to receive lands to the value previously granted for Windsor.[24]

Another four years were to elapse before Margaret's lectureships were officially founded, with their own regulations, and receiving support from lands granted to the abbey. Henry VII took some time to complete his plans to transfer his own tomb from Windsor, where it was being built still during 1501. Margaret had also to complete the complex business of arranging a suitable endowment for the abbey, in addition to the rectories, from which to finance her chantry. At this formative stage we glimpse her during 1498 supporting two lecturers, Dr Smyth at Cambridge and Dr Wilsford at Oxford, directly by payments from her coffers.[25] On 8 September 1502 indentures of foundation were drawn up in which the stipends of the lectures were directed to be paid by Westminster Abbey. The first lecturer in Cambridge under these arrangements was now named as John Fisher.

[22] *CCR, 1500–9*, 290, and above p. 190.   [23] Wolffe, *Henry VI*, 357–8.

[24] *CPR, 1494–1509*, 79; *CCR, 1500–9*, 227. The 10 May licence was not enrolled at the time, but figures in an inspeximus of 1505.

[25] SJC, D91.17, pp. 37, 55 (Smyth), 42, 46 (Wilsford). These entries from the household account for 1498–9 unambiguously refer to the two men as readers. Dr Leader's citation of a reference in the university *Grace Book* to show that Smyth paid for other lectures as vice-chancellor rather than receiving payment for them is therefore irrelevant to the issue; Leader, *A History of the University of Cambridge, to 1546*, 278 n. 38. G. D. Duncan correctly lists Wilsford as the first of the Lady Margaret professors; *The History of the University of Oxford*, III, 350.

His counterpart in Oxford, successor to Wilsford, was named as Dr John Roper. In January 1503 Sir Reginald Bray laid the foundation stone of the king's Lady chapel at Westminster, where Henry and Margaret were building new almshouses. On 1 July the abbey agreed to support the lectureships from named lands including the manor of Drayton and property in Paddington, Hendon, Willesden and Uxbridge.[26] This property in Paddington and the other lands in Middlesex had originally been conveyed to Bray in 1492. Like some of Lady Margaret's endowments for Christ's College the lands were the fruits of political plunder, skilfully used. Bray had obtained them from Thomas Stillington, cousin of Robert Stillington, bishop of Bath, who had served Richard III. Robert had been deprived briefly of his offices by Henry VII, in the aftermath of Lambert Simnel's invasion, although he was restored to favour shortly before his death in 1491.[27]

Lady Margaret had established lectures independent in status, if not in funding, to be given for one hour every day on which lectures took place during the university terms. The lectures could not be suspended without special permission of the chancellors and doctors of the faculties of theology in each place. To judge from the text taken for the first Oxford lectures – the *Quodlibeta* of Duns Scotus – they cannot be said to have marked a break with the methods of the scholastics, as did Colet's lectures on St Paul which ran at the same period. Later in the sixteenth century the Cambridge Lady Margaret Chair became the centre of theological controversy to a degree which showed its continued importance. It was held both by the vociferous Puritan Thomas Cartwright, who was expelled from the lectureship in an effort to silence him, and the neo-Pelagian Peter Baro, who strenuously defended his right to voice his opinions as Lady Margaret Professor.[28] Valuable though the professorships were to be to the universities, however, they were originally but one facet of Margaret's pious

---

[26] Foundation deed of 1502 and agreement of 1503 for Cambridge printed in Clark, *Endowments*, 59–64, 70–1. The Oxford foundation deed bearing Margaret's signature is Oxford University Archives, N.E.P./E/1.

[27] M. M. Condon, 'From caitiff and villain to pater patriae: Reynold Bray and the profits of office', in *Profit, Piety and the Professions in Later Medieval England*, ed. M. A. Hicks (Gloucester, 1990), 150–2.

[28] *Erasmus and Cambridge: The Cambridge Letters of Erasmus*, ed. H. C. Porter and D. F. S. Thompson (Toronto, 1963), 16; J. Bass Mullinger, *The University of Cambridge from the Earliest Times to 1535* (Cambridge, 1873), 435; H. C. Porter, *Reformation and Reaction in Tudor Cambridge* (Cambridge, 1958), 174–7, 376–86. For a reassessment of Colet's work, see John B. Gleason, *John Colet* (Berkeley and Los Angeles, 1989), especially 152–79.

endowments. Her decision to attach them to Westminster, rather than pursue a scheme for complete financial independence, was undoubtedly related to their place among the spiritual benefits flowing from the mighty complex of royal tombs and chantries designed for the new Lady chapel.

One of the provisions of the foundations at both universities was that the lecturers and their audience should take time off in Lent so as to be able more readily to attend to preaching duties. It was, however, only at Cambridge that this emphasis was reinforced by the second of Lady Margaret's foundations there: the university preachership. Both universities had previously been concerned about effective preaching by their clergy. In 1446 money was left to them by Thomas Collage to pay preachers, as an encouragement to the study of divinity. Oxford petitioned the pope in 1489 that its chancellor or his deputy might have power to grant licences to preach, subject not to the approval of a bishop but merely to that of the doctors of theology. Cambridge in 1503 succeeded in getting a similar privilege, under which twelve preachers licensed under the university's seal could tour the British Isles delivering sermons.[29]

The king's grant to Lady Margaret on 7 February 1504 of the power to found a university preachership, and the subsequent foundation deed of 30 October, gave permanent practical support to this and previous efforts, in a clearly defined form. The value of the foundation was £10 a year. This stipend was annexed to the lands granted before to Westminster to support Margaret's chantry and the lectureships, with the addition of land and pasture at Great and Little Chesterford and Littlebury, Essex, worth approximately £6.[30] A preacher was to be chosen triennially by the chancellor, or vice-chancellor, and the heads of houses. He was by preference to be a Doctor of Theology, but might

[29] *Epistolae Academicae*, ed. Anstey, II, 564; J. Lewis, *Life of Dr. John Fisher*, 2 vols. (London, 1855), I, 9, II, 261–3; Leader, *A History of the University of Cambridge, to 1546*, 278–9. Lewis claims that Fisher worked for the Cambridge privilege during his vice-chancellorship in 1501. Given his interest in, and support of, preaching, this is not unlikely: Thomas Cabold, named in the papal grant, was merely the university's agent in the business.

[30] The Chesterford endowment marched closely with the king's for his own chantry. John Gardyner of London had sold the land to Roger Ormeston, Margaret's chamberlain in November 1503 (WAM 3152), but Ormeston died next year and his feoffees, including Henry Hornby and William Ormeston, granted it to Margaret on 14 May 1504 (WAM, 3157). At the same time Henry provided funds for the abbey to acquire the rectory and manor of Great Chesterford itself to endow his chantry; B. Harvey, *Westminster Abbey and its Estates in the Middle Ages* (Oxford, 1977), 201, 341, 405.

be a Bachelor if these were in short supply, and was normally to be a fellow of a college. No other office was allowed him besides a college fellowship. He was to preach six sermons a year, to include one annually at St Paul's Cross or another London church, and the rest at eleven named places.

Lady Margaret's benificence nearly always demanded a specific personal return. At all the places where sermons were to be preached she had lands or wielded influence: Cheshunt and Ware (Herts), Bassingbourn and Orwell (Cambs), Maxey (N'hants), Deeping St James and St Andrew, Bourne, Boston and Swineshead (Lincs). Academic patronage entailed prayers for the patron and his or her kin, whether by an individual scholar or a community grouped in a college. As with the theology lectureships there were obligations attached to the preachership to pray on behalf of Margaret's husband who had died at the end of July 1504, the rest of her family, and the queen who had died in February 1503. Margaret's scheme for the preachership eventually linked both individual and communal obligations: once Christ's College had been established, fellows of that, her own, college were given preference as candidates for the preachership.[31]

The colleges were themselves academic chantries: natural centres for royal bounty linked to requests for prayers and masses. They were part of a larger movement: colleges of secular priests, many with schools attached, burgeoned in the fourteenth and fifteenth centuries. In the universities they could repay the generosity of benefactors more effectively than could individual masters and scholars living in halls, hostels or lodgings. However small, the collegians were a *corps d'élite* with certain strict obligations to their founders, and were guaranteed continuity as landowning corporations. They could also act as a positive force in other directions: college lectures, the seed beds of Renaissance learning in the universities, began to be formally organized in the great chantry of Magdalen College, Oxford. In addition, colleges, by training in the skills of civil and ecclesiastical law, could furnish men for public service.

Colleges were therefore a permanent attraction both for the royal house and for humbler founders. Henry VI's foundation of King's had set a precedent at Cambridge for royal munificence on a greater scale than ever before. Henry VII was destined to add to that munificence,

---

[31] The foundation deed of the preachership for Cambridge, and the agreement by which Westminster bound itself to support it, are printed in Clark, *Endowments*, 65–70, 72.

though tardily, by his gifts towards the building of King's College chapel.[32] The university always had, and needed, advocates to ensure continued bounty: John Langton the master of Pembroke had been Henry VI's close adviser; Andrew Doket, wealthy principal of St Bernard's hostel, had given land for the site of King's and laboured to create another college, Queens', under the patronage of Margaret of Anjou.[33] That queen readily adopted the new foundation, conscious of the efforts of the women foundresses of Clare and Pembroke. Elizabeth Woodville succeeded her as royal patroness, pronouncing herself 'vera fundatrix' and giving the college statutes.

Lady Margaret was to surpass her predecessors by founding two new colleges and involving herself in the fortunes of others. While she was busy founding the lectureships and preachership she became connected with Jesus and Queens' and began the great collegiate enterprise of her life: the transformation of the royal foundation of God's House into Christ's College.

Jesus College began life in 1496 as the project of a bishop eager to improve his diocese by changing a heavily indebted community of nuns, which nevertheless had great latent assets in the form of urban possessions, into an educational college and chantry. This bishop, John Alcock of Ely, had royal connections, having been tutor to one of the sons of Edward IV. He was also, like Lady Margaret, interested in the cult of the Name of Jesus and in the deepening of spiritual life through such devotion.[34] His great friend, Thomas Rotherham, archbishop of York, had himself founded a chantry dedicated to Jesus which had educational obligations attached to it. He had also been a benefactor to Cambridge university when it needed funds to build its new complex of lecture schools and libraries. Alcock prepared the way for his own foundation as early as 1487 by allowing the nunnery of St Radegund's to run down in numbers and morale rather than seriously attempting reform. To effect its replacement by the desired college, however, royal and papal licences were needed, and this was the starting point for the

---

[32] The college had reminded him tactfully of its needs in 1499, profiting by the concentration of royal attention on Henry VI's remains; *CCR, 1500–9*, 71–3.

[33] J. Twigg, *A History of Queens' College Cambridge, 1448–1986* (Woodbridge, 1987), 5–6.

[34] Jesus College Cambridge, under its first surviving statutes given by the bishop of Ely in 1515, was to celebrate the mass of the Holy Name each week. The cult of the Five Wounds of Christ, which Jesus bore as its arms until the Reformation, was also favoured by Henry VI; *Statutes of Jesus College Cambridge, 1514–15*, ed. A. Gray (Cambridge, 1935), 36.

involvement of the king and Lady Margaret. A royal licence was granted on 12 June 1496 for the bishop to replace the nuns with a college of a master, six fellows and some scholars who were to be taught grammar. On 18 January 1497 Pope Alexander VI gave assent, and Alcock was allowed to dispose of the site and property in order to erect a college. He neglected, however, to get the former members of the community to witness his action, and the shaky legal basis of his hasty dissolution concerned the king, who obtained a second papal confirmation in 1500.[35]

In 1498 Henry and his queen came to Cambridge. The university schools were newly glazed for the occasion.[36] Lady Margaret was also in attendance, as her accounts show, on 1–2 September.[37] A daily celebration of mass for the royal family including Lady Margaret was one of the duties of the new Jesus College and a bond was given to the king for the celebration of a special mass of 'salus populi' four times a year. A fellow of Jesus was dispensed from university duties to superintend the alteration of the priory buildings for the college; and at the same period Lady Margaret's cofferer was paying a scribe to write for Chubbes, its first master.[38] In May 1503 Margaret disbursed £26 towards the buildings of the new college, which continued to receive attention from a circle of courtiers. Alcock himself had been comptroller of the royal buildings and in this office had close contact with Sir Reginald Bray, who presided over the completion of St George's chapel, Windsor, and attended the laying of the foundation stone of Henry VII's chapel at Westminster. At Jesus Bray supervised alterations to the nuns' domestic buildings to make them suitable for collegiate use. Sir John Riseley, one of the king's companions before Bosworth and a trusted councillor and diplomat, financed the transformation of the conventual church to serve as a college chapel, leaving funds at his death in 1512 to complete the work. Bray's wife, Katherine, gave money towards the appropriation of Great Shelford rectory to support

---

[35] *CPR, 1494–1509*, 72; *Cal. Papal Registers*, XVI, pt 1, 433, XVIII, 297. The college was not called Jesus either in the king's patent or the first papal letter, but was apparently originally dedicated to St Radegund, the patron saint of the nunnery it replaced, to the Virgin, and to St John the Evangelist. Nevertheless, it is called Jesus at the head of its earliest surviving acount roll, 1497–8, and other evidence supports the name by that date. A. Gray, *The Priory of St. Radegund*, Cambridge Antiquarian Society (Cambridge, 1898), 31, 46 n. 1; A. Gray and F. Brittain, *A History of Jesus College, Cambridge* (London, 1979), 28. [36] *Grace Book B, part I*, 111. [37] SJC, D91.17, p. 36.

[38] *Grace Book B, part I*, 112; SJC, D91.17, 37. The latter entry is a payment to Palmer of Peterhouse 'to write out the works of Mr. Chubbis'.

the grammar school attached to the college. Lady Joan Hastings endowed a fellowship, and Riseley became joint founder of a lectureship in theology with John Batemanson, one of Lady Margaret's advisers.[39] Her interest in the college is shown in a more personal way by her partnership with one of its fellows, William Atkinson, in providing the first complete English edition of the *Imitation of Christ*.[40] Atkinson was himself chaplain to Katherine Bray, and executor to Lady Willoughby, from both of whom he acquired land with which to help endow Pembroke College, another object of patronage for the Brays.[41]

Having shared in the spiritual benefits offered to the royal family by the foundation of Jesus, Margaret turned her attention to Queens'. She took up, though on a smaller scale, the role of patroness last held by Richard III's queen Anne Neville. Richard III and, to a lesser extent, his queen, had between them endowed the college generously with lands and rents. Queens' was referred to in Richard's grant in 1484 as 'de fundatione et patronatu consortis nostre', an acknowledgement of Anne's position in succession to Elizabeth Woodville. Henry VII's queen Elizabeth of York did not become patroness of the college, nor did the king endow it.[42] Possibly the death of Elizabeth in 1503 afforded Margaret the opportunity to show her own interest: if so, her earlier restraint shows a degree of delicacy. Once Margaret did intervene in the college's affairs, she rapidly made her wishes felt. On 12 April 1505 the college's president, Thomas Wilkinson, received from Queens' an acknowledgement of his intention to resign at the wish of Lady Margaret, and of their promise to elect John Fisher in his place.[43] To accompany this sudden intrusion of her confessor, already university chancellor and bishop of Rochester, she persuaded her kinsman and former ward, Edward Stafford, duke of Buckingham, to help the college with an endowment of land in Essex.[44] The grant, made for the sake of the health of Buckingham's soul and those of his forbears, rounded off property in an area where Lady Margery Roos had already granted

[39] Contributions by Margaret, SJC, D91.20, pp. 95, 154; activity of courtiers, *VCH, Camb*, III, 421–2, Gray and Brittain, *History of Jesus College*, 32; Batemanson, *BRUC*.

[40] Above, p. 184.

[41] A. Attwater, *A Short History of Pembroke College, Cambridge* (Cambridge, 1973), 26; Atkinson as chaplain, SJC, D91.20, p. 137.

[42] Twigg, *Queens' College*, 11–12.

[43] W. G. Searle, *The History of the Queens' College of St. Margaret and St. Bernard in the University of Cambridge*, 2 vols. (Cambridge, 1867–71), I, 125–6, from CUL, Queens' College Archives, QC Bk76 fol. 22b; Twigg, *Queens' College*, chs. 1 and 2.

[44] 30 acres, abutting the road between Haverhill and Bumpstead Helion. Searle, *Queens' College*, I, 133. CUL, Queens' College Archives QC Bk1, fol. 179.

land. It went a little way towards compensating Queens' for Henry
VII's revocation in 1485 of grants made by Richard III, and was a sign
that royal favour was once more embracing the college.

Fisher remained president of Queens' for three years. At the end of
his presidency the fellows assured him that although he could not
reside owing to his other posts, they had been content to have him as
head because of the integrity of his life, the breadth of his learning
('eruditio multiiuga') and the fame of his name.[45] Through Fisher,
Erasmus made his first contact with Queens': he resided there between
1511 and 1514, and made some friends among the fellows, even if his
general impressions of Cambridge life were not very favourable.[46]
Although Queens' did not bask in royal favour to the same extent that
it had under the Yorkist kings, Fisher's presidency was intended, and
was taken, as a compliment. The king and his mother resided in the
college in 1505 and 1506 as a consequence of Fisher's position as
chancellor and president.[47] In 1508 Fisher was to allow his anxiety
about holding so many offices at once to surface. He let the fellows
know that he wished to withdraw from the presidency and devote
himself to his see. During his brief office, however, he had played host
to the royal family and superintended the greatest of Margaret's
designs at Cambridge.

That design, the creation and endowment of Christ's College, was in
fact the transformation of an earlier, more modest foundation. God's
House, founded in 1439, lay on Milne Street, of which fragments
remain in Queens' Lane and Trinity Lane. The central section of Milne
Street, including God's House, was cleared by Henry VI to form the site
of King's. The original founder of God's House was William Bingham,
a London rector from a family in the midlands who was deeply
concerned at the decay of grammar schools in his native region. He
wished to remedy the situation by providing a new college where
grammar masters could be trained to staff the schools.[48] This was a
radical step: previously grammar teaching, although a recognized
outlet for some students of the arts course, had never been the main
purpose of a separate collegiate foundation. The royal licence which
Bingham had acquired for his college associated Henry VI in the

[45] Searle, *Queens' College*, I, 137.   [46] Twigg, *Queens' College*, 21–3.
[47] Searle, *Queens' College*, I, 134, 137. For Fisher's own occasional visits see his itinerary in
   B. Bradshaw and E. Duffy, eds., *Humanism, Reform and the Reformation: The Career of
   Bishop John Fisher* (Cambridge, 1989), 236–7.
[48] For Bingham and his foundation see Lloyd, *The Early History, passim.*

benefits conferred by the prayers of the community, but Bingham was to find that this was not sufficient to ensure his project a smooth passage. It had to compete with the plans of John Langton, master of Pembroke, chancellor of the university, and one of Henry's chief spiritual advisers, for a new college to be founded by the university on a site very close by. Bingham confidently rejected the university's offers of another site between Milne Street and the river, despite the fact that in 1440 the university's scheme was replaced by one for a royal college, which would obviously take precedence with the king over Bingham's. Bingham continued acquiring property on his original site and in 1442 gained a second royal licence, which this time widened the appeal of his new college by providing for scholars in other faculties besides grammar. It was also now permitted to receive endowments from the revenues of alien priories. By 1444 Bingham had completed the purchase of the living of Helpston, Northamptonshire, the rectory of which Lady Margaret was to appropriate to Christ's College.

Bingham, however, had reckoned without the designs of Henry VI and Langton for expanding King's. These grander plans, based on the scale of New College, Oxford, allowed no room for God's House on its site: the uncertainty of royal policy for the area had allowed Bingham to retain a false sense of security. Nevertheless the king did not entirely desert God's House: letters patent of 1446 granted a new site, just outside the Barnwell gate of the town, that now occupied by Christ's. In 1448 God's House was established on a new basis as the king's foundation, embracing grammar and the other liberal arts. It was imperfectly endowed, and Bingham's efforts to secure the protection of the duke of York for estates in Wales show awareness of the king's weak authority. Bingham pursued more religious endowments, including the living of Fen Drayton, Cambridgeshire, and rectory of Navenby, Lincolnshire, but possession of the latter was successfully contested by Syon Abbey. Despite all the difficulties, however, adoption by the crown had one great advantage for the future: Lady Margaret was moved to consider herself in a special sense heir to Henry VI's good intentions. She was to 'perfect' the college, giving it final academic form and a secure endowment.

God's House was to remain a small foundation of a keeper, or proctor, and four fellows, supplemented by pensioners, or members paying for their board in the college.[49] Statutes, allowed for in the

---

[49] A register of members is given in *ibid.*, 379–81.

charter of 1448, may have been drawn up provisionally in expectation of a greater establishment, but none were sealed until 1495–6. This was the year in which John Syclyng became head of the college, and his dealings with John Fisher and with Lady Margaret led to the eventual completion of Henry VI's adopted foundation.

Fisher's and Syclyng's university business brought them together. Both were in London in 1494 or 1495 on the university's behalf when Fisher lunched with Lady Margaret, and Syclyng was subsequently commissioned by the university to work for donations to the fabric of Great St Mary's church. They also worked together during the dispute between the university and town of Cambridge which was consigned to the arbitration of Lady Margaret. In 1501 when Fisher as vice-chancellor journeyed to Richmond to put the university's case before the royal council, Syclyng was senior proctor. He served on the university syndicate appointed to handle the case, alongside Henry Hornby, master of Peterhouse and Lady Margaret's secretary.[50]

On 28 May 1503 we get a glimpse of the affairs of Syclyng's college being discussed in the countess's household. Philip Morgan, Margaret's physician, wrote advising him to go to Collyweston to meet tenants of the college and settle questions of arrears of rent. By the time the letter was written university representatives had already visited both Collyweston and Buckden, the bishop of Lincoln's manor where the countess sometimes resided. Margaret and her officers must have come to know of the financial straits of God's House during discussions of the university's dispute with the town. The fate of the college was thus drawn to Margaret's notice during the course of her familiar activity as mediator and arbitrator.[51]

Negotiations between God's House, through Syclyng, and Lady Margaret's council began in earnest in 1504. Between March and August a draft agreement for the alteration of the college was produced between the countess, the college and the university. The draft envisaged a foundation empowered to acquire land to the value of £100, composed of fellows some of whom would be priests and some scholars as yet unordained.[52] In April 1504 Margaret's surveyor was paid for viewing land at Kneesworth, Whaddon and Malton, which

---

[50] *Ibid.*, 272.   [51] *Ibid.*, 258–60; *Grace Book B, part I*, 160, 153, 174.
[52] Lloyd, *The Early History*, 287–8. The numbers varied in the draft. The first quota for the priest-fellows, twelve, was the same number prescribed in the statutes of Christ's given in 1506, but the God's House draft provided for only a handful of scholars, a maximum of fourteen, whereas there were forty-seven at Christ's.

ultimately was granted to Christ's College, as well as property intended
for the Westminster chantry. On 17 July the king had written to his
mother giving his consent for her to devote part of a licence previously
granted in favour of Westminster Abbey to the benefit of the university
of Cambridge.[53] There must have been fierce competition between the
abbey and the university's advocates for the attention of the countess
and her officers at this time: Fisher undoubtedly played a major part in
persuading the countess to refound God's House.[54]

The rapidity with which Lady Margaret and her council took up the
cause of God's House alongside the endowment of Westminster
contrasts with the uncertainties which Bingham had to face between
1439 and 1448. The household at Collyweston dealt efficiently with a
variety of business. Syclyng's great advantages were Margaret's
concern with other aspects of university affairs, the financial links
between her Westminster and Cambridge university foundations, and
the constant advocacy of Fisher. Neither should we underestimate
Margaret's direct influence with the king, which had enabled her to get
the terms of a licence in mortmain altered without charge.

During 1505 the refoundation proceeded apace. In April Syclyng
and four fellows of God's House were received at Collyweston.[55] On 1
May the king, at his mother's request, granted letters patent for her to
augment, establish and *finish* the college. This was to be done with
the assent of Syclyng and the fellows of God's House who, unlike the
occupants of the hospital of St John when it was being turned into a
college, were guaranteed an honourable place in the new foundation.
The king enlarged on his mother's motives: she was rescuing God's
House for the exaltation and increase of the Christian faith, for the
sincere love which she bore the king's uncle Henry VI while he was in
the flesh, and the confidence which she had in his sanctity in heaven.[56]
Thus the shadow of the murdered king, informing Margaret's plans
both at Westminster and Cambridge, exercised a power more
compelling by far than had the dilatory authority of the reigning
monarch. The new college was to be named Christ's, and permission
was given in the letters for the support of a maximum of sixty scholars.

[53] Underwood, 'Cambridge connections', 70.
[54] Fisher's efforts are recorded in a eulogy written probably between 1524 and 1535, SJC,
    C7.11, fols. 61–4; Underwood, 'Cambridge connections', 69.
[55] SJC, D91.21, p. 16.
[56] *Documents relating to the Colleges and University of Cambridge*, printed for the Commissioners
    3 vols. (London, 1852), III, 147.

Power was given to the countess to frame new statutes: she was already aware of those of God's House, of which, together with information about the state of its endowments, her council had taken care to be apprised.[57] The pope confirmed the king's letters on 23 August 1505. The bull stated that Lady Margaret had 'established and augmented' the college at her own expense for the study of theology as well as of the liberal sciences.[58]

God's House was experiencing a transformation, but in accord with its past. Its academic programme was to be widened, yet an important element of training in grammar was to be retained. Its personnel would remain the kernel of the new foundation for the first five years. The change of name to 'Christ's' represented a shift of emphasis rather than a contrast: dedications to God in the middle ages indicated Christ as often as God the Father. Margaret's own piety and that of some contemporaries, however, tended to focus more explicitly on the Name of Christ, while the foundation of Jesus College had, by 1500, precluded the adoption of that name. Old and new names were in concurrent use in college documents until the formal handing over of Margaret's new statutes in October 1506.[59] The most significant change in this respect came with licences granted by the bishop of Ely on 12 December 1506. The college was exempted from his power of visitation, and its feast day altered from that of St Andrew, in whose parish it lay, to Easter, appropriate to its dedication to Christ. By these licences Christ's was lifted from a status in subjection to the local bishop shared by many earlier medieval colleges, and given a position which reflected its royal foundation.[60]

The endowments of the new college were, as we might expect, worthier of the energetic countess than had been those of the gentleman parson and unstable king who were the founders of God's House. In June 1505 Margaret's receiver journeyed from Fotheringhay to Leicester, Diseworth and Kegworth 'for the buying of lyfelod'; at Kegworth this meant acquiring the advowson as well as land. Margaret's policy was to consolidate spiritual assets, the right to present to livings, with purchases of land, and to get possession of rich

---

[57] Lloyd, *The Early History*, 285.   [58] *Cal. Papal Registers*, XVIII, 164–5.

[59] Lloyd, *The Early History*, 345–8. Syclyng and his colleagues continued to use the old name in internal documents, but Margaret's agents used the new; *ibid*, 430.

[60] H. Rackham, ed. *Christ's College in Former Days* (Cambridge, 1939), 317–22, where the licences are printed, from Christ's College archives, drawer 50 misc. 1.

rectorial tithes by engineering appropriations. The case of Helpston rectory, Northamptonshire, is particularly instructive since it shows us the countess taking an interest in the very fabric of her gift. The advowson was an old possession of God's House, but the king's letters of 1 May 1505 had included a licence to Christ's to appropriate, with the usual stipulation for allowing suitable provision for a vicar. Between 1506 and 1509 Margaret obtained the ecclesiastical sanctions needed for the appropriation and also bought 7 acres in Helpston to endow the vicar. She purchased a vicarage which she proceeded to have improved by the addition of two rooms, new chimneys, doors and windows.[61] Care such as this is consistent with her reputation in dealing with other livings in Devon: the enlargement of Sampford Peverell rectory which had a splendid parlour; and her gift of a house to the priest of Torrington.[62]

Considerable outlays on the lands acquired were recorded in Margaret's household expenses, and the endowments were not free from economic and even political complications. As early as 16 October 1503 Lady Margaret bought the manor of Malton, Cambridgeshire, from Sir Thomas Tyrell for £162, with another £52 laid out to appropriate the rectory and buy other land in the neighbourhood.[63] At this stage Malton was probably intended for Westminster. After the diversion of endowments to Christ's College Malton was appropriated instead to the college, without any provision for a vicar or obligation to support the parish poor by alms. Malton was thus intended as a chaplaincy, to provide extra income for a fellow or his deputy and unstinted profits for the college. Under Margaret's will the manor house was to be repaired for use as a refuge for the fellows in time of plague. To carry her intention into effect her executors made considerable alterations to Tyrell's Hall, the farmhouse at Malton, which was equipped for a resident farmer: the hall itself was heightened, chambers repaired and a new kitchen made. The incumbent of Malton previous to its appropriation was transferred to a chantry in the chapel on Margaret's estate at Maxey.[64]

Sir James Tyrell and Thomas his son had both been charged with

[61] SJC, D91.19, p. 110. Obligations to support the parish poor were retained by the college with this rectory, unlike that of Malton; below, p. 228.
[62] M. Wood, *The English Medieval House* (London, 1981), 194, 200; Pantin, 'Medieval priests' houses', 118–46; Cooper, 42.
[63] Christ's College archives, drawer 47, envelope F.
[64] *RCHM, West Cambs*, I, 189–94; SJC, D91.19, p. 47.

treason in May 1502, and Sir James had subsequently been executed. Attainders were passed against them in 1504 and Thomas was pardoned only in April that year. He was therefore in a vulnerable position at the time of Lady Margaret's purchase, and was later forced to pay exorbitantly to reverse the process against his father. Similarly John Lord Fitzwalter, from whose son, Robert, Margaret purchased Roydon manor for Christ's, had been attainted in October 1495, after being in communication with Perkin Warbeck. In July 1505 Robert had bound himself to pay the king £5,000: in November the attainder was reversed. Meanwhile Lady Margaret was negotiating to buy the manor which was paid for by December 1505. She was also busy acquiring property from another victim of attainder. This was Thomas Howard, earl of Surrey, attainted in 1485. He was restored to favour in 1489, but only gradually worked his way back into possession of most of his family property during the course of the reign. Although he had been active at court and was treasurer from 1501, Howard had sustained great losses, having been especially richly endowed by Richard III. He had parted with an estate in Diseworth to Henry Colet of London, father of John Colet the famous dean of St Paul's. Margaret acquired the estate and granted it to Christ's with Malton and Roydon in February 1506.[65]

Christ's, therefore, was partly endowed with estates bought from men whose families either were, or had recently been, under a political cloud. It was nothing new to divert land confiscated from political opponents to charitable purposes: Richard III had done so in his handsome provision for Queens' College. Such endowments, however, always carried the risk that in a different political climate their title would come under suspicion. These fears were expressed in a legal memorandum made after Margaret's death. One of its clauses advised her executors to find out whether any suits for restitution of property were pending on behalf of Lord Fitzwalter for Roydon, or the earl of Surrey for Ditesworth, and to take suitable action to protect the title of Christ's College.[66] As ever, Lady Margaret had worked in close touch

[65] Roydon cost at least £844 and Ditesworth £740, D91.21, pp. 58, 77. A licence in mortmain to hold properties at Ditesworth, Roydon, Malton and elsewhere was granted to Christ's on 28 November 1507, *CPR, 1494–1509*, 519. The attainders are discussed in J. R. Lander, *Crown and Nobility, 1450–1509* (London, 1976), 148, 274–5.

[66] SJC, D6.12. It was concluded that Howard's restitution had been fully performed and presented no threat, but a proviso excepting Roydon from any action by Fitzwalter was entered on the parliament roll and is recorded in the executors' accounts, Cooper, 186.

with Henry VII's fiscal and political policies and had profited by knowledge of them to further her own schemes: Henry VIII's initial reversal of his father's tight-fistedness gave legitimate grounds for concern.

Compared with the relatively smooth passage of the endowment of Christ's while Margaret lived, her executors experienced delays and difficulties in the foundation of St John's. This did not mean, however, that she was able to avoid or resolve all problems. Her schemes had always depended on the king's good-will and towards the end of the reign even she was forced to pay to get what she wanted from the royal administration. Creek Abbey, Norfolk, was granted by Henry to his mother to give, with its plate and jewels, to Christ's, in July 1507, without payment of routine official fees. Yet a bargain struck between them, signed by Edmund Dudley who was an important intermediary and reaped the benefits of that office, stipulated a large payment by instalments for the grant.[67] Creek was the only religious house made over to the college and for such a prize the king and his officers demanded a recompense. When Margaret wished to grant the college the church of Manorbier, in an area where she had £93 worth of land, she had to compensate the rector with an annuity of £30, and the college had to lease the rectory burdened with an assignment of the sum.[68] In the case of Navenby church she encountered a claim to the advowson which had been contested by Syon since 1449, although God's House had subsequently been granted rights to appropriate the rectory. Both the prestigious abbey and the college could produce confirmations of their title and a simple decision risked setting one set of royal grants at nought. After evidences had been supplied to Lady Margaret's lawyers the matter was put to the arbitration of two justices and a compromise was reached: Christ's received a pension from the rectory and Syon saved face by securing the title to it and the right to present one candidate out of two or three nominated by the college. The countess bore the costs and resort to her had saved either party the burden of a fully fledged legal battle.[69]

[67] *CPR, 1494–1509*, 543; Christ's College archives, drawer 97, envelope B. The payment, £466 13s 4d, was made by the end of 1507, SJC, D91.19, pp. 29, 52. Dudley's douceur for his 'diligent labours with the king' for getting the abbey, *ibid.*, p. 22. The pope confirmed the grant, together with the college's statutes, 26 Feb. 1509. *Cal. Papal Registers*, XVIII, 59–60.

[68] Christ's College archives, drawer 44, additional 1, March 1509.

[69] Lloyd, *The Early History*, 429.

Preparations for perfecting the government and accommodation of the transformed college went hand in hand with the process of its endowment. The statutes of Christ's, as is evident from Margaret's household accounts, were drawn up under the supervision of her officers; one copy was written under her own eye at Hatfield in the summer of 1506. On 3 October that year one complete set was formally handed over to the former master and fellows of God's House by Margaret's attorney, John Fothede, 'in a certain high chamber near the gates of the college belonging to the master'.[70] Master and fellows signed the statutes of the new college: continuity between the old and new foundations was established. The countess herself began the text with 'Nos Margareta' in her own hand, giving it a rare and undoubted authenticity. Formal ratification of the statutes was completed by papal approval in February 1509, when the fellows were also given permission to use portable altars for their liturgical duties.[71]

The statutes handed over in 1506 indicate that Margaret expected to occupy the new college herself: she reserved for her own use, or that of John Fisher as visitor of the college, a suite of rooms above those allotted to the master.[72] Direct evidence for her residence is slight, but we know that she visited Cambridge frequently between 1505 and her death. She was certainly at the college at some time between October and December 1506, for payments were made to those attending her at the time of the 'hallowing' of the college and the election of her scholars. Those in attendance included trusted servants of the king as well as of his mother: Sir Robert Clifford had revealed to Henry Sir William Stanley's plot in 1494, Sir John Hussey had risen through Margaret's service to become master of the king's wards, Sir Robert Southwell was one of the king's principal auditors, while Sir John Cutte was frequently among Margaret's legal counsel. In late July 1507 a woman brought a cake to the college for her; presumably a douceur for

---

[70] John Carter, servant of Henry Hornby and one of the chapel staff, was paid for a copy of the statutes of God's House, in July 1505, and in December for a copy of those of Christ's (SJC, D91.21, pp. 37, 56). Just after Christmas 1505 the master of choristers at Fotheringhay made another copy, and John Plowfield came to Hatfield to embark on a similar task in the following July (D91.21, pp. 59, 119, 133). Thomas Gotson, the notary who witnessed the formal handing-over of statutes, was paid for certifying four copies in late October–November 1506 (D91.21, p. 135).

[71] *Cal. Papal Registers*, XVIII, 34–59. Yet another copy of the Christ's statutes had been prepared together with a 'mynet' to send to Rome, by the president of Margaret's council, SJC, D91.19, p. 72.

[72] *Early Statutes of Christ's College*, ed. H. Rackham (Cambridge, 1927), *cap. VI*, 53.

some personal cause which she would not have offered unless she thought the countess was in residence. In April 1508 offerings were made, either by Margaret or on her behalf, for the safe delivery of Lady Derby's child.[73] There is nothing out of character in Fuller's story of her leaning out of a window in the college to correct the dean for dealing too harshly with an errant scholar.[74]

Encouraged no doubt by Lady Margaret's occasional presence, the college buildings rose rapidly. They were improvements upon a substantial groundwork. God's House already had some of the essentials of a college: chapel, chambers, gateway and hall. The extent of Margaret's work is disputed, but she certainly provided a new hall and library, adapted and probably largely rebuilt the chapel, and linked chapel and hall with a two-storey range comprising the master's lodge and her own chambers. Her financial outlay in the first year of the college, between June 1505 and January 1506, has been seriously underestimated, and the household accounts show regular large sums being expended between 1506 and 1509. Eighty-six loads of timber were brought from her Bourne park estate to Christ's in 1506–7 and next year more was accounted for at Collyweston for 'reparations' to the college.[75] The workmen were in the main supervised either by Margaret's own clerk of works, James Morice, or by the master of the college. Only two named royal workmen, the glazier Bernard Flower who worked on the library in 1507, and William Swayne, employed on the chapel after Margaret's death, took part. Christ's was thus very much the work of her own men, partly supplied from her estates.[76] It was the great architectural effort of her last years, and the outlay upon it far outweighs that on other works.

[73] SJC, D91.21, p. 159; D91.19, pp. 27, 88.
[74] T. Fuller, *The History of the University of Cambridge*, ed. J. Nichols, (Cambridge, 1840), 135. Her action shows a customary vigilance and decisiveness; her words 'lente, lente' might be translated 'softly, softly'.
[75] Cf. Lloyd, *The Early History*, 314ff and *RCHM, Cambridge*, I, 26. The total spent in 1505–9, £1,625, suggests substantial works. R. Willis and J. W. Clark, *The Architectural History of the University of Cambridge*, 3 vols. (Cambridge, 1886), II, 194, mentions only a sum of £66 13s 4d for June 1505–6, but £432 was spent during that year alone: SJC, D91.22, pp. 128–9; for later expenditure, D91.21, p. 160, D91.19, p. 53, 121, D102.1, p. 18, D106.1, D91.19, p. 121, D102.1, p. 18. The larger court of St John's cost approximately £5000 in 1511–16; A. C. Crook, *From the Foundation to Gilbert Scott, A History of the Buildings of St John's College Cambridge 1511–1885* (Cambridge, 1980), 14.
[76] Flower, SJC, D91.19, p. 37; Swayne, D106.1, fol. 12v. For Swayne at Cambridge see J. Harvey, *A Dictionary of Medieval Architects*, rev. edn (Gloucester, 1984), 291–2; timber at Collyweston, D91.16.

The clearest outward sign of her proprietary concern for Christ's was her suite of four rooms above the master's lodge, located between chapel and hall, the communal centres of the college. The first room has two windows in the wall next to the hall, enabling surveillance of the collegians assembled below. The second, middle, room is distinguished externally by the oriel window into the court, bearing the arms of Lady Margaret graven in the stone beneath the sill.[77] The badges of the Beauforts and the Tudor royal house which decorate it are reproduced on the chimney piece inside the room. The third room adjoins the chapel, and a window in the wall overlooks the body of the choir; there was originally a fourth small room off the third, apparently for a bedchamber or study. The third chamber with its window enabled the countess to say her devotions while the college services were in progress below, a combination of private and public worship common in the later middle ages.[78] In the late seventeenth century an external gallery, visible in David Loggan's print of the college, linked the fourth small room with a chamber over the ante-chapel. It was later removed and we do not know its date, but Margaret built a gallery leading from her bedchamber to the 'chapel closet' at Collyweston. If this was an original feature, the north-east of the college was dominated by arrangements for her personal convenience.[79]

The college was partly equipped from Margaret's household, as it was built and endowed with her revenues. Great organs from Hatfield were conveyed to Christ's; at the same time the countess had others brought to Hatfield from London. A small plot of land necessary for the master's yard and garden was purchased through Christopher Crossley,

---

[77] Plate 15. The arms were placed similarly on the oriel above the master's original lodge at St John's, but without the crest of the chained eagle which also appears on Margaret's personal seal.

[78] Above, p. 175. In a miniature in the Vienna Hours, Mary of Burgundy is portrayed sitting with her book of hours before a window looking into a church; *The Master of Mary of Burgundy*, ed. J. G. Alexander (London, 1970), plate 1. At Christ's a glazier was paid in 1510–11 for work in a study 'over the great chamber opening into the choir of the chapel'. Accounts for the completion SJC, D106.1, fol. 11r.

[79] J. Armitage Robinson, 'History of the Chapel', in Rackham, ed., *Christ's College*, 207–12. Rooms over the western ends of chapels are found, for example, at Corpus Christi College, Oxford, formerly at St John's College, Cambridge, and at the Savoy chapel London. For the gallery at Christ's see *RCHM, Cambridge*, I, 27–8, 33. Another gallery and small transept there may have been intended for Margaret's and Fisher's use. See C. N. L. Brooke, 'The university chancellor', in Bradshaw and Duffy, eds., *Humanism, Reform and the Reformation*, 57.

one of her chaplains, and the money laid out among household expenses. Before the countess's death payment was made to engrave the college seal, a chapel cross and other furniture was provided, and one of the statute books to be chained in the chapel was bound. The greatest gifts of plate formed part of her legacy, but some had been bought before her death from John Mundy, the London goldsmith with whom both she and Henry VII had many financial dealings.[80]

There is some evidence of the purchase of books for the college, but it is tantalizingly incomplete. According to her accounts the only named books bought for the college before Margaret's death were antiphoners for the chapel, suggesting that a choir was to be formed.[81] The only evidence for the purchase of books besides the antiphoners is a block payment of £38 3s 2d for unnamed printed books.[82] The donations book in the college library, however, dating from 1623, lists thirty-nine printed books said to have been given by her. These works were relevant to the studies of three higher faculties, theology, law and medicine. They survive in the present college library, but without contemporary indication of Margaret's prior ownership, purchase or gift to the college.[83]

The college which she had built, endowed and equipped retained the most interesting and progressive features of God's House, while expanding it in numbers and in the scope of subjects studied. It continued to maintain the college lecturer of Bingham's foundation who was to take as his texts the works of Latin classical poets and orators.[84] It was still obliged to nurture students of grammar in an age when few colleges specialized in this art, although Alcock had attached a grammar school to Jesus. Margaret's enhancement of the foundation

---

[80] Organs, SJC, D91.19, pp. 37, 44; William Parker of Hatfield arranged their carriage and Robert Barton dismantled and re-set them at Christ's, *ibid.*, p. 47; land, *ibid.*, p. 34, described as orchard and garden, *ibid.*, p. 52; seal, *ibid.*, p. 8; chapel furniture, D91.21, p. 131; binding statutes, *ibid.*, p. 136; plate, D91.19, p. 21.

[81] SJC, D91.19, pp. 88, 100.

[82] *Ibid.*, p. 121. This entry, mentioning Christ's, is contained in the summary of the account. In the body of the account are two entries which together make up the sum although they do not mention the college by name: £28 3s 4d to Gerard Godfryde and Nicholas Speringe of Cambridge stationers for divers books for my lady's grace; £9 19s 10d to the same for books paid for by my lord of Rochester, *ibid.*, p. 110. Wynkyn de Worde was paid for setting seventy-six dozen 'bullions' on books at Christ's early in 1509, D102.1, fol. 7v.

[83] List printed by N. Mclean, 'Books given to the Library of Christ's College Cambridge, by the Lady Margaret', *The Library*, n.s., 8 (April 1907), 218–23. It received further notice from W. W. Skeat, 'Early printed books', in Rackham, ed., *Christ's College*, 290–1.

[84] Lloyd, *The Early History*, 299–300.

ensured that it also encouraged the other arts, while the study of grammar was reserved to six scholars who were to graduate in it before going out to teach. The college lecturer was to expand his repertoire to include elements of logic and philosophy.[85] The twelve fellows of the new foundation were distinguished from the forty-seven pupil-scholars both in their higher studies, arts leading to theology, and in their ordination as priests within a year of admission to fellowships. Bingham's original elevation of the place of grammar was thus softened, without being lost altogether, and the traditional pattern of a college established.

The evidence for the supposed influence of Erasmus on Christ's, the college classical lectureship, is thus part of the heritage of God's House, and there is little sign of such academic innovation in the new college.[86] Fisher's influence was openly declared in the document by which the college arranged an anniversary for him in 1525: he was credited with having urged the foundation upon Lady Margaret and given it laws.[87] Certainly the organization and role of the college both looks back to Michaelhouse of which he was a member and anticipates St John's whose statutes he framed. Christ's was a society of priest fellows for whom theology was to be the crown of study, and of scholars most of whom would succeed to fellowships. There were elaborate provisions for college academic exercises dovetailed with attendance at university lectures which show the same care that Fisher took over these provisions in the later college. His injunctions as Visitor at Christ's in 1510 show a concern with the harmony of the foundation: those members who were paying as 'pensioners' for board and lodging should be sure to participate with the fellows and scholars in all worship and scholarly exercises.[88]

Lady Margaret stamped the college with signs of her authority. Her statutes made Fisher Visitor for life long before he was granted the chancellorship of the university for life in 1514. Her rooms were assigned to him, a privilege of residence not usually given to Visitors but in this case a sign that he was her deputy in college affairs. The statutes reserved the appointment of the master and fellows to Margaret during her life. They directed that half the fellows and

---

[85] *Early Statutes*, ed. Rackham, 107, 99–100.
[86] According to the college donations book Fisher gave the college a trilingual Bible; it is not there now. [87] Printed in *Early Statutes*, ed. Rackham, 127–33.
[88] SJC, D57.172, article 10.

scholars were to be chosen from nine northern counties, a provision which Fisher later claimed reflected Margaret's own desire, and among these Richmond was granted a separate status.[89] Fisher's injunctions of 1510 reminded the college that the foundress had ordered that valuables removed from the treasury for college use should be duly recorded. It was perhaps a sign of her concern about the fate of such of her own property as should come to rest there.[90] Too much has been read into some provisions in the statutes which have been attributed to her 'womanly' influence, such as arrangements for laundry and care of the sick, and directions that two students should share a chamber. Similar provisions are found in the statutes of King's College sixty years earlier, which furnished a mine of detailed legislation for subsequent codes.[91] Her concern for the security of the scholars in time of plague, however, is perhaps better founded, since Edmund Tudor had died of it and she owned a book of tracts on the subject. The codicil to her will among its many other provisions specifically directed that Malton manor be repaired as a plague refuge.[92]

The obligations of the college as a chantry for Margaret and her family were clearly set out in the king's original charter of 1 May 1505. Prayers and worship were to be offered for the countess, her former husband Edmund Tudor, the king's father, for her parents and other progenitors, for Henry's deceased queen, and for William Bingham founder of God's House. To these the statutes added the names of John Brokeley, a principal benefactor of God's House, and of Henry VI. The statutes elaborated the performance of these duties, which meant for every fellow a daily celebration of mass. While the fellows appointed to the new college were to receive stipends for prayers *only* for the named beneficiaries, those remaining from God's House were allowed to act as chantry chaplains for others.[93] It was made clear that worship was the prime duty of the new college. Besides inheriting images and other chapel furniture from Lady Margaret's own chapel it possessed a permanent Easter sepulchre, in honour of the college's official feast of the Resurrection. Thus the devotion to Christ which Margaret had

---

[89] The claim was made in a letter from Fisher to Richard Croke in *c.* 1527–9, *Funeral Sermon*, ed. Hymers, 210–16.

[90] SJC, D57.172, article 6; *Early Statutes*, ed. Rackham, 57.

[91] *VCH Camb*, III, 430. On parallels in statutes cf. *Early Statutes*, ed. Rackham, 91, 113, and *Documents relating to the Colleges and University*, II, 596; *Early Statutes*, 95, and *Documents*, II, 563; *Early Statutes*, 53, and *Documents*, II, 589.   [92] *Will*, 125 section 151.

[93] *Early Statutes*, ed. Rackham, 89.

publicly encouraged was given permanent expression in the ritual of her college.[94]

It is remarkable testimony to the efforts of Margaret and her advisers that Christ's had progressed so far in building and endowment by the time she died. Certain things were left unfinished: the chapel had to be completed by her executors and legal processes affecting the endowments continued. Margaret Warton of Coventry, whose second husband was a member of the royal household, left in 1507 some lands at Allesley (Wark.) for the benefit of the college. Lady Margaret was supervisor of her will and negotiations began for carrying out the bequest during 1508, but the property was not conveyed to the college until 1512.[95] The countess's last years were busy ones, and it is not to be supposed that she was preoccupied only with the royal college founded at Cambridge. In 1506 she established her chantry at Westminster, perfecting the plan by which the abbey would support her lecturers and preacher at the universities.[96] She kept in touch with academics of Oxford as well as Cambridge, inviting them to preach in her household. One of them, Edmund Wilsford of Oriel, her first theology lecturer at Oxford, was to be named as her confessor among the legacies of her will in February 1509.

Nevertheless, the amount of royal attention converging on Cambridge during 1505–8 entitles us to regard the impact of the countess and her advisers as an early sixteenth-century 'Cambridge phenomenon'. The foundation of Christ's took place against the background of an unprecedented number of royal visits.[97] In June 1505 Lady Margaret visited Queens' and boatmen rowed her down the Cam to grace disputations in the university schools. In April 1506 the king stayed at Queens' before attending mass in King's College chapel; in the summer his mother stayed again in the college attended by a greyfriar. In 1507 the king, Margaret and the prince of Wales were present at the university commencement held in the Greyfriars' church. It was

---

[94] The sepulchre was finished, with an image of Christ, Mary and four knights, during 1510. It was made by Ralph Bolman, or Bowman, freemason (Harvey, *Medieval Architects*, 292), apparently on the premises of the Carmelites from where it was carried to the college; SJC, D106.1, fol. 13, has the following: 'Item, to Nicholas aprice for the cariege of thymage of c[r]ist with the iiij knyghts and the supulcre with themage of oure ladie from the white friers to the college after they were fully fynysshed and mad by Rafe Bolman fremason xviijd.'   [95] Underwood, 'Politics and piety', 51.

[96] Expenses for drawing up the indenture, SJC, D91.21, p. 149.

[97] For a discussion of these visits see M. G. Underwood, 'John Fisher and the promotion of learning', in *Humanism, Reform, and the Reformation*, ed. Bradshaw and Duffy, 43 n. 22.

probably on this occasion that Fisher, officiating at the ceremonies as chancellor, delivered his oration commemorating royal bounty to the university. The speech made an affectionate reference to Margaret's small stature. In the context she must have appeared as the tiny spring of a great fountain of royal munificence: the speech was an acknowledgement of past gifts and an appeal for more. Henry's donations for the university church and for King's College chapel were alluded to, but the chapel still remained unfinished. On 24 March 1509 the king capped previous gifts with a donation of £5,000 and the total he gave while living was £6,850: double the average annual income from all Margaret's estates.[98] Cambridge had been kept under the king's notice by his mother's interest, and by the eloquence of its chancellor whom she had made her chief confidant. If Fisher was the architect of her foundations, her own influence was responsible for their endowment. In the case of Christ's she had taken advantage of current political circumstances, snapping up the manors of men in need of ready cash, and she had even, with some difficulty, persuaded Dudley and the king to part with a religious house and its possessions.

There are indications that Fisher's task as advocate of Cambridge was not always an easy one. He had to contend with the Oxford academics about his mistress. These, after the foundation of Christ's, pressed her to transform the priory of St Frideswide, on the site of the present Christ Church, into a college.[99] Fisher, however, succeeded in retaining her interest in Cambridge and drew her attention to a second, more ancient, foundation in the town in need of improvement: the hospital of St John the Evangelist.

The hospital had long since ceased to fulfil its charitable purposes on the scale for which the burgesses had founded it. For a short time the home of scholars before they moved to Peterhouse in 1284, it had been recognized as part of the university once more in the mid-fifteenth century. Its income was supplemented by the rents of lodgers which it took in, in the manner of a university hostel, while continuing to provide a liturgy for the townsfolk, to serve a rural parish, and to fulfil chantry obligations. These, and an annual dole to the poor, seem to

---

[98] *Oration*, above, p. 40; gifts, Colvin, Ransome and Summerson, eds., *King's Works*, III, pt 1, 188.

[99] SJC, C7.11, fol. 62. A letter of 1508, addressed by Oxford university to the countess, thanking her for past favours, may well have been a subtle instance of this pressure; *Epistolae Academicae, 1508–96*, ed. W. T. Mitchell, Oxford Historical Society, n.s., XXVI (Oxford, 1980), 2–3.

have been the limits of its functions, and by 1505 only three brethren, now called 'fellows', were resident.[100] It was no longer actively acquiring land, although it had done so as recently as 1483–4, and some of its plate was in pledge. Yet its economic situation, like that of God's House, was by no means desperate; with additional endowments, the prospects for transforming it into a house of learning seemed fair to Margaret and her university-dominated household.

The first signs of Lady Margaret's interest in the hospital occur in 1505, when she was procuring the king's charter to transform God's House into Christ's. In that year one of the remaining brethren of St John's visited Margaret and the archbishop of Canterbury in connection with the reform of the house. The master of the hospital subsequently resigned and Margaret's stepson, James Stanley the bishop of Ely, who was also the hospital's patron, assumed its management. It took some time to formalize the master's departure, but during 1507–8 the bishop's vicar general and officers of Lady Margaret were installed as 'vices magistri'.[101] The next stage was negotiation between Lady Margaret and the bishop to allow her to adopt the foundation and 'translate' it into an academic college, adequately endowed. In the event she died in the midst of her preparations. The fledgling foundation, a weak youngster indeed, was caught up in the wider consequences of her death and its impact on a new Tudor reign.

---

[100] For the history of the hospital and its decay see M. Rubin, *Charity and Community in Medieval Cambridge*, Cambridge Studies in Medieval Life and Thought, 4th series, (Cambridge, 1987), especially 13, 234–5, 294–5.

[101] SJC, D106.10, fol. 5; D102.3, pp. 7–8; D3.75.

8

THE LEGACY

Death in the later middle ages was a voyage from one world into another for which careful preparations had to be made. It was expected to occur at any time from the age of thirty onwards and landowners with great estates and many dependants often set their affairs in order years before their actual decease. To secure the descent of their lands complicated trusts had to be established; to secure their passage to eternity chantries had to be founded and sometimes chapels built. A lifetime's patronage of particular cults and religious orders was often summed up in lavish gifts to abbeys, colleges and shrines. Wills were documents long in formation, contingent sometimes on the changes and accidents of many years. The testator's last wishes, verbally expressed, could have as much force as provisions written down long before. If he or she were politically active it was even more important that wills should be continually modified to suit the circumstances of the times. Humphrey Coningsby recalled of Lady Margaret that 'most commenly aboute the feste of the Natyvyte of oure lorde the same Princesse yerely uppon vii or viii yere before her decesse and more caused her testament and Will to be red unto her and renewed after her mynde and plesure'.[1]

She had begun as early as 1472 to safeguard her possessions in Devon and Somerset, to be used for the purposes of her will. When those had been carried out the lands were to revert to her son Henry, earl of Richmond.[2] The estates had been conveyed to new trustees in 1490, but between then and 1508 her plans unfolded in greater detail.[3] They included the endowment of a chantry for her parents at

---

[1] SJC, D4.10; *Notes*, 227.
[2] Jones, 'Richard III and Lady Margaret Beaufort', 28–9.
[3] SJC, D56.211, 203.

Wimborne Minster, and her own chantry in the royal chapel at Westminster Abbey, by which her university foundations were also to be supported.[4] In 1505 Margaret drew up a deed by which John Fisher and others were made trustees for her lands at Maxey and Torpell in Northamptonshire, so that these, too, could be devoted to the purposes of her will. In that year St John's hospital in Cambridge was already being brought to her attention, and her plans for Westminster were nearing completion. The agreement reached with the abbey in 1506 included prayers to be said for all her deceased husbands except John de la Pole.[5]

The almshouses and chantries at Westminster founded by the king and his mother set the seal on their lifetime partnership: as they had jointly watched over each other's affairs, so now jointly they set about atoning for their sins in hope of securing a heavenly reward. During 1501–2 her household accounts show £353 13s spent on the building work of her almshouse, which she personally inspected on one occasion.[6] The king had asked the pope as early as 1490 for indulgences as powerful as those obtainable at the shrines at Rome to be available for the place of his mother's burial: these were incorporated in Margaret's agreement with Westminster in 1506.[7]

Margaret's parents were remembered in all her foundations. The first family chantry, later to be overshadowed by Westminster and Christ's College, was at Wimborne Minster, where Duke John and his wife Margaret were buried. Their daughter paid to keep lights burning at their tomb and in 1497 she obtained, among licences for her other foundations, permission to endow a chantry for their souls to the value of £10.[8] Lands at Curry Rivel (Som.) were granted to trustees for the purpose in 1504. In February 1508 a greater endowment was begun: Sir Charles Brandon sold her the manor and advowson of Goathill (Dors.) for £100 to support one priest at Wimborne to 'sing there for my lady's ancestors forever'.[9] Neither of the properties was mentioned as an endowment for the chantry in Margaret's will of 6 June 1508,

---

[4] See above, pp. 208–9.   [5] *CCR, 1500–9*, 289–93.
[6] PRO, SC6/Eliz. I/3368. We are grateful to Miss M. M. Condon for drawing our attention to this isolated household account; also A. P. Stanley, *Historical Memorials of Westminster Abbey* (London, 1868), 414, H. F. Westlake, *Westminster Abbey* (London, 1923), 370; WAM, 33320.
[7] *Cal. State Papers, Venice*, I, 193, no. 581; *CCR, 1500–9*, no. 770.ii.
[8] M. K. Jones, 'John Beaufort's death and tomb at Wimborne', *Somerset and Dorset Notes and Queries*, 31 (March 1982), 218–19; *CPR, 1494–1509*, 79; *Will*, 117.
[9] PRO, E135/3/21, fol. 2; SJC, D91.19, pp. 73, 115.

however, where it was envisaged that her executors might have to finish the project. The will added the stipulation that the chantry priest was to teach grammar free of charge. In December altar furniture was bought; instructions annexed to the will in January or February 1509 spoke of the need for a further royal licence to cover the purchase of more furnishings, support of an usher for the school, repair of a schoolhouse, and books.[10]

The projected endowment for Wimborne was interrupted by the progress of Margaret's larger foundations. Christ's remained to be completed; in June 1508 the bishop of Ely discussed the scheme to translate St John's hospital into a college, and before Christmas signed an agreement to that effect.[11] In January Margaret purchased the manor of Bassingbourne in Fordham which was to be conveyed to the new college in 1512; in March Hugh Ashton was making enquiries at London to obtain the priory of Broomholm (Norf.) for St John's.[12] In the midst of these preparations, in February 1509, Goathill, the proposed endowment for Wimborne, was sold for £200.[13] The household gained £100 in ready money to devote to other endowments, but Wimborne for the present gained only the lands at Curry Rivel. The foundation charter for the chantry, drawn up by Margaret's executors in 1511, underlined the importance of the academic foundations by giving the nomination of the chantry priest schoolmaster to Christ's College.[14] Not until 1526 did James Morice, Margaret's former clerk of works, provide Wimborne with another endowment, lands in the parish of Badgworth (Som.).[15] Thus a chantry with local school obligations, much missed by the inhabitants in 1547 after its suppression, was forced into the background by the competing claims of a larger new academic foundation.

At the beginning of 1509 the countess fell ill, seriously enough for estimates for funeral expenses to be drawn up. She soon made a satisfactory recovery, but delegated some aspects of her affairs: from January 1509 three of Lady Margaret's executors, John Fisher, Henry

---

[10] SJC, D4.7.

[11] SJC, D4.10, *Notes*, 216–50. Both these facts appear only in the depositions made in Chancery in 1512, and no agreement of 1508 has survived.

[12] Unsuccessfully: it was not dissolved for twenty years; D. Knowles and R. N. Hadcock, *Medieval Religious Houses, England and Wales*, 2nd edn (London, 1971), 96, 98.

[13] It was sold to William Lang, of Candle Purse, SJC, D56.201.

[14] The clause was not printed by J. Hutchins, *The History and Antiquities of the County of Dorset*, 3rd edn, 3 vols. (London, 1861–74), III, 270–3, but is in the original charter, DRO, P204/GN1/1.   [15] PRO, E135/3/21. fol. 10v.

Hornby and Hugh Ashton, began signing the accounts of a new cofferer, Robert Fremingham, in place of their mistress. All three were thus at the centre of affairs in the household at a crucial time and were to be closely connected with the foundation of St John's after Margaret's death: Fisher seeking help at court, Hornby supervising affairs in Cambridge, Ashton assisting Hornby to manage such revenues as were available. Yet Margaret herself continued to take an active interest in this last of her enterprises: John St John recalled her saying during Lent 1509 'at her board and other places' that, should she live, she would make St John's 'as good and of as good value' as Christ's.[16]

On 10 March she made an agreement with her stepson, the bishop of Ely. This document, preserved in several versions, one of which was signed by Margaret alone and another by four of her executors and the bishop, set out terms on which he would consent to the hospital being turned into a college. He agreed to transfer to her his position as patron of the hospital so that she might found a college. The see of Ely had its rights safeguarded: the college was, unlike Christ's, to be subject to the bishop's jurisdiction as Visitor. Personally the bishop was to be commemorated as benefactor and co-founder; he was also to present three scholars, one of whom, if fit and learned, was to be elected to the college. The agreement also safeguarded the chantry and parochial duties incumbent on the hospital, and the commemoration of all its benefactors.[17] Having gained her stepson's consent, in however provisional a form, Margaret sought the necessary royal licence for a new foundation. Between the accession of Henry VIII, on 22 April 1509, and her death her solicitor drew up a petition to the new king to establish the college. It was to be a society of fifty persons, studying arts and theology as at Christ's, but also the canon and civil law.[18]

By then Margaret's attention had been drawn to affairs of state. In early April she was in London at her house of Coldharbour, but before Henry VII's death on 21 April she had moved to be near him at Richmond. There news was brought of the 'honourable services' done when her son's corpse was borne to Westminster for burial. Her name

---

[16] Chancery deposition of John St John, SJC, D4.10, *Notes*, 244.

[17] Its continued liturgical importance is shown by the fact that in April 1511 the townspeople began to grumble that a master was not put into the new foundation, although Easter was approaching and they expected to hear mass and receive the sacraments; letter from Hornby to Fisher, SJC, D105.106.

[18] SJC, D4.2. The provision for studying law was omitted both from the pope's bull, 24 June 1510, and the foundation charter, 9 April 1511.

had headed the list of those appointed to discuss arrangements for the interment. From Richmond Margaret moved to the greater security of the Tower, while her grandson's rule was established. In late May she was paying rewards to servants 'nigh about his grace' and on 8 June was at court at Greenwich.[19] On 11 June Henry VIII married Catherine of Aragon. On 23 June, when they went from the Tower of London to the palace of Westminster on the day before their coronation in the Abbey, Lady Margaret was there to watch the procession. A house was hired for her in Cheapside, the wide city street along which so many pageants passed, where she could stand with her granddaughter Princess Mary.[20] Here she waited, as she had witnessed the queen's coronation in 1487, from a secluded vantage point 'behind a lattice', attended by her waiting-women. It was a position which concealed her part in the establishment of the dynasty. Her fears for its fortunes beset her happiness at the occasion: Fisher recalled that the coronation gave her great joy, 'yet she let not to saye that some adversyte wolde followe'.[21] The last years of her son's reign had indeed been clouded by the deaths of his wife and two of his children; the early splendours of her grandson's were soon to be shadowed by his own fears for the succession.

For the present, however, her fears must have sounded out of key with the mood of triumph. After the coronation she moved to Westminster, occupying Cheyneygates, a lodging of the abbot's which was part of the vast secular and spiritual complex of the abbey and palace.[22] Here, overwhelmed perhaps by the effect of a round of festivities and banqueting on an already weakened constitution, she fell sick. Henry Parker later attributed her illness directly to eating a cygnet. 'Waters and powders' were bought to relieve her, but she did not recover and died on 29 June.[23] Two accounts of her last hours

---

[19] SJC, D102.1, fols. 11–14. See above, p. 92. The fact that she was about the court in this capacity makes it possible that she could, as reported by Stowe and Lord Herbert of Cherbury, have influenced Henry VIII's first choice of counsellors. Stow, *Annals*, 487, J. A. Guy, *The Cardinal's Court*, (Hassocks, 1977), 23.

[20] SJC, D102.1, fol. 17. Mary was called 'Princess of Castile', a vestige of the, by then, defunct proposal to marry her to the Archduke Charles.

[21] *Mornynge Remembraunce*, 306.

[22] It had been let in 1486 to Queen Elizabeth Woodville; J. Armitage Robinson, *The Abbot's House at Westminster* (Cambridge, 1911), 22–3.

[23] BL, Add. MS 12060, fol. 23v; SJC, D102.1, fol. 15; WAM, 19606; H. E. Pearce, 'The death of Lady Margaret', in Rackham, ed., *Christ's College*, 15–20.

reflect different strands in her nature: firm religious faith, and fear of what the future might bring. Fisher, stressing her deep devotion to the person of Christ, recalled that when the last rites were administered 'with all her herte and soule she raysed her body...and confessed assuredly that in that sacrament was conteyned Chryst Jhesu, the Sone of God, that dyed for wretched Synners upon the Crosse, in whome holly she putte her truste and confydence'.[24] Reginald Pole, writing in the aftermath of the spoliation of the church which Margaret had helped to endow, reported a darker scene. Weeping many tears as she was dying, Margaret had commended the young king to Fisher's guidance, fearing that the adolescent Henry, left in supreme authority, would easily turn his face from God.[25]

Lady Margaret had died on the threshold of the place she had chosen for her burial. The elaborate provisions which had been made, some months before, for the distribution of alms as her body proceeded to Westminster from the place of her decease were thus rendered unnecessary.[26] Most of the ceremonial, and the charity which accompanied it in London, took place, however: distribution of alms and payments for masses and prayers in the religious houses and parishes of the capital, the deliverance of certain prisoners from the gaols, the doles to the poor. For some, Lady Margaret's funeral was a day of jubilee.[27] On 3 July her body was moved from Cheyneygates to the abbey refectory, where it lay amid the glitter of great candles until it was transferred for burial in the royal Lady chapel of the abbey on the ninth.

The customary pomp for a great noble's burial accompanied the interment: scutcheons of her arms, banners and pennants surrounded the hearse, black and white cloth of gold were draped in vivid contrast upon it and upon the tomb, as yet uncased in stone and unembellished by effigy or other ornament. The tomb was perfected by the workmanship of Pietro Torrigiano, who also executed those of Henry VII and Queen Elizabeth in the same chapel. The contract for the tomb of Lady Margaret and the figure of the countess resting upon it was

[24] *Mornynge Remembraunce*, 309. Henry Parker stated that she died as the Host was being elevated, BL, Add. MS 12060, fol. 23v.

[25] 'Apologia Reginaldi Poli ad Carolum C. Caesarem', in *Epistolarum Reginaldi Poli...Collectio*, ed. Cardinal Quirini (Brescia, 1744, repr. Gregg Press, Farnborough, 1967), 94–5.

[26] The estimates for her funeral costs, £1,033, had been drawn up at Hatfield on 24 January 1509. The actual costs were £1,021; SJC, D4.7, pp. 38, Cooper, 190.

[27] Cooper, 188–9.

drawn up with the Florentine sculptor on 23 November 1511.[28] Erasmus, then in England at Fisher's invitation, composed an epitaph for the monument which celebrates Margaret's foundations at Wimborne Minster and the universities of Oxford and Cambridge. The praying gilt-bronze figure reclines still within the pillared surround appointed in the contract. At her feet lies the yale of Kendal, and all about her are badges of the Beaufort portcullis. Around the tomb are panels of the arms of her parents and grandparents, her husbands Edmund Tudor and Thomas, earl of Derby, Henry V and Katherine of Valois, Henry VII and Elizabeth of York, Henry VIII and Catherine of Aragon, and Arthur prince of Wales.[29]

Fisher took leave of his friend and patron publicly in the sermon he preached at her month's mind in July 1509. In it he praises her nobility of lineage, conduct and spirit. It breathes respect for the great feudatory who ably governed her household and dispensed justice, blended with admiration for her practice of piety and charity. Fisher presents these characteristics as two sides of the same medal. He pictures the impact of her death on the world at large:

> All Englonde for her dethe had cause of wepynge. The poore Creatures that were wont to receyve her Almes, to whome she was always pyteous and mercyfull; the Studyentes of both the Unyversytees, to whom she was as a Moder; all the Learned Men of Englonde, to whome she was a veray patroness; all the vertuous and devoute persones, to whome she was as a lovynge Syster; all the good relygyous Men and Women, whome she so often was wonte to vysyte and comforte; all good Preests and Clercks, to whome she was a true defendresse; all the Noblemen and Women, to whome she was a Myrroure and Exampler of honoure; all the comyn people of this Realme, for whome she was in theyre causes a comyn Medyatryce, and toke right grete displeasure for them; and generally the hole realm hathe cause to complayne and to morne her dethe.[30]

Fisher goes on to balance sorrow with joy in a celebration of her piety, and assurance of her reception in heaven. He urges his hearers 'put we

[28] SJC, D56.21, printed in R. F. Scott, 'On the contracts for the tomb of Lady Margaret Beaufort, Countess of Richmond and Derby, mother of Henry VII and foundress of the colleges of Christ and St. John in Cambridge', *Archaeologia*, 66 (1915), 366–8. For the royal effigies see C. Galvin and P. Lindley, 'Pietro Torrigiano's portrait bust of King Henry VII', *Burlington Magazine*, 130 (December 1988), 892–901.

[29] Cooper, 123–4, describes the tomb and prints the epitaph; Cornelius Symondson's contract for the grate, is printed in Scott, 'Contracts', 373–4, from SJC, D56.22.

[30] *Mornynge Remembraunce*, 301. For an analysis of the structure of the sermon, see Richard Rex, *The Theology of John Fisher* (Cambridge, 1991), 42–4.

asyde all wepynge and teeres, and be not sad, ne hevy as Men withouten hope'. In the time-honoured tradition of Christian piety the preacher uses the faith of one to strengthen that of many.

The death of the countess was followed by the appraisal of her worldly possessions. Margaret had caused inventories of her goods to be made during the last decade of her life both at Collyweston and Hatfield, and these were of use to her executors. Oliver Scales made a new valuation of her wardrobe of robes, which included seven black velvet gowns, some trimmed with ermines. These and other services to the executors culminated in his being entrusted with the oversight of the works of St John's College. The total assets in plate, jewels and rich materials came to £14,724. Hangings and tapestries which had graced her household were disposed of to those in and outside it. The History of Paris and Helen and the Story of Nebuchadnezzar were sold for £40 to Thomas, earl of Surrey. Fisher bought the History of Saul for £12, while parts of the Story of Matthew Gough went to William Bedell.[31] Less valuable, but a sign of Margaret's great position, was the herd of swans bearing her badge which cruised the waters of the Thames. After her death her squire Nicholas Aughton took many boats to capture them, their departure echoing that of their mistress. All such tasks had to be accounted for by her executors who now had to face the legal processes leading to the probate of her will. The business was not completed until 1512, during which time they had the difficult job of carrying out her last intention to establish St John's.

The will Margaret had signed in June 1508 prescribed the details for the celebration of her funeral rites, anniversary of her death, maintenance of her chantries at Westminster and Wimborne, and support of her university lecturers and preacher. The foundation and endowment of Christ's was rehearsed and Margaret's executors were directed to see that its members were properly governed according to the statutes. Grants of land to certain of her servants were mentioned, and one for the support of Margaret White, the anchoress of Stamford whom Margaret was accustomed to visit.[32] The revenues of her father's

---

[31] Cooper, 181. The charge to the executors of £17,664 recorded in the roll of accounts prepared for the crown includes in addition the balance of £2,800 due from the wardship of Lady Lisle granted by the king, and of money received by Robert Shorton, master of St John's until 1516; *L and P Henry VIII*, II, ii, 1297; list of goods sold, SJC, D102.16.

[32] These were made out of her grandmother's estates at Maxey and Torpell, Northamptonshire.

lands, put in trust since 1472, together with the profits from sale of her moveable goods, were to be devoted to the uses of her will, until such time as it was fully performed. After that, the estates would automatically revert to the king as Margaret's sole heir. No mention was made of the nascent project for translating the hospital of St John into a college, and the terms of the will as it stood were clearly insufficient to establish and endow the foundation.

A schedule of bequests was added to the will in February 1509. These covered the whole scope of Lady Margaret's bounty, with the greatest emphasis on Christ's College, which was placed first in the list. It received a great weight of chapel plate, images, crucifixes and chalices, and an elaborate incense boat: 'a great ship gilt with a litell gilt spone; on evry ende of the shippe is a litel gilt lyon'. More items, including a set of six spoons and two salts, were listed in an inventory of plate handed over to the master of Christ's in August 1509. The college still has six late fifteenth-century apostle spoons, a great beaker garnished with roses and crowned with a tuft of marguerites, which bears in addition the Beaufort portcullis, and two salts 9 inches high. None of these can be exactly matched with items in the inventory, but their date and heraldic and decorative features support their identification as surviving pieces of the foundress's bequest. Jesus College, the first to arouse her interest, received a modest bequest of £2. The Beaufort Hours, one of her most precious personal possessions, was ordered to be chained in the Lady chapel at Westminster.[33] Service books, plate and vestments were left for her chantry there, to the abbey of Bourne, the college of Tattershall, from which some of her own choristers had come, Wimborne Minster, and the parish church of Collyweston. Friars of all four orders, at Ware, Richmond (Surr.), Northampton, Greenwich and Stamford, received sums of money, as did the Carthusians at Mountgrace, Sheen and London and the Bridgettines of Syon. Recluses were not forgotten: bequests were made to the two anchoresses at Stamford for whom she had built new chambers, and to others at St Albans, Westminster, London Wall and Faversham.

[33] *Will*, 120, 'item oon booke havyng in the begynnyng certeyne Images with prayours to them and aftir theym the prymare and the psaltere to be chayned within the chapell'. For bequests to Christ's, see Plates 10–12, and Scott, 'On a list of the plate, books and vestments bequeathed by the Lady Margaret', 349–67, from SJC, D57.43; J. E. Foster and T. D. Atkinson, *Old Cambridge Plate*, an Illustrated Catalogue of the *Loan Collection of Plate Exhibited in the Fitzwilliam Museum, May 1895* (Cambridge, 1896), 4–7, 12–13.

The claims of family and household followed those of piety. Henry VIII received her 'french book', prefaced with an illuminated version of Genesis, the second volume of Froissart, a great volume of Boccaccio, Lydgate's *Siege of Troy* and five golden cups.[34] Queen Margaret of Scotland, Catherine of Aragon and Princess Mary of Castile received cups and jewels. Among the many bequests to Margaret's officers and servants her kinsman, John St John, received plate, precious cloths and a volume of the *Canterbury Tales*, while mistress Parker, wife of Henry Parker, got a volume of Gower in addition to other goods. Among those receiving annuities were Edith Fowler, who had had charge of the almswomen and was to be commemorated with her husband in a brass at Christ's College, and Perrot Doryn, a French companion from whom Margaret presumably acquired skill of use in her translations. Edmund Wilsford, named as Margaret's confessor, received a cup bearing the arms of Humphrey duke of Gloucester. This was subsequently exchanged by Wilsford and was consigned with the other plate to Christ's College, where it still remains.[35]

The will as proved in the archbishop of Canterbury's court on 22 October 1512 incorporated these bequests as well as the agreement to found St John's drawn up between Margaret and the bishop of Ely in March 1509; and another codicil explaining her last wishes for the foundations of St John's and Wimborne school, and for the completion of Christ's College. In November the court of chancery decreed that the revenues from the lands placed in trust could be used to perform these purposes.[36] By the time of probate royal and papal approval for the alteration of the hospital into St John's College had already been gained, and Lady Margaret's executors had sealed the charter of foundation on 9 April 1511. The codicil to the will made clear that the college was to be built, 'sufficiently endowed' and equipped from the revenues of Lady Margaret's estates in trust. In addition, all plate and other goods not previously bequeathed were to be divided between Christ's and St John's. Neither the codicil, however, nor the decree in chancery which released the revenues to the executors in November,

---

[34] *Will*, 121. Henry Parker recalled that Margaret read out of her 'french books' after supper. The Boccaccio was possibly Lydgate's version of the *Falls of Princes*; Axon, 'The Lady Margaret as a lover of literature', 34–41.

[35] A sum in compensation for the exchange was paid to Wilsford by the executors; Cooper, 188.

[36] *Will*, 103–26. For a full discussion of extant versions of the will, see Appendix 4, pp. 288–90.

defined precisely for how long they could be so used: when was the college to be reckoned as fully established and endowed? The executors had a longer view of this than had the king's financial officers. The withdrawal of the revenues by Henry VIII as Margaret's heir was to be the last in a series of obstacles to carrying out her wishes for St John's.

Fisher, who with Hornby and Ashton bore the brunt of the task, found the obstacles daunting enough to set them out in a vivid memorandum long afterwards.[37] From this it is clear that Margaret's death had plunged the scheme into uncertainty. To begin with, the bishop of Ely showed himself slower to co-operate in the alteration of the hospital once his powerful stepmother's influence was removed. Unlike Christ's, St John's could not be portrayed as a 'completion' of an earlier royal foundation: for all the respect shown to the bishop's rights and the benefactors of the hospital it was a new kind of establishment. Lady Margaret and her advisers had no compunction in diverting the revenues of the old house to a different purpose, and in this respect they resembled Wolsey as precursors of the great dissolution of religious houses. On a practical level they had some justification: the hospital had few brethren and was not relieving the poor of the town or the sick. Its routine of spiritual intercession was to be continued, just as Henry VIII would continue to allow chantries to function after the dissolution, and an annual dole for the poor was to be maintained by the college. These provisions were deemed adequate compensation.

The bishop of Ely, however, had other things to take into account. He was determined, before surrendering patronage belonging to his see, to secure solid rights in return. After some negotiation with Lady Margaret's executors he gained the right not only to nominate three fellows of the new college during his life, but for succeeding bishops to continue to nominate one. This power was not removed until 1860. He also worked to secure the best possible terms for the three remaining brethren of the old hospital. At first he seems to have tried to help them to stay in the house. Their eviction could be delayed because a satisfactory bull to dissolve the hospital did not arrive from the pope until the summer of 1510. On 15 December, however, he wrote to the brethren saying that he had done his utmost: they must now leave the

---

[37] SJC, C7.11, fols. 38–40, *Notes*, 209–12. Richard Fox, bishop of Winchester, was with Hornby the supervisor of Margaret's will, and Fox's part must not be underestimated. He organized negotiations between the executors and the bishop of Ely and later, to obtain endowments, between St John's and Cardinal Wolsey.

house, and he had arranged satisfactory pensions for them. The pensions to Christopher Wright, William Chandler and John Kensham were confirmed by the pope on 18 July 1511: £7 each, annually, of the fruits of the former hospital. The pope also empowered them to accept church livings.[38] Finally Richard Henrison, official of Ely, wrote to Fisher that 'they departed from Cambridge towards Ely the xii day of Marche [1511] at iiii of the clokke at afternoone by water'.[39]

There were others besides the bishop who looked askance after Margaret's death at the scheme to which many of her resources were being diverted. The new foundation of St John's College received from Henry Hornby, on behalf of the executors, plate and vestments to furnish its chapel, including images of St Margaret, St Anne, St Peter, St Anthony and St George, as well as some plate for secular use. General authority to equip and endow St John's was given to the executors in the codicil attached to Margaret's will which was included in the probate copy. The goods were distributed, however, at the discretion of the executors. The fate of the goods became a bone of contention between them and other members of her household who, according to Fisher's account, expected more than had been agreed. Since the revenues of the lands placed in trust could not be fully used until the chancery decree had released them, it was with the goods, and money from the sale of some of them, that the new college began to be built and equipped. On this issue of distribution of goods 'factions and bands' such as Margaret's care had suppressed during her lifetime broke out into the open. Her servants, jealous of the way in which Fisher and his Cambridge colleagues were using their mistress's property, took their case to the king.[40]

The king and his officials had at first co-operated swiftly with Margaret's project for a new college, and letters patent allowing the executors the site and possessions of the hospital were granted on 7

---

[38] Letter, SJC, D105.96; *Cal. Papal Registers*, XVIII, 175–6. An agreement incorporating the arrangement was sealed by the bishop and convent of Ely, 31 December 1510–5 January 1511, SJC, D6.18. Pensions continued to be paid at the rate of £6 13s 4d until the spring of 1513. From 1514 onwards only Christopher Wright was paid, with an additional salary as curate of Horningsea. In 1527 he took the living of Swaffham, and was still paid the pension. Payments ceased in 1531 (Bursars' Accounts, SJC, SB3.5).

[39] The hospital had been mutually bound with that of St John's, Ely, since 1343, to celebrate masses and prayers for brethren who had died; Rubin, *Charity and Community*, 181.

[40] Lady Margaret's plate listed in SJC, C7.11, fol. 6; question of goods discussed in Fisher's memorandum, *Notes*, 210.

August 1509, in the first flush of the young Henry's regal generosity. Yet his interest, as the ultimate inheritor of his grandmother's lands, was in the background from the start: in February 1510 Hornby had told the brethren of the hospital that if they delayed the foundation of St John's, the king would enter and take the profits of her estates, and the university lose the benefit of her last wishes.[41] The revenues were secured by the chancery decree of November 1512; the king was then confronted with the complaint by Lady Margaret's servants that they had not received their fair share of her goods. It must have seemed that the executors were busily diverting everything they could lay hands on for the benefit of the new college: the servants' allegations, says Fisher's memorandum, made Henry 'a very heavy lord against me'.[42] This cannot have helped the college when it needed the continuing favour of the king to withhold his claim to Lady Margaret's estates. In the event he enforced it after two years, in 1515, and to understand why we must consider the fiscal situation at this period of the reign.

Henry's first two years as king had been marked by a relaxation of his father's tight-fisted policies, symbolized by the rigorous financial system headed by Henry VII's ministers Empson and Dudley. As a concession to popular feeling the two men were executed by Henry VIII in one of the first acts of his reign. Some of the powers confided to the royal chamber, with which Empson and Dudley had been closely connected, were again placed under the direction of the exchequer.[43] At the same time large grants were made from the royal domain without reserving rents, and there was the ever-pressing need to reward the new king's servants to ensure him support.

In this context the lands which Lady Margaret had held had their share of burdens: profits from some of them were being devoted to charitable purposes, while many of her servants were being rewarded directly from offices pertaining to her estates. Confirmations in office like that to Nicholas Aughton, Margaret's messenger and yeoman, of a bailiffship at Combe Martin (Dev.), merely preserved continuity on

---

[41] Letter, SJC, D105.94, 19 February (1510).

[42] The proved version of the will stipulated that the servants were to be rewarded out of the goods according to Fox's discretion, *Will*, 125. Fisher's memorandum says that he was also to be consulted. The servants had gathered that all the goods were to be divided amongst them, and blamed Fisher that they were not.

[43] For the alterations in royal policy see B. P. Wolffe, *The Crown Lands, 1461–1536* (London, 1970), 76–88. The extent of the volte-face from Henry VII's policies must not be exaggerated, however: J. Guy, *Tudor England* (Oxford, 1988), 80–1, G. R. Elton, *The Tudor Constitution* (Cambridge, 1962), 130.

the estates and reinforced loyalty to the new king. Grants specified for life, or in survivorship with another person, however, were more generous. They were also, in terms of the crown's future reservoir of patronage, more costly recognitions of past service. Miles Worsley, Margaret's cofferer until January 1509, received the office of bailiff for life at Torrington (Dev.). Richard Bothe, bailiff of Wykes and Frampton (Lincs.) under Lady Margaret, was made feodary for the honour of Richmond in the county. He was to hold his offices in survivorship with Thomas Palmer, who was also in receipt of fees charged upon Margaret's estates at her death. In 1515, when they were charged with heavy arrears, Bothe addressed a petition to the crown stressing that he had first been preferred to his offices by Lady Margaret whose servant he had been for sixteen years. At Fremington (Dev.), the bailiffship was held by Roger Ratcliffe, another yeoman of Margaret's who had entered the queen's service and in 1510 was granted the countess's house of 'the Roiall' in London. On surrendering his patent in 1516 he was succeeded in survivorship by John and Robert Thomas, who had also been receiving fees from Margaret's estates. Sir John Hussey, who began his career in Lincolnshire in Margaret's service, was after her death granted the office of steward of Bourne, Deeping, Boston and the honour of Richmond, to hold in survivorship with his son and heir William.[44]

By Michaelmas 1511 slacker control had resulted in a sharp decrease of royal revenue. It became necessary to revive certain of Henry VII's financial practices, especially as during the next two years the economy was put on a war footing due to hostilities with France. In this atmosphere royal officials were eventually likely to question a long-term diversion of funds such as that involved in establishing St John's. According to Fisher's memorandum the immediate circumstance was the complaint of Lady Margaret's former servants about the executors' misuse of her goods, but the real issue was the profits of the lands. The executors were called before Sir Robert Southwell, general surveyor of the crown lands, and asked 'to show cause why we should keep the king's inheritance from him to the value of £400 yearly'. After investigation Southwell declared himself satisfied that the revenues were being used wisely, but in 1514 he was succeeded by Sir

---

[44] *L and P Henry VIII*: Merbury, *ibid.* 191, no. 414/21; Aughton, 13, 68, no. 132/83; Worsley, 68, no. 132/80; Bothe and Palmer, 68, no. 132/88, and Bothe's petition and debts PRO, C82/420 and SC6/Hen. VIII/6864; Ratcliffe, *L and P Henry VIII*, I, i, 170, no. 381/14; Hussey, 345, no. 604/31; Thomas, *ibid.*, II, ii, 428, no. 1543.

Edward Belknap. Belknap had been in charge of exploiting the feudal rights of the crown, as surveyor of the king's prerogative late in Henry VII's reign, and was vigilant in prosecuting royal interests. The servants of Lady Margaret seized the chance to bring their complaints to this new officer; the executors were, in Fisher's phrase, 'more straitly handled'.[45] They now found that the legal measures which had been taken to protect the revenues for the use of the college could not do so forever. The royal officials decided that the time had come to claim the king's inheritance, which would also help to recoup some of the losses suffered from the royal lands over the past five years.[46]

Fisher felt understandable frustration at this latest impediment to completing Margaret's vision of making St John's 'as good and of as good value' as Christ's.[47] The college's beginnings had been characterized by none of the ordered efficiency with which the countess had established and endowed the sister college. The foundation charter of 1511 spoke of a society of fifty persons studying the liberal arts and theology. The reality until 1515 was a college of five fellows awaiting completion of their buildings, and receiving half as much money for their commons as the former brethren of the hospital were receiving in pensions. Margaret's manor of Bassingbourne in Fordham had been conveyed to the college in 1512 after probate of her will, augmenting slightly the revenues of £80 a year from the hospital.[48] The sale of Lady Margaret's goods produced further money for building. This was increased by the generosity of the first benefactors: Fisher gave £500 by January 1513, money which he later claimed the countess had given him and which he decided to devote to the college.[49] By the time the king claimed his inheritance Henry Hornby had also deposited towards the buildings £1,112 drawn from almost two years' profits of the lands placed in trust. The college showed its obligation to the

---

[45] G. R. Elton, *The Tudor Revolution in Government* (Cambridge, 1953), 29; W. C. Richardson, 'The surveyor of the king's prerogative', *EHR*, 66 (1941), 67.

[46] At Michaelmas 1515 the total revenue from land in the crown's hands stood at approximately £25,000 as compared with £40,000 at Henry VII's death, Wolffe, *The Crown Lands*, 85. The executors granted Margaret's enfeoffed estates to the king on 11 July 1515; *Cal. Ancient Deeds*, IV, 23 (A6312).

[47] In time college lore exaggerated the loss: in 1564 the fellows of St John's besought the visiting Queen Elizabeth to restore to them the lands themselves, but she refused. E. Miller *Portrait of A College* (Cambridge, 1961), 4.

[48] Keen exploitation of hospital properties raised values at Newnham and Horningsea, Camb., and by 1514 the rental stood at £100.

[49] SJC, D106.5; *Early Statutes*, ed. Mayor, 240; Underwood, 'Cambridge connections', 78.

foundress before its first statutes were granted by expending sums to support Margaret's almspeople at Hatfield in their intercessions for her soul.[50]

Fortunately for Fisher and the college, the king was also still respectful enough towards his grandmother's intent to agree to compensate for the withdrawn revenues. A wardship worth £2,800 was paid at roughly £400 a year until 1519, when the death of the ward ended payment. In 1515 and 1516 the foundation supported between five and eleven fellows and three to four scholars at different times, and the wardship provided the funds to secure from the king a more solid endowment.[51] This was the decayed royal hospital of Ospringe, on the London to Dover road. It was granted with its possessions on the understanding that the college maintained a chantry there, just as it had to fulfil the religious obligations of the old hospital at Cambridge. On 29 July 1516 the college was formally opened and thirty-one fellows were elected. Some of these did not long remain, but the community was now to be permanently over a score strong. With the Ospringe estates assured to the college revenues were doubled, and in 1519 the resident membership stood at twenty-six fellows and twenty-three scholars.[52]

Fisher had appointed his archdeacon, Nicholas Metcalfe, master in 1518; together they set out to augment the college still further. Acting under legal advice they sought new endowments from Cardinal Wolsey and ultimately secured two small and decayed religious houses with estates in Surrey and Berkshire and in east Kent.[53] Richard Fox took a hand in the negotiations, the last in a series of acts helpful to both Fisher and the college. Fisher himself gave more money, sufficient to buy estates worth £60 a year, and his total gifts in both money and plate amounted to £1,700.[54] With these acquisitions the precarious austerity of the college came to an end. By 1524 an income of £300 a year had been reached, the target appointed under the first college

[50] £18 between 1511 and 1516, SJC, D6.31.
[51] The wardship also helped to clear remaining debts of the Cambridge hospital, pay for a copy of the college's first statutes and buy for its library Greek and Latin texts, an astrolabe and a map of the world; SJC, D57.33.
[52] According to Metcalfe's accounts, SJC, D107.8; but at the formal opening of the college thirty-one fellows had been named, SJC, 56.196.
[53] Broomhall nunnery, Berkshire, and Higham nunnery, Kent; Knowles and Hadcock, *Medieval Religious Houses*, 253, 256, 254, 259; summary of the estates conveyed with them to the college, H. Howard, *Finances of St John's College, 1511–1926* (Cambridge, 1935), 287, 290.   [54] SJC, D106.5, fol. 4v; C7.2, fol. 43.

statutes at which the fellows were to receive stipends as well as a subsistence allowance. Success was due not only to the untiring efforts of Fisher, Fox and Hornby and their colleagues in Margaret's household, but to the co-operation of Wolsey and Henry VIII.

When the college had been formally opened, the external walls of buildings in its first court were mostly complete.[55] The buildings themselves bear the emblems of the foundress. The great gate is surmounted by a wealth of heraldry similar to that at Christ's: it depicts the arms of the foundress, supported by the yales of Beaufort[56] (but lacking her crest of a chained eagle), surrounded by the royal badges of crowned rose and portcullis. The background is at St John's more lavishly strewn with the marguerites allusive to her name, and the coronet above the shield of arms is composed of these flowers. Margaret's arms were repeated, as at Christ's, on the front of the oriel window above the entrance to the master's lodge.[57] The suite of first-floor rooms belonging to the master was reserved for Fisher's use when he should visit the college, a privilege similar to that granted to him by Lady Margaret for the use of her own rooms at Christ's.

The statutes of the new college, and those of the personal foundation which Fisher established between 1521 and 1524 to support his own fellows, scholars and lecturers, bore witness to Lady Margaret's intentions.[58] The earliest statutes declared that she had wished to establish a school of theology from whose heart learned men should issue and communicate their knowledge to the people. Armed with that authority Fisher set out the duty of a quarter of the fellows to preach public sermons in English.[59] Her wishes were followed also in the preference given at St John's, as at Christ's, to candidates for fellowships and scholarships from nine northern counties. To be sure, Yorkshire was Fisher's home county and many of his colleagues both in the university and in Margaret's household were northerners, as were the earliest benefactors to the college. Yet the special place given to Richmondshire, of which Fisher was not a native, as a county in its own right, is surely a tribute to the countess of Richmond. In the

---

[55] SJC, D56.196, printed in *Funeral Sermon*, ed. Hymers, 256–61.

[56] For yale, see below, p. 291.

[57] Plates 16, 17; 'Souvent me souvient', the foundress's motto, appears only on the oriel at Christ's.

[58] For an examination of Fisher's foundation and its impact on the college, see Underwood, 'Fisher and the promotion of learning', 36–8.

[59] *Early Statutes*, ed. Mayor, 377.

college's prayers Margaret and her parents were to be commemorated, along with her royal son and grandson, and the king she much revered, Henry VI, his wife Margaret of Anjou and their son Edward.

In Fisher's statutes for his own foundation he recorded his debt to Lady Margaret in more intimate terms. His fellows were especially to remember her in their masses as one to whom he had been obliged as much as to his own mother.[60] When the university in 1528 offered to establish exequies for Fisher in St John's, as a mark of its respect, he responded graciously, but asked that they be celebrated instead in Margaret's name, he being granted a share in the spiritual benefits of prayers said for her.[61] Two years after Fisher had framed his statutes, in 1526, he wrote a dedication to Richard Fox in which he returned to the special quality of his debt to Lady Margaret. She had not, he said, been the agent of his preferment to a bishopric as some thought; but, quite as valuable in its own right, she had honoured him with her friendship and admitted him to her counsels. He had amply and publicly praised her virtues in his sermon at her month's mind, but he now wished to add a personal testimony. The words of this conscientious preacher and pastor give us the measure of the impression that Margaret Beaufort had made upon him: 'I freely admit that once she had adopted me both as her confessor and her moral and spiritual guide, I learned more of what leads to an upright life from her rare virtues than I ever taught her in return.'[62]

Fisher's eloquent tribute was echoed in humbler fashion by those of her servants who, in their wills and elsewhere, spoke with reverence of their former mistress. The Sussex gentleman Edward Lewkenor in 1522 willed that masses should be said for his soul 'in the chapel of scala celi in the abbey of Westminster, where the famous and excellent princess Margaret countess of Richmond is buried'.[63] Henry Parker Lord Morley, who had served her table, recalled that while she kept her state and conversed with bishops at her board, she knew the names and needs of her many dependants and took care to visit them when they were sick. John Harrington, author of a sixteenth-century addendum

---

[60] *Ibid.*, 242: 'cui non secus atque propriae genetrici fuerim obnoxius'.

[61] Lewis, *Life of Fisher*, II, 307, document xxiii.

[62] Dedicatory Epistle to 'De Veritate Corporis et Sanguinis', *Johannis Fischeri Opera* (Wirceburg, 1597), 747.

[63] *Transcripts of Sussex Wills*, ed. W. H. Godfrey, III, *Sussex Record Society Publications*, 43 (1938), 58. The lady chapel at Westminster is meant by the scala celi chapel; see above, p. 193 and n. 69.

to the Crowland chronicle, singled out the moral awe her presence inspired: no man dared do wrong for fear of her chiding.[64] William Bedell, her treasurer of household, struck a particular note of personal affection in the terms of his will. In Margaret's service he had grown into a man of substance, with lands in Hertfordshire and Essex. Bedell was rewarded for his past service by being made bailiff of Cheshunt, formerly one of her manors, in July 1509. When he came to draw up his will he, like Lewkenor, wished to be buried in 'my lady's chapel called scala celi'. There a priest was to sing for his soul and that of Lady Margaret, and for his father, mother and wife, as if Margaret were a member of his own family. His gold cup and chains were to be sold and the money given discreetly to the poor and to be spent in other deeds of alms 'most requisite for the soul of my most singular good lady Margaret countess of Richmond, by whom I had all that I have'.[65]

---

[64] See above, p. 136.   [65] PRO, Prob. 11/19, 8 Ayloffe, 4 Dec. 1513.

CONCLUSION

Lady Margaret's foundations at Christ's and St John's College, Cambridge, were a fitting memorial to both her cultural and political involvements. Her death in June 1509 played a large part in denying her second foundation the smooth and rapid progress that Christ's had enjoyed. Margaret's rigorous supervision of the work at Christ's, supported by a highly trained council, had combined speed and efficiency with political ruthlessness to gain a landed endowment for the new college. Nevertheless Henry VIII's willingness to respect the wishes of his deceased grandmother was ultimately to transcend the confusion and division that followed the countess's death. The young king's attitude showed the respect felt for the foundress of the new dynasty. But to understand fully Margaret's legacy one has to place it firmly in the context of the fears and uncertainties, the constant struggle of her own life.

The striking quality that emerges from her portraits and particularly from the tomb effigy is the strength of character in the face. The sharply etched lines, the pronounced cheekbones and slightly hooded eyes convey considerable force of personality. Her features are intelligent but worldly and astute, an impression reinforced by the coats-of-arms and the badges that surround them. It is the face of a political survivor. Margaret had a natural and deep-seated pragmatism. She was always business-like and respected those whose toughness and efficiency ensured they would get things done. Her longest-serving and most loyal servant, Reginald Bray, was described as 'playn and rowth in speech'. His inventory of goods, compiled after his death in 1503, gives no hint of cultured or chivalric interests. Margaret prized him for his administrative ability and reliability in times of crisis. John Hussey, another long-standing officer who had risen from Margaret's service to the king's, and Henry Uvedale, her lieutenant at Corfe, were notorious for their strong-arm tactics in the localities. The contrast with the cultured presence of men such as John Fisher and Henry Hornby reveals the range of personalities within her household. Amidst these men Margaret exerted a commanding influence. It is worth recalling the force of Fisher's recollection that if division or strife arose secretly amongst her head officers, 'she with great polycye dyde boulte it oute'. One of the problems faced by late medieval dowagers was their vulnerability in the face of exploitation or corrupt practice by their servants. That Margaret could rise above this was a tribute to her charisma, that inspired quite exceptional devotion from many in her service. But it was also a product of her unrelenting vigilance, her personal supervision of all matters of importance and willingness to use spies and informants to root out any malpractice.

Her life was notable for its constant activity, whether riding to court or touring her properties with her respective husbands, Stafford and Stanley, or later accompanying her son, the king, on his progresses. It was unusual for a woman in late medieval England to travel so much. It reflected her freedom, after the separation from her son in 1462, from the responsibilities of raising further children but was also characteristic of her desire to attend to business personally. This was combined with a scrupulous attention to detail. Her closet next to her bedchamber contained a series of cupboards with boxes for different documents so they could be readily inspected. Lady Margaret was no great bibliophile of the order of her contemporaries, Anne of Brittany or Margaret of Burgundy, and her outlook was practical rather than learned. She was quick to grasp the value of printing as a means of disseminating pious instruction, ordering large assignments of works for her own household. The printers were to appeal to her as a woman of action when they competed for her patronage. Such qualities are seen in Margaret's interest in the Feast of Jesus. Her chapel was to become a centre for the devotion and her petition to the pope in 1494 led to the full establishment of the cult.

Lady Margaret's practical abilities were demonstrated most strongly in the management of her properties. Her estate administration must rank as one of the most efficient in the entire late middle ages. Her reforms of accounting practice and centralizing of receipts were given teeth by a frequent resort to the law and the unstinting efforts of her officers, willing to implement measures that were often harsh or severe. The expanding landed revenue provided the basis for the works of charity and education in the last years of her life. Margaret's interest in her properties was ruthless and acquisitive, sentiments caught well by Professor Lander: 'landowners...looked upon their "lifelode", the complex of family estates, as an almost sacred trust to be defended at all costs and by all means'.[1] Her methods set an example to her former ward, Edward Stafford, duke of Buckingham, when he took possession of his lands. Yet Stafford's vigilant pursuit of profit was not tempered by any sense of justice, and he alienated many of his servants and tenants. Fisher was to stress Margaret's accessibility, her concern to provide suitors with a fair hearing and her ability to harmonize the divergent outlooks of those around her. The discipline of her personal routine found outward expression in the order of her own household.

Margaret's relationships with her various husbands had sacrificed personal predilection to the cause of political necessity. The early child marriage to John de la Pole Margaret neither comprehended nor recognized. The brief match to Edmund Tudor was more complex psychologically. Margaret always reverenced his name and memory as the progenitor of her only child. In her first will of 1472 it was he beside whom Margaret wished to be buried. Yet the consequence of her giving birth at such a young age was a legacy of physical and emotional damage. In her fourteen-year marriage with Sir Henry Stafford Margaret found the stability of a close relationship alongside that of a political protector. It is likely that the couple spent the earliest days of their marriage at the Stafford castle of Maxstoke, and the extraordinary attention Margaret paid to rebuilding this residence (deliberately slighted by Richard III) during the first years of her son's reign may have recalled the happiness she found at this period of her life. The fourth and most famous marriage, to Thomas Lord Stanley, was the product of careful negotiation: her new husband provided an influential ally at the Yorkist court. The relationship was more one of respect than affection. It nevertheless had a strong influence on Margaret, allowing her political and cultural contacts that she would later draw on to great effect.

During Henry VII's reign Margaret's position as Stanley's wife was subordinated to her role of matriarch of the house of Tudor. Her

---

[1] J. R. Lander, *Conflict and Stability in Fifteenth-Century England* (London, 1974), 169.

assertion of the legal rights of a *femme sole* and her later vow of chastity gave her an unprecedented freedom within an aristocratic marriage. She was to be found as frequently in the company of the royal family as with her husband, and her abiding concern for the future of the dynasty pervaded all her activities. On her copy of the statutes of Christ's College was the extended motto, 'God save our noble king harry the vij and preserve Margaret his moder Also preserve harry arturis broder'. At the heart of this lay Margaret's powerful relationship with her son, all the more remarkable in view of the little time they had spent together before 1485. Three particular moments of crisis helped forge the bond between them: the dangerous circumstances immediately before and after Henry's birth; the turbulence of the period 1469–71, when Margaret strove to secure her son's safety and the risks she ran conspiring on his behalf in 1483. There was an heroic quality to the relationship, rightly perceived by the Tudor poet Bernard André.

A comparison can be made with the efforts of another mother, Margaret of Anjou, to protect her only child. Faced with the incapacity of her husband and Yorkist slanders against her son, Margaret had fought to secure recognition for the young prince. His birth on 13 October 1453 had occurred at a time when Henry VI's breakdown had prevented him from recognizing his heir. Margaret had sought to make the christening as magnificent as possible, inviting no less than ten duchesses and eight countesses and purchasing a superbly embroidered and jewelled christening mantle. Accusations over the legitimacy of her son, which may have been circulated by Warwick as early as 1455, caused her great offence and prompted her to take a more active political role. In the summer of 1459 she organized a progress through Cheshire to display the five-year-old prince of Wales and to distribute his livery badge of the white swan. Her manifesto before the second battle of St Albans in 1461 angrily attacked the pretensions of the Yorkists, who had sought 'the utter undoing of our said son'. After the failure of the Lancastrian cause at Towton mother and child were forced to adopt the life of wandering exiles. The most famous episode, often retold by Margaret of Anjou, was her appeal for the life of her son when both were captured by robbers after the battle of Hexham, in 1464. One of the thieves took pity on them, allowing them to escape. All Margaret's efforts were in vain, for her son was cut down in the aftermath of Tewkesbury in 1471.

The similarity of their situations cannot have escaped Margaret Beaufort, who took under her protection members of the Vaux family of Harrowden, whose parents had ranked among Margaret of Anjou's most loyal servants. But despite the Lancastrian queen's heroic determination two important factors had contributed to her political downfall. The first was her attempt to assert power and dignity normally reserved for the anointed king. Although there was no impediment to designating the succession through the female line, fifteenth-century opinion was resistant to the idea of a queen regnant rather than consort. Such a prejudice can be sensed in the discussions of the 1406 parliament and in the writings of Fortescue. Margaret's demands for a regency in 1453, in which she would be able to appoint chancellor, treasurer and other great officers, 'all that the king should make', install bishops and choose sheriffs assumed a measure of authority for a woman that was alien to English custom. Her insistence, on a visit to Coventry in 1457, that she be accorded honour as if she were the king surprised and shocked contemporaries. This was exacerbated by her overriding lack of compassion, seen in her decision, after the second battle of St Albans, to execute Yorkists who had been pardoned by Henry VI. It was an important lesson and one not lost on Margaret Beaufort. Always circumspect, she chose to promote her son's interests rather than advance her own. Never needlessly vindictive, she was able to bring together differing parties, both in the rebellion of 1483 and in the composition of her household after 1485. Her prudence and ability to win loyalty and harmonize faction were the keys to her success.

Margaret had been impressed by the more subtle authority and greater range of cultural interests possessed by Cecily Neville, dowager-duchess of York, whom she had encountered at court in the 1470s. Cecily combined pious and devotional concerns (she was a generous donor to Queens' College, Cambridge) with a forceful upholding of her rights, whether exploiting wardships or protecting her tenants at law. She held a commanding behind-the-scenes influence within the Yorkist polity, and Edward IV and his brother Richard duke of Gloucester regularly discussed matters of state with her. These two determined ladies held each other in great respect. In her will, in 1495, Cecily left Margaret a beautiful breviary bound in cloth of gold.

Margaret's devotion to her son's cause was steadfast. In the last years of the reign she shouldered the burdens of government at

Collyweston and assisted in the great state occasions, the marriage of
Arthur and Catherine and the entertaining of Philip of Castile. She was
always mindful of 'good policy'. Writing to the king from Calais in
January 1501 Margaret commended a man named Fielding: 'Verily,
my kynge, he ys a gued and a wyse, well rewled gentlyman, and full
trewly hath served you...as well at your fyrst as all oder occasions...and truly, my good kyng, he helpeth me ryght well yn seche
matters as y have besynes wythyn thys partyes.' Both shared a highly
calculating vein of thought, discussing financial levers in relations with
France as if they were planning moves in one of their games of chess.

Their relationship was to remain one of action to the very end. Yet
although Margaret was to outlive her son and witness the coronation
of her grandson, uncertainty and fear for the future never completely
left her. Her sense of foreboding, even at moments of ostensible
triumph, was noted by Fisher. Tears of penitence were a conventional
demonstration of contrition. Yet Margaret's tears, however well they fit
into the well-known image of medieval men and women bewailing the
turn of fortune's wheel, were linked to particular climactic events in
her life and Fisher's words bear the marks of a genuine recollection. It
was a reaction more emotional than rational. Beneath the remarkable
self-control and discipline, the charismatic and forceful personality,
was a more concealed but darker trait. Hints are found amidst the piety
of her daily regimen. Her individual acts, the ministering to the poor
and sick with her own hand, were not uncommon among great ladies
of rank and a similar routine was followed by Margaret of York,
duchess of Burgundy. What was more significant was the degree of
pain borne performing them: the sixty-three aves undertaken by an
elderly lady who purchased cramp rings in an effort to combat her
arthritis. There was something obsessive about Margaret's maintenance of such a punishing personal schedule.

A deep sense of loss had afflicted her life on a personal as well as
political level. An only child, she had no memory of her father and had
later learnt, through her association with Crowland, of the tragedy of
his death. Her husband Edmund Tudor had succumbed to the plague
two months before the birth of her son. The difficulties of the birth
prevented her from having any more offspring. Within a few years her
child was taken from her, and over the next two decades they would
be together for little more than a matter of weeks. The shadow of the
family she never had or raised cast a long reach. It accounts for the

emotional intensity of her relationship with her son, that occasionally bordered on the hysterical. It also explains the strength of her affection for the St Johns, her family of the half-blood that she came to adopt as her own. To protect their fortunes she was even prepared to defy Henry VII. Her concern to promote the interests of their kin led her to one of the few serious political miscalculations she made in her life. The marriage between Richard Pole, her nephew of the half-blood, and Margaret Plantagenet, almost certainly came about through her influence. It was a match fraught with dynastic risk and the Poles were to cause as much trouble to Henry VIII as the de la Poles had for his father.

The sense of foreboding that so struck Fisher was as much a product of Margaret's personal circumstances as a testimony to the difficult times she had lived through. It was a deep-seated unease that she would never be completely rid of. Yet the scale of her educational patronage, which was to gather apace in the last years of her life, offered a form of resolution. Her guiding influence was John Fisher. A quite remarkable depth of feeling existed between the two of them. For Margaret it was a profoundly emotional as well as spiritual experience, based on her own free choice and the powerful impression generated from their earliest meeting, that she was to recall in her second vow of chastity: 'I avowe to you, my lord of Rochester, to whom I am and have been, since the first time I see you admitted, verely determined to owe my obedience.' She confided in him in a way that betokened trust and intimacy and clearly found him a civilizing and elevating influence. For Fisher, who knew Margaret in the very private context of hearing her confession, the experience left him feeling as much pupil as teacher. He was no Wykeham or Fox, a prelate practised in the ways of society. Margaret had taken him from the sheltered world of university life into the activity of her household. Once there he had certainly influenced the direction of her bounty back to Cambridge. But she in turn had wanted to do something for him, to advance his prospects by giving him a richer bishopric. This was her arena, the world of preferment, patronage and court negotiation, as much as the precious secluded hours of reflection and confession.

The choice of a university foundation as a memorial, both personal and dynastic, can be explained in the growing fifteenth-century trend towards collegiate endowments as a form of perpetual chantry. However, Margaret's foundations, both at Christ's and St John's, may have had a deeper psychological attraction. Fisher described her care for the university scholars, to whom she was 'as a mother'. The story of her intervention on behalf of a student at Christ's to mitigate his punishment is based on a respectable tradition. Margaret's own childhood had been overshadowed by the uncertainties and violence of the times. Her success was rooted in an awareness of the mutability and danger of high politics: 'she never was yet in that prosperyte but the gretter it was the more always she dredde the adversyte'. In that spirit she turned her attention to the provision of a stable environment for the young students in her care.

Yet if Fisher and Lady Margaret have usually been cast together as actors in the overarching drama of building up Cambridge University, the situation was more complex. Of all Margaret Beaufort's biographers Cooper came nearest to showing the breadth of her interests, busy as she was up to the eve of her death with a host of different matters. Whilst Fisher concentrated on her works of mediation, reconciliation and charity Henry Parker recalled her regality and power as well as her benificence, her public role as a great lady. Close though Fisher and Margaret were, their worlds were divergent ones. After Lady Margaret's death Fisher was clearly resented within the household, because of the claim of her dependants to goods which he and his fellow executors had earmarked for her charitable foundations. Yet even while she lived he had had a far from unique *entrée*: a month before her death Edmund Wilsford of Oxford was named as her confessor in a list of personal legacies. Margaret's dealings were sometimes with men of whom Fisher disapproved. Her stepson, James Stanley, had impressed her with his support for the collegiate church at Manchester and she raised no objection to his elevation to the bishopric of Ely. However, he was a worldly man, and of unproven learning, not the sort of reforming pastor she and Fisher were encouraging in their schooling of the clergy in the universities. Nicholas West, Stanley's successor, was a graduate of Eton and King's: Fisher took care to say of him, in his last code of statutes for St John's, that he obtained his see 'suis meritis'.

Fisher was less than comfortable in his attempts, in his monthmind sermon, to deflect from Margaret the charge of avarice, which had been levelled against her great-uncle, Cardinal Beaufort, her uncle, Edmund Beaufort, duke of Somerset and more recently her own son. He may not have seen the jewel house or closet glittering with precious gems, but he had carried to Henry VII documents concerning the Orléans ransom, which Margaret was trying to extract from the French king, and as an executor of her will knew the vast extent of her moveable wealth, valued at some £15,000. He was also well aware that Margaret's colleges were endowed with purchased land, acquired on highly favourable terms, or with revenues temporarily dedicated to that purpose, rather than by permanent alienation of her estates. These properties were conserved as her legacy to the new ruling house. It was the strongest loyalty of Margaret's later life. Just as she had fought for her son's interests in the Yorkist period she subsequently devoted her energies to ensuring the survival of a Tudor monarchy. However, one also senses something of the compulsive hoarder, collecting ancient debts and pursuing tenuous titles to lands as a safeguard against the uncertainties of political fortune. It was a harsh, unattractive side of her personality. Yet such traits must be set against her outstanding qualities, her courage, presence of mind, family loyalty and a deeply felt awareness of the spiritual responsibilities of high office. Whatever her flaws, the story of Lady Margaret's life is a powerful and moving testimony to the foundress of one of England's greatest ruling dynasties.

APPENDIX 1

ITINERARY OF LADY MARGARET, 1498–9

The following itinerary for half a year in 1498–9 is based on SJC D91.17, cofferer's account 24 June 1498 to 12 Jan. 1499. We are grateful to Margaret Condon for supplying us with a list of the king's movements, entered as K, from PRO E/101/414/14, 16, and C82.

1498: 24–30 June   Westminster, Sheen, Windsor, Easthampstead, Windsor, Sheen

1–7 July   Westminster, the Tower; K at Westminster and Sheen

8–11 July   Westminster, Sheen (Charterhouse), Windsor; K at Westminster

12–14 July   Westminster, K

15–17 July   Westminster, Sheen, Syon; K at Westminster

18 July   Eton, Windsor; K at Westminster

19 July   Westminster, K

20–8 July   Westminster, K

29 July   the Tower; K at Westminster

30 July   the Tower; K at Westminster

31 July   Stratford Abbey; K at the Tower and Stratford Abbey

1 Aug.   Havering of the Bowre (Havering-atte-Bower, Ess.), Stratford Abbey; K at Havering

2 Aug.   Sir James Tyrell's (Herongate, Ess.), K

3 Aug.   Mr Bardvyle's (William Bardwell?) (Chelmsford), K

4–5 Aug.   the earl of Ormonde's, K; and K at Montgomery's (Faulkbourne castle, Ess.)

6 Aug.   Castle Hedingham (the earl of Oxford), K

7–13 Aug.   Castle Hedingham (LM changes her carriage, which is sent to Collyweston, for a litter), K; K also at Laneham, 12–13 Aug.

14–16 Aug.   Bury St Edmunds, K

17 Aug.   Our Lady of Woolpit; K at Bury

18 Aug.   Thetford, K

19 Aug.   Buckingham castle, K

20–1 Aug.   Norwich, K; K also at Sir William Knyvett's

22 Aug.   Sir William Boleyn's (Blickling Hall, Norf.), K; K also at Aylsham (Norf.)

23–4 Aug.   Walsingham, K

25–7 Aug.   King's Lynn, K; K also at Oxborough Hall on 27 Aug.

28 Aug.   Margaret Lady Bedingfeld's (widow of Sir Edmund Bedingfeld) (Oxborough Hall, Norf.), K; K at Brandon ferry

29 Aug.   Brandon ferry, K; K also at Ely, Mr (Sir Roger?) Cotton's place

30 Aug.   Mr Cotton's place, K; K also at Newmarket

31 Aug.   Ely, K

1–2 Sept.   Cambridge, K

3–4 Sept.   Huntingdon, K

5–6 Sept.   Peterborough, K

7–12 Sept.   Collyweston, K; K at Drayton (Leics.), the earl of Wiltshire's, on 11 Sept., and at Gt Harrowden (N'hants.), and Wellsborough (Leics.) on 12 Sept.

13 Sept.   Gt Harrowden, K

14 Sept.   Northampton, K

15–18 Sept.   Edgrete; K at Edgrete on 16 Sept., otherwise at Banbury (Oxon.)

19 Sept.   Banbury, K

20 Sept.–2 Oct.   Woodstock, K

3–4 Oct.   Langley (Herts.), K

20–1 Oct.   Northampton; K remaining at Woodstock

22 Oct.   Kettering; K at Wycombe (Bucks.). On 23 Oct. K departs for Westminster via Windsor and Sheen, arrives 31 Oct.

23 Oct. 1498–12 Jan. 1499   Collyweston

APPENDIX 2

LADY MARGARET'S ESTATES

The following list of the location of estates is based upon the valor drawn up by George Quarles, the royal auditor, in 1520, PRO E36/177, with the exception that estates known to have been alienated before that date, and so excluded from the valor, have been included here with the identification +.

The list is arranged as follows: A, properties originally held by Margaret's father, John duke of Somerset, with those held by, or in right of, Margaret's grandmother, Margaret Holland, distinguished by an H; B, lands known as Exeter lands, deriving from John Holland duke of Exeter and his heirs and granted to Margaret in 1487; C, lands of the honour of Richmond mostly granted to Margaret in 1487; D, lands from other sources.

A

BEDFORDSHIRE
Wrestlingworth

CAMBRIDGESHIRE
Orwell

CARDIGANSHIRE
Gwynionydd
Yscoed

DEVON
Aller Peverell
Holbeton and Flete

Sampford Peverell manor
Sampford Peverell borough and hundred of Halberton

DORSET
Corfe castle
Purbeck

ESSEX
Colnwake   H
Lamarsh   H
Stratford, rent in   H
Waltham   H

GLOUCESTERSHIRE
Cirencester, fee-farm in   H

HAMPSHIRE
Andover   H
Basingstoke   H
Bedhampton   H

HERTFORDSHIRE
Tidburst and Kendall manor

KENT
Chedlington
Dartford   H

LEICESTERSHIRE
Enderby

LINCOLNSHIRE
Billingborough   H
Bourne   H
East Deeping   H
West Deeping   H

NORFOLK
Lynn
Ormesby   H

NORTHAMPTONSHIRE
Chapel- or Little Brampton
Eydon
Maxey   H
Overston
Torpell   H

RUTLAND
Redlington

SOMERSET
Abdyke
Bath, fee-farm in   H
Bulston
Curry Rivel
Langport Eastover
Langport Westover
Martock
Milborne Port
Queen Camel   H

STAFFORDSHIRE
Maidcroft or Medecroft
Walsall, fee-farm or part of manor

SURREY
+Bagshot meadow and wood
Woking

WORCESTERSHIRE
Droitwich, fee-farm in   H

YORKSHIRE
Cottingham   H
Scotton

B

DERBYSHIRE
Dalbery and Dalberyleys
Wrixworth

DEVON
Barnstaple
Blakeborneboty
Bovey Tracey
Combe Martin manor and borough
Dartington
Fleet
Fremington manor and hundred
Holdsworthy
Langacre
South Molton manor and borough
Torrington manor
Wincle Tracey

MIDDLESEX
London, the lodging of Coldharbour

NORTHAMPTONSHIRE
Aldwinkle
Thorpe Achurch

PEMBROKESHIRE
Manorbier
Pennally

SOMERSET
hundreds of Stone and Catsasshe

C

CAMBRIDGESHIRE
Bassingbourn, two-thirds of fee of honour of Richmond, with its
appurtenances in Cambs, Herts, Ess and Suff (granted to Margaret,
widow of Edmund earl of Richmond in dower, 1459)
Bassingbourn, one third of fee of honour of Richmond, with its
appurtenances in Cambs, Herts, Ess and Suff (granted in 1487)

HERTFORDSHIRE
Cheshunt, manor

Appendix 2

LINCOLNSHIRE
   Boston cum Jeserhall
   Boston cum membris
   Frampton
   Fulbeck
   Gayton soke
   Kirton soke
   Leddenham
   Mumby soke
   Skirbeck
   Washingborough
   Wykes

WESTMORLAND
   Kendal, barony, two-thirds of the Richmond fee, granted 1459; one
      third of the Richmond fee granted 1487

D

DORSET
   Canford (incl. in grant 1487, but subject of another grant 1506, in
      exchange for other lands, see below; Margaret claimed it as the
      heiress of Cardinal Beaufort who bought Canford)
   Poole (granted in 1487, bought by the cardinal with Canford. These
      manors, like Ware, were granted to the exclusion of the claim of
      Edward earl of Warwick)

HERTFORDSHIRE
   Hunsdon (granted 1503, in exchange for Woking, itself recovered
      1509)
   Ware (granted 1487)

LINCOLNSHIRE
   Tattershall castle and manor

NORTHAMPTONSHIRE
   Collyweston

SOMERSET
+ Charlton
+ Henstridge

WILTSHIRE
+ Amesbury
+ Winterbourne Earls
(granted to Margaret as Cardinal Beaufort's heir by act of parliament 1492; she held them until 1506)

APPENDIX 3

OFFICERS, SERVANTS AND SCHOLARS IN LADY MARGARET'S HOUSEHOLD, *c.* 1499–1509

'household accounts' = account books and rolls in SJC, D91, D102, *passim*

Aderton, Richard
Messenger on several occasions; yeoman usher to the princess of Wales, *c.* 1501; bequest to by Sir Roger Ormeston (SJC, D102.11, household accounts.)

Ashton, Hugh
BRUC; receiver-general from 1502, but many receipts still managed by Hugh Oldham; sole receiver-general after 1504; controller by the end of 1508 and in 1509; presented by Lady Margaret to Lythe rectory, Yorks., succeeding John Fisher, 1504 (ex inf. David Smith, Borthwick Inst., register of Archbishop Savage); chaplain of Cresmere, archdeacon of Richmond till 1511, archdeacon of York, 1516, benefactor to SJC, d. 1522. His chantry in the old chapel of SJC contained his monument and effigy which were moved to the new chapel in 1868 (C. C. Babington *The History of St. John's College Chapel* (Cambridge, 1874), p. 18; *RCHM, Cambridge*, II, 191).

Aughton, Nicholas
Yeoman to Lady Margaret, escorted Princess Margaret towards Scotland; bailiff and parker at Combe Martin, Dev., conf. in that office by Henry VIII; took Lady Margaret's swans from the Thames at her death (*L and P Henry VIII*, I, i, 68, 132/83; I, i, 13; SJC, D57.21).

Baldwyn, Peter
Servant at Coldharbour, scribe and illuminator, binder and dresser of books (SJC, D91.20, p. 25, D91.19, pp. 7, 17).

Bedell, William
Receiver, lands of the duke of Buckingham in wardship, 1487–92, receiver-general, 1493–8 (WAM, 32355), treasurer of household in 1493 and from 1498–1509 (WAM, 32364, household accounts; *Will*, 123); surveyor-general for dowager-duchess of Buckingham, 1496 (PRO, SC6/Hen. VII/1842, m. 5v). Married Cecily Crathorne, *c.* 1506 (PRO, CP40/979, fol. 543, 980, fol. 444); bailiff of Cheshunt (Herts.), 1509 (*L and P Henry VIII*, I, i, 69, 132/97; possibly bailiff of Kimbolton (Hunts.), 1517–18 (B. J. Harris, *Edward Stafford, Third Duke of Buckingham* (Stanford, 1986), appendix c, 229). His will, proved 11 July 1518, attributed all his wealth to Lady Margaret (PRO, Prob. 11/19, 8 Ayloffe).

Bekinsall, Robert
BRUC; almoner in 1508–9 (household accounts, D91.19, p. 82), became almoner to the queen after Lady Margaret's death. As fellow of Michaelhouse received an exhibition from the household in 1502–3 (SJC, D91.20, p. 24). By his will he left 20s to Michaelhouse and provision at an Oxford or Cambridge college for a scholar he was maintaining at Eton.

Bell, ?Alexander
BRUO; chapel clerk and choirmaster at Magdalen College, Oxford, 1486–7, receiving wages from the household at Fotheringhay College in 1505 when he wrote a mass copied by the children of the chapel there (SJC, D91.21, pp. 39, 44).

Bothe, Edward
Keeper of the jewel house in 1509 (SJC, D57.43).

Bothe, Richard
Bailiff of Wykes and Frampton, Lincs., in 1502, 1507; attended the president of Lady Margaret's council at Leicester when he examined an affray between servants of Lord Hastings and the bishop of Lincoln, 1502 (SJC, D91.20, p. 61).

Bray, Reginald
DNB; receiver-general to Lady Margaret and Sir Henry Stafford, 1467–71, also to Margaret and Stanley, and to Lady Margaret until *c.* 1499, when he was especially responsible for lands granted to her by the crown in 1487 (WAM, 32365; PRO, SC6/1771). His successors

were first his deputy Nicholas Compton, then from 1501 Hugh Oldham and Hugh Ashton (SJC, D102.10).

Brudenell, Robert
Lawyer, sergeant at law, king's sergeant, 1505, and justice of king's bench, 1507, chief justice of the common pleas 1521, associated with the council learned of Henry VII and regularly employed by the crown as its attorney, as well as by Lady Margaret. She supported him for the post of *custos rotulorum* at Keston, Lancs., in 1504 (SJC, D91.20, p. 156, Chrimes, *Henry VII*, 150).

Burgon, —
Scholar, supported at Oxford in 1498–9 (SJC, D91.17, p. 20); there was a Thomas Burgon who was a ward in 1508 (SJC, D91.19, p. 115).

Burton, —
Child of the chapel, livery of medley (SJC, D91.20, p. 25), 1502; reward given to his mother, 1503 (SJC, D91.20, pp. 25, 116).

Bury, Thomas
Child of the chapel and scholar at Eton, 1504–9 (SJC, D91.20, p. 175; D102.1).

Carter, John
Servant of the chancellor and dean of chapel, Hornby, presented with a benefice in 1503 (SJC, D91.20, p. 156); paid in July 1505 for writing out statutes of Godshouse (SJC, D91.21, 37); for 'leechcraft' in Cambridge, 1507 (SJC, D91.19, p. 37); for translating 'certen books into English', 1508 (SJC, D91.19, p. 89).

Chamber, or Chambre, John
?Physician, called 'one of the chief advisers to the foundress', in a letter from SJC of 1551 (T. Baker, *History of St. John's College, Cambridge*, ed. J. E. B. Mayor, 2 vols. (Cambridge, 1869), I, 349). Delivered from Ludgate prison, 1507 (SJC, D91.19, p. 10).

Chamber, Thomas
Groom of the spicery by indenture, 1507 (SJC, D91.19, p. 14).

Cholmondeley, Richard
Steward of Cottingham (Yorks), granted 1509, as held from Lady Margaret before her death (*L and P Henry VIII*, I, ii, 1282, 2964/87); wife was widow of Sir Walter Strickland and he had custody of Strickland's heir (*ibid.*, I, i, 279, 449/6). Cholmondeley's first entry into office under the crown in 1487, as receiver-general of the king's

lordships in Yorkshire and Durham, is said to have been due to Lady Margaret's patronage (A. J. Pollard, *North-Eastern England during the Wars of the Roses* (Oxford, 1990), 387–8).

Clarell, James
Cofferer, in 1494 and 1498–9 (WAM, 22830; SJC, D91.17); Lady Margaret's suits against for debts, *c.* 1501 (chancery, PRO, C1/205/71), common pleas, 1506 (PRO, CP40/978/462v, 695); part of his arrears collected in 1501 (SJC, D102.2, p. 8).

Clement, 'Sir'
Of the chapel, 1508 (SJC, D91.19, p. 89).

Clerk, William
Subdean of the chapel in 1506 and 1508 (SJC, D91.21, p. 11; D91.19, p. 70).

Coke, Henry, probably the same as Henry Ludlow, q.v.

Coldharbour, Peter of, *see* Baldwyn, Peter

Collingwood, Roger
BRUC; scholar, fellow of Queens' College, 1497–1510, permitted to study at Paris, 1502–3, and 'abroad', 1507; granted stipend of 40s from the household in 1507–8, 1508–9 (SJC, D91.19, pp. 34, 94). His *Arithmetica Experimentalis* was dedicated to his former master, Bishop Fox.

Colman, Thomas
BRUC; scholar of Gregory hostel, of the queen and Lady Margaret, 1498–9 (SJC, D91.17, p. 37).

Compton, Nicholas
Receiver-general, deputy to Reginald Bray in 1493–4 (PRO, SC6/1771), makes most of the deposits recorded by Hornby, 1499–1502 (SJC, D102.10), after which succeeded by Ashton as receiver-general.

Coningsby, Humphrey
Lawyer, sergeant at law 1496, justice of king's bench in 1509, associated with the council learned; regularly employed as an attorney by Lady Margaret. He was one of the arbitrators in her award between Cambridge university and town, 1503, and claimed in 1512 to have been 'of counsell and of fee' with her many years before her death (Chrimes, *Henry VII*, 150; *Notes*, 227).

Conway, —
Child of the chapel, 1503, loan to as late of the chapel, 1507 (SJC, D91.20, p. 106; D91.19, p. 61).

Cotterell, Robert
Of the chapel, schoolmaster of choristers at Fotheringhay, 1505 (SJC, D91.21, p. 39).

Crossley, Christopher
BRUC; chaplain, 1504, when he delivered Bury to Eton (SJC, D91.20, pp. 112, 175); entered study of canon law 1494–5, rector of Market Deeping.

Danyell, William
Yeoman of the chariot, 1498–9 (SJC, D91.17, pp. 30, 51).

Denman, Thomas
BRUC; scholar, physician, probably the master Denman in the riding household of 1498–9 (SJC, D91.17). In his will he left money to Edward Vaux his servant and an annuitant of Lady Margaret, to Henry 'coco domine mee' (Coke, above?), clothes and bedclothes (a sparver) to William Elmer, and 40s for a mass in 'capella domine mee' (Cooper, 215; Denman's will, 12 July 1500, PCC, Register F, fol. 25).

Denton, James
BRUC; scholar, lawyer, retained as 'my lady's scholar at Orleans' by Lady Margaret in connection with her suit to recover money from the king of France, 1502–3, 1503–4 (SJC, D91.20, pp. 39, 84; M. K. Jones, 'Orléans Ransom', 267); DCL at university of Valence, 1505, *grace ad eundem* at Cambridge; king's chaplain and almoner to Mary queen of France, 1514.

Denton, mistress
Paid by the household as attendant to Henry VII's daughter Margaret in Scotland 22 May 1505 (SJC, D91.21, p. 24).

Doryn, Perrot, alias Perrot the Frenchwoman
Chamberer at Henry VII's funeral and until Margaret's death (*L and P Henry VIII*, I, i, 13, no. 20; SJC, D91.4, p. 12); in the household in 1503 with a French priest as confessor, possibly a companion and language tutor for Margaret (SJC, D91.20, pp. 120, 126b); granted 5 marks in ready money and an annuity of £4 from the enfeoffed lands for life 'if she tary within this realme', under Margaret's will, performed by the executors 23 Oct. 1509 (*Will*, 123; SJC, D3.78).

Elmden, Nicholas
Of the chapel, loan to in 1507 (SJC, D91.19, p. 29).

Elmer, or Hylmer, William
Physician, paid for medicines, 1505 (SJC, D91.21, p. 74); he was left a bequest by Thomas Denman. Lady Margaret granted him messuages and lands at Maxey for his life in 1505 (SJC, D3.81).

Everingham, John
Cater, granted compensation by Lady Margaret's executors against Nicholas Saunder her clerk of the kitchen, SJC, D91.7, fol. 10v. He and the controller of household gave money for building to Mr Wyott of Christ's College 1507 (SJC, D91.19, p. 7).

Falconer's son, the, *see* Sedington, John

Farthing, Thomas
Singing man of the chapel, granted an annuity, formerly held by Elizabeth Massey, for services to Lady Margaret 1511 (*L and P Henry VIII*, I, i, 442, 883/25), gentleman of the chapel royal at the funeral of Prince Henry, 1511 (*ibid.*, I, i, 382/707); possibly the same as 'William' Farthing 'late of the chapel' to whom a prest of £13 6s 8d was made in 1507 (SJC, D91.19, p. 61).

Fawne, John
BRUC; scholar, rewarded in 1498 while a fellow of Queens' College (SJC, D91.17), received £3 towards costs of his BTh, along with £2 to settle debts of his brother Ralph, April 1504, (SJC, D91.20, p. 152), first Lady Margaret preacher.

Fell, William
BRUC; almoner, of Oxford, incorporated at Cambridge 1497–8, mentioned as almoner in 1507 (SJC, D91.19, p. 18).

Fisher, John
BRUC, DNB, but cf. the itinerary of Fisher in Bradshaw and Duffy, eds., *Humanism, Reform and the Reformation*, 236–49; chaplain and confessor to Lady Margaret, *c.* 1500, bishop of Rochester, 1504, chancellor of Cambridge university for life, 1514. Fisher's first meeting with Lady Margaret was in 1494 or 1495, probably the latter (*Grace Book B, part I*, xxii). Richard Fitzjames was confessor at some stage during his tenure of the see of Rochester (1497–1503), but Fisher had already become confessor when the king considered making him

bishop (Lady Margaret's vow, and the king's letter to her, Cooper, 95–8).

Fothede, John
BRUC; controller in 1504–6, while master of Michaelhouse (SJC, D102.10, pp. 101, 181v); handed over statutes of Christ's College to the fellows, 3 Oct. 1506; university preacher in 1509–10.

Fowler, Edith
Servant, gentlewoman to Lady Margaret, mentioned paying for needs of the almsfolk and in rewards, including one to Margaret Stukeley, 1503, and to 'my lord prince's nurse', 1505 (SJC, D91.20, pp. 120, 171; D91.21, p. 25). She was granted an annuity of £10 under Margaret's will, with her husband Thomas, from lands at Maxey, 23 Jan. 1506 (*Will*, 123; SJC, D3.83). A brass at Christ's College, *c.* 1520 commemorates the Fowlers (*RCHM, Cambridge*, I, 29).

Frances, George
Servant, granted bailiffry of Thorpewaterfield alias Achurch, N'hants, and Ridlington, Rut, and keepership of Calgarth and Windermere for services to Lady Margaret, 31 Aug. 1509 (Cooper, 218; *L and P Henry VIII*, I, 82, 158/89).

Fremingham, Robert
Treasurer of the chamber, 1509, succeeding Miles Worsley (SJC, D102.1); travelled to London to obtain Repull advowson from the bishop of Worcester, and gave attendance on the king and his council on Lady Margaret's business, 1507 (SJC, D91.19, pp. 9, 16, 17); defendant with Richard Bothe in a suit by Worsley and Margaret his wife, Easter term 1507 (PRO, CP40/980).

Freston(e), Christopher
Scholar of my lady at the grammar school at Sheen, briefly resident at Christ's College before returning to continue his learning, 6 Jan. 1509 (Hornby's accounts, SJC, D57.34, fol. 4v).

Frogenhall, Alexander
Servant, received expenses, 1505 (SJC, D91.21, p. 79); was left plate, linen and a printed copy of Magna Carta in French (*Will*, 122).

Frogenhall, mistress
Servant, expenses on her apparel 1506 (SJC, D91.21, p. 157).

Gilpyn, Gilbert
Clerk of the kitchen/steward of household to Lady Margaret and

Stafford at Woking, 1466–71 (WAM, 12181–90), given money by her command to repair the manor on the king's visit, 1493 (WAM, 32364), still resident in charge of the stable 1498–9 (SJC, D91.17, p. 28). In *c.* 1800 a brass of Gilpyn in Woking church was recorded. It showed him with a bugle horn about his neck and a hound at his feet and was inscribed 'pray for Gilbert Gilpyn, parker at Woking park, who died 10 August 1500' (Manning, and Bray, *The History and Antiquities of Surrey*, I, 138). This brass was lost by 1926 (Mill Stephenson, *A List of Monumental Brasses in the British Isles* (London, 1926), 500).

Gower, Richard
Clerk of the kitchen, 1498–9 (SJC, D91.17, p. 58).

Gower, Jane
Servant, supported at a cost of 20s in London, 1502 (SJC, D91.20, p. 40).

Guildford, Lady Jane
Lady-in-waiting, bequeathed £20 (*Will*, 121; Cooper, 133); granted in 1514 annuity of £20 for services to the late king and queen and others, but not Lady Margaret by name (*L and P Henry VIII*, I, ii, 1514, 3499/59).

Heven, Edward
Servant, accompanying Lady Margaret in July 1498 (SJC, D91.17, p. 23) and agent in Lincolnshire, bailiff of Boston, 1503–9 (PRO, SC6/Hen. VII/1772, 1773; SJC, D91.19, p. 115); benefactor to the collegiate church of Tattershall (Done, *A Guide to the Collegiate Church*, describes his memorial tablet); confirmed in the bailiffry of Boston for services to her 24 July 1509 (*L and P Henry VIII*, I, i, 69, 132/99), granted the bailiffry at Tattershall (*ibid.*, 132/100).

Hilton, Robert
Yeoman of the wardrobe, 1498–1509 (household accounts and inventories taken at Collyweston 1500, and Hatfield 1509, SJC, D91.6; D91.4).

Hobson, Thomas
Auditor in 1496 of lands held by Lady Margaret and Stanley, excluding those of the king's grant in 1487 (WAM, 32366), granted for his services auditorship of all her lands 24 July 1509 (*L and P Henry VIII*, I, i, 75, 158/2, and keepership of Bourne park, Lincs., *ibid.*, 76, 158/4); gained the wardship of John Stowell one of her wards (*Calendar of Ancient Deeds*, V, 343 (A12575).

Holland, Oliver
Yeoman usher of the chamber in 1505 (SJC, D91.21, p. 79).

Holt, John
Bailiff of Canford, grant 21 July 1509 for services to Lady Margaret (*L and P Henry VIII*, I, i, 68, 132/87).

Hornby, George
Paid to look after horses of Stanley and Margaret at Deeping in 1483, also claimed fishing rights there at Talyngton (PRO, SC6/909/16). Plea against him by Robert Benell in 1487 (PRO, CP40/902/281).

Hornby, Henry
BRUC; secretary and dean of chapel by 1499, chancellor from 1504 to 1509 (SJC, D102.10, and other household accounts), master of Peterhouse, 1501–18, master of Tattershall College, 1502–8, 1512–18, dean of Wimborne, 1509–18. He founded a school at Boston while alderman of the guild of the Blessed Virgin there, the master's salary to be paid from his chantry at Peterhouse (T. A. Walker, *Register of Peterhouse*, 2 vols. (Cambridge, 1927), I, 95, and Peterhouse archives, Boston School Miscellanea, 1 and 2). He endowed an anniversary at Clare Hall for his parents George and Emma, Lady Margaret, himself, his friends and benefactors in 1517 (Peterhouse archives, Collegium A10, E2, E3). Hornby vacated the living of East Deeping, Lincs., in 1481, to which he may have been presented by Margaret duchess of Somerset; credited with the authorship of an office for the Name of Jesus, *c*. 1488 (Pfaff, *New Liturgical Feasts in Late Medieval England*, 83).

Hussey, Sir John
Steward of the manors of Maxey and Deeping, with an annuity from those lands, entered Margaret's service in 1486 or 1487 (Jones, 'An early Fenland drainage scheme', 14 and notes). He was granted stewardship of Boston, Bourne and Deeping, 16 Oct. 1510 (*L and P Henry VIII*, I, i, 604/31).

Jackson, John
Scholar of Lady Margaret at Oxford, 1498–9 (SJC, D91.17, p. 50). A Mr Jackson went to Rome to pray for her in 1505 (SJC, D91.20, p. 66).

Knight, John
Auditor to Lady Margaret 1487–8 (WAM, 32355), and to the king and several peers (will, PRO, Prob. 11/11, 1 and 7 Horne, 8 Sept. 1496). His widow prosecuted for debt by Lady Margaret in 1502 (PRO, CP40/1962, fol. 12d).

Knyvett, William
Steward of household, 1502 (PRO, Req./2/4/246); influential Norfolk
landowner, previously served as councillor to Henry duke of
Buckingham; took part in rebellion of 1483 (Rawcliffe, *Staffords*, 227).

Leonard of the Vestry alias Leonard Le Fevor
Book-binder, and supplier of books 1502–9 (household accounts),
including a book in which to write the names of those retained by Lady
Margaret and the cofferer's own account book (SJC, D91.20, p. 11, Feb.
1502). He bound five books 'of my lord of Rochester's sermons' in
1508 (SJC, D91.19, p. 112). He was granted by Lady Margaret's
feoffees certain tenements and lands at Maxey for life, 20 Oct. 1509
(SJC, D3.79), and a document was prepared at Fisher's direction to
witness Lady Margaret's grant of an annuity of 40s to him out of
Maxey 'to serve in the vestry of Christ's College' (SJC, D57.34, fol. 5v).
In 1527–8 'Leonard of Christ's College' was paid by the churchwardens of Holy Trinity parish, Cambridge, for writing, repairing and
binding service books and an 'organ book' (Cooper, 123 n. 1). Leonard
of the Vestry is not to be confused with Leonard Delese, printer, from
whom primers were bought in 1504 (SJC, D91.20, p. 171), and who
is probably also the Leonard who provided 'six French books' in 1505
(SJC, D91.21, p. 16).

Lewkenor, Edward
A Sussex landowner, who provided in his will for trentals to be
celebrated for him in the chapel of scala celi at Westminster 'where the
famous and excellent princess Margaret Countess of Richmond is
buried' (PRO, Prob. 11/20, 28 Maynwaryng).

Lewkenor, Thomas
Active rebel against Richard III in 1483; attendant on the duke of
Buckingham while the latter was a ward of Lady Margaret, 1494
(WAM, 22830).

Ludlow, Henry, alias Coke, Henry
Cook, probably the man referred to in the will of Thomas Denman. He
was left an annuity by Lady Margaret (*Will*, 123), granted property at
Maxey for his life by Lady Margaret's feoffees, 23 Jan. 1506, and
arrears of wages for six months by the executors, 1510 (SJC, D3.77;
Cooper, 199).

Lynne, Richard
Vice-chamberlain to Lady Margaret; payment made to him for costs of

a sewers commission, 1504 (SJC, D91.20, p. 165). From *c.* 1497 he was steward of Lady Margaret for Bassingbourn manor, Camb., which she held as part of the honour of Richmond. Here he rebuilt the manor house 'Richmonds', whose site had been granted to his father John Lynne, a London merchant, in 1455. He also owned a moiety of Castle manor, another part of the Richmond fee (*VCH, Camb,* VIII, 15). His monumental brass is in Bassingbourn church (*Monumental Inscriptions and Coats of Arms from Cambs.,* ed. W. M. Palmer (Cambridge, 1932), 220). In his will he left land at Wendy to the churchwardens of Bassingbourn to maintain obits for himself and his family, 20s to improve the roads around Bassingbourn, and various local personal bequests including malt for his godchildren (PRO, Prob. 11/16, 12 Bennet); d. 1509.

Mason, John
Singing man of the chapel and scholar, had exhibition at Tattershall College, 1504–7, grammar master employed for him, 1505 (SJC, D91.20, p. 175; D91.21, pp. 9, 40). In 1507 he obtained a dispensation and journeyed from Tattershall to Hatfield, where Lady Margaret made offering when he sang his first mass (SJC, D91.19, pp. 29, 32, 34, 35).

Massey, Elizabeth
Servant, gentlewoman, mentioned paying for flax for the almswomen, for their houselling ('hoselyng') for Easter and for shoes for poor folk, 1507–8 (SJC, D91.19, pp. 22, 92). Under Margaret's will she received 10 marks cash and an annuity of 10 marks from property at Maxey, granted by Margaret's feoffees, 23 Jan. 1506 (*Will,* 123; SJC, D3.82).

Mawdesley, James
?Receiver, assaulted at Caister, 1495 (PRO, CP40/934/41d), paying money to cofferer 1498–9 (SJC, D91.17), bailiff and collector at East Deeping, 1505–6 (PRO, SC6/Hen. VII.359).

Merbury, Robert
Yeoman to Lady Margaret at Henry VII's funeral (*L and P Henry VIII,* I, i, 13) and probably in 1507 (SJC, D91.19, 12), yeoman usher of the queen's chamber when made feodary of the duchy of Exeter (*ibid.,* I, i, 191, no. 414/21).

Merbury, William
Controller, in 1498–9 to 1504; rode to the Lincolnshire sessions in 1502 (SJC, D91.20, p. 11).

Morgan, Philip
BRUC; physician to Lady Margaret; glister pipe bought by him, 1503 (SJC, D91.20, p. 90); expenses paid to Cambridge before the commencement, 1507 (SJC, D91.19, p. 27). The university had written to Lady Margaret, who granted a pension to him in 1500–1, which may mark the beginning of his service after the death of Thomas Denman (Cooper, 71 and n. 2).

Morice, James
Servant of the earl of Derby 1492 (WAM, 5474); clerk of works at Collyweston and Lady Margaret's other residences, at the sluice at Boston and at Christ's College (household accounts); granted office of controller of customs at the port of Boston, 1504 (*CPR, 1494–1509*, 386), and weigher of wool there, (*L and P Henry VIII*, I, i, 48, no. 94/29), and with Hugh Edwards sewer of the chamber and surveyor of Lady Margaret's possessions, 8 Dec. 1509 (*L and P Henry VIII*, I, i, 135, no. 289/20), this being confirmed in 1510, 1515. He settled at Roydon. His son Ralph was a scholasticus of Christ's College, 1522 (*L and P Henry VIII*, I, i, 108, ex inf. Richard Rex). On 21 March 1554/5 by his will he gave to his grandson James and to Philip, Oliver and John Morice some lands there, and to his son Ralph a close and house called Fosters (PRO, Prob. 11/39, 48 Wrastley).

Moyne, Richard
Scholar of Lady Margaret at the London Charterhouse; personal bill for clothes and exhibition for him, 1502–3 (SJC, D91.20, pp. 55, 86).

Oldham, Hugh
BRUO; sued in 1488 in common pleas for a bond, given 11 May 1485, as parson of the church of Lanivet, Cornwall; claimed immunity as servant of William Smith, keeper of the hanaper (PRO, CP40/905/137); supervisor of repair of royal mills at Wimborne, 1488 (*Materials*, II, 262). He accounted to William Bedell for lands of the earl of Westmorland, 1490–1 (WAM, 32364); receiver for Lady Margaret's west-country estates, including the 'Exeter lands', in succession to John Hayes attainted for treason, 1492 (*RP*, VI, 455a; WAM, 32364, 32390); one of the king's receivers in 1493 (Wolffe, *The Crown Lands*, 140). He continued to act as Lady Margaret's receiver till 1504; mentioned as chancellor of the household, April 1503 (SJC, D91.20, p. 87); archdeacon of Exeter, 1492, bishop, 1504; buried in his chantry

chapel in Exeter cathedral; chief benefactor of Manchester grammar school.

Orlow, Henry
Singing man of Norwich, of the chapel in 1505 when his costs were paid to Collyweston (SJC, D91.21, p. 8).

Ormeston, Roger
Chamberlain to Lady Margaret at least from 1501 to his death in 1504 (SJC, D102.10, D102.2); paid as constable of Corfe castle by her command, 1492–3 (WAM, 32364). As the servant of Lady Margaret he received lands in Suffolk forfeited by Sir Robert Chamberlain, rebel, in 1495. Roger married Robert's widow Elizabeth and had to arrange a settlement with Ralph their son in 1496 (*CPR, 1494–1509*, 64, *CCR, 1485–1500*, 266). In 1502 he collected on Margaret's behalf the fine of a knighthood (SJC, D56.213). He was steward of Cambridge University in 1504 until his death by 28 May (*Reports and Communications of the Cambridge Antiquarian Society*, I (Cambridge, 1859), 274). In his will he bequeathed a standing cup with gilt cover to Lady Margaret, a gown to Richard Aderton and a ring to his cousin Hugh Oldham (PRO, Prob. 11/14, 15 Holgrave). Margaret sued his widow and other executors for a debt of £22 in 1506 (PRO, CP40/978, m. 736).

Parker, Alice, née St John
Servant, gentlewoman, wife of Henry Parker. Under Margaret's will she was left six bowls, parcel gilt, a gold collar ornamented with devotional symbols, 'hearts' and 'IHS', a bed and other precious cloths (*Will*, 122).

Parker, Henry (Lord Morley from 1518)
Sewer to Lady Margaret in *c.* 1491, her cupbearer at the coronation of Henry VIII, 1509, he was son of William Parker and Alice Lovell, Lady Morley. For his career and writings see *Forty-Six Lives*, ed. H. G. Wright, EETS, o.s., 214 (1943), Introduction.

Pellet, Thomas
Scholar, kinsman of Lady Margaret, maintained at Cambridge in 1502, 1503, in the latter year via John Hechyn of Jesus College (SJC, D91.20, pp. 21, 38, 61, 120), in 1507 via Mr Wyott and Mr Scott of Christ's (SJC, D91.19, p. 43); he journeyed to Hatfield to see Lady Margaret (*ibid.*, p. 43). In 1510 he was professed as a Whitefriar of Cambridge, at the expense of her estate (Hornby's accounts, SJC, D57.34, fol. 5v),

and remained at his studies in 1514–15 (*ibid.*, fol. 14). He was possibly of Tattershall: a John Pelet was presented at a court leet there in 1503 (KRO, U1475/M158, view of 11 May).

Peper (Pepur), ?Christopher
Scholar, maintained at Oxford, 1503 (SJC, D91.20, pp. 157, 172), 1505 via John Longland at Magdalen (SJC, D91.21, p. 66). He was possibly of Tattershall: a Robert Pepur was among tenants at an inquisition in 1503 (KRO, U1475/M168, 10 Oct.). A Christopher Pepur was receiver of the deanery of Wimborne, and accounted for building the schoolhouse there in 1513–14 (SJC, D57.34, fols. 13v–14).

Philip, David
Swan farmer to Margaret duchess of Somerset at Deeping, 1483 (PRO, SC6/909/16), farming part of site of manor of West Deeping 1488–9 (PRO, SC6/Hen. VII/358); granted by Lord Stanley and Lady Margaret office of warden of Maxey castle and supervisor of the marsh there, and of the fens in their domains of Deeping and Bourne, by 1494 (PRO, SC6/Hen. VII/450); bailiff at Collyweston, 1488 (WAM, 32365) and in charge of repairs there, 1490–3, and of the expenses of Henry Stafford, younger brother of Edward duke of Buckingham, 1493 (WAM, 32364); squire of the king's body (*The Reign of Henry VII from Contemporary Sources*, ed. A. F. Pollard, 3 vols. (London, 1913–14), II, 16–17; *RP*, VI, 496), master of the king's swans in Lincolnshire (*RP*, VI, 360b), 1503; member with Lady Margaret and Richard Fox, of the Corpus Christi Guild of Boston 1502 (Thompson, *History of Boston*, 121, 318); kept wards of Lady Margaret in his house at Stamford, and was buried in St Mary's church there (Leland, *Collectanea*, VI, 27).

Pole (Poole), William
Gentleman usher of the chamber to Lady Margaret, appointed to be the king's sergeant at arms to give attendance on the queen, 18 June 1509 (*L and P Henry VIII*, I, i, 48, nos. 94/70, 71); made bailiff of Holsworthy Dev, 21 July 1509 (*ibid.*, I, i, 76, no. 158/10).

Preched, Prechett, Thomas
Of the chapel in 1502 (SJC, D91.20, p. 39), was paid 10s at his departure in 1506 (SJC, D91.21, p. 107). In 1500 he had a chamber at Collyweston (clerk of works' accounts, 1500–1, SJC, D102.9, p. 17). In 1503 he was abbot of misrule at Christmas (SJC, D91.20, p. 126).

Radcliffe *see* Ratcliffe
Ratcliffe, —
One of Margaret's gentlewomen at the funeral of Henry VII (*L and P
Henry VIII*, I, i, 13).

Ratcliffe, Roger
Servant to the queen and to Lady Margaret, handled payments from
the household 1502 (SJC, D91.20, p. 20); granted the bailiwick of
Fremington, Dev, as he held it of Margaret, for services to her, and her
house called 'the Roiall' in London, 5 Feb. 1510 (Cooper, 219; *L and
P Henry VIII*, I, i, 170, no. 381/14).

Richards, Griffith
Clerk of the signet to Lady Margaret and to the queen (*L and P Henry
VIII*, I, i, 41, no. 82); made bailiff of Collyweston and park-keeper,
1509 (*ibid.*, I, i, 67, no. 132/60).

Rowley, —
Of the chapel; reward for singing there as 'sir Edward's servant' in
December 1498 (SJC, D91.17, p. 60), was paid 10s at his departure in
1506 (SJC, D91.21, p. 107).

Rowse, Thomas
With Edward Vavasour made keeper of Overston park and warren,
N'hants, for services to Lady Margaret, 3 Aug. 1511 (*L and P Henry
VIII*, I, i, 453, no. 857/8).

Rygote, Robert
Scholar, priest of Syon, claims in a letter to Henry VIII to have been
'sometime scholar to your grandmother' (*L and P Henry VIII*, VII, no.
1092, ex inf. Richard Rex).

St John, Sir John, of Bletsoe (*see* Genealogical table 2, p. xx)
Kinsman, chamberlain to Lady Margaret after the death of Roger
Ormeston in 1504, and one of her executors (*Will*, 109). *See also* entry
below.

St John, John, esquire, of Lydiard Tregoze (see Genealogical table 2,
p. xxi)
Kinsman, servant, 'in household' many years until Margaret's death,
according to his testimony to chancery in 1513, taken at Exeter when
he was about thirty-four. He seems to have been one of the feoffees of
Lady Margaret in 1505 but was not her executor of the same name, for

he does not call himself either her executor or her chamberlain in his deposition; was left by Margaret a book of the *Canterbury Tales* (*Will*, 122).

Sanders (Saunders, Sander), Nicholas
A clerk of the kitchen in 1509, receiving money for expenses of the household from two weeks before Lady Margaret's death until her month mind (Cooper, 190, 226). He was paid for cloth in 1502 (SJC, D91.20, p. 26), for two books in 1505 (SJC, D91.21, p. 10), and received materials 'to write in the crown of our lady', 1507 (SJC, D91.19, p. 43). He oversaw works at the manor of Croydon in the absence of James Morice at Fotheringhay and at Boston, 1505 (SJC, D91.22, p. 55). His name appears on a fragment of the statutes of St John's College, as 'admitted' (*c.* 1520? SJC, C1.40).

Sandes, George
Made ranger of 'Le Old Parc', forest of Windermere, for services to Lady Margaret, 24 July 1509 (*L and P Henry VII*, I, i, 67, no. 132/78).

Sant, Randall
Servant or ward, bound apprentice to Boniface Stanley, 1506 (SJC, D91.21, p. 91).

Scales, Oliver
Rent collector for Queens' College, Cambridge, in 1502–3 (CUL, Queens' College archives, QC Bk1); paid in connection with acquisition of Manorbier for Christ's, 1508 (SJC, D91.19, p. 112), and with making Thomas Lynne a ward of Lady Margaret, 1509 (SJC, D102.1, fol. 4). He was a notary public (Cooper, 145) active in the establishment of St John's College especially as clerk of works 1512–16 under Robert Shorton, master (SJC, C17.1; D6.30; Willis and Clark, *Architectural History*, II, 246).

Sedington, John
Scholar, possibly the same as 'the falconer's son', supported at school at St Albans at 10d a week for eighteen weeks from mid-Feb. to 28 June 1508 (SJC, D91.19, pp. 75, 86, 92, 115). Sedington was paid for ten weeks' board at 8d a week, before dying and being buried at St Albans in the autumn (SJC, D91.19, p. 104).

Sherade, Thomas
Child of the chapel; conveyed home to his father dwelling beside Melton Mowbray, at Stapelford, 1507 (SJC, D91.19, p. 45).

Shirley, Lady Anne
Wife of Sir Ralph Shirley and daughter of Sir Henry Vernon of Haddon;
Lady Margaret gave Anne a book of hours inscribed in Margaret's own
hand with a request for prayers (SJC Library, MS N.24; K. Harris, 'The
origins and make-up of Cambridge University Library MS Ff. 1.6',
Trans. Cambridge Bibliographical Society, 8 (1983), 306). The costs of
Anne's board at the George inn (Croydon) were met in 1508 (SJC,
D91.19, p. 90).

Shirley, Richard
Servant, paid for diets of between nine and eleven persons in London,
Norfolk and Oxfordshire from June 1498 to September 1499 and for
provisions for horses and wages of the horse-keeper at Westminster in
July 1498 (SJC, D91.17, *passim*). He was Margaret's bailiff at Ware and
keeper of the park there reserved for her horses, until 1509 when he
was succeeded by William Compton (Cooper, 36–7; *L and P Henry VIII*,
I, i, 276). A Mr Shirley was rewarded as clerk of the king's kitchen in
1502 (SJC, D91.20, p. 109). Lady Margaret and a Richard Shirley both
sued Humfrey Monk of Pudrug, Dev., in 1494, she for assaulting her
servant at Holdsworthy, he for giving livery at Gt Torrington against
the royal statute (PRO, CP40/930, 87, 87d). It is possible therefore
that Shirley's earlier service with the countess was in the west country.
    It has been supposed that Lady Margaret gave her book of hours to
his wife, but the recipient is more likely to have been Lady Anne, wife
of Sir Ralph Shirley (M. R. James, *Manuscripts in the Library of St. John's
College* (Cambridge, 1913), 311, and *see also* previous entry).

Stanbank, Richard
BRUC; scholar, fellow of Queens's College, 1500–19, granted leave to
study theology overseas for three years in July 1508 (Queens' College
archives, QC Bk76, fol. 27r), in which year he was also paid 20s by
Lady Margaret as her scholar at Paris (SJC, D91.19, pp. 95, 115).

Stanhope, mistress
Servant, gentlewoman, paying rewards, 1506–8 (SJC, D91.21, p. 104;
D91.19, pp. 31, 85). She may have been related to Henry Stanhope,
brother of Maud Lady Willoughby of Tattershall (*HMC, Report on the De
L'Isle and Dudley MSS*, I, 176–7); granted a gown 'by my lady's order',
according to an inventory of early 1509 (View of Robes, Jan. 1509,
SJC, D91.4, p. 5).

Stukeley, Margaret and Richard

Servants, a reward was paid to Margaret when Lady Margaret visited the king in 1505 (SJC, D91.21, p. 33). Richard Stukeley (Stewkeley) had a wage of 20s in 1498 (SJC, D91.17, p. 46). They were granted property at Maxey for the term of Margaret's life by the feoffees, 23 Jan. 1506 (SJC, D3.80). Under Lady Margaret's will, however, they were to receive an annuity of £4 until the longer-lived should die (*Will*, 123), and a new agreement was made by the executors, 18 March 1514 (SJC, D3.84).

Sylvester, Gabriel

BRUC; scholar, master of Clare Hall, 1496–1506, preached before Lady Margaret in lent 1502 as 'Mr. Gabriel of Clare Hall' (SJC, D91.20, 14). He received money from Margaret's officers to give to the master of Christ's College for building in 1505 or 1506 (SJC, D91.22, p. 129), and was on her council at least to advise on that foundation (Lloyd, *Christ's College*, 284, n. 1).

Thwaytes, John

BRUC; John Tweytes, BCL 1506–7, scholar, retained in France, 1502–4, in connection with Margaret's suit to recover money from the French king (SJC, D91.20, pp. 65, 127; Jones, 'Orléans ransom', 267 and notes).

Urmston, Roger, *see* Ormeston

Vavasour, Edward

Servant, granted keepership of park and warren at Overston, N'hants., for services to Lady Margaret, 4 Aug. 1509 (Cooper, 217; *L and P Henry VIII*, I, i, 122, no. 257/32).

Vaux, Edward

Servant, granted bailiwick of manor of Langton in le Old York, 30 July 1509, for services to Lady Margaret (Cooper, 217; *L and P Henry VIII*, I, i, 70, no. 132/118).

Walcote, Humphrey

Servant, paid for his trouble 'sitting in the parts of Lincoln apon the retayners', he gave rewards to the priors of Kettleby and Sempringham, 1509 (SJC, D91.19, p. 105); plaintiff with his wife Elizabeth in a plea of waste vs. Margaret Lancastre, executrix of John Seleston, 1507 (PRO, CP40/979, m. 533).

Walcote, John
Servant, relative of above; said to have lived in Margaret's household
for sixteen years, to have been one of the jurors empanelled by
Margaret in 1500 to decide the boundaries in Kesteven, and to have
made additions to the Crowland chronicle (R. Gough, *Observations on
Croyland Abbey and Bridge and Other Additions to the History of the Abbey*
(London, 1784), 172–3).

Wall, William
Chaplain to the earl of Derby, presented by proxy to the living of West
Ludford, Som., in 1487–8 (*Register of Robert Stillington*, Somerset
Record Society, vol. 52 (1937), 144, 152); receiver for Kendal at least
from 1492 to 1501, when Margaret refers to the discharge of his
account (Sizergh Castle, Strickland MSS, IV, 1492–3; Cooper, 66).

Walter, Jane
Chamberer to Lady Margaret at Henry VII's funeral (*L and P Henry VIII*,
I, i, 13, no. 20).

Walter, John
Servant, in attendance in 1498, rode to Lancashire to the earl of Derby
(SJC, D91.7, pp. 37, 40).

Watwood, William
Singing boy of the chapel, sent to school at Eton, 1502 (SJC, D91.20,
p. 36).

Welby, Richard
Receiver for the honour of Richmond in Lincolnshire, 1478–9, 1484–5
(PRO, DL29/639/10378. 10379), came from one of the principal
families of Moulton (*Ingulph's Chronicle of the History of Croyland*, 507).
'Master Welby', a member of this family though possibly not Richard,
was a messenger from the king to Lady Margaret in 1501 (Cooper, 66).

Westbury, Maurice
BRUO; scholar, granted leave of absence from Oxford at Margaret's
request to tutor certain young gentlemen of her household, 1494
(*Epistolae Academicae*, ed. Anstey, II, 614).

Wheatley, Thomas
BRUC; scholar 'of my lady at Cambridge', ?a questionist 1492; the
household paid his commencement fee of 40s in 1498 (SJC, D91.17, p.
19).

Whitstones, James
BRUC; scholar and lawyer, incepted in canon Law, 1491–2; in 1501 Margaret chose him to present her case in the French *parlement* (Cooper, 66). In July 1503 he was president of her council (SJC, D91.20, 104), and in 1509 drew up at her command documents for the conversion of St John's hospital into a college (*Notes*, 229).

Wilsford, Edmund
BRUO; scholar, fellow of Oriel College, 1483–1516, provost from 1507; Lady Margaret's divinity reader at Oxford, paid by the household, in 1498–9 (SJC, D91.17, p. 46); by March 1509 he was confessor to Margaret, who left him the cup later acquired by Christ's College (*Will*, 123; Rackham, ed., *Christ's College* 309).

Windsor, mistress Ursula
My lady's goddaughter, payments to her while Margaret was at Sheen, 1498 (SJC, D91.17, p. 24); payments by her for household needs included those for binding a book, mistress Stanhope's nurse, and Lord Stanley's month mind, 1504 (SJC, D91.20, p. 187).

Worsley, Miles
Cofferer, succeeding James Clarell, 1499–1509, called treasurer or treasurer of the chamber from 1506 (household accounts, *passim*). *See* Fremingham, Robert.

Young, John
BRUO; scholar and preacher, fellow of Winchester and New College, 1485–1502, rector of All Hallows, Honey Lane, London, preached before Lady Margaret, Lent 1506 (SJC, D91.21, p. 102).

Zouche, Lionel
Kinsman, ?ward, receives livery in 1509 (SJC, D91.4, p. 7).

APPENDIX 4

VERSIONS OF THE LAST WILL OF LADY MARGARET IN ST JOHN'S COLLEGE ARCHIVES

The texts of five versions are compared with the SJC copy of that proved in 1512 (no.5 below), the most complete version, printed as *Will* in the college quatercentenary volume *Collegium Divi Johannis Evangelistae, 1511–1911*. It is fuller than the copy entered in the register of the Prerogative Court of Canterbury.

1. SJC, D6.27, in book form, signed by Lady Margaret on each page. As *Will* up to 'covenyent', 118 section 105, followed immediately by the clause of attestation (123 section 138), excluding mention of Bassingbourne. The core of this document represents the will as it stood in 1508, before the purchase of that manor in January 1509. A note of the purchase as printed (118 section 105) is loose in the front of the book, signed by Margaret in a hand markedly shakier than the other signatures. June 1508–?April 1509, with later insertions.

    The names of the executors (SJC, D6.27, p. 16) were inserted in blanks left for the purpose. They were : Richard Fox, bishop of Winchester, John Fisher, bishop of Rochester, Charles Somerset Lord Herbert, Sir Thomas Lovell, Sir Henry Marney, Sir John St John, Henry Hornby and Hugh Ashton. Subsequent insertion of the names explains why Sir Henry Marney is referred to in *Will* as chancellor of the duchy of Lancaster, although he was not appointed until May 1509.

    A schedule of legacies added in February 1509 follows the will, altered later to accord with the final disposition of goods as recorded in *Will*. No personal legacy to Henry VII was recorded in SJC, D6.27.

288

2. SJC, D4.3, a roll. As *Will* up to 'requyred' (p. 118 section 106); n.d. ?end of 1508, unsigned.

3. SJC, D4.5, a roll. ?Copy first prepared for probate. Text as SJC, D6.27. To this is added the memorandum, 124 section 145, as far as 'the will of the said princess', 126 section 155. Unsigned, n.d., ?shortly after Lady Margaret's death, 29 June 1509.

4. SJC. D4.7, in book form, pp. 1–31, 39–48. ?Draft of will as proved in 1512. As *Will*, but the memorandum (124 section 145 – 126 section 153) is in the first person plural, showing its origin in one prepared during Margaret's life. In this version there is mention of the establishment of St John's but not specifically of its endowment with the enfeoffed lands or its equipment from her goods. The final version as printed in *Will* is included towards the end of the document.

   SJC, D4.7, pp. 31–8 is an estimate of funeral expenses, made at Hatfield, 17 January 1509. These mention 40 torchbearers, 50 gentlemen servants out of the check roll, 110 yeomen and grooms, 6 head officers and counsellors, 10 gentlemen of the household, 12 gentlemen of the chapel, 8 choristors, 8 knights, 8 chief captains, 12 gentlewomen, 4 ladies. Expenses of the household for three months (as required in *Will*, 108 section 36) are £144, wages for six months (end of section 105) £152. Expenses to Westminster of 600 people for two days at 8d each a day, £40; expenses of 12d each at London for two days, £60; 200 persons coming home from London £6 13s 4d. Allowances are given for charity to parish churches adjoining the place of our decease (*Will*, 104 section 10), and other items as in *Will*, 104–6. The sum total of the estimate is £1,033, compared with actual expenses £1,021 (Cooper, 190). Unsigned, n.d., 1509–12.

5. SJC, D4.6, a roll. The probate copy, printed as *Will*, with the seal of the archbishop of Canterbury and grant of probate attached, 22 October 1512.

   The will proved on this date as registered in the Canterbury register, however, has some omissions. The text is as *Will* up to 118 line 105 ('convenyent'), omits the section about the Bassingbourne purchase and the list of legacies, and begins again at *Will*, 124 line 145, with the memorandum about the foundation of St John's. It ends with a record of the commission of administration of goods to Richard, bishop of Winchester, 30 July 1518, when the executors had completed their accounts; PRO, Prob.11/16 31 Bennet. The same text is printed in *A Collection of All the Wills now Known to be Extant, of the Kings and Queens of England*, ed J. G. Nichols (London, 1780), 356–88, except that the document of 1518 is omitted.

6. SJC, D91.23, a register, pp. 1–24. As *Will*, except for the attached grant; the legacies section is printed in Cooper, Appendix, 129–36.

LADY MARGARET'S ARMS AND SEAL

Lady Margaret's arms were those of her father with certain differences. The coat was England and France (modern) quarterly, differenced by a border compony argent and azure. Her father had as supporters a gold crowned eagle, derived from a badge of Edward III, and a silver yale with gold spots, possibly originally a variant of the Lancastrian badge of the antelope. The yale was first used by John, duke of Bedford, and was associated with his earldom of Kendal.[1] Margaret, for whom Kendal was important as the endowment which had accompanied her father's elevation to the dukedom of Somerset, adopted two yales as supporters. She had as crest the eagle issuing from a royal coronet, gorged with another ducal coronet to which a chain is attached. Queen Margaret of Anjou's crest, as seen in the arms of Queens' College, Cambridge, was an eagle issuing from a royal coronet, but ungorged. Lady Margaret also used the Beaufort badge of the portcullis, to which her son sometimes added the words 'altera securitas'. The words signified that as a portcullis was an additional strength to a fortress, so Henry regarded his Beaufort blood as an additional support to his title to the crown, vindicated in battle.[2] Another personal badge of the foundress, clusters of daisies known as 'marguerites', which were also incorporated in some of her plate, are found freely scattered as a

---

[1] J. P. Brook-Little, *Royal Heraldry, Beasts and Badges of Britain* (London, 1977), 18. The pun 'Kend-eale' or 'Kend-yale', adduced in support of the connection with Kendal seems far-fetched, but the yale has no other royal association and entered the royal bestiary with the grant of that earldom to Bedford.

[2] T. Willement, *Royal Heraldry* (London, 1821), 86.

background to the arms over the gates of Christ's and St John's Colleges.[3]

Margaret's seal presents one interesting variation over time. It is a replica of her arms, except that in 1472 the eagle atop the arms does not issue from a coronet, and the legend runs 'sigillum Margarete comitisse Richmond et Derbii, filie et heredis John ducis Somerset', whereas in 1502 the coronet, of fleurs de lys and daisies, is present and the legend is completed by '...et mater Henrici septimi regis Anglie et Hibernie'.[4]

---

[3] *The Cambridge Armorial*, ed. C. Humphery-Smith, H. E. Peek, G. H. Wright and C. W. Scott-Giles (London, 1985), 60, 74–5; J. W. Cartmell, 'The gate', in Rackham, ed., *Christ's College*, 294; J. W. Clarke, 'Chimney-piece in master's lodge', in *ibid.*, 250–1.

[4] SJC, D56.195, seal on revoked will of 1472; SJC, D5.13, D5.14, deeds establishing professorships at Oxford and Cambridge.

APPENDIX 6

PORTRAITS OF LADY MARGARET

Of the many likenesses of Lady Margaret only the important sixteenth-century portraits are considered below. We are grateful to Mr F. Hepburn for comments on the development of the early portraiture of Lady Margaret, and to Mr Mitchell and the Librarian at Christ's College for information about the portraits there.

1. Tomb effigy by Pietro Torrigiano, at Westminster Abbey. Torri-giano's effigy, lying in its pillared surround on the tomb, was described in the contract between him and the executors as 'an image lying in the tabernacle', and the other features of the tomb were specified.[1] It was all to be made 'according to a patron drawen in a cloth' which remained with the executors. This patron or pattern was almost certainly one of those commissioned by the executors from the Dutch painter Meynnart Wewyck, payment for which was recorded in their accounts. Meynnart was also paid at the same time for making Margaret's 'picture and image', and 'for payntynge the pyketour of my lady the kinges grauntmother in Crystys college', but these have not survived.[2] The full-length now at Christ's (no.5 below) is likely to be a later picture.

2. (Plate 2) Half-length, in the master's lodge of Christ's College.[3] This is of the first half of the sixteenth century. It has strong similarities with the miniature by Lucas Hornbolte, c. 1530 (Plate 4).[4] The figure holds an open book, but the gaze is directed half-left out of

---

[1] See above, p. 238 n. 28.   [2] Cooper, 198, 200–1.

[3] J. W. Goodison, *Catalogue of Portraits in Christ's, Clare, and Sidney Sussex Colleges,* Cambridge Antiquarian Record Society, VII (Cambridge, 1985), 37.

[4] R. Strong, *Artists at the Tudor Court,* Catalogue of an Exhibition at the Victoria and Albert Museum (1983), no. 13.

the portrait. The face, with prominent cheekbones, resembles the Sittow portrait of Henry VII, 1505.[5] It is in the tradition of a number of royal portraits of the fifteenth century known through early sixteenth-century copies.[6] Both the lodge portrait and the miniature are likely to have been based on an original portrait by Wewyck. They show Margaret's headdress as a gabled coif and a wimple of widowhood; over the wimple is a pleated barbe of mourning of transparent material, clearly visible on close inspection as a garment reaching from chin to chest. The detail of the barbe and its position relative to the wimple have been misunderstood in later portraits (except Lockey's, no.4). The barbe is shown in these as an appendage to the bottom of the wimple, divided from it by a broad edging band. Such a rendering makes no sense either of the form of the widow's wimple – plain like that of a nun – or of the barbe, which reached above the chin.

3.   Half-length, in the Combination Room, St John's College. This is the same pose as no.2, but the face is younger, and lacks the resemblance to the Sittow portrait of Henry VII. The headdress is done less accurately, without a tippet, or point of the hood, at the back such as appears in no.2. An inscription runs round the frame: 'Margareta mater Henrici septimi, comitissa Richmondiae et Darbiae, Fundatrix Collegiorum Chri et Joanis Cantabrigiae, obiit anno Dni 1509 Kalend. Julii'.

A very similar portrait, *c.* 1580, with the same inscription, is in the Old Schools, Cambridge University.[7] Although John Wolf was paid by the executors for two portraits, it is unlikely that these are the pictures in question. Another portrait, alike in clothing, except that the tippet is clearly defined, but with sterner features, is in the National Portrait Gallery. It has been dated as possibly second half of the sixteenth century.[8]

4.   (Plate 3) Full-length, kneeling before a prie-dieu covered in cloth of gold on which is an open missal, against a background also of cloth of gold, on which are the Beaufort arms surmounted by a coronet, with a swan and yale as supporters. Beneath the arms is a portcullis with chains. This picture is in the hall of St John's

[5] National Portrait Gallery, reproduced in Chrimes, *Henry VII*, 268.

[6] F. Hepburn, *Portraits of the Later Plantagenets* (Woodbridge, 1986).

[7] J. W. Goodison, *A Catalogue of Cambridge Portraits*, I, *The University Collection* (Cambridge, 1955), 2–3.   [8] R. Strong, *Tudor and Jacobean Portraits* (London, 1969), I, 18.

College. It is by Roland Lockey, *c.* 1597. On the back is the inscription 'impensis Iulianae Clippesbie generosae virginis Norfolcensis, Rolandus Lockey pinxit Londini'. The college rental, 1597–8, has an entry for 'making a new crest for the new picture of the foundress, 5s'.[9]

This is the best documented of the late sixteenth-century portraits of Lady Margaret. It may be derived from the lost one of her 'sitting upon her knees', recorded in the 1549–50 inventory of the royal collection.[10]

5. Full-length, in the hall of Christ's College, Cambridge. The figure, with a peaked headdress and wimple covering the chin and holding an open book, is turned half-left. It is not in devotional pose, but stands looking out of the picture. In the top left-hand corner is her coat of arms. This portrait was thought by Gordon Kipling to be the work of Meynnart Wewyck.[11]

Others assigned the portrait to the later sixteenth century, citing the compelling evidence of tree-ring dating of the wood panel on which the portrait was painted. The report by Dr John Fletcher on the tree-ring test in 1977 gave a tentative date for the painting of 1580–90.[12]

The headdress has been misunderstood in a manner similar to that of many late copies, and the face has none of the character of that in no.2 or in the Hornbolte miniature.

[9] J. W. Goodison, 'Cambridge Portraits', *The Connoisseur*, 139 (1957), 214–15; SJC, SB4.2, rental 1597–8, fol. 505v.   [10] Strong, *Tudor and Jacobean Portraits*, I, 20–1.

[11] Kipling, *The Triumph of Honour*, 66.

[12] Report by J. M. Fletcher, Research Laboratory for Archaeology and the History of Art, Oxford, 1977; P. Tudor-Craig, *Catalogue of the National Portrait Gallery Exhibition on Richard III*, 2nd edn (London, 1977), 82, 91; Goodison, *Catalogue of Portraits in Christ's, Clare and Sidney Sussex Colleges*, 34–6.

SELECT BIBLIOGRAPHY

MANUSCRIPTS

Cambridge

Cambridge University Library
MS Oo.6.89, 'Memoir of the Public Life and Private Character of Margaret
    Countess of Richmond and Derby, by J.B.' Unfinished memoir by John
    Britton, with notes and correspondence.
Add. MS 7592, letter of Lady Margaret to the mayor of Coventry about the
    complaint of Owen Birch, 22 August, no year.

Cambridge University Library, Queens' College archives
QC Bk1, Magnum Journale (annual accounts), 1484–1518
QC Bk76, 'Miscellanea A'
QC Bk77, 'Miscellanea B'
QC box 29, 'Early documents'

Christ's College archives
Drawer 1, Allesley deeds, B, C, D
Drawer 44, Manorbier deeds, C, F, G, Additional 1
Drawer 47, Malton deeds, F
Drawer 97, Creek Abbey and Calthrop deeds, B

Christ's College Library
Donations Book, and books in the library there listed as of Lady Margaret's
    bequest

Fitzwilliam Museum
MS 261, tracts about plague, *c.* 1500

Peterhouse archives
Boston School Miscellanea, 1, 2, letters, 1518, receipts 1517–42
Collegium E2, benefaction of Henry Hornby, 1517

St John's College archives (SJC)

Household accounts
D91.16, account of the treasurer of the household (William Bedell), 1506–7
D91.17, account of the cofferer (James Clarell), 1498–9
D91.19, accounts of the treasurer of the chamber (Miles Worsley), 1507–9
D91.20, accounts of the cofferer (Miles Worsley), 1502–5
D91.21, accounts of the cofferer, 1505–7
D102.1, account of the treasurer of the chamber (Robert Fremingham), 1509
D102.2, account of the chamberlain, including expenses at Coldharbour, 1501
D102.6, account of the chamberlain, 1502
D102.10, book of receipts and payments, 1499–1509

Accounts of the clerk of works (James Morice)
D91.13, 1504–5
D91.14, 1502–4
D91.22, 1505–7
D102.9, 1500–1

Deeds and other records
C7.2, register of inventories, *c.* 1528–96
C7.11, the Thin Red Book, college register, *c.* 1516–42
D3.75, deed of the bishop of Ely removing the master of St John's hospital, 1507
D3.78, grant of annuity to Perrot Doryn, 1509
D4.1, petition by Lady Margaret, with the sign manual of Henry VIII, for the foundation of St John's College, 1509
D4.10, exemplification of proceedings in chancery (1511–12), 1513
D6.12, questions for counsel by Lady Margaret's executors, ?1509
D6.18, agreement between Lady Margaret's executors and the bishop of Ely, for the suppression of the hospital and foundation of the college, confirmed by the prior and convent of Ely, 1510–11
D6.27, original will of Lady Margaret, 1508, with later additions
D6.31, account of Robert Shorton, master, 1511–16
D15.49, first will of John Lord Welles, 1492
D56.3, will of Elizabeth, duchess of Norfolk, 1506
D56.6, indulgence for contributions to the war against the Turks, 1476
D56.20, indulgence granted to Lady Margaret and King Henry VII by Pope Julius II, 1504
D56.21, agreement between Pietro Torrigiano and Lady Margaret's executors for making her tomb, 1511
D56.156, 161, bonds of Elizabeth Scrope and Richard Wentworth to abide by an arbitration, 1502
D56.158, agreement for the disposition of lands of Margaret, duchess of Somerset, 1482
D56.184, indulgence for the feast of Jesus, 1494

D56.185, grant of confraternity to Lady Margaret and her husband Lord Stanley by the Carthusian Order, 1478

D56.186, will of Sir Henry Stafford, 1471

D56.195, first will of Lady Margaret, 1472

D56.196, instrument for the official opening of SJC, 1516

D56.200, marriage settlement of Lady Margaret and Lord Stanley, 1472

D56.205, grant by Lady Margaret of certain estates to trustees for her will, 1472

D56.213, receipt for fine for the knighthood of Sir John Markham, 1502

D57.33, account of part of the money from the wardship of Lady Lisle assigned to SJC, 1515–17

D57.34, account of Henry Hornby, of money received for the use of Lady Margaret's executors, 1509–16

D57.43, inventory of plate and jewels received by Christ's College, 1509

D57.172, articles given by Fisher after his visitation of Christ's College, 1510

D91.2, 3, 6, 10, 15, inventories of goods taken at Lady Margaret's death, n.d., *c.* 1509

D91.23, pp. 110–11, copy of a letter from King Henry VII to Lady Margaret, n.d. [1504]

D91.24, accounts of Lady Margaret's executors, 1509–19

D94.397, petition by Sir Robert Southwell to the executors of Lady Margaret, ?1509

D102.3, accounts including those of a brother of St John's hospital, 1505–11

D102.11, list of officers attending on Queen Elizabeth and Princess Catherine, 1501

D102.13, inventory of chapel stuff, n.d., *c.* 1509

D106.1, accounts for the completion of works at Christ's College, 1509–11

D106.3, pp. 9–15, account of part of the money from the wardship of Lady Lisle assigned to SJC, 1518–20

D106.5, account of money received by Nicholas Metcalfe from benefactors to SJC, 1518–23

D106.10, annual accounts of St John's hospital, 1505–10

D107.8, account of Nicholas Metcalfe, as master, 1518–23

St John's College Library
MS N.24, Lady Margaret's book of hours (James, *Catalogue of the Manuscripts in the Library of St. John's College*, no. 264), early fifteenth century

Clwyd Record Office

D/DM/426, receiver's account for Hawarden and Mold, 1476–7

Coventry, City Record Office

A6, accounts of the Corpus Christi guild, 1488–1553

A79/12, letter from Lady Margaret to the mayor of Coventry, n.d.

Dorset Record Office

P204/CW23, churchwardens' accounts, Wimborne Minster
P204/GN1/1, charter of foundation of Wimborne chantry, 1511

Durham, Muniments of the Dean and Chapter

Registrum Parvum IV, Prior's Letter Book, 1484–1519

Guildford Muniment Room

3242/19, 20, leases and agreements relating to Kendal, 1471

Kent Record Office

U1475/M167, court roll of Tattershall, 1494
U1475/M168, court roll, 1503
U1475/M169, court roll, 1505
U1475/Q19/2, Tattershall college precentor's account, 1495–6
U1475/Q21/4, ordinances for Tattershall college, drawn up at the instance of
    Lady Margaret, 1501

Lancashire Record Office

DDK/2/14, dispensation for marriage of Thomas Stanley and Elizabeth Welles,
    1498
DDK/1746/14, ministers' accounts for the duchess of Exeter, 1471–2
DDK/1746/17, receiver's account for properties of Margaret, countess of
    Richmond in Somerset, 1504
DDX/13/3, arbitration award by Lady Margaret, 1474

Lichfield Record Office

B/A/1/11, register of Reginald Boulers, bishop of Coventry and Lichfield

Lille, France, Archives Départementales du Nord

B2064-8, receiver-general's accounts of the duke of Burgundy

Lincolnshire Archives Office

Sp.S.503/101, boundary commission, September 1500

Liverpool City Library

920/MOO/574, award by Lady Margaret, 1473
920/MOO/1091, receiver's account for Hawarden and Mold, 1472–3

London

British Library
Add. MS 4712, fols. 3–32, royal household ordinances, 1493
Add. MS 5825, fol. 224v, Lady Margaret's vow of chastity (copy of SJC, C7.11, fol. 47r)
Add. MS 12060, a book of miracles and examples of virtue for the guidance of a ruler, dedicated to Queen Mary by Henry Parker Lord Morley
Add. MS 21480, book of payments, 1499–1505, kept for the king by John Heron
Add. MS 29976, fols. 65–80, extracts from records relating to Corfe castle and Purbeck
Add. MS 33772, 'Liber Precum', prayers and hymns for the office of the feast of the Name of Jesus, with the proper of the mass, dedicated to Lady Margaret by John de Gigli
Add. MS 35814, statement of account of sums owed by the Orléans family to Margaret duchess of Somerset for the ransom of Jean, count of Angoulême, 1447
Add. MS 45133, fol. 141v, ordinances for mourning, 1502–3
Add. MS 46399A, material relating to Chirk, C14–15
Add. MS 59899, accounts and memoranda, 1502–5, kept for the king by John Heron
Cotton MS Vesp.F.XIII, fol. 60, holograph letter from Lady Margaret to King Henry VII, n.d. [1499]
Ibid., fol. 61, letter from Lady Margaret to Richard Shirley, her bailiff at Ware, n.d. [1506–7]
Egerton MS 2341, schedule for design of windows, church of the Greyfriars, Greenwich, 1503
Harleian MS 602, fol. 1, exemplification of part of an account for Tidburst, Herts.
Harleian. MS 6072, fol. 21, the apparel of great estates of women in time of mourning, late sixteenth century
Royal MS 2A XVIII, the Beaufort Hours
Sloane MS 403, fol. 338b, medical recipes for Lady Margaret, Lady Howard, King Edward IV and others, n.d.
Stowe MS 144, fols. 100–2, depositions brought before Lady Margaret in a case of persons impugning the Tudor dynasty

Public Record Office
C1, early chancery proceedings
C39, inquisitions post mortem, Henry VI
C47, miscellanea of the chancery
C67, patent rolls (supplementary)
C81, warrants for the great seal, series I
C82, warrants for the great seal, series I
CP40, common pleas rolls

DL1/2, duchy of Lancaster pleadings, Henry VII
DL12/1, duchy of Lancaster warrants (under privy seal etc.), Henry VII
DL29, duchy of Lancaster ministers' accounts
E101/414/6, book of payments by John Heron, 1495–7
E135, ecclesiastical documents, department of the king's remembrancer of the
    exchequer
E159, memoranda rolls of the king's remembrancer
E368, memoranda rolls of the lord treasurer's remembrancer
E404, warrants for issue
KB9, ancient indictments
KB27, king's bench plea rolls
KB29, king's bench controlment rolls
Prob. 11, microfilms of registers of wills proved in the prerogative court of
    Canterbury
Req. 2, proceedings of the court of requests, Henry VII
SC1, ancient correspondence
SC6, ministers' and receivers' accounts
SC8, ancient petitions
SC11, rentals and surveys (rolls)
SC12, rentals and surveys (portfolios)
SP46, state papers domestic (supplementary)

Westminster Abbey
Westminster Abbey MS 39, prayer book owned by Lady Margaret and Lord
    Stanley, late fifteenth century

Westminster Abbey Muniments

Household accounts
WAM, 12181–90, household accounts of Sir Henry Stafford at Bourne and
    Woking, 1466–71
WAM, 22830, a bill of prests by Lady Margaret's cofferer, 1493–4

Estate accounts
WAM, 5472, miscellaneous receipts and expenses of Reginald Bray, receiver
    of Sir Henry Stafford, 1468–9
WAM, 5479, miscellaneous receipts of Reginald Bray, 1469–72
WAM, 32348, account of William Bedell for the lands of Edward Stafford,
    1495–6
WAM, 32349, account of Richard Harpur for the lands of Edward Stafford,
    1485–8
WAM, 32350, valuations of Lady Margaret's lands, 1485–8
WAM, 32355, account of receipts and charges on lands of Lady Margaret,
    both of her inheritance and the king's grant, 1487–8
WAM, 32364, account of William Bedell 1490–3
WAM, 32365, account of fees and lordships borne jointly by Lord Stanley and
    Lady Margaret, 1488

WAM, 32377, account of Sir Reginald Bray for receipts and charges on lands of Lady Margaret, both of her inheritance and the king's grant, 1495–6

WAM, 32389, account of William Bedell, Lady Margaret's treasurer, 1487–90

WAM, 32407, miscellaneous receipts and expenses of Bray, as receiver of Lord Stanley, 1473–4

Deeds and other records

WAM, 574, resignation of Hugh Oldham from the benefice of Swineshead, 1500

WAM, 575, sale of land and advowson of Swineshead by Thomas West Lord de la Warre and his wife to Lady Margaret, 1492

WAM, 4681, licence by Westminster Abbey to Gerbert Crosly to take possession of the rectory of Cheshunt, lately resigned by Hugh Oldham, 1500

WAM, 4683, exemplification of proceedings about presentation to Cheshunt, 1494

WAM, 4688, quitclaim by the dean and chapter of Windsor to Lady Margaret, of rights in the benefice of Cheshunt, 1494

WAM, 4691, admission of Hugh Oldham to the benefice of Cheshunt, 1494

WAM, 4693, sentence in favour of the presentation of Hugh Oldham to Cheshunt, 1494

WAM, 6658, admission of Lady Margaret, Sir Henry Stafford and Henry Tudor to confraternity of the order of the Holy Trinity, Knaresborough, Yorks, 1465

WAM, 6660, admission of Sir Henry Stafford and Lady Margaret to confraternity of the hospital at Burton Lazars, Leics, 1466

WAM, 12245, confession of the prior of Stoneley before Lady Margaret, 1500

WAM, 16016–73, correspondence of Sir Reginald Bray, c. 1485–1503

WAM, 19606, refectorer's account roll, 1508–9

WAM, 32378 (dorse), draft of pardon from Edward IV to Henry Tudor, n.d.

WAM, 32390, receipts of 'Exeter lands', 1492–3

WAM, 33320, expenses of Abbot Islip, 1500–2

Longleat House, North Muniment Room

Misc. MS I, wardrobe account, 1452–3

Northamptonshire Record Office

Fitzwilliam MS 370, letter of William Paston, c. 1493

Oxford

The Bodleian Library

MS Bodley 13, fols. 22–31, oration made before King Henry VII at Cambridge, n.d. [?1507]

MS Lat. Liturg. e. 10, Fairfax book of hours

Oxford University archives
N.E.P./E/1, foundation deed for the Lady Margaret professorship, 1502

Paris

Archives Nationales
Collection Dom Lenoir, vol. 22, fol. 307, 'a government enquiry of 1433 into
    the conduct of Edmund Beaufort in Normandy'
P1370, no. 1882, will of John, duke of Bourbon, 1434

Bibliothèque Nationale
MS Fr. 6970, report to Louis XI, 1 July 1463

San Marino, California

Henry Huntington Library
HM 745, book of expenses of those attending the funeral of Henry VII

Sizergh Castle, Cumbria

Strickland MSS IV–VI, receivers' accounts for Kendal, 1491–5

Spalding Gentlemen's Society

Strong Room, book 79, John Harrington's chronicle, compiled 1509, copied
    and translated by Sir Thomas Lambarde, 1607

Staffordshire Record Office

D593/A/1/29/5, letter of Lady Margaret to the keeper of Madeley Park, 1492
D641/1/2/76, 78, 181, receiver's accounts for the Stafford lands

Stamford, Burghley House

Unclassified fifteenth-century deeds, enfeoffment by Margaret, duchess of
    Somerset, 1447

Wiltshire Record Office

G23/1/2, ledger book of Salisbury Corporation

PRINTED SOURCES

Primary

Account Rolls of the Obedientiaries of Peterborough, ed. J. Greatrex (N'hants
    Record Society, 1984)
André, Bernard, 'Vita Henrici Septimi', in *Memorials of King Henry VII*, ed. J.
    Gairdner, Rolls Series (London, 1858)

'Annales Rerum Anglicarum', in *Letters and Papers Illustrative of the Wars of the English in France*, ed. J. Stevenson (Rolls Series, 2 vols. in 3, 1864)

Annals of the Lords of Warrington, part 2, ed. W. Beamont Chetham Society, o.s., 87 (1873)

Basin, T., *Histoire des règnes de Charles VII et de Louis XI*, ed. J. Quicherat, 4 vols. (Paris, 1933–44)

Benet, J., 'Chronicle for the years 1400–1462', ed. G. L. and M. A. Harriss, in *Camden Miscellany*, XXIV, Camden Society, 4th series, 9 (1972)

Blanchardin and Eglantine, ed. L. Kellner, EETS, e.s., 58 (London, 1890)

Calendar of Ancient Deeds in the Public Record Office, I (London, 1890); III (London, 1900); IV (London, 1902); V (London, 1906)

Calendar of State Papers, Milan, I, *1385–1618*, ed. A. B. Hinds (London, 1912)

Calendar of State Papers, Spanish, I, *Henry VII, 1485–1509*, ed. G. A. Bergenroth (London, 1862)

Calendar of State Papers, Venice, I, *1202–1509*, ed. R. Brown (London, 1864)

Cambridge University Grace Book B, part I, ed. M. Bateson, Luard Memorial Series II, Cambridge Antiquarian Society (Cambridge, 1903)

Chastellain, G., *Oeuvres*, ed. K. de Lettenhove, 7 vols. (Brussels, 1863–5)

The Chronicle of John Stone, Monk of Christ Church, 1415–71, ed. W. G. Searle (Cambridge, 1902)

Chronicles of London, ed. C. Kingsford (Oxford, 1905)

A Collection of All the Wills now Known to be Extant, of the Kings and Queens of England, ed. J. G. Nichols (London, 1780)

Collection of Letters from Original MSS, of Many Princes, Great Personages and Statesmen, ed. L. Howard (London, 1753)

Collegium Divi Johannis Evangelistae, 1511–1911, St John's College Quatercentenary publication (Cambridge, 1911)

The Coronation of Richard III, The Extant Documents, ed. A. F. Sutton and P. W. Hammond (Gloucester, 1983)

De Imitatione Christi, ed. J. K. Ingrams, EETS, e.s., 63 (1893)

Descriptive Catalogue of Derbyshire Charters, ed. I. H. Jeayes (London, 1906)

Documents of the Diocese of Lincoln, 1450–1544, ed. A. Clark, EETS, o.s., 149 (1914)

Documents relating to the Colleges and University of Cambridge, printed for the Commissioners, 3 vols. (London, 1852)

Early Statutes of Christ's College, ed. H. Rackham (Cambridge, 1927)

Early Statutes of St. John's College, Cambridge, ed. J. E. B. Mayor (Cambridge, 1859)

An English Chronicle of the Reigns of Richard II, Henry IV, Henry V and Henry VI, ed. J. S. Davies, Camden Society, o.s., 64 (1856)

English Historical Literature in the Fifteenth Century, ed. C. L. Kingsford (Oxford, 1913)

Episcopal Register of St. David's, 1397–1518, ed. R. F. Isaacson, Cymmrodorion Record Series, 6, 2 vols. (London, 1917), II, *1407–1518*

Epistolae Academicae Oxonienses, ed. H. Anstey, 2 vols., Oxford Historical Society, XXXV–VI (Oxford, 1898)

Epistolae Academicae, 1508–96, ed. W. T. Mitchell, Oxford Historical Society, n.s., XXVI (Oxford, 1980)

Erasmus and Cambridge: The Cambridge Letters of Erasmus, ed. H. C. Porter and D. F. S. Thomson (Toronto, 1963)

Excerpta Historica, ed. S. Bentley (London, 1831)

'Genealogical and historical notes from ancient calendars', entries from BL, Royal MS 2A XVIII, printed by F. Madden in *Collectanea Topographica et Genealogica*, I (1834)

The Funeral Sermon of Lady Margaret Beaufort, ed. J. Hymers (Cambridge, 1840)

Hall's Chronicle, ed. H. Ellis (London, 1809)

Historical Collections of a Citizen of London, ed. J. Gairdner, Camden Society, n.s., 17 (1876)

'The Homage Roll of the Manor of Warrington', ed. W. Beamont, in *Miscellanies relating to Lancashire and Cheshire, I*, Lancashire and Cheshire Record Soceity, 12 (1885)

Ingulph's Chronicle of the History of Croyland, ed. H. T. Riley (London, 1854)

The Itinerary of John Leland, 1535–43, ed. L. T. Smith, 5 vols. (London, 1906–10)

Leland, J., *De Rebus Brittanicis Collectanea*, ed. T. Hearne, 6 vols. (London, 1774)

Letters and Papers Illustrative of the Reigns of Richard III and Henry VII, ed. J. Gairdner, 2 vols., Rolls Series (London, 1861–3)

Letters and Papers, Foreign and Domestic, of the Reign of Henry VIII, ed. J. S. Brewer and J. Gairdner, 21 vols. (London, 1862–1910), I, pt i

Letters of Richard Fox, 1486–1527, ed. P. S. and H. M. Allen (Oxford, 1929)

The Manuscripts of St. George's Chapel Windsor Castle, ed. J. N. Dalton (Windsor, 1957)

Materials for a History of the Reign of Henry VII, ed. W. Campbell, 2 vols, Rolls Series (London, 1873–7)

'Mornynge Remembraunce had at the moneth mynde of the Noble Prynces Margarete Countesse of Rychemonde and Darbye, emprynted by Wynkyn de Worde', in *The English Works of John Fisher, part I*, ed. J. E. B. Mayor, EETS, e.s., 27 (1876), 289–310

'The most pleasant song of Lady Bessy', ed. J. O. Halliwell, *Percy Society*, 20 (1877)

The Northumberland Household Book, ed. T. Percy (London, 1770)

Notes from the College Records, Continued from The Eagle [St John's College Magazine], *vol. xxxvi*, ed. R. F. Scott, (St John's College, 1915)

'Pedigrees of noble families related to the blood royal', extracts from BL, Harley MS 1074, printed in *Collectanea Topographica et Genealogica*, I (1834)

Original Letters Illustrative of English History, ed. H. Ellis, 11 vols. (London, 1824–46), 2nd series, I

The Paston Letters, 1422–1509, ed. J. Gairdner, 6 vols. (London, 1904)

Privy Purse Expenses of Elizabeth of York, ed. N. H. Nicolas (London, 1830)

Proceedings and Ordinances of the Privy Council of England, ed. N. H. Nicolas, 7 vols. (Record Commission, 1834–7)

Records of the Borough of Leicester, ed. M. Bateson, 3 vols. (London, 1899–1905)
Records of the Borough of Nottingham, ed. W. H. Stevenson, 5 vols. (London, 1882–1900)
Register of Oliver King, Bishop of Bath and Wells, 1496–1503, ed. H. Maxwell-Lyte, Somerset Record Society, 54 (1939)
The Reign of Henry VII from Contemporary Sources, ed. A. F. Pollard, 3 vols. (London, 1913–14)
Rotuli Parliamentorum, ed. J. Strachey *et al.*, 6 vols. (London, 1767–77)
The Scale of Perfection, ed. G. Sitwell (London, 1953)
The Shepherd's Calendar, ed. G. C. Heseltine (London, 1930)
Somerset Medieval Wills, 1501–30, ed. F. W. Weaver, Somerset Record Society, 19 (1903)
Stow, J., *The Annals or General Chronicle of England* (London, 1615)
Testamenta Vetusta, ed. N. H. Nichols, 2 vols. (London, 1826)
Transcripts of Sussex Wills, ed. W. H. Godfrey, III, *Sussex Record Society Publications*, 43 (1938)
Vergil, Polydore, *Three Books of English History*, ed. Sir H. Ellis, Camden Society, o.s., 39 (1844)
Anglica Historia, ed. D. Hay, Camden Society, n.s., 74 (1950)
Warkworth, J., *A Chronicle of the First Thirteen Years of the Reign of King Edward the Fourth*, ed. J. O. Halliwell, Camden Society, o.s., 10 (1839)
Wills from Doctors' Commons, 1495–1695, ed. J. G. Nichols and J. Bruce, Camden Society, o.s., 83 (1863)

Unpublished theses

Jones, M. K., 'The Beaufort family and the war in France, 1421–50' (Bristol PhD, 1982)
Musgrave, C. A., 'Household administration in the fourteenth century with special reference to the household of Elizabeth de Burgh, Lady Clare' (London MA, 1923)
Rogers, N. J., 'Books of hours produced in the low countries for the English market in the fifteenth century' (Cambridge MLitt, 1982)
Thomas, D. H., 'The Herberts of Raglan as supporters of the House of York in the second half of the fifteenth century' (Cardiff MA, 1968)
Thurgood, J. M., 'The diet and domestic household of the English lay nobility, 1265–1531' (London, MPhil, 1982)

Secondary

Alcock, N. W., 'Maxstoke castle, Warwickshire', *Archaeological Journal*, 135 (1978)
Anglo, S., *Spectacle, Pageantry and Early Tudor Policy* (Oxford, 1969)
Anstruther, G., *Vaux of Harrowden* (London, 1953)
Archer, R. E., 'Rich old ladies: the problem of late medieval dowagers', in *Property and Politics: Essays in Later Medieval English History*, ed. A. J. Pollard (Gloucester, 1984)

'The estates and finances of Margaret of Brotherton, *c.* 1320–1399', *Historical Research*, 60 (1987)

Armitage-Smith, S., *John of Gaunt* (London, 1964)

Armitt, M. L., 'Fullers and freeholders of Grasmere', *TCWAS*, n.s., 8 (1908) *Rydal* (Kendal, 1916)

Armstrong, C. A. J., 'The piety of Cicely, Duchess of York', in *England, France and Burgundy in the Fifteenth Century* (London, 1983)

Aston, T. H., Duncan, G. D., and Evans, T. A. R., 'The medieval alumni of the university of Cambridge', *Past and Present*, 86 (1980)

Attwater, A., *A Short History of Pembroke College, Cambridge* (Cambridge, 1973)

Axon, W. E., 'The Lady Margaret as a lover of literature', *The Library*, n.s., 8 (Jan. 1907)

Bacon, Sir Francis, *History of the Reign of King Henry the Seventh*, ed. R. Lockyer (London, 1971)

Bagley, J. J., *The Earls of Derby, 1485–1985* (London, 1985)

Baker, G., *History and Antiquities of the County of Northampton*, 2 vols. (London, 1822–30)

Baker, T., *History of St. John's College, Cambridge*, ed. J. E. B. Mayor, 2 vols. (Cambridge, 1869)

Ballard, G., *Memoirs of Learned Ladies* (London, 1775)

Barron, C. M., 'The "golden age" of women in medieval London', *Reading Medieval Studies*, 15 (1989)

Bennett, H. S., *English Books and Readers, 1475–1557* (Cambridge, 1969)

Bennett, M. J., *The Battle of Bosworth* (Gloucester, 1985)

Bond Paul, W., 'The church, Langport Eastover, county of Somerset', *SANHS*, 40 (1984)

Bradshaw, B., and Duffy, E., eds., *Humanism, Reform and the Reformation: The Career of Bishop John Fisher* (Cambridge, 1989)

Bromley, J., 'The heraldry of Ormskirk church', *THSLC*, 58 (1906)

Brooke, C. N. L., *The Medieval Idea of Marriage* (Oxford, 1989)

Brooke, C. N. L., Highfield, R., and Swaan, W., *Oxford and Cambridge* (Cambridge, 1988)

Brown, A. L., 'The reign of Henry IV', in *Fifteenth-Century England, 1399–1509*, ed. S. B. Chrimes, C. D. Ross and R. A. Griffiths (Manchester, 1972)

Buck, Sir George, *The History of King Richard III*, ed. A. N. Kincaid (Gloucester, 1979)

Burgess, C., 'A fond thing vainly invented: an essay on Purgatory and pious motive in late medieval England', in *Parish, Church and People*, ed. S. J. Wright (London, 1988)

Chrimes, S. B., *Henry VII* (London, 1977)

Clark, J. W., *Endowments of the University of Cambridge* (Cambridge, 1904)

Cobban, A. B., *The Medieval Universities* (London, 1975)

Cokayne, G. E., *The Complete Peerage of England, Scotland, Ireland, Great Britain and the United Kingdom*, ed. W. Gibbs *et al.*, 12 vols. in 13 (London, 1910–59)

Colvin, H. M., Ransome, D. R., and Summerson, J., eds., *The History of the King's Works*, 6 vols. (London, 1963–82)

Condon, M. M., 'Ruling elites in the reign of Henry VII', in *Patronage, Pedigree and Power in Later Medieval England*, ed. C. D. Ross (Gloucester, 1979)

'From caitiff and villain to pater patriae: Reynold Bray and the profits of office', in *Profit, Piety and the Professions in Later Medieval England*, ed. M. A. Hicks (Gloucester, 1990)

Cooper, C. H., *The Lady Margaret: A Memoir of Margaret, Countess of Richmond and Derby*, ed. J. E. B. Mayor (Cambridge, 1874)

Coward, B., *The Stanleys, Lords Stanley and Earls of Derby, 1385–1672, the Origins, Wealth and Power of a Landowning Family* (Manchester, 1983)

Crawford, A., 'The private life of John Howard', in *Richard III: Loyalty, Lordship and Law*, ed. P. W. Hammond (London, 1986)

Crofts, P. J., 'A copy of Walter Hylton's Scala Perfectionis', *Sale Catalogue, Bernard Quaritch Ltd* (London, 1958)

Curwen, J. F., *Kirkbie-Kendal* (Kendal, 1900)

Danbury, E., 'The decoration and illumination of royal charters in England, 1250–1509', in *England and her Neighbours, 1066–1453*, ed. M. Jones and M. Vale (London, 1989)

David, C., *St. Winefride's Well: An Illustrated Description* (Kildare, 1971)

Deneuil-Cornier, A., *The Renaissance in France* (London, 1969)

Done, R., *A Guide to the Collegiate Church of the Holy Trinity, Tattershall* (Coningsby, 1983)

Dowling, M., *Humanism in the Age of Henry VIII* (New York, 1986)

Draper, P., *The House of Stanley* (Ormskirk, 1864)

Dugdale, W., *The Baronage of England*, 2 vols. (London, 1675–6)

Dyer, C., *Standards of Living in the Later Middle Ages* (Cambridge, 1989)

Elton, G. R., *The Tudor Revolution in Government* (Cambridge, 1953)

Emden, A. B., *A Biographical Register of the University of Cambridge to 1500* (Cambridge, 1963)

Galvin, C., and Lindley, P., 'Pietro Torrigiano's portrait bust of King Henry VII', *Burlington Magazine*, 130 (1988)

Gardner, H. M., 'The text of the Scale of Perfection', *Medium Aevum*, 22 (1936)

'Walter Hilton and the mystical tradition in England', *Essays and Studies*, 22 (1936)

Girouard, M., *Life in the English Country House* (Harmondsworth, 1980)

Given-Wilson, C., and Curteis, A., *The Royal Bastards of Medieval England* (London, 1984)

Goodman, A., *The Wars of the Roses* (London, 1981)

Goodwin-Austen, R. A. C., 'Woking Manor', *Surrey Archaeological Collections*, 7 (1874)

Gray, A., and Brittain, F., *A History of Jesus College, Cambridge* (London, 1979)

Griffiths, R. A., 'The sense of dynasty in the reign of Henry VI', in *Patronage, Pedigree and Power in Later Medieval England*, ed. C. D. Ross (Gloucester, 1979)

The Reign of Henry VI (London, 1981)

'The crown and the royal family in later medieval England', in *Kings and Nobles in the Later Middle Ages*, ed. R. A. Griffiths and J. Sherborne (Gloucester, 1986)

Griffiths, R. A., and Thomas, R. S., *The Making of the Tudor Dynasty* (Gloucester, 1985)

Haggard, D. J., 'The ruins of Old Woking Palace', *Surrey Archaeological Society Collections*, 55 (1958)

Halsted, C., *Life of Margaret Beaufort, Countess of Richmond and Derby* (London, 1839)

Hampton, W., *Memorials of the Wars of the Roses* (Upminster, 1979)

Harris, B. J., *Edward Stafford, Third Duke of Buckingham* (Stanford, 1986)

Harris, K., 'The origins and make-up of Cambridge University Library MS. Ff. 1.6', *Trans. Cambridge Bibliographical Society*, 8 (1983)

Harrison, F. L., *Music in Medieval Britain* (London, 1963)

Harriss, G. L., *Cardinal Beaufort* (Oxford, 1988)

Harvey, B., *Westminster Abbey and its Estates in the Middle Ages* (Oxford, 1977)

Harvey, J., *A Dictionary of Medieval Architects*, rev. edn (Gloucester, 1984)

Hicks, M. A., *False, Fleeting, Perjur'd Clarence* (Gloucester, 1980)

'The Neville earldom of Salisbury, 1429–71', *Wiltshire Archaeological Magazine*, 73 (1980)

'Edward IV, the duke of Somerset and Lancastrian loyalism in the north', *Northern History*, 20 (1984)

'The piety of Margaret Lady Hungerford', *Journal of Ecclesiastical History*, 38 (1987)

Horrox, R., *Richard III. A Study in Service* (Cambridge, 1989)

Hosker, P., 'The Stanleys of Lathom and ecclesiastical patronage in the north-west of England during the fifteenth century', *Northern History*, 18 (1982)

Hoult, J., *The Vill, Manor and Township of Knowsley* (Liverpool, 1930)

Howard, M., *The Early Tudor Country House* (London, 1987)

Hubbard, E., *The Buildings of Wales: Clwyd* (London, 1986)

Hutchins, J., *The History and Antiquities of the County of Dorset*, 3rd edn, 3 vols. (London, 1861–74), III

Ives, E. W., *The Common Lawyers of Pre-Reformation England* (Cambridge, 1983)

Jenkinson, H., 'Mary de Sancto Paulo, foundress of Pembroke College, Cambridge', *Archaeologia*, 66 (1914–15)

Jones, M. K., 'John Beaufort, duke of Somerset and the French expedition of 1443', in *Patronage, the Crown and the Provinces in Later Medieval England*, ed. R. A. Griffiths (Gloucester, 1981)

'Edward IV and the Beaufort family: conciliation in early Yorkist politics', *The Ricardian*, 6 (1983)

'Henry VII, Lady Margaret Beaufort and the Orléans ransom', in *Kings and Nobles in the Later Middle Ages*, ed. R. A. Griffiths and J. Sherborne (Gloucester, 1986)

'Lady Margaret Beaufort, the royal council and an early Fenland drainage scheme', *Lincolnshire History and Archaeology*, 21 (1986)

'Richard III and Lady Margaret Beaufort: a reassessment', in *Richard III, Loyalty, Lordship and Law*, ed. P. W. Hammond (London, 1986)

'Richard III and the Stanleys', in *Richard III and the North*, ed. R. Horrox (Hull, 1986)

'Collyweston – an early Tudor palace', in *England in the Fifteenth Century*, ed. D. Williams (London, 1987)

'L'imposition illégale de taxes en "Normandie Anglaise": une enquête gouvernementale en 1446', in *'La France Anglaise' Au Moyen Age. Actes du 111e Congrès National des Sociétés Savantes* (Paris, 1988)

'Sir William Stanley of Holt: politics and family allegiance in the late fifteenth century', *Welsh History Review*, 14 (1988)

'Somerset, York and the Wars of the Roses', *EHR*, 104 (1989)

Jones, M. K., and Underwood, M. G., 'Lady Margaret Beaufort', *History Today* (1985)

Keiser, G., 'Patronage and piety in fifteenth century England: Margaret duchess of Clarence, Symon Wynter, and Beinecke MS. 317', *Yale University Library Gazette* (October 1985)

'The mystics and the early English printers', in *Exeter Symposium IV, Papers read at Dartington Hall*, ed. M. Glasscoe (July 1987)

Kingsford, C. L., 'On some London houses of the early Tudor period', *Archaeologia*, 71 (1920–1)

Kipling, G., *The Triumph of Honour* (Leiden, 1977)

Lander, J. R., *Crown and Nobility, 1450–1509* (London, 1976)

Government and Community, England, 1450–1509 (London, 1980)

Leader, D. R., *A History of the University of Cambridge*, I: *The University to 1546* (Cambridge, 1989)

Lewis, J., *Life of Dr. John Fisher*, 2 vols. (London, 1855)

Little, A. G., 'The introduction of the Observant Friars into England', *Proceedings of the British Academy*, 10 (1921–3)

Lloyd, A. H., 'Two monumental brasses in the chapel of Christ's College', *Proceedings of the Cambridge Antiquarian Society*, 33 (1933)

The Early History of Christ's College, Cambridge (Cambridge, 1934)

Loades, D. M., *The Tudor Court* (London, 1986)

Lodge, E., *Portraits of Illustrious Personages of Great Britain*, 4 vols. (London, 1821–34), II

Lovatt, R., 'The Imitation of Christ in late medieval England', *Transactions of the Royal Historical Society*, 18 (1968)

Lowe, D. E., 'Patronage and politics: Edward IV, the Wydevills and the council of the Prince of Wales, 1471–83', *Bulletin of the Board of Celtic Studies*, 29 (1981)

Lowry, M. J. C., 'Caxton, St Winifred and the Lady Margaret Beaufort', *The Library*, 6th series, 5 (1983)

McConica, J., ed. *The Collegiate University*, T. H. Aston, ed., *The History of the University of Oxford*, III (Oxford, 1986)

McFarlane, K. B., *Lancastrian Kings and Lollard Knights* (Oxford, 1972)

The Nobility of Later Medieval England (Oxford, 1973)

MacGibbon, D., *Elizabeth Woodville (1437–92)* (London, 1938)

McNiven, P., *Heresy and Politics in the Reign of Henry IV. The Burning of John Badbury* (Bury St Edmunds, 1987)

Manning, O., and Bray, W., *The History and Antiquities of Surrey*, 3 vols. (London, 1804–14)

Mertes, K., *The English Noble Household, 1250–1600* (London, 1988)

Mumford, A. A., *Hugh Oldham* (London, 1936)

Myers, A. R., 'The household of Queen Margaret of Anjou, 1452–3', in *Crown, Household and Parliament in Fifteenth Century England*, ed. C. H. Clough (London, 1985)

Orme, N., *English Schools in the Middle Ages* (London, 1973)

Owen, H., and Blakeway, J. B., *A History of Shrewsbury*, 2 vols. (London, 1825)

Painter, G. D., *William Caxton* (London, 1976)

Pantin, W. A., 'Medieval priests' houses in south-west England', *Medieval Archaeology*, 1 (1957)

'Instructions for a devout and literate layman', in *Medieval Learning and Literature: Essays Presented to Richard William Hunt*, ed. J. J. G. Alexander and M. T. Gibson (Oxford, 1976)

Pfaff, R. W., *New Liturgical Feasts in Later Medieval England*, Oxford Theological Monographs (Oxford, 1970)

Plomer, H., *Wynkyn de Worde and his Contemporaries* (London, 1925)

Pompen, A., *The English Versions of the Ship of Fools* (London, 1925)

Porter, H. C., *Reformation and Reaction in Tudor Cambridge* (Cambridge, 1958)

Pugh, T. B., *The Marcher Lordships of South Wales, 1415–1536* (Cardiff, 1963)

'The Marcher Lords of Glamorgan and Morgannwy, 1317–1485', *Glamorgan County History*, III, ed. T. B. Pugh (Cardiff, 1971)

Putnam, B. H., *Early Treatises on the Practice of the Justices of the Peace in the Fifteenth and Sixteenth Centuries* (Oxford, 1924)

Rackham, H., ed., *Christ's College in Former Days* (Cambridge, 1939)

Raines, F. R., *The Rectors of Manchester and the Wardens of the Collegiate Church of that Town*, part I, Chetham Society, n.s., 5 (1885)

Rawcliffe, C., *The Staffords, Earls of Stafford and Dukes of Buckingham, 1394–1521* (Cambridge, 1978)

Reid, R. R., *The King's Council in the North* (London, 1921)

Richmond, C., 'Religion and the fifteenth century gentleman', in R. B. Dobson, ed., *The Church, Politics and Patronage in the Fifteenth Century* (Gloucester, 1984)

Rickert, M., 'The so-called Beaufort Hours and York Psalter', *Burlington Magazine*, 104 (June 1962)

Rigby, S., '"Sore decay" and "fair dwelling": Boston and urban decline in the later middle ages', *Midland History*, 10 (1985)

Rogers, A., 'Late medieval Stamford: a study of the town council, 1465–92', in *Perspectives in English Urban History*, ed. A. Everitt (London, 1973)

Rosenthal, J. T., *The Purchase of Paradise: Gift-giving and the Aristocracy, 1307–1485* (London, 1972)

Nobles and the Noble Life, 1295–1500 (London, 1976)

Ross, C. D., *Edward IV* (London, 1975)

Routh, E. M. G., *A Memoir of Lady Margaret Beaufort, Countess of Richmond and Derby, Mother of Henry VII* (Oxford, 1924)

Rubin, M., *Charity and Community in Medieval Cambridge*, Cambridge Studies in Medieval Life and Thought, 4th series (Cambridge, 1987)

St John Hope, W. H., *Windsor Castle* (London, 1913)

Scofield, C. L., 'Henry, Duke of Somerset, and Edward IV', *EHR*, 21 (1906)
  The Life and Reign of Edward IV, 2 vols. (London, 1923)

Scott, R. F., 'On a list of the plate, books and vestments bequeathed by the Lady Margaret to Christ's College', *Communications of the Cambridge Antiquarian Society*, 9 (1899)
  'On the contracts for the tomb of Lady Margaret Beaufort, Countess of Richmond and Derby, mother of Henry VII and foundress of the colleges of Christ and St. John in Cambridge', *Archaeologia*, 66 (1915)

Searle, W. G., *The History of the Queens' College of St. Margaret and St. Bernard in the University of Cambridge, 1446–1662*, 2 vols. (Cambridge, 1867–71)

Simon, L., *Of Virtue Rare: Margaret Beaufort, Matriarch of the House of Tudor* (Boston, Mass., 1982)

Staniland, K., 'Royal entry into the world', in *England in the Fifteenth Century*, ed. D. Williams (London, 1987)

Stanley, A. P., *Historical Memorials of Westminster Abbey* (London, 1868)

Sutton, A. F., and Visser-Fuchs, L., *The Hours of Richard III* (Gloucester, 1990)

Swanson, R. N., *Church and Society in Late Medieval England* (Oxford, 1989)

Thompson, E. M., *The Carthusian Order in England* (London, 1930)

Thompson, P., *The History and Antiquities of Boston* (Boston, 1856)

Thomson, J. A. F., 'Bishop Lionel Woodville and Richard III', *BIHR*, 59 (1986)

Tuck, A., *Richard II and the English Nobility* (London, 1973)

Twigg, J., *A History of Queens' College Cambridge, 1448–1986* (Woodbridge, 1987)

Tyerman, C., *England and the Crusades, 1095–1588* (Chicago, 1988)

Underwood, M. G., 'The Lady Margaret and her Cambridge connections', *Sixteenth Century Journal*, 13 (1982)
  'Behind the early statutes', *The Eagle* (SJC magazine), 69 (1983)
  'Politics and piety in the household of Lady Margaret Beaufort', *Journal of Ecclesiastical History*, 38 (1987)
  'John Fisher and the promotion of learning', in *Humanism, Reform and the Reformation: The Career of Bishop John Fisher*, ed. B. Bradshaw and E. Duffy (Cambridge, 1989)

Venables, E., 'Bourne: its abbey and castle', *Associated Architectural Societies, Reports and Papers*, 20 (1889)

Virgoe, R., 'The recovery of the Howards in East Anglia, 1485–1529', in *Wealth and Power in Tudor England*, ed. E. W. Ives, R. J. Knecht and J. J. Scarisbrick (London, 1978)

Visser-Fuchs, L., 'The casualty list of the battle of Barnet', *The Ricardian*, 8 (1988)

Walpole, H., *A Catalogue of the Royal and Noble Authors of England, with Lists of their Works* (Edinburgh, 1796)

Warnicke, R. M., 'The Lady Margaret Beaufort, Countess of Richmond, (d. 1509) as seen by John Fisher and by Lord Morley', *Moreana*, 19 (1982)
'The Lady Margaret, Countess of Richmond; a noblewoman of independent wealth and status', *Fifteenth-Century Studies*, 9 (1984)
'Sir Ralph Bigod: a loyal servant to King Richard III', *The Ricardian*, 6 (1984)
Weightman, C., *Margaret of York, Duchess of Burgundy, 1446–1503* (Gloucester, 1989)
Westlake, H. F., *Westminster Abbey* (London, 1923)
Wilkie, W., *The Cardinal Protectors of England: Rome and the Tudors before the Reformation* (Cambridge, 1974)
Willis, R., and Clark, J. W., *The Architectural History of the University of Cambridge*, 3 vols. (Cambridge, 1886)
Winchester, A. J. L., *Landscape and Society in Medieval Cumbria* (Edinburgh, 1987)
Wolffe, B. P., *The Crown Lands, 1461–1536*, (London, 1970)
The Royal Demesne in English History (London, 1971)
Henry VI (London, 1981)
Woodman, F., *The Architectural History of Canterbury Cathedral* (London, 1981)

INDEX

à Kempis, Thomas, 184–5, 197–8
Abell, William, painter, 32
Aclane, John, 106
Aderton, Richard, 88, 161, 268
Alcock, John, bishop of Ely, 213
Alday, Richard, 151
Allesley, 229
alms and almsfolk, 155, 156, 165, 167, 169, 179, 233
Amesbury, 102
André, Bernard, 1–2, 58, 70
Angoulême, Jean, count of, 138
Anne Neville, queen of Richard III, 214
apprentices, 167
arms, see heraldry
Arthur, prince of Wales, 76–8, 172, 182, 238; household, 111
Ashridge, 198
Ashton, Hugh, 106, 124, 128, 130, 169, 201, 234, 235, 268, 288
Atkins, Jane, lady-in-waiting, 144
Atkinson, William, 184, 214
Aughton, Nicholas, 239, 244, 268

Bacon, Sir Francis, 4
badges, see heraldry
Badgworth, 234
Baker, Thomas, 5–6
Baldwyn, Peter, 183, 268
Ballard, George, 6–7, 15
Barclay, Alexander, 186
Barnet, battle of, 55, 119, 143
Bassingbourn manor, 95, 265–6
Baugé, battle of, 27
Baynard's Castle, 66, 146
Beauchamp, Anne, daughter of Henry, duke of Warwick, 36
Beauchamp, Eleanor, duchess of Somerset, 45

Beauchamp, Henry, duke of Warwick (d.1446), 36
Beauchamp, Margaret, duchess of Somerset, mother of Margaret Beaufort, 28, 50–1, 60, 72, 94, 95, 125, 126, 127, 138, 238
Beauchamp, Richard, bishop of Salisbury, 206
Beauchamp family, of Bletsoe and Lydiard Tregoze, 28
Beaufort, Anne, 101
Beaufort, Charles, 72, 288
Beaufort, Edmund, duke of Somerset (d.1455), 25, 30, 42, 101, 102, 164
Beaufort, Edmund, duke of Somerset (d.1471), 45, 52–7, 72
Beaufort, Henry, cardinal, 25, 27, 28, 102, 181, 198
Beaufort, Henry, duke of Somerset (d.1464), 23, 43–6, 72, 139
Beaufort, Henry, earl of Somerset (d.1418), 27
Beaufort, John, duke of Somerset (d.1444), 26–30, 72, 238; book of hours acquired by, 160; disgrace and death, 29, 35; lands, 94
Beaufort, John, earl of Somerset (d.1410), 19, 20, 22–4, 27, 108
Beaufort, Margaret: and arbitration, 91, 98, 135, 163, 222; arms, see heraldry; birth of, 34–5; and bishops, 194; books and literary interests of, 6–7, 9, 32, 143, 147, 160, 162, 163, 173, 174, 176–7, 179–87, 199, 241; building and engineering associated with, 71–2, 80, 83–4, 104, 111, 123–4, 127–30, 154–5; chapel, 114, 131, 154–5, 158, 169, 176–8, 183; character, 1–11, 65, 68, 81, 108, 188, 256–9; and

314